# RETHINKING THE RENAISSANCE AND REFORMATION IN SCOTLAND

# RETHINKING THE RENAISSANCE AND REFORMATION IN SCOTLAND

## Essays in Honour of Roger A. Mason

Edited by
Steven J. Reid

THE BOYDELL PRESS

First published 2024
The Boydell Press, Woodbridge

ISBN 978 1 83765 161 0

The Boydell Press is an imprint of Boydell & Brewer Ltd
PO Box 9, Woodbridge, Suffolk IP12 3DF, UK
and of Boydell & Brewer Inc.
668 Mt Hope Avenue, Rochester, NY 14620–2731, USA
website: www.boydellandbrewer.com

A catalogue record for this book is available
from the British Library

# *Contents*

## Part III
## Literature, Politics and Religion: Renaissance and Reformation

# *Contributors*

*Stephen Boardman* is Professor of Medieval Scottish History at the University of Edinburgh. He has published on various aspects of the history of fourteenth- and fifteenth-century Scotland.

*Dauvit Broun* is Professor of Scottish History at the University of Glasgow. He specialises in historical texts of little or no literary merit written and copied from the sixth to the sixteenth centuries.

*Michael H. Brown* is Professor of Scottish History at the University of St Andrews. He researches the politics and political society of Scotland and the insular world from c. 1250 to c. 1500.

*Alison Cathcart* is Professor of Early Modern Scottish and Archipelagic History at the University of Stirling. She researches various aspects of the Atlantic archipelago during the 'long' sixteenth century.

*Jane E.A. Dawson* is John Laing Professor Emerita of Reformation History at the University of Edinburgh. She published a major biography of John Knox in 2015.

*Catriona M.M. Macdonald* is Reader in Late Modern Scottish History at the University of Glasgow. Her recent work focuses on the evolution of Scottish historiography since 1832.

*Kate McClune* is Senior Lecturer in Medieval Literature at the University of Bristol. She has published widely on Older Scots and Middle English literature, and the Arthurian legend in Scotland. Her recent research focuses on animal conservation and the medieval archive.

*Tricia A. McElroy* is an Associate Professor of English and Associate Dean for Humanities and Fine Arts at the University of Alabama. Her research focuses on Renaissance Scotland, specifically on political satire and the intersections of literature and history.

*Sally Mapstone* is Principal and Vice-Chancellor of the University of St Andrews. She has published extensively on Older Scots literature and Scottish book history.

*Joanna Martin* is an Associate Professor in Middle English and Older Scots at the University of Nottingham. She has a particular interest in Older Scots poetry, family books, and text editing.

*Esther Mijers* is Senior Lecturer in Scotish History at the University of Edinburgh. She specialises in the relationship between Scotland and the wider world in the long seventeenth century. She has published widely on the exchange of goods, people and ideas between Scotland and the Continent, especially the Netherlands, and the Americas.

*Steven J. Reid* is Professor of Early Modern Scottish History and Culture at the University of Glasgow. He has published widely on intellectual, religious, and political culture in the reigns of Mary, Queen of Scots and James VI and I.

*Bess Rhodes* is a research fellow at the University of St Andrews. Her research focuses on Scotland in the fifteenth and sixteenth centuries, with a particular concentration on religious and landscape history.

*Nicola Royan* is Professor of Older Scottish Literature at the University of Nottingham and President of the Scottish Text Society. She has published widely on texts in Older Scots and in Latin, and has a particular interest in the reception of humanism.

# Acknowledgements

THIS volume originated in a day conference with the same title held in Roger's honour in Parliament Hall, St Andrews, on 13 October 2018. I am grateful to Malcolm Petrie and the School of History at the University of St Andrews for the support and assistance they provided in organizing the conference, and to Malcolm and Caroline Palmer for guiding me through the process of submitting the volume to Boydell. My thanks also go to Sally Mapstone for hosting the post-conference reception and dinner at the Principal's House, and to Ellen Collingsworth for acting as my secret agent in all things Roger, including serving as photograph-finder and biographical fact-checker.

The contributions by Dauvit Broun, Ali Cathcart, Jane Dawson, Catriona Macdonald, Esther Mijers, Steven Reid, Bess Rhodes and Nicola Royan were all presented in early drafts at the conference. They were joined at the conference by Katie Stevenson and Jamie Reid-Baxter, whose contributions have not appeared in the final volume but which were warmly received by Roger on the day. Stephen Boardman, Michael H. Brown, Kate McClune, Tricia A. McElroy and Joanna Martin, all of whom were on Roger's 'most wanted' list as potential contributors, willingly agreed to write chapters in the wake of the conference for inclusion in the volume. I am hugely grateful to my fellow contributors for their encouragement, their constructive response to revisions and feedback, and above all their patience as the volume slowly came together, despite the various crises of the past five years.

Nicola Royan would like to note her thanks to the British Academy for Mid-career Fellowship funding which allowed her to pursue and develop the research for her chapter.

Finally, our collective thanks go to Roger – for the constructive criticism, support, advice, and friendship he has given us all.

# *Abbreviations*

| | |
|---|---|
| BL | British Library, London |
| Boardman and Goodare (eds), *Kings, Lords and Men* | Steve Boardman and Julian Goodare (eds), *Kings, Lords and Men in Scotland and Britain, 1300–1625: Essays in Honour of Jenny Wormald* (Edinburgh, 2014) |
| Brown and Tanner (eds), *Scottish Kingship* | Michael Brown and Roland Tanner (eds), *Scottish Kingship 1306–1542: Essays in Honour of Norman Macdougall* (Edinburgh, 2008) |
| *CSP Scot.* | Joseph Bain *et al.* (eds), *Calendar of State Papers Relating to Scotland and Mary, Queen of Scots, 1547–1603*, 13 vols (London, 1862–1954) |
| CSSR | *Calendar of Scottish Supplications to Rome* |
| Calderwood, *History* | David Calderwood, *History of the Kirk of Scotland*, 8 vols, ed. T. Thomson and D. Laing (Edinburgh, 1842–49) |
| *Diurnal* | Thomas Thomson (ed.), *Diurnal of remarkable occurrents that have passed within the country of Scotland since the death of King James the Fourth till the year MDLXXV* (Edinburgh, 1833) |
| *DPS* | Arthur Johnstone and John Scot of Scotstarvit (eds), *Delitiae Poetarum Scotorum*, 2 vols (Amsterdam, 1637) |
| *ER* | John Stuart *et al.* (eds), *The Exchequer Rolls of Scotland*, 23 vols (Edinburgh, 1878–1908) |
| Erskine and Mason (eds), *George Buchanan* | Caroline Erskine and Roger Mason (eds), *George Buchanan: Political Thought in Early Modern Britain and Europe* (Farnham, 2012) |

| | |
|---|---|
| EUL CRC | Edinburgh University Library, Centre for Research Collections |
| *Foedera* | *Foedera, Conventiones, Litterae et Cuiuscunque Generis Acta Publica*, ed. T. Rymer, Record Commission edition (London, 1816–69) |
| GUA | University of Glasgow Archives |
| *IR* | *Innes Review* |
| *Knox: On Rebellion* | Roger A. Mason (ed.), *John Knox: On Rebellion* (Cambridge, 1994) |
| Knox, *Works* | David Laing (ed.), *The Works of John Knox*, 6 vols (Edinburgh, 1846–64) |
| *L&P Henry VIII* | J.S Brewer *et al.* (eds), *Letters and Papers, Foreign and Domestic, of the Reign of Henry VIII* (22 vols; London, 1864–1932) |
| Mason, *Kingship and the Commonweal* | Roger A. Mason, *Kingship and the Commonweal: Political Thought in Renaissance and Reformation Scotland* (East Linton, 1998) |
| Mason and Reid (eds), *Andrew Melville* | Roger A. Mason and Steven J. Reid (eds), *Andrew Melville (1545–1622): Writings, Reception and Reputation* (Farnham, 2014) |
| Mason and Smith | Roger A. Mason and Martin S. Smith (eds), *A Dialogue on the Law of Kingship among the Scots: A Critical Edition and Translation of George Buchanan's 'De jure regni apud Scotos dialogus'* (Aldershot and Burlington, VT, 2004) |
| NLS | National Library of Scotland |
| NRS | National Records of Scotland |
| *ODNB* | *Oxford Dictionary of National Biography* (Oxford, 2004) [www.oxforddnb.com; all articles cited by their unique site identifier in square brackets, correct at time of publication] |
| *PSAS* | *Proceedings of the Society of Antiquaries of Scotland* |
| Reid and McOmish (eds), *Corona Borealis* | Steven J. Reid and David McOmish (eds), *Corona Borealis: Scottish Neo-Latin Poets on King James VI and His Reign, 1566–1603* (Glasgow, 2020) |
| *RSCHS* | *Records of the Scottish Church History Society* |
| *RPC* | J.H. Burton *et al.* (eds), *Register of the Privy Council of Scotland*, 38 vols (Edinburgh, 1877–98) |

| | |
|---|---|
| *RPS* | Keith M. Brown (ed.), *The Records of the Parliament of Scotland to 1707* (2007–2015) [www.rps.ac.uk/] |
| *RMS* | J.M. Thomson *et al.* (eds), *Registrum Magni Sigilli Regum Scotorum (Register of the Great Seal of Scotland)*, 11 vols (Edinburgh, 1882–1914) |
| *Rot. Scot.* | D. Macpherson *et al.* (eds), *Rotuli Scotiae in Turri Londinensi et in Domo Capitulari Westmonasteriensi Asservati*, ed. D. Macpherson, 2 vols (London, 1814–19) |
| *RSS* | M. Livingstone *et al.* (eds), *Registrum Secreti Sigilli Sigilli Regum Scotorum (Register of the Privy Seal of Scotland of Scotland)*, 8 vols (Edinburgh, 1908–82) |
| *SP Henry VIII* | *State Papers of Henry VIII, vol. II, part III: Correspondence between England and Ireland 1515–1538* (London, 1834) |
| STC | Short Title Catalogue (http://estc.bl.uk/F/?func=file&file_name=login-bl-estc) |
| *St Giles Reg.* | David Laing (ed.), *Registrum Cartarum Ecclesie Sancti Egidii de Edinburgh* (Edinburgh, 1859) |
| *Scotichronicon by Walter Bower*, ed. Watt | *Scotichronicon by Walter Bower in Latin and English*, ed. D.E.R. Watt, 9 vols (Aberdeen/Edinburgh, 1987–98), vol. vii, *Books XIII and XIV*, ed. A.B. Scott and D.E.R. Watt with Ulrike Morét and Norman F. Shead (Edinburgh, 1996) |
| *SHR* | *Scottish Historical Review* |
| SHS | Scottish History Society |
| TNA | The National Archives, London |
| UStA | University of St Andrews, Special Collections |

The publisher is grateful to the Institute of Scottish Historical Research, University of St Andrews, for generous financial support towards the production costs of the volume.

# I

# Memory and Identity: Mason and the Historians

# Introduction

## *Rethinking the Renaissance and Reformation in Scotland: Roger A. Mason's Work and Legacy*

Steven J. Reid

THE Silver Fox, the Boss, Dr M, he of the full moustache and sardonic eyebrows – all these epithets have been used to describe Roger Mason by his colleagues and students. However, he is best-known to the academic community as Professor of Scottish History at the University of St Andrews, where he taught for almost four decades between 1979 and 2018; as the founding director of their Institute for Scottish Historical Research; and as a leading scholar of Scotland's intellectual and cultural engagement with the Renaissance and Reformation. Roger's research in the field of pre-modern Scottish History has been ground-breaking and iconoclastic. He re-cast late-medieval Stewart kingship within the framework of Renaissance monarchy and Christian humanism; pioneered the application of intellectual- and literary-historical approaches to early modern Scottish studies; and has produced novel and highly influential analyses of a wide canon of key texts, from Mair's *History of Greater Britain* to the writings of John Knox and George Buchanan. This volume, produced to mark Roger's retirement, celebrates his 'rethinking' of the Scottish Renaissance and Reformation by applying the core elements of his historical approach to a broader temporal period between the fourteenth and early seventeenth centuries, and to a range of unstudied or little-known texts. It explores new aspects of Scotland's cultural transition from medieval to Renaissance, the role of historical memory in defining and redefining Scottish identity, the interface between literature, politics and religion in a period of confessional strife and, above all, the importance of ideas in shaping the political and religious outlook of pre-modern Scots. This introductory essay serves both as a personal appreciation of Roger – not just as a research leader but as a colleague, mentor, and teacher – and outlines how the chapters in the volume both interact with and respond to Roger's extensive body of work.

STEVEN J. REID

## Roger A. Mason: Historian, Colleague, Mentor

ROGER attended school at Robert Gordon's College, Drumtochty Castle, and Rannoch, and like most Scottish children of the mid-twentieth century was exposed to virtually no Scottish history while growing up. This trend continued when Roger went to Edinburgh University in 1972 to study Modern History and Politics, but increasingly he became drawn to history and particularly to the period of the Renaissance and Reformation as his course went on. In his final year as an undergraduate he came into contact with two academics who had a profound influence on his historical approach: H.T. (Harry) Dickinson, author of *Liberty and Property: Political Ideology in Eighteenth-Century Britain* (London, 1977); and N.T. (Nick) Phillipson, who, until his death in 2018, was a giant in the study of the society and culture of the Scottish Enlightenment, and who served as Roger's PhD supervisor between 1976 and 1983.[1] Although the courses Roger took with both men were rooted in the eighteenth century, it was through them that Roger engaged with the cultural history of ideas and the authors of the 'Cambridge School' of historiography, key amongst them John Dunn, Quentin Skinner, and John Pocock. Their central contention was that ideas in historical texts were not atemporal, and that their prevailing social and cultural contexts were essential for their interpretation.[2] Phillipson arranged for Roger to spend a year with Pocock in 1978–9 as a graduate student at Johns Hopkins University, when Pocock had only recently published his *The Machiavellian Moment* (1975) and his article inaugurating the concept of a 'New British History'.[3] While studying at the Folger Shakespeare Library in Washington DC in the same year, Roger also met Skinner, who had just published his seminal two-volume *The Foundations of Modern Political Thought*,[4] which fundamentally rewrote our understanding of medieval and Reformation-era conceptions of society, authority, and resistance. Thus, at a key formative point in his intellectual development Roger was immersed in both a contextually based approach to sources and a pan-British approach to Scottish history, methodological frames that would remain an integral part of his work.

After his return from the US Roger succeeded Jane Dawson as the second Glenfiddich fellow in Scottish History at the University of St Andrews, a

1 Thomas Ahnert, 'Editor's Introduction: Nicholas Phillipson and the Sciences of Humankind in Enlightenment Scotland', *History of European Ideas* 48:1 (2022), 1–2.

2 See John Dunn, *The History of Political Theory and Other Essays* (Cambridge, 1996); John Pocock, *Politics, Language and Time* (Chicago, IL, 1971 edn.); Quentin Skinner, 'Meaning and Understanding in the History of Ideas', *History and Theory* 8:1 (1969), 3–53.

3 John Pocock, 'British History: A Plea for a New Subject', *The Journal of Modern History* 47:4 (1975), 601–21.

4 Quentin Skinner, *The Foundations of Modern Political Thought*, 2 vols (Cambridge, 1978).

post that would be held by a series of other distinguished Scottish historians.[5] There Roger joined Professor T.C. (Chris) Smout and Dr Norman Macdougall as the junior member of a newly established Department of Scottish History. Roger's fellowship ended in 1983, but after spending a brief but instructive spell teaching Italian Renaissance history at Newcastle Polytechnic (now the University of Northumbria), Roger returned to St Andrews in 1984 as a full-time lecturer in Scottish History, where he would teach until his retiral in 2018. Roger played an integral role in the development of Scottish History at the university, where staffing in the subject more than doubled over the following four decades. He also contributed teaching across the full spectrum of the curriculum, including survey courses on Scottish history, honours modules on the political and intellectual culture of Renaissance and Reformation Scotland and on Anglo-Scottish unionism in the early modern period, and special subjects on history and national identity in pre-union Britain and on Mary, Queen of Scots. One of the most memorable of these courses (at least in my opinion) was 'Culture and Society in Renaissance Scotland, 1450–1550', which he co-taught with Norman Macdougall. Each week consisted of Roger and Norman sitting at either end of a long table in St John's House, with Roger trying to convince a rather sceptical Norman that there was, in fact, such a thing as a Renaissance in fifteenth- and sixteenth-century Scotland. Another highlight was being taken to see (and hold, though do not tell the insurers) the university's collection of spectacular medieval maces as part of the end of course field trip. Amidst all this activity, one contribution stands out. Roger was the creator in 2007 of the Institute of Scottish Historical Research, which – complete with its own Masters programme and its own publishing outlet in the form of Boydell's 'St Andrews Studies in Scottish History' series – remains a vital and active centre for the discipline and has published several first monographs by promising young scholars in the past decade.[6]

Roger has always advocated framing Scotland's history within the context of the wider world, both as a means of uncovering broader cultural processes shared between Scotland and its neighbours, such as those seen in the transmission of Renaissance thought, and to highlight where Scotland made a decisive contribution to those cultural trends.[7] His work as an academic colleague at St Andrews took a similar inclusive approach, and he was as active a participant in the Centres for Reformation Studies and Book History as he was in Scottish History. Roger also frequently traversed the

[5] Including Keith Brown, John Brims, Catriona Burness, Steve Boardman and Andrew Mackillop.

[6] Amy Blakeway, *Regency in Sixteenth-Century Scotland* (Woodbridge, 2015); Alexander D. Campbell, *The Life and Works of Robert Baillie (1602–1662): Politics, Religion and Record-Keeping in the British Civil Wars* (Boydell, 2017); Miles Kerr-Peterson, *A Protestant Lord in James VI's Scotland: George Keith, Fifth Earl Marischal (1554–1623)* (Woodbridge, 2019).

[7] Roger A. Mason, 'The State of Scottish History: Some Reflections', special supplement to *SHR* 92 (2013), 167–75.

interdisciplinary boundary between Scottish History and Literature, with benefits to both. Nick Phillipson initially encouraged Roger to take this approach when contextualising the ideas of George Buchanan for his doctoral research, advice which ultimately produced a broad and rich thesis on the long context of Buchanan's ideas as framed against Mair, Boece, Knox and other key authors of the sixteenth century.[8] Roger's endeavours into these texts were greatly facilitated by the extensive corpus of Middle Scots texts created by generations of editors for the Scottish Text Society, and he further encouraged historical engagement with them in several 'literary' theses that he supervised, on topics ranging from the works of Sir David Lindsay to the political works of John Leslie.[9] Roger met Sally Mapstone for the first time at a conference in the early 1980s, and their shared interest in fifteenth-century kingship literature led to a long-standing friendship. Roger was an examiner and post-viva source of advice to several of her students, affectionately known as the 'Mapstone Mafia', several of whom have contributed to this volume. Another key colleague and friend of Roger's was the inimitable Jenny Wormald. The two frequently contributed chapters to each other's edited collections, with Roger writing a masterly chapter-length survey of Renaissance and Reformation Scotland for Jenny's *Scotland: A History*.[10] Although the two may not have wholly agreed on a view of Mary, Queen of Scots, it is apparent to anyone who reads their work just how much of an interplay there is between their ideas on renaissance monarchy, pageantry and display, and the nature and extent of royal power.

Influence and legacy come in many forms, and one of Roger's greatest legacies, alongside his body of published work, is as a mentor of students (especially postgraduate students) and young colleagues. Roger often remarked to his Masters and doctoral students that academia was a calling and not just a job, an idea that came increasingly under challenge during his career as a result of growing administrative and workload burdens, increasingly prescriptive REF exercises, and the constant assault on the perceived 'value' of arts and the public sector by successive UK governments. Despite this, Roger always strove to ensure that his students felt valued and included in a lively and engaging academic community, and that they felt a reciprocal responsibility to participate in and enrich that community with their own scholarly input. Roger made attendance mandatory at seminar series and centre social events (something he himself participated in assiduously) and co-organised stimulating and sometimes quite raucous annual reading

8 Roger A. Mason, 'Kingship and Commonweal: Political Thought and Ideology in Reformation Scotland' (unpublished Edinburgh University PhD thesis, 1983).

9 Carol Edington, 'Sir David Lindsay of the Mount: Political and Religious Culture in Renaissance Scotland' (St Andrews PhD thesis, 1991), published as *Court and Culture in Renaissance Scotland: Sir David Lindsay of the Mount* (Amherst, MA, 1994); Margaret J. Beckett, 'The Political Works of John Lesley, Bishop of Ross (1527–96)' (unpublished St Andrews PhD thesis, 2002).

10 Roger A. Mason, 'Renaissance and Reformation: The Sixteenth Century', in *Scotland: A History*, ed. Jenny Wormald (Oxford, 2005), pp. 107–42.

weekends for staff and postgraduates at the Burn and Hospitalfield House in Arbroath. He encouraged his students to give papers wherever possible and to participate in large events like the International Conference on Medieval and Renaissance Scottish Languages, Literature and Culture (ICMRSLLC), which Roger has regularly attended from 1996 and addressed with two plenary lectures. Roger also encouraged younger colleagues to be actively involved with the work of the Scottish History Society, for which he served as President between 2013 and 2018. Above all, Roger inculcated a view in his students that they had a responsibility to repay the time, effort and funding invested in their research by publishing their work, and long after their degrees would serve as a proof-reader and commentator on successive drafts to ensure that this happened.

Yet Roger's influence was often more subtle and more profound than that, and many of his former PhD students recall frequent modest, but key, interventions around the nature and direction of their work. Roger challenged every one of his PhD students at the outset of their research with the simple question: 'why do you want to do this?', and painted a suitably pessimistic picture of potential job prospects for anyone thinking academia was a route to a stable career. However, while he made sure that they understood no job was guaranteed at the end of their degree, he always made them feel that the pursuit and discovery of new historical knowledge was a valuable reward in itself. Roger provided similar critical scrutiny and support mid-PhD when students decided to break into challenging new sources which turned out to be career-defining for the scholars involved, whether these were highly complex Neo-Latin poems, indecipherable kirk session records, or the myriad property transactions in and around early modern St Andrews.[11] With Roger, each supervision was as much a social and pastoral event as it was a mandatory check-in on progress. Many students can recall receiving the full heat of what Roger called his 'professorial scowl' from beneath those famed bushy eyebrows, usually over strong coffee in a café on Market Street, as they sought to explain their latest chapter or research finding. Yet despite the occasional terror that scowl invoked, it was never hostile – merely inquisitive, and usually deeply interested in whatever the student had to say.

Roger has achieved particular distinction as an editor working collaboratively with other scholars, and has produced no less than nine edited collections and special editions of journals.[12] He served as co-editor (with Colin Kidd) of the *Scottish Historical Review* between 1998 and 2003, and is lead editor of the New Edinburgh History of Scotland series, a

[11] Steven J. Reid, *Humanism and Calvinism: Andrew Melville and the Universities of Scotland, c.1560–c.1625* (Farnham, 2011); Steven J. Reid and David McOmish (eds), *Neo-Latin Literature and Literary Culture in Early Modern Scotland* (Leiden, 2016); John McCallum, *Reforming the Scottish Parish: The Reformation in Fife, 1560–1640* (Farnham, 2010); Bess Rhodes, *Riches and Reform: Ecclesiastical Wealth in St Andrews, c.1520–1580* (Leiden, 2019).

[12] See 'Roger A. Mason: A Select Bibliography', section 1.

collection of textbooks which have become the reference point for modern undergraduate study thanks to the combination of narrative and anecdotal case studies on Scottish society and culture in every work. Roger was also one of the founding editorial board members of the 'St Andrews Studies in Reformation History' series, first published by Ashgate and then Brill. Roger was as much of a mentor in his editorial work as he was in his teaching and supervision, providing a number of young colleagues with opportunities to be published in the same volume as the collection of academic heavyweights that Roger seemed effortlessly able to cajole into contributing, and co-editing with Caroline Erskine and Steven Reid in the case of his volumes on George Buchanan and Andrew Melville.[13] Roger understood that edited collections often take their own time and shape, and was patient and constructive in his comments. He also made sure that nothing intemperate or rash was said. He had a natural talent for getting to the heart of what the collection was about in clear simple terms and for organising this material in the best way, a process he continued in advice to the editor of this volume.

## Rethinking the Renaissance and Reformation in Scotland: Roger's Approaches Reconsidered

The essays in this volume interrogate and build on several key areas of Roger's scholarship. Roger is a scholar with an exceptionally broad temporal reach, and has written on topics ranging from the Declaration of Arbroath to the expression of Scottish identity in the decades before the Incorporating Union of 1707 (and even in several articles linking the two).[14] However, he focussed most of his attention on the cultural projection of power between the reigns of James III and James VI and I, on articulating how Scots expressed their culture and identity in a British and European context, and how they used their past to do so. The chapters in this volume reflect these broad themes. Part I situates Roger's work within the context of the development of Scottish history as a field of study in the past four decades, and in the broader historiography of Scottish Reformation studies. Part II engages with several key themes in Roger's writings on medieval nation building and the development of Scottish kingship from the fourteenth to the early sixteenth century, including issues of resistance to royal authority, rituals of royal display and the emergence of Stewart kings as 'Renaissance monarchs'. Part III moves on to the impact of the Reformation on Scottish political and religious culture in the reigns of Mary, Queen of Scots and James VI, particularly emphasising the importance of literary sources – both

13 Mason and Reid (eds), *Andrew Melville*; Erskine and Mason (eds), *George Buchanan*.

14 'The Declaration of Arbroath in Print, 1680–1705', *IR* 72 (2021), 158–76; 'Beyond the Declaration of Arbroath: Kingship, Counsel and Consent in Late Medieval and Early Modern Scotland', in Boardman and Goodare (eds), *Kings, Lords and Men*, pp. 265–82.

vernacular and neo-Latin – in illuminating the intellectual world of post-Reformation Scots. However, while parts II and III are broadly chronological in arrangement, with each examining the pre- and post-Reformation period in turn, the core themes of textual history, history and memory, and the projection of power are interspersed among the chapters across the entire volume. In what follows we examine the key contributions Roger has made to each of these themes, and how the chapters advance, extend, and challenge his work, bringing innovative approaches and new insights to the study of Scotland's medieval and early modern past.

### *Texts Need Context*

Roger's willingness to embrace contextual and literary approaches to texts was apparent from the publication of his very first article in 1980, in the inaugural volume of *History of Political Thought*, which collectively assessed John Knox's *Appellation to the Nobility and Estates*, *Letter to the Commonalty*, and *First Blast of the Trumpet*.[15] Roger argued that Knox's political theology was wholly 'guided by his sense of prophetic vocation' and 'took the form of moral imperatives made binding by a covenant with God', where the people had a moral duty to resist a leader who broke that divine compact. However, Knox's ideas on resistance remained unsystematic and ambiguous, and while he appealed to the Scottish nobility to act as 'inferior magistrates' in defending religion, he never fully articulated the use of deposition or tyrannicide to do so. Roger would develop his articulation of Knox's 'covenanted' view of government in a series of subsequent articles and in his edition of Knox's writings *On Rebellion*, published in the 'Cambridge Texts in the History of Political Thought' series in 1994, and now regarded as the standard edition of Knox's 'political' writings.[16]

Buchanan would remain another central figure in Roger's scholarship, beginning with his exegesis in 1982 of Buchanan's *De Iure Regni Apud Scotos Dialogus* ('Dialogue on the Law of Kingship Among the Scots') in the volume *New Perspectives on the Politics and Culture of Early Modern Scotland* which he co-edited with John Dwyer and Alexander Murdoch.[17] Roger highlighted that although the *De Iure* suggested Scotland had an elective kingship, like Knox's writings it did not offer a clearly defined or systematic exposition of Scottish constitutional law. Instead, it conformed

[15] Roger A. Mason, 'Knox, Resistance and the Moral Imperative', *History of Political Thought*, 1 (1980), 411–36.

[16] Roger A. Mason, 'Covenant and Commonweal: The Language of Politics in Reformation Scotland', in N. Macdougall (ed.), *Church, Politics and Society: Scotland 1408–1929* (Edinburgh, 1983), pp. 97–126; *Knox: On Rebellion*; Roger A. Mason, 'Knox, Resistance and the Royal Supremacy', in Roger A. Mason (ed.), *John Knox and the British Reformations* (Aldershot, 1998), pp. 154–75.

[17] Roger A. Mason, '*Rex Stoicus*: George Buchanan, James VI and the Scottish Polity', in John Dwyer, Roger A. Mason, and Alexander Murdoch (eds), *New Perspectives on the Politics and Culture of Early Modern Scotland* (Edinburgh, 1982), pp. 9–33.

more closely to the humanist 'mirror for princes' (*specula principis*) genre, was heavily influenced by natural law and Classical arguments over scriptural ones, and tried to inculcate an attitude of Senecan Stoicism in its dedicatee, the young James VI.

As with his work on Knox, Roger would go on to examine Buchanan in a range of contexts. These included an assessment of his impact on Andrew Melville and the second generation of reformed Presbyterian intellectuals active in the personal reign of James VI, and the role of the *De Iure* and Buchanan's own history of Scotland in the propaganda war against Mary.[18] Roger also punctured the belief that a wide range of anonymous vernacular polemics circulating at the time of the Marian Civil War were by Buchanan simply because they showed some affinity with his ideas.[19] However, perhaps his greatest gift to Scottish History is his critical edition of the *De Iure*, edited with Martin Smith and first published in 2004, which gave scholars access for the first time to a clear and fully referenced translation of Buchanan's major ideological statement on the nature of kingship and how to deal with tyrants.[20] The importance of this edition was recognised by the Saltire Society in its sponsoring of an accessible translation-only edition of the text, published two years after the release of the facing text edition.[21]

Following Roger's lead, four of the chapters in this volume provide new contextually led examinations of texts, all of which are thematically linked to Buchanan, Mary, Queen of Scots, and the broader shift in intellectual culture towards a Protestant aesthetic in the post-Reformation period. Roger's examination of the pre-publication history of the *De Iure* revealed just how long a gestation period it had, with some 12 years lapsing between its initial drafting around the time of Mary's abdication and its publication for the young King James. Tricia McElroy takes a similarly forensic approach to Buchanan's chief literary opponent, John Leslie, bishop of Ross, whose 1569 *A defence of the honour of the right highe, mightye and noble Princesse Marie Quene of Scotlande* laid the groundwork for all subsequent apologia for the queen. In the most detailed analysis of the work to date, McElroy reveals that the *Defence* was a similarly complex text, which Leslie composed from a range of English legal defences of Mary's claim to the English throne by authors including Edmund

18 Roger A. Mason, 'George Buchanan, James VI and the Presbyterians', in Roger A. Mason (ed.), *Scots and Britons: Scottish Political Thought and the Union of 1603* (Cambridge, 1994), pp. 161–86 [Mason, *Kingship and the Commonweal*, ch, 7]; Roger A. Mason, 'George Buchanan and Mary Queen of Scots', *RSCHS* 30 (2000), 1–27; Roger A. Mason, 'How Andrew Melville Read His George Buchanan', in Mason and Reid (eds), *Andrew Melville*, pp. 11–45. See also 'People Power: George Buchanan on Resistance and the Common Man', in Robert von Friedeburg (ed.), *Widerstandsrecht in der fruhen Neuzeit* (Duncker and Humblot, 2001), pp. 163–81.

19 Roger A. Mason, 'George Buchanan's Vernacular Polemics 1570–1572', *IR* 54 (2003), 47–68.

20 Mason and Smith.

21 Roger A. Mason and Martin S. Smith (eds), *A Dialogue on the Law of Kingship among the Scots: George Buchanan's* De Iure Regni apud Scotos *with a new introduction* (Edinburgh, 2006).

Hale and Anthony Browne, as well as his own work. Leslie's arguments on Mary's rights to rule are diametrically opposed to those of Buchanan in every regard. Where Buchanan suggested that Mary's gender naturally inculcated in her a lust and cruelty that led inexorably to her downfall, Leslie emphasises her positive attributes as a wife, mother and daughter and argues that her gender naturally disinclines her from violence. Ultimately, however, Leslie's core argument hinges on the view, directly challenging Buchanan, that subjects simply cannot depose or remove their divinely appointed sovereign.

Roger showed just how unusual Buchanan's views on royal authority and on tyrannicide were by the standards of his contemporaries, particularly in terms of Buchanan's limiting of the application of Paul's injunction in Romans 13 to obey the magistrate to the immediate historical context of Nero's Rome. Recent work on the ideas of kingship among neo-Latin Scottish authors, including the volume on Andrew Melville co-edited by Roger, has shown that there were a wide spectrum of views on the nature and exercise of kingship in Scotland, even amongst radical Presbyterians who have traditionally been viewed as in ideological lock-step with Buchanan.[22] The chapters by Steven Reid and Kate McClune contribute directly to this debate with new case studies of the articulation of ideas on kingship in neo-Latin and vernacular contexts. Reid focuses on Buchanan's 'interlocutor' in the *De Iure*, Thomas Maitland, and his neo-Latin sylva on the coronation of James VI in 1567, his *Iacobi VI, Scotorum Regis Inauguratio* ('The Consecration of James VI, King of Scots'). Maitland was allegedly furious to learn that he was portrayed in manuscript versions of the *De Iure* as supporting Buchanan's views and denied ever endorsing them, particularly after his family aligned themselves with the Marian cause from 1570 onwards. However, his poem – the only one known to exist commenting on the events of Mary's abdication and James' accession – shows that he had a more complex and ambiguous relationship with the elder humanist, that wavered between supporting his views and defending the monarchy. While Maitland uses the imagery of Virgil's *Aeneid* to demonise the earl of Bothwell as a sub-human murderer and would-be infanticide of the young king, and suggests, with some sympathy, that Mary is a victim of Bothwell's machinations, his text also clearly declares support for James' accession and for Buchanan's views that an unfit monarch should face removal or death, a view which he later retracted.

McClune's examination of the genre of 'New Year's Gift' poetry, also known as *étrennes* or *strena*, between 1500 and 1583 provides us with another new source of corrective advice to the monarch in early modern Scotland. In mapping the incidence of this genre in Scotland against comparative examples in England and France and by Scots in neo-Latin, McClune acknowledges that Scottish poets across the sixteenth century were contributing to a much broader pattern of patronage-seeking from monarchs across Europe at the turn of the year, a traditional day of liberality and largesse in the royal calendar. Yet McClune's

22 See also Reid and McOmish, *Neo-Latin Literature*; Reid and McOmish (eds), *Corona Borealis*.

contextual analysis of this corpus shows that Scots deviated significantly from their European counterparts in not producing these merely to solicit gifts and pensions. As the poems by Gavin Dunbar to James IV, Richard Maitland of Lethington to Marie de Guise, and John Stewart of Baldynneis and Walter Quin to James VI show, there was a consistent thematic link among Scottish authors in using these poems as a means by which to advise and even chastise the monarch for failing to manage religious conflict and the court successfully. These poets did so in bold and often direct ways that reflect the considerable willingness of Scottish intellectuals to hold their rulers to account.

The focus on major 'political' texts of the post-Reformation era, such as those by Buchanan or Knox, has in the past led to a neglect of the wide range of other Protestant texts – devotional, lyrical, autobiographical, emotional – that were produced at a growing rate in the late sixteenth and early seventeenth centuries. Happily, this neglect is now being remedied, thanks to works such as John McCallum's exploration of the emotional world of James Melville via his *Autobiography and Diary*, and Alasdair A. MacDonald's anthology of early seventeenth-century vernacular verse by Scottish authors.[23] Joanna Martin adds to this growing body of work with the first full critical reading of an overlooked but significant contribution to Scots Calvinist poetry, Alexander Hume's *Hymnes, or Sacred Songs, wherin the right vse of Poesie may be espied*, a collection of verse and prose which was printed in Edinburgh in 1599.[24] Martin demonstrates that the *Hymnes* is a carefully designed collection of a minister's writings, its sequence of prose and poetry precisely crafted and structured to explore the identities, roles and relationships of the 'Godly' poet and his reader, in terms of both delineating a method of private piety and drawing the reader into a sense of community with other members of the faithful elect.[25] The text is thus emblematic of the growing shift, evident by the second half of the reign of James VI and confirmed by recent studies of kirk discipline in a behavioural context, of Scottish communities embracing Protestantism as a core part of national identity. This key cultural process was one identified by Roger in his own studies of historical and political writings of the early seventeenth century.

### *'Usable Pasts' and the Manipulation of History*

Another key aspect of the 'contextual' approach developed by the 'Cambridge School' is the recognition of how inherently contingent all texts are on the place and time in which they are written.[26] Never is this idea more apparent than in Roger's exploration, across a wide range of articles, of what he termed

[23] John McCallum, *Exploring Emotion in Reformation Scotland: The Emotional Worlds of James Melville, 1556–1614* (Palgrave, 2022); Alasdair A. MacDonald (ed.), *Jacobean Parnassus: Scottish Poetry from the Reign of James I* (Glasgow, 2022).

[24] STC 13942.

[25] See, for example, George David Mullan, *Narratives of the Religious Self in Early Modern Scotland* (Farnham, 2010).

[26] See notes 2–4.

Scotland's 'usable pasts', where Scottish authors shaped and reshaped the collective store of national events and memory to serve their political and ideological needs.[27] How these 'pasts' (Roger uses the plural advisedly) were expressed and harnessed shifted considerably, depending on whether an author had (for example) a scholastic or humanist background, or a pro- or anti-English viewpoint. However, a core thread linking virtually all of them is their need to stress the sovereignty and fierce independence of the ancient Scottish nation from England, and the two nations' equal standing.

As Roger notes, the scholastic theologian John Mair, in his *History of Greater Britain* (1521), was surprisingly in favour of a monarchical union between the two kingdoms, as a remedy to what he saw as the untrammelled power of Scotland's nobility and its weak and ineffective church hierarchy.[28] He also presented the histories of Scotland and England in parallel, underscoring the fact that the two had a shared and overlapping past. However, Mair rejected the fable that the kingdoms of mainland Britain had been founded by Brutus of Troy and divided among his three sons, and that Scotland had returned to his eldest son Locrinus, the king of England, on the premature death of Albanactus, his second son. This fiction had been used by English monarchs from Edward I onwards to assert England's feudal superiority, and Mair refused to countenance either it or the idea that Scotland had been founded by the Trojan Prince Gathelus and Scota, the daughter of an Egyptian pharaoh. However, the same feudal myth would be used by Henry VIII, the Protector Somerset, John Henrisoun and other pro-English authors during the period of the Rough Wooings to justify their invasion of Scotland and argue that a forced marriage of Mary to the young Edward VI would simply be a return to an ancient and natural British political settlement.[29]

In the same period the turn towards Renaissance Humanism created two histories of Scotland, by Hector Boece and George Buchanan, that were diametrically opposed in both approach and content to such pro-union readings.[30] Both men combined the content of medieval chronicle narratives

[27] Roger A. Mason, 'Usable Pasts: History and Identity in Reformation Scotland', *SHR* 76 (1997), 54–68. See also Roger A. Mason, 'From Chronicle to History: Recovering the Past in Renaissance Scotland', in Rudolf Suntrup and Jan Veenstra (eds), *Building the Past / Konstruktion der eigenen Verganganheit* (Frankfurt am Main, 2006), pp. 53–66.

[28] Roger A. Mason, 'Kingship, Nobility and Anglo-Scottish Union: John Mair's *History of Greater Britain* (1521)', *IR* 41 (1990), 182–222 [Mason, *Kingship and the Commonweal*, ch. 2].

[29] Roger A. Mason, 'Scotching the Brut: Politics, History and National Myth in Sixteenth-Century Britain', in Roger A. Mason (ed.), *Scotland and England 1286–1815* (Edinburgh, 1987), pp. 95–129; Roger A. Mason, 'The Scottish Reformation and the Origins of Anglo-British Imperialism', in Roger A. Mason (ed.), *Scots and Britons: Scottish Political Thought and the Union of 1603* (Cambridge, 1994), pp. 161–86 [Mason, *Kingship and the Commonweal*, ch. 9]; Arthur H. Williamson, *Scottish National Consciousness in the Age of James VI: The Apocalypse, the Union and the Shaping of Scotland's Public Culture* (Edinburgh, 1979).

[30] Mason, 'Scotching the Brut'; Roger A. Mason, 'Civil Society and the Celts: Hector Boece, George Buchanan and the Ancient Scottish Past', in E. J. Cowan and R. J. Finlay

of Walter Bower and John of Fordun with the approach of moralising Classical histories, chief among them Livy's *Ab Urbe Condita*, to write a heavily rhetorical and largely fabulous account of Scotland's past. Both projected the cultural values of humanism onto a primitive and idealised Gaelic past, going back to the reign of the mythical Fergus I in 330 BC, which they believed contemporary Scots would do well to emulate for its 'Spartan' simplicity and virtue. While Mair had been deeply critical of Highland culture as 'indolent, undisciplined and aggressive', Boece and Buchanan believed that the Highlands and Islands retained the last vestiges of that golden age of Gaelic society. Both men also suggested that Scotland had a long tradition of 'aristocratic conciliarism', though only Buchanan went so far as to argue that monarchical authority had been fully elective, and suggested there was an explicit link between their behaviour as good or bad monarchs and their ultimate and often providential fate as a result.

The Scottish Reformation of 1559–60 and the Union of Crowns in 1603 disrupted and challenged the narrative of Scotland's past, but the championing of Scotland as a sovereign kingdom rarely wavered as it headed towards the Incorporating Union of 1707.[31] Elizabeth I showed little or no interest in the spurious feudal claims that had been so championed by her father, but ironically it was after James VI's accession as James VI and I that it became 'far from axiomatic' that seventeenth-century Scotland possessed sovereignty – this was certainly not a view held by either the successive Stuart monarchs or Oliver Cromwell.[32] Amongst English intellectuals in the seventeenth century there was little evidence of engagement with the idea of the power relationship between the two nations, save for an unquestioned assumption that England was the dominant partner, by virtue of both its much larger population, wealth, and imperial trading power. For Scots this relationship was an uneasy and anxious one, and intellectual responses wavered between articulating a desire for closer union, often rooted in Protestant providentialism, and the need to ensure that Scotland's sovereignty and equality with its southern partner was respected.[33] The lawyer and intellectual

---

(eds), *Scottish History: The Power of the Past* (Edinburgh, 2002), pp. 95–119; Martin MacGregor, 'Gaelic Barbarity and Scottish Identity in the Later Middle Ages', in D. Broun and M. MacGregor (eds), *Mìorun mòr nan Gall, 'The great ill-will of the Lowlander?' Lowland Perceptions of the Highlands, Medieval and Modern* (Glasgow, 2009), pp. 7–48; Martin MacGregor, 'Civilising Gaelic Scotland: The Scottish Isles and the Stewart Empire', in E. Ó. Ciardha and M. Ó. Siochru (eds), *The Plantation of Ulster: Ideology and Practice* (Manchester, 2012), pp. 33–54.

[31] Roger A. Mason, 'Dis-United Kingdoms? What Lies Behind Scotland's Referendum on Independence', *Georgetown Journal of International Affairs* 14 (2013), 139–46.

[32] Roger A. Mason, 'Scotland, Elizabethan England and the Idea of Britain', *Transactions of the Royal Historical Society* 14 (2004), 279–93; Roger A. Mason, 'Debating Britain in Seventeenth-Century Scotland: Multiple Monarchy and Scottish Sovereignty', *Journal of Scottish Historical Studies* 35 (2015), 1–24 [quote at p. 2].

[33] Roger A. Mason, 'Lineages of Unionism: Early Modern Scotland and the Idea of Britain', *History Scotland* 8.1 (2008), 40–48; Roger A. Mason, '1603: Multiple Monarchy and Scottish Identity', *History* 105 (2020), 402–21.

Sir Thomas Craig's poems and tracts on union show clearly that he believed James inherited the English and Scottish thrones by divine right at a crucial juncture in world history. This was a view shared by Andrew Melville, John Johnston and other reformed intellectuals, who all toyed with the epithet 'Scoto-Britannus' as a way of showing their enthusiasm for what they hoped would be an enduring godly union that would directly counter the power of Catholic Europe.[34] However, Craig and Sir John Russell both argued for a union *aeque principaliter*, an idea first put forward by the Spanish jurist Juan de Solarzano Pereira in relation to the composite Habsburg monarchies in Europe, where each sovereign ruled over a series of constituent states that were equally important and sovereign in their own way.[35]

This narrative of the engagement of Scottish writers and historians with their own past is one that we owe nearly entirely to Roger, and four of the chapters engage directly with the presentation of Scottish history, memory and self-identity. Taking as his starting point Norbert Kersken's identification of a proliferation of self-consciously 'national histories' across Europe in the twelfth and thirteenth centuries, Dauvit Broun uses the methodologies pioneered by Joanna Tucker in her examination of Scotland's cartulary manuscripts to examine the earliest attempts to provide a 'national history' of Scotland from its origins until the early fourteenth century in the form of John of Fordun's *Chronica Gentis Scotorum*.[36] William Skene's nineteenth-century edition of Fordun had intentionally edited the text to make it look like a continuous narrative and had deliberately played down the disparate and fragmented nature of his source base. However, Broun's masterful study of manuscript witnesses has led to the reconstruction of a version in the British Library collection, previously thought lost in the fire of 1731, which had been separated into folios in Cotton MS Vitellius E XI and is now called Cotton MS Otho B III*. The reconstructed witness shows that a medieval codex of the first five books of Fordun and material down to the mid-fourteenth century had been compiled in just such a 'continuous' way as early as the last quarter of the fifteenth century, and that Skene's editorialising of Fordun into an early 'national history' had a medieval precedent.

[34] Steven J. Reid, 'Andrew Melville and the Law of Kingship', and Arthur H. Williamson, 'Empire and Anti-Empire: Andrew Melville and British Political Ideology, 1589–1605', in Mason and Reid (eds), *Andrew Melville*, pp. 47–74, 75–99. For editions of Melville's 'political' poetry, see *George Buchanan: The Political Poetry*, ed. Paul J. McGinnis and Arthur H. Williamson (Edinburgh, 1995), Appendix C; and Reid and McOmish (eds), *Corona Borealis*, pp. 213–43.

[35] For general background, see J. H. Elliott, *Scots and Catalans: Union and Disunion* (New Haven, CT, 2018), pp. 6–38.

[36] Norbert Kersken, 'National Chronicles and National Consciousness', in János M. Bak and Ivan Jurković (eds), *Chronicon. Medieval Narrative Sources: A Chronological Guide with Introductory Essays* (Turnhout, 2013), pp. 119–26 (quote at p. 125); Joanna Tucker, *Reading and Shaping Medieval Cartularies: Multi-Scribe Manuscripts and their Patterns of Growth. A Study of the Earliest Cartularies of Glasgow Cathedral and Lindores Abbey* (Woodbridge, 2020).

Protestantism in Scotland was, until well into the twentieth century, a defining element of national character and pride, and the Reformation of 1560 was treated in historiography as a defining moment when Catholic 'superstition' was cast off in favour of literacy and discipline.[37] Area studies and examinations of the lived experience of Protestant culture have shown that the idea of a sudden break with Scotland's Catholic past was in no way true, and that even by the early seventeenth century reformed culture was slow to take root in many parts of Scotland.[38] However, as the chapters by Jane Dawson and Bess Rhodes in this volume show, the mythology of Protestant reform was already being actively created and promoted in the immediate aftermath of the events of the Reformation Rebellion and Parliament. Rhodes' wide-ranging examination of recollections of the process of reform in diaries, council registers, kirk records, and histories by Knox and others across the later sixteenth century charts for the first time the ways in which the reform movement was initially remembered and commemorated by many of its participants. Rhodes reveals widespread optimism regarding the actions of the reformers in the immediate aftermath of 1560, and a general sense that it had 'pleased the Almighty to open the eyes of all people'. However, as the first decade of reform passed and James VI grew out of his minority into young adulthood, this optimism foundered and criticism on both sides of the Kirk began to emerge – for radical Presbyterians because the Reformation had not gone far enough, and for moderates more inclined to episcopal and royal control because there was a sense that the reform movement had brought massive disorder and chaos.

Dawson's examination of the relationship between John Knox and James Stewart, the earl of Moray and first regent of James VI, reveals how mythology was also applied to key figures in the early process of reform. The events of 1558–9 quickly forced the two men to work together in the shared interest of promoting religious reform, but their relationship quickly soured following the return of Mary, Queen of Scots to Scotland in August 1561 and Stewart's subsequent political alignment with his sister (for which he was rewarded in 1562 with the earldom of Moray). They remained opposed to one another, and Knox remained largely in political exile, until Mary's abdication, when the need to present a united 'godly' front around the infant King James saw Knox provide a sermon at his coronation and side once again with Moray. Moray's assassination in 1570 led to Knox creating an image of Moray as a 'gude' and godly regent which endured until very recently, and directly added to the mythology of the early reform movement.

[37] See discussions of this issue below, in the chapters by Catriona MacDonald and Bess Rhodes.

[38] Margo Todd, *The Culture of Protestantism in Early Modern Scotland* (New Haven, CT and London, 2003); Michael F. Graham, *The Uses of Reform: 'Godly Discipline' and Popular Behavior in Scotland and Beyond, 1560–1610* (Leiden, 1996); McCallum, *Reforming the Scottish Parish*.

That mythology remained an integral part of Scottish historical scholarship, as Catriona MacDonald argues in her assessment of the intellectual and social relationships between Andrew Lang and David Hay Fleming, well into the twentieth century. Hay Fleming's approach to historical writing was, as one might expect from one of the earliest editors for the Scottish History Society, deeply empirical and rooted in source transcription and examination, whilst Lang, an early pioneer of material culture and literary approaches to history, was more willing to countenance the role that romance and legend played in constructing historical narratives, particularly in relation to Mary, Queen of Scots. While the works written by both men on Mary were wholly opposed in both approach and assessment of the queen, and the two men deeply disagreed on the positive and 'whiggish' values of the Protestant Reformation, they shared a friendship and a respect that gives the lie to any idea of a binary division in their views and reflects an age of scholarship when historiographical battle lines over the history of the Reformation had yet to be fully drawn.

### *Renaissance Monarchy and the Projection of Stewart Power*

Another key argument in Roger's work, and one which has (as Sally Mapstone's afterword shows) caused considerable debate, is that there was in fact a Renaissance in Scotland, and that the monarchs of the Stewart dynasty participated in the cultural movement known as 'Renaissance' or 'New Monarchy'.[39] In a series of lively studies Roger portrayed the later Stewart dynasty as consciously emphasising the supremacy of the king's legal authority within the realm and beyond it, seen most strikingly in James III's declaration of Scotland having 'ful jurisdictioune and fre impire within his realme' in the parliament of 1469.[40] Under James IV and James V this process particularly accelerated via the patronage of new building programmes at the main royal palaces as physical symbols of power and display. Heraldry, chivalry and iconography played a central role in this articulation of Stewart power, with the core symbols we associate with Scotland – the cross of St Andrew, the lion rampant, and the thistle – all being deployed to the fullest extent in art and coinage for the first time. Another core element of this programme was the use of Renaissance Humanism, particularly at the courts of James IV and James V, where a range of scholars, poets and scientists were gathered under the auspices of the king for the purposes of demonstrating his cultural refinement and learning.

[39] Glenn Richardson, *Renaissance Monarchy: The Reigns of Henry VIII, Francis I and Charles V* (London, 2002).

[40] *RPS*, 1469/20. Roger A. Mason, 'This Realm of Scotland Is an Empire? Imperial Ideas and Iconography in Early Renaissance Scotland', in Barbara E. Crawford (ed.), *Church, Chronicle and Learning in Medieval and Early Renaissance Scotland* (Edinburgh, 1999), pp. 73–91; 'Renaissance Monarchy? Stewart Kingship (1469–1542)', in Brown and Tanner (eds), *Scottish Kingship*, pp. 255–78.

As Steve Boardman notes, chronologically the advent of Renaissance kingship in Scotland is usually placed, by Roger and others, in the reign of James III (1460–88). Three of the chapters in this volume argue that several of these aspects of Renaissance monarchy were evident in Scotland far earlier. Boardman argues that the pietistic elements of royal display can in fact be found in the reign of James III's grandfather, James I (1406–37), particularly in the ways that James promoted an elevated and quasi-sacral image of the monarchy through his support of the cult of St John the Baptist. This cult, which was Europe-wide, emphasised the Baptist's role as a forerunner of Christ's message and in fostering piety, ideas which correspond closely to the role of Renaissance kings as defenders of the faith. James' patronage of the Carthusian Priory at Perth, an order noted for its asceticism and discipline, may have been intended to bolster the image of James as a lawgiver and reformer.[41] In the same vein, his building of a new palace chapel at Linlithgow, and the linked rebuilding of the parish church as a collegiate foundation via a papal supplication 'bearing special devotion to St John the Baptist', all reflect interest in the cult as a means to project royal piety and authority, and directly anticipate later displays of piety such as James III's re-foundation of the chapel at Restalrig.

Monarchs were also intent on ensuring that their rights as sovereign rulers were projected – and protected – while those of their subjects were given short shrift. In Roger's articles examining political attitudes to monarchy in the fourteenth and fifteenth centuries he has shown that the more open models of counsel and consent apparent in documents like the Declaration of Arbroath simply did not gain widespread currency.[42] Roger has explored how far intellectual justifications were used to justify resistance to James I and his ultimate regicide, and here Michael Brown looks at a much earlier example of legal theory being deployed to underpin monarchical authority.[43] Robert the Bruce's use, at the Black Parliament of August 1320, of charges of lese majesty, or high treason, against a group of nobles led by William Soules of Liddesdale was without precedent in Scotland, though similar charges had been used in a contemporary English context by Edward II. Bruce was challenged as a monarch due to his being placed under excommunication by Pope John XXII in June 1318 for his refusal to heed papal censure, and his continued lack of an adult male heir. It was this continued insecurity that resulted in the need to define treason as a specific crime of disloyalty to the monarch in a 1318 entail, or 'tailzie', outlining the succession through the Stewart line, which he then used two years later. The evolution of this response shows that Bruce had a clear sense of his rights as a monarch which

[41] James' Carthusian foundation at Perth is the focus of a current project led by Professor Richard Oram and Dr Lucinda Dean. See also Richard Oram, 'Perth in the Middle Ages: An Environmental History', in D. Strachan (ed.), *Perth: A Place in History* (Perth, 2011).

[42] Mason, 'Beyond the Declaration of Arbroath'; Roger A. Mason, 'Kingship, Tyranny and the Right to Resist in Fifteenth-Century Scotland', *SHR* 66 (1987), 125–51.

[43] Mason, 'Kingship, Tyranny and the Right to Resist'.

went far beyond those of previous kings ruling in concert with the community of the realm, and presaged the imperial ambitions of the later Stewart kings to be recognised as undisputed rulers of the kingdom.

Nicola Royan also examines the intellectual dimensions of early Renaissance Humanism in Scotland, particularly in terms of rhetoric and oratory, through two Scottish diplomatic missions during the reign of James III. Via a close reading of speeches attributed to Archibald Whitelaw (as part of an embassy to Richard III) and William Elphinstone (as ambassador to Louis XI), Royan considers the way in which the authors present the Scottish people and the characterisation of their relationships with the English and the French. Both authors make extensive use of Classical allusion within their arguments, suggesting a greater accessibility to Classical material in Scotland in the 1470s and 1480s than has been acknowledged hitherto. The speeches also show that the bureaucracy of James III's government engaged directly with the intellectual fashions on the Continent, and displayed considerable self-belief in Scottish sovereignty in general and implicit critiques of Richard III in particular. Royan concludes that Whitelaw's and Elphinstone's speeches show they were part of the foundational generation of Scottish humanism, at a time when scholastic logic and disputation was still very much the dominant mode of discourse in the universities and other parts of the intellectual landscape in Scotland.

While these chapters all roll back the temporal boundaries by which we view the practice of Renaissance monarchy, the chapters by Alison Cathcart and Esther Mijers look at the application of these ideas in a transnational context, by focussing on Scottish relationships across the sixteenth century with other European nations. James V's circumnavigation of Scotland in 1540 has often been taken rather uncritically as a blunt expression of the king's imperial pretensions, but Cathcart's careful, contextually led reconstruction of his reasons for making such a voyage turns the focus outward from internal Scottish politics to James' place within disputes and debates over kingship in both Ireland and Denmark–Norway. Kingship in the latter was both hereditary and elective as kings were bound by the remit of their coronation oath in terms of the scope of their duties. Cathcart brings to the fore evidence that suggests the people of Lübeck offered Henry VIII the crown of Denmark in 1535, capitalising on his perceived commitment to the Protestant faith. The Lübeckers made the offer solely to realise their own domestic political aims, and the offer was promptly rejected by the English king when he realised the terms. However, such a claim would have given Henry the right to redeem Shetland and Orkney, territory ceded to Scotland as part of James III's marriage negotiations in 1469. James V's awareness of these events ensured he turned down the offer made to him in 1540 of 'high-kingship' of Ireland, and prompted him to refocus his attention on the dimensions of his own imperium. The expedition, therefore, had a very real and practical aim of securing the full landed territorial extent of Scotland and making the most of its internal natural resources, a process left very much in progress at his untimely death.

Renaissance symbolism and display continued to play an enduring role in Scotland's part in international politics and diplomacy, even long after the high watermark of Renaissance monarchy reached by James IV and James V had passed. Scotland and the Dutch states had a long-shared history of trade, religious culture, and interest in Renaissance Humanism which endured across the sixteenth century, yet the attendance of the Dutch ambassadors at the baptism of Prince Henry in 1594 has gone relatively unnoticed. Mijers provides the first exploration of this event from the perspective of Dutch sources, and finds that the visit of the Dutch ambassadors was no mere courtesy. Instead, it was a carefully planned trip using the pretext of the baptism, preceded by lengthy negotiations among the Estates General, that aimed to propose an offensive and defensive league between Scotland and the Dutch states (recently emancipated from Habsburg rule) against Spain. It also aimed at the resumption of previous trade agreements, central to which (in Dutch eyes at least) was the Treaty of Bins, originally concluded in 1550 between Charles V and Mary, Queen of Scots in the aftermath of the Treaty of Boulogne, and which the Dutch believed would offer them protection against Spanish reprisals if renewed. While James refused to ratify such a league or the Treaty of Bins, he did renew and maintain older trade contacts and the Scottish Staple at Veere, and the whole episode showed the important political dimensions that continued to underpin such symbolic and celebratory displays of power, even at the end of the sixteenth century.

## Conclusion: The Renaissance, the Reformation, and Rethinking Long-Term Trends in Scottish History

THE chapters in this volume all collectively respond to methodological frames developed largely by Roger: the ideas of a Scottish Renaissance and the exercise of Stewart power within that cultural context; of a constantly evolving Scottish self-identity that was particularly exercised throughout the early modern period by the changing relationship with both England and Europe; and of the historical and political significance of a wide range of writings by Scottish authors that is only fully revealed when their contents are contextually researched. Collectively they show the continued and enduring value of these approaches, while at the same time nuancing and challenging Roger's conclusions. The chapters by McClune, Reid, McElroy, and Martin show the necessity and continued vitality in early modern Scottish historical studies of the 'text needs context' approach. Each offers a fundamental re-assessment of the author or genre in question that further complicates our understanding of arguments for and against monarchical power, the nature of governance in Scotland, and the reception of the Reformation. There remains a wealth of tracts, poems and other writings that simply have not had even a basic survey using this approach, particularly in a neo-Latin context, and which have the potential similarly to disrupt our perceived understandings of these issues.

A broader question emerging from the chapters by Boardman, Brown, Royan, Cathcart and Mijers is the nature of periodization in early modern Scottish history, particularly in relation to the practice and exercise of Scottish monarchy. As these chapters show, several aspects of what we might previously have termed 'Renaissance' cultural traits – the use of theory to justify and protect sovereign authority, chivalric and pietistic displays of powers, cultural set pieces including circumnavigation and celebrations, and the articulation of humanist Classicism within a diplomatic context – can be witnessed across a much broader temporal scope than we are accustomed to thinking, much earlier than the traditional chronology of James III–James V suggests, and with continuities in practice that extend into the post-Protestant watershed of James VI's reign and beyond. Roger certainly identified the core traits of what made the Stewart dynasty successful and powerful in the fifteenth and sixteenth centuries, but the evidence of this volume suggests that we arguably need to reframe these traits within a much broader view as tools deployed to maintain authority in Scotland across the whole of the medieval and early modern period.

Finally, the chapters by MacDonald, Broun, Rhodes, and Dawson all engage with the centrality of the idea of a shared national past in historical writings by Scottish authors, and develop Roger's ideas that an anxiety to assert Scotland's independence from English sovereignty and an ardent belief in the values of the Protestant faith were core in the articulation of that past. The case studies on offer here, from Fordun through to Lang and Hay Fleming, show that the desire for a 'national history' has existed discontinuously for over three quarters of a millennium, again extending the chronological scope of this idea beyond the fifteenth and sixteenth centuries as an origin point. But they also confirm that Roger's view of Protestantism as a defining factor in Scottish identity was more central than even he suggested, from the moment of the Reformation itself until the very recent past. In this sense, the embracing of a Protestant 'self-fashioning' – in other words, taking up the idea that to be Scottish was to be Protestant and vice versa – was arguably a far more significant, sudden and enduring shift than any practical or behavioural shift triggered by the adoption of reformed discipline. The conclusion that this idea about Scottish identity ultimately had a greater endurance and power than any short-term action is surely a fitting one to end on for a volume dedicated to a historian of political thought.

# 1

# *Contesting the Reformation: Roger Mason's ('sufficiently plausible') Debt to David Hay Fleming and Andrew Lang*

Catriona M.M. Macdonald

IN 1881 the publishers of the *St Andrews Citizen* produced *An Alphabetic Guidebook to St Andrews* by David Hay Fleming – a local man whose father John had a china and stoneware business which David would sell two years later to finance a life focused on all things antiquarian. His guidebook pointed to the usual tourist attractions, including the skating rink at the west end of the Scores where workmen had unearthed a lead seal of Pope Innocent IV, a pontiff described by Hay Fleming as 'inferior to none of his predecessors in arrogance and insolence of temper'.[1] In comments such as these it was clear that Hay Fleming offered more than a map to the boulevards of the town: he also suggested he had the measure of its soul. Anticipating the black tourism of later generations, while clinging unapologetically to hegemonic Protestant 'truths', Hay Fleming began this volume by guiding visitors around sites of execution and iconoclasm, imbuing the built environment of St Andrews with the memory of religious fervour.

> … Patrick Hamilton gained the martyr's crown; but his "reek" infected all on whom it blew. … the gentle George Wishart was consumed in front of the Castle that Cardinal Beaton might luxuriously gloat over his dying agonies. The retribution, however, was swift and terrible, for he who had shown no mercy was slain without mercy in his own stronghold. Walter Mill, though aged and feeble, was committed to the flames in 1558. The following year the inhabitants of St Andrews, fired by the irresistible logic and eloquence of Knox, invaded the monasteries, and cleansed the churches of everything that seemed to savour of idolatry. In a niche over the archway between the east end of the Cathedral and the Turret Light, there was an image of the Madonna; though it has been rudely handled, a fragment is still to be seen; it is the only surviving vestige of a Popish idol in St Andrews.[2]

[1] David Hay Fleming, *An Alphabetic Guidebook to St Andrews* (St Andrews, 1881), p. 64. Here Hay Fleming borrows directly from the eighteenth-century Lutheran church historian Johann Lorenz von Mosheim (1693–1755). The site of the skating rink has been occupied since 1910 by St James Roman Catholic church.

[2] Ibid., p. v.

Yet Hay Fleming's, as one might expect, was not the only voice when it came to St Andrews' heritage around this time. In 1861 Selkirk born Andrew Lang enrolled at St Andrews University. His love of the town would last his lifetime; he is buried near the perimeter wall in the east graveyard of St Andrews Cathedral, and during his life he immortalised the town in poetry and prose, including a short history, published in 1893. The preliminary pages of Lang's *St Andrews* make it clear that 'his' is a town very different from that of Hay Fleming's imagination. Pointedly, Lang's book begins with a tranquil illustration of 'St Andrews *before* John Knox', and thereafter he offers a sceptical take on the Reformation:

> Mary Stuart is the fairest and most fascinating of the historical shadows which haunt St Andrews. … we hear of her coming and going, of her retreats to the little town of the desecrated shrines, but of what she did here we know but little. A retreat she needed, for she had come into a terrible country – among open enemies, false friends, hatred, covetousness, treason. On all sides her path was beset by dangers which were insuperable and inevitable. …
>
> [Mary] was grudgingly permitted the exercise of her own religion; but the spite of the irreconcilable Knox and the insults of the multitude dogged her devotions. … The Scottish kirk was in the hands of men who abominated all authority, ecclesiastical or secular, superior to their own. They had got rid of priests, of a sacred class with sacerdotal pretensions, but their own pretensions were really more arrogant. Anyone who liked, and whose violence of invective could persuade others, set up as a prophet.[3]

Roger Mason arrived in St Andrews in 1984 as Lecturer in Scottish History. St Katharine's Lodge, not far from the site of the old skating rink, and Mason's academic home for the next 34 years, had not even been built when Lang enrolled as a student, but in a very real sense, David Hay Fleming and Andrew Lang helped shape the environment in which Roger Mason found himself. After his death, Hay Fleming's library became the core of the town's reference library, to which at least one of Mason's undergraduate students would often have recourse, having found the university library shelves denuded by her more eager peers. And in a series of Andrew Lang lectures, the 'college of the scarlet gown' periodically honours the author of 'Almae Matres' – a poem which more than any other encapsulates an idealistic vision of the St Andrews undergraduate experience.[4] More profoundly, the work of these authors informed the intellectual environment in which Mason's own scholarship would be read by both lay and academic audiences. In short, despite the passage of many years, they contributed to an interpretive frame

3 Andrew Lang, *St Andrews* (London, 1893), frontispiece [my italics], pp. 172–3.

4 University of St Andrews, Special Collections [hereafter UStA], Lan PR4876.A6A, Andrew Lang, 'Almae Matres' (Edinburgh, 1887).

with which Mason and other early modern scholars of his generation had to engage. Whether or not the particular contribution of Fleming and Lang was obvious to Mason as he made St Andrews his home is doubtful: you will struggle to find Mason quoting either scholar.[5] Yet Mason certainly appreciated the power of centuries of partisan scholarship, and the traditions of the past in shaping the historiography of the Scottish Reformation. Indeed, it is a topic that has been at the core of many of his publications.[6] In this regard, then, Mason's debt to Fleming and Lang is 'sufficiently plausible' – the measure of rigour rather self-effacingly endorsed by Mason himself in an *Innes Review* essay on George Buchanan from 2003 where he admits that there is much in his interpretation that 'cannot be proved conclusively'.[7] This author, who knew the town library well, follows her erstwhile tutor in claiming the same measure, though with far more cause.

## Reputations

ANDREW Lang started writing Scottish history in the mid-1890s, after a successful yet foreshortened career at Oxford, and having already established a reputation in the classics, folklore studies and anthropology as well as achieving celebrity status as a writer of fairy tales and memorable reviews and articles in numerous London journals. By the 1890s, Hay Fleming's reputation as a serious scholar of both St Andrews and of the Reformation was recognised in Scotland.[8] In the 1880s Hay Fleming published a range of serious studies of ecclesiastical and local interest, exemplified by his study of the hammermen of St Andrews published by the *Fife Herald* in 1884. Thereafter, his alphabetic guide to the town was variously reworked as a 'handbook', and penny- and six-penny-editions were printed in large numbers, as were new works of a similar ilk that took in the East Neuk more generally. Hay Fleming produced a study of the martyrs of St Andrews in 1887, before – in 1889 – the first volume of his register of the ministers, elders and deacons of St Andrews was published by the Scottish History Society (SHS), the second following in 1890. By contrast, Lang's engagement with Scottish studies grew from a literary root, if one sets aside his works on angling and

[5] James Kirk, 'John Knox and the Historians' – an essay edited by Mason – paraphrases Lang approvingly but does not mention him by name in the narrative. In Roger A. Mason (ed.), *John Knox and the British Reformations* (Basingstoke, 1998), pp. 7–26, at pp. 15, 18, 20.

[6] See for example: Roger A. Mason, 'Kingship, Nobility and Anglo-Scottish Union: John Mair's *History of Greater Britain* (1521)', *IR* 41.2 (1990), 182–222; '*Certeine Matters Concerning the Realme of Scotland*: George Buchanan and Scottish Self-Fashioning at the Union of the Crowns', *SHR* 92.1 (2013), 38–65.

[7] Roger A. Mason, 'George Buchanan's Vernacular Polemics, 1570–1572', *IR* 54.1 (2003), 47–68, at p. 61.

[8] William Donaldson, 'Andrew Lang (1844–1912)', *ODNB* [34396]; J.D. Mackie (revised H.C.G. Matthew), 'David Hay Fleming (1849–1931)', *ODNB* [33165].

golf. In the 1890s he edited Walter Scott's Waverley novels, and followed this up with a biography of John Gibson Lockhart (Scott's son-in-law and biographer), at much the same time as producing an edition of the poems and songs of Robert Burns. It may seem that on the one hand we have an East Neuk antiquarian and ecclesiastical scholar and, on the other, a metropolitan polymath and something of a literary dandy, but were things that simple?

The choice by the SHS of David Hay Fleming as one of its earliest editors – the society was but four years old when it published his *Register* – is certainly worth noting as a measure of the respect in which he was held. Indeed, his commitment to record scholarship was further reaffirmed in the preface to this work, where he prioritised archival sources and emphasised that the importance of the Reformation was such that 'every authentic record must be welcome'.[9] Lang, however, had earlier confessed in his introduction to his St Andrews volume that he had made 'scarcely any use of documents in MS', gladly leaving 'the department of manuscript to a far better qualified student'.[10] Both approaches got their authors into trouble: Lang, predictably, for his cavalier attitude to scientific methods. The following poem appears in the Hay Fleming archive in the University of St Andrews, although its authorship is unclear:

> *An Epilogue*
> This book on St Andrews was written by Lang,
> A smart Selkirk lad with a slight Oxford twang.
> Concocted in haste for the sake of the penny –
> Its merits are few and its blunders are many.
> The matter is cribbed, but the style is his own,
> And for flippant conceit it stands quite alone.
> No Scotsman can read it without indignation,
> And wishing the author a sound flagellation,
> And this he has got at the hands of a native [David Hay Fleming]
> That slates the book as the work of a catiff (sic),
> Who for a living has taken to letters,
> And earns his bread by abusing his betters.[11]

Meanwhile, Hay Fleming was found not to be beyond reproach. He was taken to task for his shameful inclusion of salacious details in his accounts of the early Kirk. In March 1889, Mr Bowie of the Union Bank of Coatbridge wrote to Thomas Law of the SHS intimating that he intended to leave the Society, noting:

9 David Hay Fleming (ed.), 'Preface', *Register of the Ministers, Elders and Deacons of the Christian Congregation of St. Andrews … Part First: 1559–1582* (Edinburgh, 1889), p. v.
10 Lang, *St Andrews*, p. ix.
11 UStA, MS Dep 113/6, Anon., 'An Epilogue' (n.d.). David Hay Fleming's reviews of Lang's *St Andrews* were damning: see *British Weekly*, 1 March, 8 March, 15 March 1894.

> I am surprised that anyone at this present could have been so ill advised as to print such a thing. Surely no one wants to know the particulars of the sin & disgrace of certain men and women of three hundred years ago ... such rubbish ... speaking for myself I must say I should be ashamed if any member of my family came across it in my bookcase & I think the best thing to do is to return it to you, which I do today.[12]

A temptation at this point is simply to accept the caricature – Lang as the romantic populariser with little sympathy for the rigours and conventions of record scholarship, and Hay Fleming as characteristic of the new breed of scholars that the SHS was seeking to foster. Certainly, Lang was well aware of the scepticism of his peers.[13] But that is too simplistic. This was not as straightforward as Mason's 'take' on Buchanan and Knox – one historical (Buchanan), the other anti-historical (Knox).[14] Lang was a revisionist as much as a romantic, and Hay Fleming was in many regards a throw-back to the providential didacticism of Knox, rather than a modern scientific researcher, an apologist as much as an archivist at times. And yet, Lang clearly had an agenda as deeply held as that of Hay Fleming: he was determined to liberate Scottish history from the shackles of Presbyterian tradition.[15] Equally, one might suggest that Hay Fleming's forensic approach to history offered the Kirk, after generations of schism and declining influence, an intellectual legitimacy it badly needed. In what follows a study of the works of both scholars on the Reformation will serve to highlight that differences between Hay Fleming and Lang meant more than a clash of personalities, and that confessional bias in the discipline's most noteworthy modern texts and leading associations left a limiting legacy for Scottish history, even into the 'secular century'. Much has been said by Colin Kidd and others about the legacy the Reformation left to scholars of the Enlightenment: it is suggested here that much is to be gained by extending that inquiry into the Victorian period and beyond.[16] This essay is but a start.

[12] NRS, GD401/1/4, Scottish History Society, Correspondence (1889), Mr Bowie to T. Law, 7 March 1889.

[13] Andrew Lang, 'Preface', *History of Scotland, Volume 1* (Edinburgh, 1900), p. x. Here Lang notes that 'specialists will never combine to write a general history, and are apt, each within the fence of his special science to disdain "the populariser"'.

[14] Roger A. Mason, 'Usable Pasts: History and Identity in Reformation Scotland', *SHR* 76 (1997), 54–68 at p. 54.

[15] Catriona M.M. Macdonald, 'Andrew Lang and Scottish Historiography: Taking on Tradition', *SHR* 94 (2015), 207–36.

[16] Colin Kidd, 'Subscription, the Scottish Enlightenment and the Moderate Interpretation of History', *Journal of Ecclesiastical History* 55.3 (2004), 502–19.

## Reformation

ROGER Mason has emphasised that the Reformation was an 'antiquarian battlefield fought over with intense ferocity by the rival proponents of Presbyterianism and Episcopacy.'[17] The relationship between Hay Fleming (baptised into the Free Church but a member of the Original Secession Church from 1899) and Lang (an Episcopalian at least in death by default if not necessarily by design)[18] seems to endorse this statement: they came to blows within weeks of the publication of Lang's *St Andrews*, with Hay Fleming attacking Lang for 'seldom [missing] an opportunity of having a fling at the martyrs, reformers and covenanters'.[19] But the differences between Hay Fleming and Lang reached a crescendo in the first years of the twentieth century when both authors published well-publicised works on the Reformation era and the legacy of the reformers.[20] Looking at their perspectives on the causes, events and legacy of the Reformation, it is clear that their differences were as much philosophical as historical.

Neither author tired of stating and re-stating their respective positions. So, even in a handbook for children in 1903, Hay Fleming admitted that while 'It is true that the Reformation was not a smooth business, ... its roughness has been grossly exaggerated.'[21] Against this, Lang two years later countered that traditional histories 'are remarkable for the points which they ignore, and the contemporary authorities which they neglect. Things distasteful to traditional Scottish sentiment are left out.' Instead, claiming no 'sympathy with the suppression of the truth', he stated that *his* purpose would be 'to fill

[17] Mason, 'Usable Pasts', p. 68.

[18] This caveat rests on archival evidence where Lang's denominational sympathies are qualified. For example, in 1897 Lang, in St Andrews, wrote to Gilbert Murray, declaring himself 'true to the persecuted Church of Charles I, in Scotland. I can't persuade the Jesuit, that the differences are superficial and the agreement subliminal'. Oxford, Bodleian Library, MS Gilbert Murray 147, Andrew Lang to Gilbert Murray, 21 March 1897. In 1905 he noted: 'I have not a word to say against modern Presbyterianism, though, personally, I prefer the beautiful liturgy of the Church of England, when well or properly read, and not gabbled through, to such prayers as I have heard delivered from Presbyterian pulpits': Andrew Lang, 'My History Vindicated', *Blackwoods Magazine* (October 1905), p. 481.

[19] UStA, MS Dep 113/35/9 Notebook 9, *Fife Herald*, 27 Dec 1893.

[20] For Hay Fleming, see *Mary Queen of Scots from Her Birth to Her Flight to England* (London, 1897); *The Scottish Reformation: Its Epochs, Episodes, Leaders and Distinctive Characteristics* (Edinburgh, 1900); *Six Saints of the Covenant: Peden, Semple, Welwood, Cameron, Cargill, Smith* (London, 1901); *The Scottish Reformation* (Edinburgh, 1903); *The Reformation in Scotland: Causes, Characteristics, Consequences. The Stone Lectures at Princeton Theological Seminary for 1907–1908* (London, 1910); *Diary of Sir Archibald Johnston of Wariston Vol II.* (ed.) (Edinburgh, 1919). For Andrew Lang, see *History of Scotland from the Roman Occupation*, 4 vols (Edinburgh, 1900–1907); *The Mystery of Mary Stuart* (London, 1901); *John Knox and the Reformation* (London, 1905); *Portraits and Jewels of Mary Stuart* (Glasgow, 1906); *Sir George MacKenzie, King's Advocate of Rosehaugh* (London, 1909).

[21] David Hay Fleming, *The Scottish Reformation* (Edinburgh, 1903), p. 101.

up the popular omissions when I am able to do so'. [22] It is worth exploring what this looked like in practice.

First, it is important to state that Lang was no Catholic apologist. In a *Bookman* review of Hay Fleming's *Reformation in Scotland*, Lang referred to the Reformation as 'absolutely necessary and inevitable', and to ground this, he deployed evidence similar to that which Hay Fleming harnessed in his preface to the St Andrews register in 1889, although on very different terms.[23] Indeed, at this juncture, Hay Fleming's preface is worthy of quoting at some length, if only to highlight just how embedded views similar to those of Hay Fleming must have been in the SHS and the wider historical community at the time. Thus, in Hay Fleming's day, it was permissible for an SHS editor to speak of the 'yoke of the papacy', as he did, and to point in unqualified terms to the 'deplorable state into which the people had been allowed to sink' in the mid-sixteenth century. The Reformers, according to Hay Fleming, made 'unflagging efforts … to cure the festering sores' of the old church – the 'gross debauchery and crass ignorance of its officials' – and to instil 'high toned morality'. He notes that 'trusting to the Most High, they right resolutely undertook the task'.[24] Lang, however, caviled at the use traditional writers made of evidence of corruption in the pre-Reformation church, urging in 1911 that

> We need not force an open door; "who's a deniging of it," – of the corruption? Certainly not Mary of Guise, who tried hard to induce the Pope to reform the scandalous nuns; certainly not Archibald Hay, Principal of St Mary's College, St Andrews (1546); certainly not good Ninian Winzet, or Quentin Kennedy, or even the papal nuncio who secretly visited Queen Mary, taking his life in his hand; and certainly not Father Pollen, S.J., in our own time.[25]

Differences between the scholars appear even more acute when one turns to the events of the Reformation itself and the character of Scottish society after 1560. It is a state of affairs easily shown by merely comparing and contrasting these authors' most notable forays into public lecturing: Hay Fleming's Stone lectures, published as *The Reformation in Scotland* and delivered at Princeton Theological Seminary in session 1907–8, and Lang's lecture series, 'The Making of Scotland Presbyterian', delivered at Glasgow University in 1911. Hay Fleming accords the causes of the Reformation primary and secondary status; the characteristics of the Reformation itself are graded 'leading' and 'minor'; while the consequences of '1560' take up five separate chapters, invariably positive or not quite as bad as his critics had alleged. By contrast,

22 Lang, 'My History Vindicated', p. 480.
23 Andrew Lang, 'The Reformation in Scotland', *The Bookman* (April 1910), p. 31.
24 Hay Fleming, 'Preface', pp. v–vi, x.
25 Andrew Lang, 'Introduction', in Rev. J. Vyrnwy Morgan, *A Study in Nationality* (London, 1911), p. xv.

Lang was less measured, his lecture abstracts alone pointing to 'the intolerance of the new preachers', 'education despoiled', the 'ferocity and profligacy of the lay leaders' and the 'fatal defects of the Covenant'.[26] It is no surprise to learn that the Glasgow church ministers who gathered to listen to Lang's first lecture were conspicuous by their absence from the rest of the series.[27]

Meanwhile, Hay Fleming was only too well aware of conventional criticisms made against the early reformed church, and repeatedly was at pains to set the record straight. So, in a pamphlet from 1917, he countered the view that the Scottish Reformers were 'gloomy and fanatical bigots who frowned upon all innocent amusements', by emphasising quite simply that the greatest of the Reformers were just too busy for leisure, although they did retain their sense of humour.[28] Indeed, many loved music, he affirms, and 'even douce elders found golf … alluring'.[29] What is more, 'to art in itself, the Reformers had no antipathy; but when … certain classes of artistic objects … had become objects of worship [it was only then] they determined to make an end of them'.[30] Hay Fleming also countered common views about church discipline by suggesting elsewhere that 'tenderness was often shown [by St Andrews Kirk Session] for the feelings of the transgressor, and a manifest reluctance to proceed to extremities is not rarely revealed'. Indeed, according to Hay Fleming, the 'proceedings are pervaded by a spirit of strict impartiality' and 'decisions in difficult cases were evidently prompted by sincerity'.[31] To prove such open-mindedness he also offers as evidence the Kirk Session's approval to pray for the king's mother in 1587 (her conversion specifically), alas, as it transpired, on the day of her execution.[32] As for the Reformers destroying much of the architectural heritage of Scotland, Hay Fleming has an answer: it was the English and/or lawless Borderers.[33] In any case, the Roman Catholic Church, he alleges, had not properly maintained many Scottish churches, and as for allegations that Reformers used Catholic cathedrals as stone quarries and sources of lead for other building projects, he suggests the Catholic Church itself 'had form' in this respect.[34] So, in a paper to the Society of Antiquaries he pointed to the use of Celtic grave slabs in the construction of St Andrews Cathedral.[35]

[26] University of Glasgow, Special Collections, Sp Coll MacLehose 832, 'Lectures in Scottish History, 1911'.

[27] E.J. Cowan, 'Patriotism, Public Opinion and the "People's Chair" of Scottish History and Literature', *SHR* 93 (2014), 177–94, at p. 190.

[28] David Hay Fleming, 'The Influence of the Reformation on Social and Cultural Life in Scotland', *SHR* 15 (1917), 1–29 at pp. 12–13.

[29] Ibid., p. 15.

[30] Ibid., p. 17.

[31] Hay Fleming, 'Preface', p. x.

[32] David Hay Fleming (ed.), *Register of the Ministers, Elders and Deacons of the Christian Congregation of St. Andrews … Part Second:1582–1600* (Edinburgh, 1890), pp. 583–84.

[33] Hay Fleming, *The Reformation in Scotland*, p. vii.

[34] Ibid., p. vii.

[35] David Hay Fleming, 'Notice of a Sculptured Cross-Shaft and Sculptured Slabs

Predictably, Lang saw things rather differently. He turned Presbyterian protestations of freedom of conscience against themselves. How could reformers deny Catholics the very freedom of conscience they themselves identified as the bedrock of their own faith? And, by implication, how could modern-day avengers accuse him of treachery? After all, he claimed in the first volume of his *History of Scotland*,

> To conceal my opinion on these matters, in deference to tradition, would be to sin in such sort as the outspoken Knox never sinned; and perhaps my openness of speech may be commended by his example. Our modern freedom of thought and belief is the inestimable heritage of the Reformation, but it is a heritage which neither Reformer nor Covenanter intended to bequeath.[36]

For Lang, the corruption of the old church was no excuse for the fanaticism of the new. And unlike many historians of this period, he actively sought the silenced Catholic voice in the post-Reformation years: 'the hardships of the Catholics, after the Reformation, have been rather cavalierly treated by many of our historians', he noted in the preface to the second volume of his *History*.[37] For Lang, Scotland had exchanged one tyranny for another – a new ecclesiastical despotism. While there were comparatively few Catholic martyrs – something that Hay Fleming never tired of repeating for his own purposes – Lang suggested in an article from 1910 that instead, Presbyterian persecution 'was a steady grinding tyranny of civil disabilities, fines, imprisonment and exile'. He concluded: 'The Reformation was unchristian in its methods: that is the short and the long of it.'[38]

The differences between these two scholars are further illuminated when one looks at their engagement with two important figures of the Reformation, Cardinal Beaton and George Wishart. Lang's appreciation of Beaton is suggested in the title of the final chapter of the first volume of his history of Scotland, 'The Tragedy of the Cardinal'. Elsewhere, he is even more explicit. In an article in *Blackwoods* in 1898 Lang described Beaton as the 'most consummate statesman whom Scotland ever produced', defended him against allegations of having forged the will of James V, and, like other historians at the time, identified George Wishart – the martyr – as a possible accomplice in plots to secure Beaton's death as early as 1544.[39]

Recovered from the Base of St Andrews Cathedral', *Proceedings of the Society of Antiquaries of Scotland* 53 (1919), 385–414.

36 Lang, 'Preface', *History of Scotland, Volume 1*, p. xi.

37 Andrew Lang, 'Preface', *History of Scotland, Volume 2* (Edinburgh, 1902), p. vi. It is telling that Lang thanks both Hay Fleming and Major Martin Hume (1847–1910) in the paragraph immediately above this statement. Hume, a Catholic historian who edited the calendar of state papers relating to Spain in the years 1558–1586, would publish *The Love Affairs of Mary Queen of Scots* in 1903.

38 Lang, 'The Reformation in Scotland', p. 31.

39 Andrew Lang, 'The Truth about the Cardinal's Murder', *Blackwood's Magazine* (March

Lang's view on the murder of Beaton is clear: 'beside his opponents, Beaton shows like a gentleman', he writes.[40] And in contrast to the Anglophile Reformers, Lang exclaims, 'God rest the soul of David Beaton! He fought for Scotland.'[41] Hay Fleming, predictably, saw things rather differently. Attacking those who – like Lang, one presumes – had sought to 'whitewash' the cardinal, Hay Fleming draws up a list of Beaton's carnal sins, illegitimate children and corrupt practices. Excitedly mixing his metaphors, he claims that: 'Desperate attempts have been made to whitewash this Ethiopian, to cover up the spots of this leopard; but all such attempts have proved and must prove futile.'[42]

These differences of opinion rested on more than just prejudice, something seen most clearly in Lang's and Hay Fleming's contrasting critiques of John Knox and his writings. Here connections with Roger Mason's work become more apparent. In very practical terms, in 1898 Lang seemed to catch established Scottish historians sleeping on the job.

> In the libraries of two great Scottish universities we can swear, and save our oath, that, after forty years, the pages of [David] Laing's edition of Knox's Works are still virgin, or were recently virgin of the paper-cutter. Oddly enough, in both cases, the 'uninvaded sleep' of Knox's writings has been first disturbed by two admirers of Cardinal Beaton.[43]

In addition to *John Knox and the Reformation* (1905), Lang's critique of Knox can be found in the second volume of his *History*, and in many journal contributions dating from the first years of the twentieth century.[44] At the time, his insights were widely scorned. Hay Fleming reviewed Lang's *History* for the *British Weekly* under the title, 'Knox in the Hands of the Philistines'.[45]

---

1898), pp. 344–55, at p. 344. See also Andrew Lang, 'The Scottish Reformation' (review), *Speaker*, 26 August 1905, p. 503; 'The Cardinal and the King's Will', *SHR* 3 (1905–6), 410–22; 'Letters of Cardinal Beaton, 1537–1541', *SHR* 6 (1908–1909), 150–58.

40 Lang, 'The Truth about the Cardinal's Murder', p. 355.

41 Ibid., p. 355. Elsewhere Lang anticipates many nationalist accounts of the Reformation as a necessary step towards union with England and the end of Scottish independence. Lang repeatedly refers to the reformers as 'Anglophile', and in 1905 he emphasised that the 'preachers made possible the conquest of Scotland by England': Lang, 'My History Vindicated', p. 487. This is echoed, for example, in Compton MacKenzie, *Catholicism in Scotland* (London, 1936), p. 142: 'In 1707 the political metamorphosis of Scotland into North Britain was effected by the Act of Union which brought to a shameful conclusion that long transaction which was first made a practical possibility by the Reformers when they sacrificed their country on the altar of religious hate'.

42 Hay Fleming, *The Reformation in Scotland*, p.45.

43 Lang, 'The Truth about the Cardinal's Murder', p. 353. David Laing (1793–1878) edited the works of John Knox in six volumes for the Bannatyne and Woodrow clubs between 1846 and 1864.

44 See Andrew Lang, 'John Knox and Mr Lang', *The Speaker*, 26 August 1905, pp. 503–4; 'Knox as Historian', *SHR* 2 (1904–5), 113–30.

45 As noted, William Croft Dickinson, 'Andrew Lang, John Knox and Scottish

Echoes of Lang, however, are to be found in Mason's essay of 1997, 'Usable Pasts'. Indeed, both authors claim much the same, namely that Knox's *History* has 'rarely been studied as a text'.[46] That said, there are differences in their approaches. Lang refers to Knox's *History* as a 'party pamphlet', points to numerous errors in Knox's dating of events, and cross references many of Knox's observations with his letters to Mrs Locke, Cecil, and others.[47] (It is clear that Lang had learned much since his first foray into the history of St Andrews.) For much of Lang's 1904–5 *SHR* article 'Knox as Historian', however, his intent is clear: what we find is an assured defence of Mary of Guise against Knox's allegations of misrule, and an attack on Knox as historian as 'singularly false and deliberately misleading'.[48] Elsewhere, Lang was uncompromising in his critique of Knox's prose:

> The style of the great Reformer is remarkable for the luscious freedom of its invective. Nobody who has ever heard Knox scold can mistake him for any other artist. Persons who know Knox merely in the genteel twilight of Mr Hume Brown's biography are like Sir John Falstaff at an innocent stage of his career. They 'know nothing'. These, alas, are the majority! … for vernacular abuse Knox was unmatched in his age.[49]

Mason concurs with Lang to the extent of agreeing that 'Knox was no historian', and was hampered by a faith in 'crude dualities' through which he ordered both his own world and that of generations of Scottish Protestants that followed after.[50] But it matters less to Mason that Knox erroneously recorded dates and sequences of events than that he rooted Scotland's new Protestant identity in Biblical rather than historical precedent. Both Mason and Lang realise that a Protestant Scotland had to be fashioned – Lang's Glasgow lectures were carefully titled 'The *Making* of Scotland Presbyterian', while Mason observes that 'For Knox there was a very real sense in which, in the eyes of the Lord and thus in the eyes of His prophet, Scotland did only become Scotland in 1560.'[51] In this regard, Mason's critique takes us closer to understanding Hay Fleming's world view by deploying something of Lang's barbed scepticism while successfully agreeing with neither.

---

Presbyterianism' (Edinburgh, 1952), p. 6. See also David Hay Fleming, 'Review', *Athenaeum*, 19 August 1905, pp. 230–31.

46 Mason, 'Usable Pasts', p. 55.

47 Lang, 'Knox as Historian', p. 114.

48 Ibid., p. 128. Lang defends Mary of Guise in a number of publications: of particular relevance, see Andrew Lang, 'The Alleged Treachery of Mary of Guise (1559)', *The Atheneaum*, 26 May 1900, p. 657 and 'Mary of Guise' *The Atheneaum*, 9 June 1900, pp. 720–21.

49 Lang, 'The Truth about the Cardinal's Murder', p. 353. The reference is to Peter Hume Brown, *John Knox: A Biography* (London, 1895).

50 Mason, 'Usable Pasts', pp. 64, 58.

51 Ibid., p. 67.

## Friends

HAY Fleming and Lang were irreconcilable scholars, but on a personal level, they were friends, often spending time together during Lang's regular trips to St Andrews. A short glimpse at Lang's acknowledgements in various publications shows that Hay Fleming often corresponded with Lang about matters historical. And Lang was known to defend Hay Fleming against the criticism of the metro-centric presses of the capital that seemed often to think of Scottish history as something of an acquired taste. For example, in October 1899, Lang wrote to Gilbert Murray, the classicist, newly arrived in Oxford after a decade as Professor of Greek at the University of Glasgow:

> An ass in *The Athenaeum* actually abused Hay Fleming for quoting State Papers as they stood, because they were Scotch, as if the English Ambassador wrote Scots. Fleming was writing for historians, as an electrician writes for electricians: he was not doing a popular sketch, though providing material for popularisers. ... It makes me ill to read this kind of thing in reviews: it is like the *Quarterly* driveling about the Waverley novels as 'Anglified Erse'.[52]

It would not be an exaggeration to suggest that the scholars needed one another – that each would have been a very different writer had the other not been around at much the same time. In 1909 Lang wrote to James Maitland Anderson – the university librarian in St Andrews: 'I hope Fleming is getting on with his book, and that he abuses me like mad, which would be very good for him.'[53] While taking their academic differences very seriously indeed, they also joked about them. In 1906 Lang wrote to Hay Fleming about a new book he was working on – a children's version of his Life of Joan of Arc: he noted, 'I have been careful to say that Jeanne lived before Knox and knew no better.'[54] There is also evidence that the cut and thrust of the review columns was not allowed to affect their friendship; in fact it may have contributed positively to it. In 1911 Lang complained to Hay Fleming that his lectures in Glasgow were 'a horrible bore' and asked how Hay Fleming was 'getting on with Mr Knox': 'There is nobody to reason with, to be candid. The others make, as the Irish Jesuit said, "a compilation of omissions"'.[55] In 1912, three months before Lang's unexpected death, Hay Fleming wrote to Lang requesting permission to re-print Lang's replies to his reviews. Lang declined, explaining: 'When I began to dabble in Scots history I knew next to nothing, and was ignorant of sources and methods.' Still, he alleged that Hay Fleming had dealt more leniently with Peter Hume Brown. But Lang continued:

[52] Bodleian Library, MS Gilbert Murray 147, Andrew Lang to Gilbert Murray, 27 October 1899.
[53] UStA, MS 628, Andrew Lang to James Maitland Anderson, 13 October 1909.
[54] UStA, MS Dep 113/22/1/24, Andrew Lang to David Hay Fleming, 27 February [1906].
[55] UStA, MS Dep 113/22/1/22, Andrew Lang to David Hay Fleming, 30 October 1911.

> I hope there has never been an unkind thought on my side, nor an unsportsmanlike criticism on yours which is rare among men of letters! And I owe you unbounded gratitude in making me as I went on, try to keep up to a certain level of accuracy, which is not natural to me.[56]

Hay Fleming responded, reassuring Lang that no-one would think the earlier reviews reflected Lang's current understanding, although, 'As for Hume Brown', Hay Fleming noted, 'I have pointed out mistakes in his books, but have never found such provoking howlers in them as in yours.'[57]

## Legacy

This blend of mutual dependence and mutual antagonism lasted beyond the grave. Following Lang's death in 1912, it is striking just how often Hay Fleming continued to refer to him in various publications, particularly on matters on which they actually agreed.[58] So, in a Knox Club pamphlet from 1922, Hay Fleming points out that even Lang had 'frankly testified' that Knox was a man of 'pure life'.[59] A good many years passed before any academic historian of merit dared attack the Reformers with as much ferocity as Lang, and Hay Fleming needed something to kick against in the meantime.[60] Indeed, he grew increasingly intolerant in old age. In 1916 he attacked in no uncertain terms William Forbes Leith's publication, *The Pre-Reformation Scholars in Scotland in the 16th Century* (1915), thus:

> Father Forbes Leith's well-deserved reputation for chronic inaccuracy will be greatly enhanced by this latest production … There were really good and scholarly men among the pre-Reformation clergy in Scotland, but an almost incredible number of them were woefully immoral, and latterly very many of them were disgracefully ignorant.[61]

[56] UStA, MS Dep 113/22/1/26/2, Andrew Lang to David Hay Fleming, 11 April [1912].
[57] UStA, MS Dep 113/22/1/26/3, David Hay Fleming to Andrew Lang, 16 April 1912. Hay Fleming took 'Notes for Criticism of Andrew Lang's *John Knox and the Reformation*' (n.d.), where he noted: 'Mr Lang's quotations are not remarkable for accuracy. Sometimes words or clauses are omitted, sometimes inserted. In one case, nearly two pages are compressed into three lines, and these lines are given within inverted commas. The spelling is usually modernised, but not always successfully.' UStA, MS 38977/2/3/10.
[58] David Hay Fleming, 'Were Cardinal Beaton and Archbishop Hamilton not Libertines: An Exposure of the Controversial and Historical Methods of Abbot Hunter Blair, a Rejected Contribution to the *Catholic Herald*, and Some Remarcks on the Arrogance and Ignorance of that Popish Paper' (Edinburgh: Scottish Reformation Society (reprinted from *The Bulwark*), 1929), pp. 30–31.
[59] David Hay Fleming, 'John Knox Cleared from the Slanders of the Rev. W.L. Sime' (Edinburgh: Knox Club Publication no. 54, 1922), p. 5.
[60] An exception here can be found in Hay Fleming's attack on David Oswald Hunter Blair. See Hay Fleming, 'Were Cardinal Beaton and Archbishop Hamilton not Libertines'.
[61] David Hay Fleming, 'A Jesuit's Misconception of Scottish History and a Fellow

Such personal attacks were extended to other Catholic writers (particularly Jesuits) and others (even Kirk ministers) who supported them.[62] It is fair to say that in his final years, Hay Fleming's historical scepticism bled into contemporary bigotry, as he criticised the 'Church of Rome' on celibacy and its stance on 'mixed marriages', referring to it as 'a huge overgrown sect', in a pamphlet in 1931.[63] It was, perhaps, a predictable if regrettable end to a career often marked by sermonising as much as scholarship. Yet this was, of course, the era of the Church of Scotland's report, *The Menace of the Irish Race to our Scottish Nationality* (1923), which witnessed the rise of militant political Protestantism.[64] History was foundational to the sectarianism of the inter-war period, and in the years that followed, history also served to endorse a popular yet exclusive Protestant world view. This meant that few historiographical tensions evident at the start of the century were resolved by the time Roger Mason commenced his academic career as an undergraduate student at the University of Edinburgh in 1972.

In 1951 William Croft Dickinson, Professor of Scottish History and Palaeography at the University of Edinburgh, delivered the Andrew Lang lecture at the university of St Andrews on the subject of 'Andrew Lang, John Knox and Scottish Presbyterianism'. Croft Dickinson – a man whose own 'take' on the Reformation was known to be 'pungent', and who experienced a walk out by Catholic students – criticised Lang for immersing himself too deeply in the detail of Knox's history (a strange complaint from an acknowledged expert in MS study).[65] Lang was also criticised for judging Knox 'by modern standards'.[66] 'Surely', Croft Dickinson scoffed,

> [Lang] did not expect the critical approach of a Ranke in the time of Knox? ... how could Lang look for an objective account from a man writing in the very heat of the battle, and a battle ... which, to Knox, was being fought, not for gain of earthly things ... but for the very assurance of life eternal?[67]

Jesuit's Apology for the Inexactitudes Exposed' (reprinted from *The British Weekly*, 1916). The second Jesuit referred to in the title is Father Pollen, who had researched alongside Lang on a number of projects. For example, in 1911, Lang shared with Hay Fleming that they were working on the Lennox papers together. UStA, MS Dep 113/22/1/10.

[62] David Hay Fleming, 'George Wishart the Martyr, a Reply to Father Power, S.J., and His "Protestant" Admirer, the Minister of Smailholm' (reprinted from *The Bulwark*: Knox Club Publication No. 56, 1923).

[63] David Hay Fleming, 'The Church from which the Reformation Delivered Scotland' (Edinburgh: Scottish Reformation Society, 1931), p. 1. See also David Hay Fleming, 'The Church of Rome and Marriage' (Knox Club, 1911).

[64] S.J. Brown, '"Outside the Covenant": The Scottish Presbyterian Churches and Irish Immigration, 1922–1938', *IR* 42.1 (1991), 19–45.

[65] John Imrie, 'William Croft Dickinson: A Memoir 1897–1963', *SHR* 45 (1966), 1–12 at p. 8.

[66] Dickinson, 'Andrew Lang, John Knox and Scottish Presbyterianism', p. 7.

[67] Ibid., p. 8.

Croft Dickinson suggested that Lang's *John Knox and the Reformation* was motivated by its author's antipathy to Knox's cause and his dislike of Knox's certainty.[68] He concluded by suggesting that Lang 'feared' Presbyterianism's 'democratic nature and distrusted its virility. [Lang's] sympathies were always with an aristocracy, and Knox, for good or ill, had raised a people.'[69]

As an undergraduate at St Andrews, Dickinson was a student of J.D. Mackie and, following graduation, became his assistant. Of all the Scottish historians of the mid-twentieth century, Mackie (Professor of Scottish History and Literature at the University of Glasgow, 1930–1957 and Historiographer Royal, 1958–1978) was arguably the foremost academic populariser of traditional views of the Reformation in a new multi-media environment while being old enough to have corresponded with Hay Fleming in the last years of his life.[70] Mackie was among the first to exploit the power of the popular press, radio, and television, and was regularly in demand by the BBC. Indeed, in 1960 – the quatercentenary of the Scottish Reformation – the BBC features producer, George Bruce, solicited a peroration from Mackie, emphasising the need to 'make people understand the self respect and the status the Reformation conferred upon common man'.[71] Mackie duly obliged, writing, amongst other things, that: 'To disparage the Reformation is to denounce the very qualities which have enabled the children of a small poor country to set their mark on the history of the world.'[72] It was a conclusion Mackie shared in other media too, and repeated in a piece for the *Glasgow Herald* in 1972 in which he recalled favourably the earlier revisionism of Andrew Lang who by this time had been dead for 60 years.[73] Indeed, Mackie delivered at least two radio talks for the BBC on the subject of Andrew Lang, noting in 1944:

> I knew him only slightly, towards the end of his career, and mainly as a historian with whose outlook I wasn't always in accord. ... He made some errors in fact – I daresay everyone does – but not, I think, any vital error. The real criticism of his work is that he wrote as an advocate rather than as an historian, pleading a case while he seemed only to tell a story .... In any case, his vigorous criticisms had a stimulating effect.[74]

68 Ibid., p. 11.

69 Ibid., p. 29. In his inaugural lecture in 1944, Dickinson emphasised that a 'magnificent trait' of the Scots was their 'love of freedom, an independence in all things'. W.C. Dickinson, 'The Study of Scottish History' (Edinburgh, 1944), p. 8.

70 See University of Glasgow Archives [henceforth GUA], DC32/9/35.

71 GUA, DC32/6/23 George Bruce to J.D. Mackie, 23 September 1960.

72 GUA, DC32/6/23, Running Order (attachment), p. 2.

73 The final words of Mackie's 1951 Historical Association pamphlet 'John Knox' bear striking comparison: 'Those who disparage Knox would do well to remember that in denouncing him they denounce also the qualities which have enabled the children of a small poor country to set their mark upon the history of the world.' (J.D. Mackie, 'John Knox' (Historical Association), 1951, p. 24. See also GUA, DC32/11/6, *Glasgow Herald*, 7 September 1955.

74 GUA, DC32/5/82, J.D. Mackie, 'Scottish Portraits Series: Andrew Lang – Historian,

By this time, Mackie's former assistant, W.C. Dickinson, occupied the Scottish History chair at Edinburgh University, and three years later he hired Gordon Donaldson, whom he had known before the war in the Institute of Historical Research and who worked with him on the galley proofs of his edition of Knox's *History* (1949) for Nelson's.[75] It was Donaldson's Reformation scholarship, particularly his *Scottish Reformation* of 1960, that would be identified as something of a turning point in the history of the Reformation in Scotland. Despite disagreeing with Donaldson on many other issues, Roger Mason conceded in 1997 that: 'Among professional historians, it was only in the early 1960s that a Protestant "whig" teleology finally began to give way to a more balanced view of the Reformation. The publication of Gordon Donaldson's *The Scottish Reformation* ... saw the tide beginning to turn.'[76] Yet Donaldson himself was rightly more cautious, and nor is it clear that he necessarily wished the tide to turn completely. In an undated lecture entitled 'The Scottish Reformation: Some Second Thoughts', Donaldson – perhaps characteristically – came close to offending those who praised him most:

> ... the reviewers saw the book as more important than the author saw it. I suppose in doing so what the reviewers really disclosed was that they had not read enough of what had been written before.[77]

Sidney A. Burrell, the reviewer in the *Journal of Modern History*, might have agreed. He was one of the few who, while acknowledging the weight of scholarship in Donaldson's book, noted that the 'evidence here presented has not been unknown to Presbyterian scholars in and out of Scotland.'[78] More copious footnotes and greater precision did not hide that much that was set out in *The Scottish Reformation* had been said already by earlier writers. Donaldson elsewhere admitted this debt to the past, and to Hay Fleming in particular: writing to historian James Kirk in 1976, Donaldson confessed that 'I have often remarked that if you think you have discovered anything new about the Scottish Reformation you should then look at Hay Fleming where you will probably find it.'[79] A second point of continuity was observed by Donaldson's reviewer in the *Scottish Journal of Theology*, A.C. Cheyne, who saw in *The Scottish Reformation* a 'passionate controversialism perhaps

---

Poet, Man of Letters', 31 March 1944.

75 Edinburgh University Library, Centre for Research Collections [hereafter EUL CRC], Gen1627/1/1/2, Gordon Donaldson, 'Retirement', 11–12. See also W. Croft Dickinson, *John Knox's History of the Reformation in Scotland* (London, 1949).

76 'Usable Pasts', n. 1.

77 EUL CRC, Gen1627/3/8, Gordon Donaldson, 'The Scottish Reformation: Some Second Thoughts', p. 1.

78 Sidney A. Burrell, 'Review', *Journal of Modern History* 33 (1961), 188.

79 EUL CRC, Gen16331/7/26, Gordon Donaldson to James Kirk, 11 June 1976.

unequalled since Hay Fleming'.[80] And a third echo of the past can be found in Donaldson's acceptance of the Reformation as simply necessary: he noted,

> Any twentieth-century reader who reviews the evidence will assuredly agree with the general consensus of sixteenth century opinion that 'reformation' was necessary. He will very likely go further and conclude that for a situation so desperate the remedy could hardly be other than drastic.[81]

While Donaldson's Episcopalian faith sets him apart from Hay Fleming, they shared a view of the Reformation that was common currency in Scotland until relatively recently, and one that was even shared, as we have seen, by Andrew Lang (at least in part), namely, that *a* reformation (if not *the* Reformation) was inevitable. Such a consensus was important if tenuous: obvious and significant differences divided its adherents. Indeed, one might suggest that any consensus built upon a hypothetical reading of the past scarcely warrants the name – a spectrum of approaches, large areas of disagreement and philosophical tensions were evident within. Yet its effect was real: sustained by the academic community in Scotland's universities and the slow growth of Catholic historical scholarship, it served to circumscribe the potential for radical revisionism. The impression of fierce scholarly disagreement belied the continuing conservative influence of generations of earlier writers. The *Innes Review* – the journal of the Scottish Catholic Historical Association – was scarcely ten years old when the Kirk marked the 400th anniversary of the Reformation in Scotland, and aside from the work of David Oswald Hunter Blair, Malcolm Vivian Hay and Compton Mackenzie, in 1960 there had been little of substance seriously to counter conventional wisdom on the Reformation for decades.[82]

## Conclusion: 'a haunted town to me'

THE historiography of the Scottish Reformation as it emerged between its ter- and quater-centenaries evolved within an intellectual environment infused with but not entirely defined by religious partisanship. While it may be tantalizingly suggestive of uncomfortable if comforting binaries, attributing

[80] A. C. Cheyne, 'Review', *Scottish Journal of Theology* (1963).

[81] Gordon Donaldson, *The Scottish Reformation* (Cambridge, 1960), p. 27.

[82] In a recent work on Catholic historical studies in Scotland, the author highlights only two significant works in this period: Malcolm Vivian Hay, *A Chain of Error in Scottish History* (London, 1927) and the aforementioned Mackenzie, *Catholicism in Scotland*. See Clifford Williamson, *The History of Catholic Intellectual Life in Scotland, 1918–1965* (London, 2016), p. 206. Hunter Blair is principally known for his translation of Alphons Bellesheim, *History of the Catholic Church of Scotland*, 4 vols (Edinburgh, 1887–90). See also Darren Tierney, S. Karly Kehoe and Ewen A. Cameron, 'The Scottish Catholic Archives and Scottish Historical Studies', *IR* 65.2 (2014), 79–94.

simple denominational appellations (Catholic or Protestant, Presbyterian or Episcopalian) to either writers or 'histories' does not sufficiently account for the historiography of these years.[83] Instead, Colin Kidd's analysis of scholarship during the Scottish Enlightenment seems just as fitting in this period. He notes, proving one can have it both ways, that:

> Given the confessional animus which drove antiquarian polemic there was a remarkably high degree of cross-fertilisation and co-operation in Scottish historical circles. ... partisan conflict did provoke advances in scholarly criticism.[84]

The scholarship of and relationship between David Hay Fleming and Andrew Lang was symptomatic of this state of affairs and can only be captured by appreciating that the work of each was at once a reaction against and in part constitutive of that of the other. Their legacy was probably what neither of them might have wished. My 'sufficiently plausible' conclusion is that Roger Mason stands as the inheritor of this dynamic both in his rejection of its certainties and his acknowledgement of the dangers of a maverick disregard for the insights of past scholars. A hallmark of his work is that he has avoided the temptation to reconcile the irreconcilable – to essentialise – and in so doing he has, in the last 40 years, confounded the certainties of many established voices. His St Andrews has always been that of *both* Hay Fleming *and* Lang; his legacy is to have claimed the Reformation for *neither*.

> St Andrews by the Northern Sea,
> That is a haunted town to me!
>
> Andrew Lang, 'Almae Matres'

[83] In this regard I would take issue with aspects of the analysis offered in both Williamson, *The History of Catholic Intellectual Life in Scotland* and Douglas W.B. Somerset, 'Changing Views on the Scottish Reformation during the Twentieth Century', *Scottish Reformation Society Historical Journal* 7 (2017), 1–55.

[84] Colin Kidd, 'Antiquarianism, Religion and the Scottish Enlightenment', *IR* 46 (1995), 139–54 at p. 154.

# II

# Kingship and Political Culture: From Medieval to Renaissance

# 2

# *A New Perspective on John of Fordun's* Chronica Gentis Scotorum *as a Medieval 'National History'*[1]

Dauvit Broun

ONE of the many fundamental contributions by Roger Mason to scholarship is his pioneering research on Latin histories of the kingdom as a source for insights into the nature of Scottish political culture. As a result, he has revealed patterns of political thought that bring us closer to the views and assumptions of the kingdom's elite than would be possible by focusing exclusively on more intellectual works of political theory. In the process he has shaped our understanding of the most important historical texts in Latin in ways that are likely to endure for as long as these works are read or their reception studied, from John of Fordun writing in the mid-1380s to George Buchanan two centuries later. This chapter will not attempt to discuss the substance of any of these histories. Instead, it will ask what might be learnt about the genre of medieval 'national' histories – as this is generally understood by historians – by looking beyond print editions to extant manuscripts.

## Medieval 'National' Histories

ALTHOUGH John of Fordun was not the first to write a history of the kingdom from its origins, his *Chronica Gentis Scotorum* is the earliest to survive intact.[2] It appears in Norbert Kersken's monumental study, published in 1995, of what he described as 'works of long-term history, providing an overview of the

[1] I am extremely grateful to Joanna Tucker for commenting on a draft of this chapter and suggesting many improvements, and also to the editor and referee for some further improvements. All blemishes and shortcomings are, of course, solely my responsibility.

[2] *Johannis de Fordun Chronica Gentis Scotorum*, ed. William F. Skene, The Historians of Scotland, vol. 1 (Edinburgh, 1871); *John of Fordun's Chronicle of the Scottish Nation*, trans. Felix J. H. Skene, The Historians of Scotland, vol. 4 (Edinburgh, 1872). For the antecedents of Fordun's history, see Dauvit Broun, *Scottish Independence and the Idea of Britain from the Picts to Alexander III* (Edinburgh, 2007), pp. 215–68. Note that the dating there of Fordun's principal source ('proto-Fordun') to 1285 is flawed: see Dauvit Broun, 'Scotland's First "National" History? Fordun's Principal Source Revisited' (forthcoming), where sometime in or shortly after 1326 is suggested.

"national" past from the very beginnings to the time of their writing'.[3] Kersken argued that these texts – which he referred to as 'national histories' – began 'almost simultaneously' to be written across much of Europe in the first quarter of the twelfth century.[4] He showed that, by the end of the thirteenth century, it was rare for a kingdom *not* to have been provided by one of its *literati* with an extensive written account of its past from its origins to within living memory.[5]

Kersken's outstanding achievement in identifying and describing each of these works across most of Europe in the Middle Ages was only feasible by researching them as printed editions, rather than by trying to deal with a myriad of manuscripts. He was aware of the significance of these texts as editions, taking care to note when they were first printed, as well as basing his work on the most recent publications. It has recently been shown by Joanna Tucker, however, how our understanding of a genre of medieval historical texts can be transformed by taking manuscripts as our starting point. This chapter is an initial consideration of how a similar approach has the potential to offer fresh perspectives on medieval 'national' histories, using John of Fordun's work as a case study.

## A New Approach

KERSKEN explained that 'national histories' could take a variety of shapes and sizes, and were written in the vernacular as well as in Latin. Typically they were narratives of a people and/or territory and its rulers. Sometimes

[3] Norbert Kersken, *Geschichtsschreibung im Europa der 'nationes'. Nationalgeschichtliche Gesamtdarstellungen im Mittelalter*, Münstersche historische Forschungen (Cologne, 1995); the title may be translated as *Writing History in the Europe of* Nationes. *A Comprehensive Survey of National Histories in the Middle Ages* (I am grateful to Simon Taylor for help with this). A summary in English is: Norbert Kersken, 'High and Late Medieval National Historiography', in Deborah Mauskopf Deliyannis (ed.), *Historiography in the Middle Ages* (Leiden, 2003), pp. 181–215. The quotation is from Norbert Kersken, 'National Chronicles and National Consciousness', in János M. Bak and Ivan Jurković (eds), *Chronicon. Medieval Narrative Sources: A Chronological Guide with Introductory Essays* (Turnhout, 2013), pp. 119–26, at p. 125.

[4] Kersken, 'National Chronicles', pp. 119–20. Kersken does not discuss Ireland, where a comprehensive account of the island's history as a kingdom was developed in the early and mid-eleventh century: see Broun, *Scottish Independence*, pp. 44–45; Peter J. Smith, 'Early Irish Historical Verse: The Evolution of a Genre', in Próinséas Ní Chatháin and Michael Richter (eds), *Ireland and Europe in the Early Middle Ages: Texts and Transmission* (Dublin, 2002), pp. 326–41; and John Carey, '*Lebor Gabála* and the Legendary History of Ireland', in Helen Fulton (ed.), *Medieval Celtic Literature and Society* (Dublin, 2005), pp. 32–48.

[5] Kersken, 'High and Late Medieval National Historiography', pp. 208–9, regarded Scotland as an exception; he also saw the emphasis on the Scots as a people in Fordun's history (citing the account of Scottish origins) as having few parallels, and attributed this to the experience of the Wars of Independence. Scotland is not so remarkable, however, if Fordun's work was derived ultimately from a lost history from Scottish origins to Mael Coluim III (1058–93) written probably in the 1260s by Richard Vairement: Broun, *Scottish Independence*, pp. 248–63. The emphasis on the Scots as a people in the origin-legend can be explained simply as a response to how Ireland, not Scotland, was understood to be the original homeland: the focus on ancient beginnings could not, therefore, be initially about the kingdom itself, but the people.

they were the centre of gravity in a Christian history of the 'world' (as in the *Polychronicon* by Ranulph Higden [d. 1364]). Kersken also cited a few instances where the work took the form of a year-by-year chronicle (the Welsh *Brut y Tywysogion* would be an example) so that chronology takes priority over narrative.[6] Although Kersken saw medieval 'national' histories as a particular kind of history writing, he recognised that they could be expressed in different forms.

There is a suggestive parallel here with modern historians' approach to another kind of medieval text: the cartulary. This has been treated as a self-evident genre, with catalogues produced for French-speaking lands and for Britain and Ireland.[7] Like Kersken's 'national' histories, it has been readily recognised that cartularies take a variety of forms. What appears to define them is that they contain copies of charters and other documents relating to a family's or institution's properties and privileges. Recently, however, Joanna Tucker has highlighted how dynamic and varied these manuscripts can be. As a result, in her study of scholarly approaches to cartularies, she has advised that 'typologies should be taken lightly as impressions, not hard and fast classifications'.[8] Joanna Tucker has also emphasised how our understanding of cartularies has been filtered by their published editions in ways which obscure the manuscripts themselves.[9] Her proposed solution is not to turn our backs on the infrastructure of editions and catalogues that are the legacy of generations of scholarship, or to abandon the very idea of the 'cartulary', but to develop what she describes as 'a new way of working with the existing printed resources, one that is grounded in an awareness of the medieval cartulary as a dynamic manuscript that could take a variety of forms'.[10] She has shown that, when we do this, cartularies can be understood to be 'active',

[6] Kersken, 'National Chronicles', pp. 123–24. Kersken does not discuss Wales: the examples he gives are the Russian Primary Chronicle and the chronicle of Cosmas of Prague. For *Brut y Tywysogion* see Broun, *Scottish Independence*, pp. 43–44; Thomas Jones (ed.), *Brut y Tywysogyon, Peniarth MS 20* (Caerdydd [Cardiff], 1941); Thomas Jones (ed.), *Brut y Tywysogyon or The Chronicle of the Princes, Red Book of Hergest Version* (Cardiff 1955). In general, see Thomas Jones, 'Historical Writing in Medieval Welsh', *Scottish Studies* 12 (1968), 15–27.

[7] Henri Stein, *Bibliographie générale des cartulaires français ou relatifs à l'histoire de France* (Paris, 1907); G.R.C. Davis (ed.), rev. Claire Breay, Julian Harrison and David M. Smith, *Medieval Cartularies of Great Britain and Ireland* (London, 2010). See Joanna Tucker, *Reading and Shaping Medieval Cartularies: Multi-scribe Manuscripts and their Patterns of Growth. A Study of the Earliest Cartularies of Glasgow Cathedral and Lindores Abbey* (Woodbridge, 2020), pp. 9–10; the 'Davis' catalogue for Britain and Ireland is discussed in Joanna Tucker, 'Understanding Scotland's Medieval Cartularies', *Innes Review* 70 (2019), 135–70, at 149–56.

[8] Tucker, 'Understanding Scotland's Medieval Cartularies', p. 154.

[9] Ibid., pp. 136–49; the way this material was published was first problematised in Alasdair Ross, 'The Bannatyne Club and the Publication of Scottish Ecclesiastical Cartularies', *SHR* 85 (2006), 202–33, taking a purely textual perspective.

[10] Tucker, 'Understanding Scotland's Medieval Cartularies', p. 136.

often comprising the work of multiple scribes who were contributing to a growing manuscript across many generations.

Cartularies as selections of document texts were potentially a more flexible environment for scribes to work in than an extensive narrative of a kingdom's history. It is not difficult, however, to see a parallel between Kersken's study – and the editions he depended on – and the cartulary publications discussed by Tucker. Her call for a new way of working grounded on an awareness of the manuscripts could usefully be applied to medieval 'national' histories, too. At one level it is easy to see how studying manuscripts would expand the horizons of Kersken's work. The advent of book history has led to an increasing awareness of how manuscripts can provide rich material for understanding the reception of texts, revealing how they were produced and read, and by whom.[11] Laura Cleaver's recent study of English and Norman historical works through the lens of illuminated manuscripts produced between 1066 and 1272 is an impressive example of what can be achieved by viewing these texts in this way.[12] Joanna Tucker's call to a greater awareness of manuscripts, however, is more fundamental, with the potential to go to the heart of our understanding of medieval 'national' histories.

It would not be surprising if the editions used by Kersken, especially those published a century or more ago, offered only a limited view of the text as found in the manuscripts. More manuscripts may have come to light in the intervening period. A more fundamental issue is how editors may have sought to rationalise any significant variety or inconsistency they encountered, just as Joanna Tucker has recently highlighted in relation to cartularies. It is worth bearing in mind that some of these histories were published by scholars committed to establishing or maintaining national histories as a discipline; this raises the possibility that there could be instances where the work has been fashioned into a coherent national narrative by the editor to an extent which would have been unknown to its medieval scribes and readers.[13] When seen simply as texts, therefore,

[11] In a medieval context this has been particularly productive in studies of vernacular manuscripts. The leading scholar in this field in Scotland is Roger Mason's colleague Margaret Connolly: see for example Margaret Connolly and Linne R. Mooney (eds), *Design and Distribution of Late Medieval Manuscripts of England* (York, 2008). The possibilities of this approach are developed further in Margaret Connolly, *Sixteenth-Century Readers, Fifteenth-Century Books: Continuities of Reading in the English Reformation* (Cambridge, 2019).

[12] Laura Cleaver, *Illuminated History Books in the Anglo-Norman World, 1066–1272* (Oxford, 2018).

[13] This dimension is disappointingly absent from Stefan Berger with Christoph Conrad, *The Past as History: National Consciousness in Modern Europe* (Basingstoke, 2015), the eighth and final culminating volume of the series 'Writing the Nation: National Historiographies and the Making of Nation States in 19th and 20th Century Europe' (general editors Stefan Berger, Christoph Conrad and Guy P. Marchal). Although medieval 'national histories' are commented on briefly as such (at pp. 29–31, without referencing Kersken's work), the publication of these texts by scholars in the modern era

Joanna Tucker's words in relation to cartularies are equally important for our understanding of 'national' histories when she argues that 'there is further ground to cover still in separating out the *publications* from the *manuscripts* themselves, recognising both as distinct creations that must be taken on their own terms'.[14] Manuscripts not only provide a wider perspective on this material as a source for the views and assumptions of those who produced and read them; they also make it possible to begin to understand these works as medieval texts in their own right.

## John of Fordun's History

THIS chapter is an initial study of how our view of one of Kersken's medieval 'national' histories as a text can change as well as be enriched by studying the surviving manuscripts. John of Fordun's *Chronica Gentis Scotorum* provides a continuous narrative from the ancient origins of the Scots to David I's death in 1153 in five books. Book V was finished sometime between 1384 and September 1387.[15] An incomplete sixth book gives an account of St Margaret's ancestors, with increasing detail of kings of England from Alfred the Great to the Norman Conquest. The witnesses of Fordun's text before it was copied and expanded by Walter Bower in his *Scotichronicon* in the 1440s can be listed here for ease of reference, using the *signa* devised by Donald Watt in his edition of *Scotichronicon*.[16]

is absent from their discussion of 'source editions', which focuses only on major initiatives to publish documents (pp. 134–35, 169–70).

14 Tucker, 'Understanding Scotland's Medieval Cartularies', p. 148 (her emphasis).

15 The dating of Fordun's history has been hampered by the assumption that he was responsible for drafting the material which originally ran up to 1363 (later extended to the mid-1380s), and that its unfinished state was because he died that year (see, for example, D.E.R. Watt, 'Fordun, John (d. in or after 1363), Chronicler', *ODNB* [9875]. There are no grounds, however, for regarding the material to 1363 as Fordun's work: see Dauvit Broun, 'A New Look at *Gesta Annalia* Attributed to John of Fordun', in B.E. Crawford (ed.), *Church, Chronicle and Learning in Medieval and Early Renaissance Scotland* (Edinburgh, 1999), pp. 9–30. Book V chapter 50 is a genealogy of David I which Fordun says he received some time ago (*dudum acceperam*) from Walter Wardlaw, who he refers to as 'lord cardinal of Scotland' (*Johannis de Fordun Chronica*, ed. Skene, 251): Wardlaw was created cardinal on 23 December 1383 and died on 22 May × 20 September 1387 (possibly on 21 or 23 August): *Scotichronicon by Walter Bower in Latin and English*, ed. D.E.R. Watt, 9 vols (Aberdeen/Edinburgh, 1987–98), vii, *Books XIII and XIV*, ed. A.B. Scott and D.E.R. Watt with Ulrike Morét and Norman F. Shead (Edinburgh, 1996), p. 519 (note on lines 7–11) and p. 521 (note on lines 62–63); presumably news that he was cardinal would not have reached Scotland until January 1384. It can be deduced from this that, although Fordun probably acquired the genealogy before Wardlaw became cardinal, he did not write book V chapter 50 until January 1384 at the earliest; the lack of any mention to Wardlaw as deceased (e.g., 'of good memory') in Fordun's fulsome reference to him, in turn, suggests that book V chapter 50 was written no later than September 1387.

16 *Scotichronicon by Walter Bower*, ed. Watt, ix, pp. 196–202. Note that Watt used the *sigla* to

**FA**: Wolfenbüttel, Herzog August Bibliothek, MS Helmstedt 538.
Books I–V and the incomplete book VI, followed by a collection of documents (beginning with the Declaration of Arbroath, but mainly relating to the case led by Baldred Bisset at the Curia in 1301), and material running from St Margaret's English royal ancestors to the mid-1380s.

**FB**: London, British Library, MS Cotton Vitellius E XI (first element): its original order is ff. 3–23, lacuna, 28–33, 35–37, 169, 38–51, 176, 173, 52–65, 170–71, 66–83, 175, 174.
Books I–V of Fordun's history, with a lacuna in book II between f. 23 and f. 28.[17]

**FC**: Cambridge, Trinity College MS O. 9. 9 (also known as MS 1421).
Books I–V and the incomplete book VI, with the collection of documents and material running from St Margaret's English royal ancestors to the mid-1380s found in **FA** and **FG**, but configured differently; there is also some material from book VI of *Scotichronicon*.[18]

**FD**: Dublin, Trinity College, MS 498: second element (pp. 223–398).
Book V of Fordun's history followed by material for 1153–1363 (very similar to the second element of BL Cotton Vitellius E XI that follows **FB**: see above) and the collection of documents found in **FA**, **FC** and **FG**, with additional items.[19]

**FE**: London, British Library MS Harleian 4764: first element (ff. 1–113).
Books I–V only.[20]

refer to manuscript volumes as they are today, rather than specifically to witnesses of Fordun's text as they were originally created. Sometimes the manuscript witnesses originally included more than Fordun's history (as in the case of **FA**, **FC**, **FD** and **FG**); in other cases, however, Fordun's history was only one, originally physically independent element in a current volume. This is either because other elements were added incrementally later, as occurred in the case of **FE** and **FF**, or because originally distinct manuscripts have been bound together: **FB** is only the first element of BL Cotton Vitellius E XI, a composite volume consisting of four different manuscripts relating to Scottish and English history and Anglo-Scottish relations (see British Library Search – "IAMS040-001103082" (bl.uk); Cotton Manuscript Vitellius E XI – British Library (bl.uk)); these have been bound together for convenience, presumably by Sir Robert Cotton (1571–1631) (see further, pp. 56–57, below).

[17] Dauvit Broun, *The Irish Identity of the Kingdom of the Scots in the Twelfth and Thirteenth Centuries* (Woodbridge, 1999), pp. 21–22, for distinguishing **FB** from ff. 24–27 and ff. 84–95, 172, 96–115, and 116–66 as an originally different manuscript (although mistakenly referring to ff. 96–115 as part of **FB**): see below, p. 54.

[18] *Scotichronicon by Walter Bower*, ed. Watt, ix, p. 202: this consists of the list of chapter titles for book VI and the first eight chapters. This is followed by Fordun's text of book VI.

[19] The first element (consisting of a revised form of books I to IV) was added later: see below, p. 54.

[20] A second element was added in 1497 × 1515, extending the narrative to 1437: see below, p. 54.

**FF**: Aberdeen, Aberdeen University Library, Scottish Catholic Archives MS MM2/1: first element (up to f. lxxvii$^r$, stopping before the end of a gathering). Books I–V only.[21]

**FG**: London, British Library, MS Add. 37223.
This has the same contents as **FA**, and was probably its exemplar.[22]

A further manuscript discovered more recently will be discussed in due course.[23] As far as the dating of these witnesses is concerned, paper manuscripts (**FB**, **FC** and **FD**) can be assisted by watermarks: the earliest (**FD**) is most likely to have been produced in the 1430s, and the latest (**FC**) has been dated to 'probably 1480 × 1496'.[24] According to Rod Lyall, the watermarks suggest that **FB** 'must have been written, in part at least, before 1450'.[25] The earliest parchment manuscripts appear to be **FA** and **FG**, which have been dated to probably the mid-fifteenth century;[26] the latest (**FE**) has been dated tentatively to sometime between 1497 and 1515 (the date of the second element of the codex).[27]

Fordun's history is a stark example of how a modern editor rationalised a text into a more coherent account of the kingdom's history than was reflected in the manuscripts at his disposal. The editor in question was William Forbes Skene (1809–92), 'a quintessential citizen of Edinburgh', whose family hailed from Rubislaw near Aberdeen.[28] He earned his keep as a lawyer, admitted Writer to the Signet in 1831 and establishing his own law firm around 1858, while he was also a Depute Clerk of the Court of Session (1853–67).[29] In his spare time he devoted himself to the study of medieval historical texts not only in Latin but also in Gaelic/Irish and Welsh: his interest was ignited by coming across an edition of Irish sources while lodging (on Sir Walter Scott's recommendation) with the minister of Laggan in 1830.[30] The only genre he did not turn his hand to was

[21] A second element was added in 1509, extending the narrative to 1437: see below, p. 54.
[22] **FG** came to light soon after Skene's edition was published (see below), and was first discussed in W.F. Skene, 'Notice of an Early MS of Fordun's Chronicle', *PSAS* 10 (1872–74), 27–30. See *Scotichronicon by Walter Bower*, ed. Watt, ix, p. 200, for a clear indication that this was the exemplar (or ancestor) of Skene's base manuscript, **FA** (more information is given in Broun, *The Irish Identity*, p. 28). Both are about the same date, which makes it more probable that this was the exemplar of **FA**.
[23] See below, pp. 56–58.
[24] For **FD**, see below, pp. 58–59; for **FC**, see *Scotichronicon by Walter Bower*, ed. Watt, ix, p. 202.
[25] R.J. Lyall, 'Books and Book Owners in Fifteenth-Century Scotland', in Jeremy Griffiths and Derek Pearsall (eds), *Book Production and Publishing in Britain 1375–1475* (Cambridge, 2007), pp. 239–56, at pp. 246 and 254 n. 34.
[26] *Scotichronicon by Walter Bower*, ed. Watt, ix, pp. 199, 200: in Lyall, 'Books and Book Owners', p. 254 n. 13, the date is expressed as '1450 or a little later'.
[27] *Scotichronicon by Walter Bower*, ed. Watt, ix, p. 198; in Broun, *The Irish Identity*, p. 25, however, it is dated to the third quarter of the fifteenth century.
[28] W.D.H. Sellar, 'William Forbes Skene (1809–92): Historian of Celtic Scotland', *PSAS* 131 (2001), 3–21 (quotation at 5).
[29] Sellar, 'William Forbes Skene', pp. 6, 12.
[30] Sellar, 'William Forbes Skene', p. 5, quoting from Skene's account of his last visit to Sir

cartularies, perhaps because these benefitted from the attentions of other scholars at the time, particularly Cosmo Innes (1798–1874).[31] Skene was elected a fellow of the Society of Antiquaries of Scotland in 1833, and appointed Historiographer Royal for Scotland in 1881. David Sellar, in a 2001 discussion of his life and work, has commented that 'one cannot fail to be impressed by the range of Skene's scholarship, by his extraordinary energy, by the boldness of what he attempted, and by the durability of so much of what he achieved'.[32] As a historian Skene is remembered mainly as the author of *Celtic Scotland. A History of Ancient Alban*, a narrative and thematic treatment of Scottish history to 1286 published in three volumes between 1876 and 1880 (with a second edition published between 1886 and 1890). His most enduring contribution, however, is his edition of John of Fordun's *Chronica Gentis Scotorum* and the material which follows it in **FA** (which he chose as the base manuscript, believing it to be 'the most complete copy of the work as left by Fordun').[33] This is likely for the foreseeable future to remain an indispensable resource for accessing the kingdom's history as this was most fully understood in the late fourteenth century.

Like Cosmo Innes in some of his editions, Skene sought to bring a coherent chronological order to his material.[34] Donald Watt has observed that Skene re-arranged what he found in his principal manuscript (**FA**) so that it became an undisturbed narrative focused on Scottish events through to Fordun's own time of writing.[35] This, however, conformed to only one of the manuscripts known to Skene – a manuscript which has subsequently been shown to be a composite of two manuscripts produced at different times. (The first is listed as **FB**, above; the second was part of another manuscript and consists of material running from 1153 to 1363.)[36] Skene revealed his motives in relation to one of the changes he made: in the case of Fordun's book VI (which, it will be recalled, was largely an account of English kings from Alfred the Great to 1066) he explained that these 'have no relation to the history of Scotland, and are placed in the Appendix, so as not to interrupt the continuous narrative of the events of Scottish history'.[37] It was Skene, therefore, and not Fordun, who created a text that fully matches Kersken's profile of a medieval 'national' history running from ancient origins to the time of writing.

---

Walter Scott the following year, written by Skene in April 1890 and published in a lengthy footnote in *The Journal of Sir Walter Scott, 1825–32, from the Original Manuscript at Abbotsford*, ed. David Douglas (Edinburgh, 1891; reprinted with corrections, 1910), pp. 813–15.

[31] Richard A. Marsden, *Cosmo Innes and the Defence of Scotland's Past, c.1825–1875* (Farnham, 2014), ch. 4.

[32] Sellar, 'William Forbes Skene', p. 17.

[33] *Johannis de Fordun Chronica*, ed. Skene, p. xlvi: Skene's text is not based only on **FA**, however, but seems to have also been influenced by *Johannis de Fordun Scotichronicon Genuinum*, ed. Thomas Hearne (Oxford, 1722), an edition of **FC**: see Broun, *The Irish Identity*, pp. 17–18.

[34] Tucker, 'Understanding Scotland's Medieval Cartularies', pp. 139–49, esp. pp. 140–43.

[35] *Scotichronicon by Walter Bower*, ed. Watt, vol. iii, *Books V and VI*, ed. John and Winifred MacQueen and D.E.R. Watt (Edinburgh 1995), pp. xvi–xvii.

[36] See below, p. 56.

[37] *Johannis de Fordun Chronica*, ed. Skene, p. xlvi.

It is apparent from a careful reading of Skene's explanation for rearranging what he found in **FA** that he imagined that Fordun's intention had been to produce a continuous narrative. Skene felt moved to do so because Fordun's history, as it stands, is incomplete. All manuscripts bar one (**FD**) include books I to V. A few lack book VI; those that include it only do so with a considerable body of extra material, which served to extend the chronological range to the late fourteenth century.[38] Book VI breaks off after 15 chapters at the point where the narrative reached the Norman Conquest of England; this led to St Margaret's flight to Scotland and would therefore have begun to overlap with Fordun's book V (which covers the kingdom's history from Margaret's husband Mael Coluim III, who reigned 1058–93, to their son David I, 1124–53). A couple of manuscripts (**FA** and **FG**) end book VI in mid-sentence, which suggests that it was not meant to finish at this point: in **FC** the incomplete final sentence is omitted.[39] It is unclear how Fordun intended to continue the work. Finally, there is one manuscript (**FD**) that originally began with book V so that the kingdom's history ran only from the reign of Mael Coluim III. This truncated version will be set aside for discussion later.[40]

In three manuscripts (**FA**, **FC** and **FG**) the incomplete book VI was followed by material extending to the mid-1380s. No concern, however, was given to presenting this extension as a straightforward chronological continuation of Fordun's work. The first part overlaps with the narrative in Fordun's books V and VI; as a result, readers were confronted with two very similar accounts of St Margaret's ancestors, with detail on kings of England from Alfred the Great to 1066. No secret, either, was made in these manuscripts of the fact that most of the material following Fordun's book VI was, in fact, books V–VII of a history of the kingdom by an earlier author that is otherwise lost: this previous work has been dubbed 'proto-Fordun' because it was evidently Fordun's principal source.[41] 'Proto-Fordun', as found in **FA**, **FC** and **FG** as an extension of Fordun's history, however, provided a continuous narrative only as far as February 1285 before breaking off to finish with a series of documents beginning with the Declaration of Arbroath (1320) and concluding with Baldred Bisset's *Pleading* written at the Curia in 1301.[42] The material in **FA**, **FC** and **FG** running from October 1285 to the mid-1380s is ultimately from another source that was predominantly

[38] This is true not only of the manuscripts of Fordun's history which give a version of the text earlier than Bower's *Scotichronicon* (listed above), but also of Bower's *Scotichronicon* itself and its derivatives (listed and described in *Scotichronicon*, ed. Watt, ix, pp. 186–98).

[39] *Johannis de Fordun Chronica*, ed. Skene, p. 401 (note that Skene was unaware of **FG** when editing the text). For **FG** as the likely exemplar of **FA**, see n. 22, above.

[40] See below, pp. 58–59.

[41] The book-division between books VI and VII is lost. See Broun, 'Scotland's First "National" History?' for more detail; this develops the analysis in Broun, 'A New Look at *Gesta Annalia*'. The extant portion that overlaps with Fordun's books V and VI was certainly used heavily as a source by Fordun: see the apparatus in *Johannis de Fordun Chronica*, ed. Skene, pp. 406–37; Broun, *Scottish Independence*, pp. 227–29.

[42] Broun, 'Scotland's First "National" History?': see n. 2, above.

annalistic in form (especially from the early fourteenth century): this originally ended in 1363 (as in **FD**).[43] The original configuration of all this material after Fordun's book VI has only been preserved in **FC**: in **FA** and **FG** the documents beginning with the Declaration of Arbroath no longer sit incongruously in the middle of events in 1285.[44]

In sum, therefore, **FA**, **FC** and **FG**, both in content and structure, provide a strikingly uneven way of maintaining a continuous narrative of the kingdom's history beyond David I's death in 1153. An extensive account of pre-1066 kings of England appears twice as part of the kingdom's history, first in Fordun's book VI and then at the beginning of the material copied from 'proto-Fordun'; there is also a significant overlap between 'proto-Fordun' and Fordun's book V.[45] It comes as no surprise that Skene took pains to present this in a more chronologically coherent form. He made both Fordun's book VI and the part of 'proto-Fordun' that overlaps with Fordun's books V and VI into separate appendices, and removed the series of documents beginning with the Declaration of Arbroath to another appendix, providing only their headings and linking passages.[46] The result was an account of Scottish events running uninterrupted from the accession of Mael Coluim IV in 1153 to the mid-1380s. Skene labelled this *Gesta Annalia*, and regarded it as Fordun's unfinished draft, rather than largely the remains of Fordun's principal source ('proto-Fordun').[47]

## Continuous Histories of the Kingdom between the Mid-Fifteenth and Early-Sixteenth Centuries

IF we wish to find the earliest surviving history of the Scots from origins to near-contemporary times as a single work, the obvious answer is *Scotichronicon* by Walter Bower, abbot of Inchcolm (d. 1449), completed in 1447. Bower included Fordun's books I to V and incomplete book VI (with his own additions), and

43 It has been updated piecemeal to 1385, although the final item relates to February 1384: *Johannis de Fordun Chronica*, ed. Skene, p. 383. The lost history from 1285 to 1363 and its use by Wyntoun and an unpublished succinct chronicle will be discussed in more detail on another occasion.

44 See Broun, 'Scotland's First "National" History?', modifying Broun, 'A New Look at *Gesta Annalia*'.

45 The relationship is noted in detail by Skene in his apparatus to appendix III: *Johannis de Fordun Chronica*, ed. Skene, pp. 406–37.

46 *Johannis de Fordun Chronica*, ed. Skene, pp. 406–37 (appendix III, entitled *Johannis de Fordun Capitula ad 'Gesta Annalia' Præfixa*) and pp. 402–5 (appendix II entitled *Documenta quædam a Johanne de Fordun Exscripta*); Fordun's incomplete book VI was removed to pp. 387–401 (appendix I, entitled *Johannis de Fordun Capitula ad Librum Sextum Parata*).

47 In his prologue to *Scotichronicon*, Bower says that Fordun 'left much material by way of texts that were not yet fully developed', *multa reliquit in scriptis nondum tamen usquequaque distincta* (*Scotichronicon by Walter Bower*, ed. Watt, ix, p. 2): Bower's exemplar was related to **FA**, **FC** and **FG** in which the incomplete book VI of Fordun's history was followed by material from Margaret's ancestors to the mid-1380s, which Bower (like Skene) evidently assumed was by Fordun.

extended the narrative up to James I's death in 1437 – a work of 16 books altogether. He presented Fordun as the 'master', and diligently distinguished Fordun's prose from his own, identifying Fordun's passages as being of the *autor* or *scriba* and his own as that of the *scriptor*.[48] *Scotichronicon* itself was not Bower's last word on the kingdom's past: it formed a preliminary step towards his ultimate account of Scottish history, a much more coherent work in 40 books which survives (almost) intact in the codex known as the Book of Coupar Angus.[49] In the prologue to this 40-book work Bower went even further in idolising John of Fordun, portraying him as travelling across Britain and Ireland in a quest to recover the kingdom's history after the losses inflicted by Edward I.[50] Bower's 40-book work was the first of a number of attempts to recompose *Scotichronicon* into a more consistent and fluent account of Scottish history. The most accomplished is known to scholars as the Book of Pluscarden, probably completed in 1461.[51] It is notable that the focus on kings of England from Alfred the Great to 1066 in Fordun's book VI was incorporated into Bower's 16-book *Scotichronicon*, his 40-book version of *Scotichronicon* and the Book of Pluscarden. None of these medieval accounts of the kingdom's history shared Skene's view that pre-Conquest kings of England 'have no relation to the history of Scotland'.[52]

Fordun's history in all its manifestations, not just those edited by Skene, survives in at least two dozen manuscripts datable to between the 1430s and 1530s. Apart from those that include only Fordun's history, or Fordun's history followed by material running to 1363 or to the mid-1380s, there are also those which consist of Bower's *Scotichronicon* (six manuscripts) or the Book of Pluscarden (five manuscripts, plus a translation into French); others are viewed simply as 'abbreviations' of Bower's *Scotichronicon*, or as an abbreviation of an abbreviation.[53] All these manuscripts show what the kingdom's history meant to their scribes and readers in the late Middle Ages.[54]

[48] *Scotichronicon by Walter Bower*, ed. Watt, ix, pp. 4–5.

[49] *Scotichronicon by Walter Bower*, ed. Watt, ix, pp. 193–96 (Edinburgh, NLS Adv. MS 35.1.7).

[50] *Scotichronicon by Walter Bower*, ed. Watt, ix, pp. 12–15.

[51] *Liber Pluscardensis*, ed. Felix J.H. Skene, Historians of Scotland, vol. 7 (Edinburgh, 1877); *The Book of Pluscarden*, trans. Felix J.H. Skene, Historians of Scotland, vol. 10 (Edinburgh, 1880). The author is unknown: Sally Mapstone, 'The *Scotichronicon*'s First Readers', in Crawford (ed.), *Church, Chronicle and Learning*, pp. 31–55, at p. 35, tentatively suggested Sir Gilbert Hay as a possibility, but recognised that this is problematic.

[52] See below, pp. 56–58, quoting *Johannis de Fordun Chronica*, ed. Skene, p. xlvi.

[53] This includes all the manuscripts described in *Scotichronicon by Walter Bower*, ed. Watt, ix, pp. 148–49, 186–202, plus another manuscript of Fordun's history (see below, pp. 56–57), and all the pre-Reformation manuscripts in Marjorie Drexler, 'The Extant Abridgements of Bower's *Scotichronicon*', *SHR* 61 (1982), 62–67. A diagram of how these manuscripts (limited to those in Latin) relate to each other, based on current published knowledge, is in Dauvit Broun, 'Rethinking Medieval Scottish Regnal Historiography in the Light of New Approaches to Texts as Manuscripts', *Cambrian Medieval Celtic Studies* 83 (Summer 2022), 19–47, at p. 27.

[54] For a more focussed and detailed discussion, see Mapstone, 'The *Scotichronicon*'s First Readers'.

Those that are witnesses to the pre-*Scotichronicon* text of Fordun's history show the clearest divergence from Kersken's model of a medieval 'national' history running from ancient origins to the time of writing. Although most manuscripts of Fordun's history without Bower's continuation can be dated to the mid-fifteenth century, it was certainly still being copied after *Scotichronicon* had been completed.[55] It will be recalled that, although three manuscripts (**FA**, **FC** and **FG**) included a continuation (overlapping with books V and VI of Fordun's work) and a series of documents, three did not (**FB**, **FE** and **FF**), and originally finished with David I's death. Another manuscript (**FD**) originally consisted only of Fordun's book V followed by material running to 1363 (discussed below): this was later extended with the addition of the equivalent of Fordun's books I to IV derived from Bower's 40-book work.[56] Two of those consisting originally of Fordun's books I–V were later extended beyond 1153 to the fifteenth century by the addition of material derived ultimately from Bower; one of these extensions (**FF**) is dated to 1509 and the other (**FE**) can be dated to sometime between 1497 and 1515.[57] The original manuscripts would therefore have existed for anything between a decade or a generation or more as simply books I to V of Fordun's history. **FB**, the third manuscript from Scottish origins to David I's death, has also been extended, in this case by cannibalising the material labelled by Skene as *Gesta Annalia* (running from 1153 to 1363) from another manuscript. This almost certainly did not occur until both **FB** and the cannibalised manuscript were in the possession of Sir Robert Cotton (1571–1631), the renowned antiquary whose collection became part of the British Museum when it was founded in 1753.[58] On the face of it, therefore, **FB** was not only produced as a manuscript of Fordun's books I to V without any additional material, but was unchanged as a history ending in 1153 for as long as it was in Scottish ownership.[59]

55 *Scotichronicon by Walter Bower*, ed. Watt, ix, p. 202; see also below, pp. 48–49.

56 *Scotichronicon by Walter Bower*, ed. Watt, ix, p. 200 (dated to 'perhaps before 1465', referring to advice from Rod Lyall).

57 *Scotichronicon by Walter Bower*, ed. Watt, ix, pp. 196, 197; see also vol. v, *Books IX and X*, ed. Simon Taylor and D.E.R. Watt, with Brian Scott (Aberdeen, 1990), p. 460 (note on line 50).

58 His library has been described as 'arguably the most important collection of manuscripts ever assembled in Britain by a private individual': C.J. Wright (ed.), *Sir Robert Cotton as Collector. Essays on an Early Stuart Courtier and His Legacy* (London, 1997), vii (editor's foreward).

59 Its earliest known owner, William Schevez, archbishop of St Andrews (1479–97), at some stage also owned manuscripts of *Scotichronicon* and the Book of Pluscarden: Margaret Connolly, 'A Manuscript Owned by William Scheves Now at Maynooth', *The Library* 17 (2016), 331–35, at 335. The manuscript of *Scotichronicon* is London, British Library Harleian MS 712 (*Scotichronicon by Walter Bower*, ed. Watt, ix, pp. 189–90) and the manuscript of the 'Book of Pluscarden' is Glasgow, University Library, MS Gen. 333 (Lyall, 'Books and Book Owners', pp. 246–47). Schevez would not, therefore, have needed **FB** for an account of the kingdom's history after 1153. Unfortunately nothing is known of the manuscript's history in the sixteenth century before it was acquired by Sir Robert Cotton, so it is possible that after Schevez's death its owner might not have had such ready access to other histories of the kingdom that extended beyond 1153.

At the end of the day, therefore, there was some demand (at least in the mid-fifteenth century) for manuscripts consisting only of books I to V of Fordun's history. The overwhelming interest, however, among the readers and owners of the surviving manuscripts of the kingdom's history was not in Fordun's history on its own, but in a narrative of some kind that extended at least to 1437. In most cases the narrative failed to reach near-contemporary times, falling short by a number of generations before the likely date when the manuscript was produced. This does not mean there was little or no desire for an ongoing continuous history – simply that updating the narrative of a work on this scale was not viewed as a straightforward task. A vivid indication of both the aspiration to continue the kingdom's history and the reticence in writing this is the provision of a blank 'book' at the end of one of the earliest manuscripts of *Scotichronicon* (London, British Library, MS Royal 13 E X, the 'Black Book of Paisley',[60] datable to some point after October 1447 and the death of Pope Nicholas V in March 1455).[61] It will be recalled that *Scotichronicon* consisted of 16 books; in this manuscript there are running headers for a 'book XVII' on the blank pages at the end (with *liber* in the middle of the top margin of the verso and *xvii* in the same place on the recto). Writing the kingdom's history at this level, however, demanded something more than *ad hoc* notes or piecemeal accounts of events. Bower himself, near the end of *Scotichronicon*, made it clear how he expected his work to be continued. He imagined that it should be each monastery's duty to 'make a dated record of all noteworthy things during a king's reign' which would then, on the king's death, be brought together into an official record by a commission appointed by parliament or general council.[62] This was not seen as a task, therefore, which a scribe should attempt on their own.

At this stage in the discussion the main point to take away from looking at the question of a continuous history through the lens of manuscripts is that scribes often found ways to extend Fordun's narrative to beyond 1153 by copying material that already existed in some form. Bower and the anonymous author of the Book of Pluscarden took this one step further by refashioning what they found and (particularly in Bower's case) composing fresh material. The results were uneven, however. A kingdom's continuous history would be all the more compelling if it could be experienced either within a single work or as a chronologically consistent narrative. Bower's *Scotichronicon* and its derivatives offered the former, if not the latter (bearing in mind the detour into pre-Conquest kings of England).[63] The expedient of adding material

[60] This name for the manuscript is given by John Gibson (notary, a chaplain of Glasgow Cathedral) whose abbreviated version of the text (Edinburgh, NLS, Adv. MS 35.6.8) was completed on 4 March '1501' (i.e., 1502): Drexler, 'The Extant Abridgements', p. 64.

[61] *Scotichronicon by Walter Bower*, ed. Watt, ix, pp. 186–87.

[62] *Scotichronicon by Walter Bower*, ed. Watt, vol. viii, *Books XV and XVI*, ed. D.E.R. Watt (Aberdeen, 1987), p. 339.

[63] By virtue of including Fordun's incomplete book VI: *Scotichronicon by Walter Bower*, ed. Watt, iii, pp. 308–43.

from another work to Fordun's history offered neither, at least as found in the manuscripts known to Skene. It was, it seems, left to Skene to fashion a medieval 'national history' that was a single chronologically consistent work.

## A 'New' Manuscript of Fordun's History[64]

ANOTHER manuscript, however, has recently been identified that shows that the way Skene presented the text as a continuous history does, after all, have a medieval precedent.[65] Every discovery increases our knowledge, but also serves as a graphic reminder of how we are limited by what survives. This is a particular issue when trying to understand how a text was treated by medieval scribes. This newly identified codex also serves to emphasise that, although it should come as no surprise that a nineteenth-century editor might reorder the text (in Skene's words) 'so as not to interrupt the continuous narrative of the events of Scottish history', we should be wary of regarding a modern response to this material as inherently incompatible with what would have been possible in the Middle Ages. The differences between medieval and modern are not necessarily as clear-cut as might be supposed.

Until Julian Harrison's seminal work in cataloguing the Cotton manuscripts there was no way for scholars to find this 'new' manuscript of Fordun's books I to V.[66] It was badly damaged in the fire in 1731 that consumed parts of Sir Robert Cotton's library; 91 surviving folios were bound in 1866, but without identifying the text, which meant that it remained unknown to Skene.[67] Its shelf-mark in Cotton's library could not be established, and so the volume was initially designated as Cotton MS Otho B III: the original Cotton MS Otho B III seems to have been regarded as lost in the fire of 1731. About a century later, however, a study of the detritus of charred manuscript leaves

64 What follows is based on Julian Harrison's description (in his catalogue entry: see next notes) and a full discussion of the manuscript that is currently part of an unpublished analysis (in progress) of witnesses to Fordun's history prior to the earliest extant manuscripts in the mid-fifteenth century.

65 Julian Harrison came across it in 2005 while working on his catalogue of Cotton manuscripts and, seeing that it was a history of Scotland, showed it to me for identification.

66 Julian Harrison's catalogue entry for this manuscript can be accessed online: http://searcharchives.bl.uk/primo_library/libweb/action/display.do?tabs=detailsTab&ct=display&fn=search&doc=IAMS040-001102857&indx=6&recIds=IAMS040-001102857&recIdxs=5&elementId=5&renderMode=poppedOut&displayMode=full&frbrVersion=&dscnt=0&frbg=&scp.scps=scope%3A%28BL%29&tab=local&dstmp=1581279391090&srt=rank&mode=Basic&&dum=true&vl(freeText0)=Otho%20B%20iii&vid=IAMS_VU2 (accessed 28 December 2020).

67 The date of the binding is given in Harrison's catalogue entry (see previous note); a note on the recto of the first flyleaf after f. 91, dated March 1884, that the manuscript has 91 folios – presumably made at the same time as a pencil foliation in the top right corner of the guards – is in the same hand as pencil notes occasionally identifying the book and chapter number (based presumably on internal evidence). Occasionally an earlier pencil foliation appears on the burned paper folios.

surviving from the fire allowed parts of the original Cotton MS Otho B III to be identified and bound in 1962. The same shelf-mark cannot be given to two manuscripts, of course, so in order to distinguish the copy of Fordun's history from what remains of the 'real' Cotton MS Otho B III, a crucial asterisk has been added: if anyone wishes to consult this manuscript of Fordun's work they should ask for Cotton MS Otho B III*.

The discovery of a 'new' manuscript of Fordun's history would be significant on its own – but there is more. Studying it has led to the realisation that in BL Cotton MS Vitellius E XI the extension of Fordun's history (covering the years 1153–1363, labelled *Gesta Annalia* by Skene) and four folios of Fordun's book II (ff. 24–27) originally belonged to the same manuscript as Cotton MS Otho B III*. Not only do the sections dovetail together textually, but ff. 24–27 and *Gesta Annalia* as far as f. 139v in Cotton MS Vitellius E XI are by the same scribe as Cotton MS Otho B III*.[68] The issue is put beyond doubt by the watermarks, showing that the paper in these sections of Cotton MS Vitellius E XI is from the same stocks as Cotton MS Otho B III*, with the exception of only five folios (Cotton MS Vitellius E XI, ff. 141, 144, 164–66). The watermarks suggest that the manuscript was written no earlier than 1473: its likeliest date-range therefore would be sometime between the mid-1470s and mid-1480s. Unfortunately there are no surviving marks of ownership.

Putting all this together, a medieval codex containing books I to V of Fordun's work followed by material covering the years 1153–1363 (labelled *Gesta Annalia* by Skene) emerges from the wreckage of the fire in 1731. For convenience it can be given the *siglum* **FH**. Parts of it are lost forever (about a fifth of the text of books I to V, particularly in book V where a third is lost, and books I and III where about a quarter has disappeared). Nevertheless, what remains is quite substantial. The key difference between this and other manuscripts of books I to V of Fordun's history followed by similar material is that the narrative of the kingdom's history flows on without a break after 1153. This has been achieved (in much the same way as in Skene's edition) by removing Fordun's book VI and omitting the material from 'proto-Fordun' as far as 1153, which overlapped with Fordun's books V and VI. The references to books in 'proto-Fordun' have gone, so this material no longer appears so obviously to be part of another work. Although the end of Fordun's book V in **FH** is lost, the list of chapter-titles survives, which shows that book V was still regarded as ending in 1153. The extension from 1153 to 1363 is not presented in this manuscript as part of Fordun's history, therefore, but more like a supplement. The series of documents beginning with the Declaration of Arbroath has been omitted, too: there is, however, an inexplicable gap (equivalent to about ten lines of writing) which corresponds with where the documents appear in **FC**, in the middle of the account of events in 1285. It seems likely, therefore, that the documents, too, have been sacrificed

68 The gradual change in writing explains why it has not been clear before that Cotton MS Vitellius E XI ff. 24–27 was by the same scribe as from f. 84r: in Broun, *The Irish Identity*, pp. 21–22, they are treated as originally from different manuscripts.

in order to achieve an undisturbed narrative. The result for the reader is a chronologically uninterrupted account of the kingdom's history from its ancient origins to David II's second marriage in 1363.

When was this undisturbed narrative originally created? If this manuscript were the only example where Fordun's book V was followed directly by material beginning with the inauguration of King Mael Coluim IV in 1153, then it would be impossible to tell if this innovation had been made by the scribe of this manuscript or copied by them from their exemplar. Fortunately this manuscript is not alone. **FD** (which survives as the second element of Dublin, Trinity College, MS 498) begins only with Fordun's book V. This, however, is also followed by the material covering the years 1153–1363 (labelled *Gesta Annalia* by Skene) found in **FH**: indeed, it shares many distinctive readings (particularly in the section between 1285 and 1363).[69] There can be little doubt, therefore, that both manuscripts represent an earlier text which consisted of books I to V of Fordun's history and the material from 1153 to 1363. There is one feature that is present in **FD** but absent from **FH**: the series of documents beginning with the Declaration of Arbroath. These documents were presumably also in the earlier text, placed at the end, as in **FD**.

Can this earlier text, surviving only in **FD** and **FH**, be dated? One of the passages found uniquely in both these manuscripts shows that it cannot have been written earlier than 1389. It occurs in the account of the Battle of Poitiers (1356), where a passing reference is made to Archibald Douglas 'the Grim' as earl of Douglas.[70] Archibald's claim to the earldom was confirmed in parliament in early April 1389.[71] As far as the latest date for this undisturbed narrative from Scottish origins to 1363 goes, this is determined by whichever of its extant witnesses (**FD** and **FH**) is the earliest. It will be recalled that the watermarks in **FH** suggests that it was probably produced sometime between the mid-1470s and mid-1480s. **FD**, however, must be earlier. Martin Colker, in his catalogue description of the manuscript, refers to watermarks that are comparable to those dated by Briquet mainly to the 1420s.[72] This is consistent

[69] This is considered in detail in the unpublished analysis of witnesses to Fordun's history referred to in n. 42 (above).

[70] *Johannis de Fordun Chronica*, ed. Skene, p. 377 n. 3.

[71] Michael Brown, *The Black Douglases* (East Linton, 1998), pp. 76–86.

[72] Martin L. Colker, *Trinity College Library Dublin: Descriptive Catalogue of the Mediaeval and Renaissance Latin Manuscripts*, 2 vols (Dublin, 1991), ii, p. 918, refers to two main types of watermark: one relates to the later addition ('Briquet nos 7226–27'), and the other to the original manuscript ('Briquet nos 14292 sqq.'). C.M. Briquet, *Les Filigranes. Dictionnaire historique des marques du papier dès leur apparition vers 1282 jusqu'en 1600*, 4 vols (Geneva, 1907), iv, p. 725, no. 14292 (dated to 1411); no. 14293 (dated to 1417, 1424, 1426 and '1463?'); no. 14294 (1420 and 1424–39); no. 14295 (1422). Although Colker does not cite any of these as corresponding exactly to the watermarks in the manuscript, its close similarity with those dated by Briquet predominantly to the 1410s and 1420s suggests that the paper of the original manuscript was of a similar date. The paper need not have been used immediately, so the optimum dating of the manuscript is the 1420s or 1430s.

with the likely date of the handwriting, which points to sometime in the first half of the fifteenth century.[73] On the available evidence, therefore, a date in (or possibly a little before) the 1430s can be suggested for **FD**. This would make it the earliest extant manuscript of any part of Fordun's history. The undisturbed narrative from Scottish origins to 1363, consisting of Fordun's books I to V and what Skene dubbed as *Gesta Annalia* (1153–1363), was therefore originally written sometime between around 1390 and around 1430. Before Cotton Otho B III* was identified as a manuscript of Fordun's books I to V, it was possible to say that Skene's edition published in 1871 was the first occasion when a chronologically undisturbed continuous history of the Scottish kingdom had been attempted using medieval material. It can now be recognised that this had been achieved at least 440 years earlier.

## Conclusion

A range of scribal responses to Fordun's history has come to light in this discussion. The most striking is the creation of an uninterrupted narrative of the kind published by Skene. This may have been copied in full only once (in **FH**). It seems not to have caught on, judging by the codices that survive today. Another less creative response was to provide a much cruder and uneven way of supplementing Fordun's work. As far as extant or traceable manuscripts are concerned this was the most influential, leading to a number of adaptations, including Bower's much more ambitious *Scotichronicon*.[74] An alternative and more straightforward reaction was to reduce Fordun's text so it remained a continuous narrative only as far as 1153, shorn of its foray into English history. After Bower completed his 16- and 40-book continuations, scribes enjoyed even more choice, and a range of abbreviations and combinations were fashioned. All this suggests not only that medieval 'national' histories could take different forms, as Kersken observed,[75] but that even when they were standalone texts on the scale of a codex, there was no established expectation of what they should be like, or even that they should provide a continuous chronology of the kingdom's past up to recent times.

There is an obvious danger in drawing general conclusions about medieval 'national' histories from Fordun's history alone. There is a strong suspicion that it would have been unusual for a narrative to cease (as Fordun's did) more

[73] Pers. comm. Joanna Tucker, 1 May 2020 (without knowledge of the watermark evidence). The coincidence between the optimum dating suggested by the watermarks and the middle of the range suggested by the handwriting is particularly reassuring.

[74] This will be discussed in more detail on a future occasion.

[75] Norbert Kersken, 'National Chronicles and National Consciousness', in János M. Bak and Ivan Jurković (eds), *Chronicon. Medieval Narrative Sources: A Chronological Guide with Introductory Essays* (Turnhout, 2013), pp. 119–26.

than two centuries earlier than the time of writing. This could, nevertheless, make it a particularly revealing test case. When viewed through the lens of surviving manuscripts, it provides a rare opportunity to see how far there was an expectation that the kingdom's past should be continued to near-contemporary times, and what form this could take. The variety of responses shows what was possible within this genre more readily than if there had been a complete canonical text that was simply copied and periodically updated. It also allows us to see how some scribes – and not just authors such as Bower – engaged with the kingdom's history and could be innovators as well as editors or copyists.

This chapter will have served its purpose if it has shown the value of undertaking similar studies of other medieval 'national' histories and how they have been edited. Joanna Tucker's work, however, suggests that focussing on the manuscripts themselves on their own terms could have deeper implications. For her, 'the cartulary might be seen as essentially a starting point for engaging with a wide landscape of documentary material produced by communities and individuals throughout the middle ages'.[76] The same could be true for 'national' histories, too, taking this as a starting point for opening up a vista of scribal engagement with a kingdom's continuous past that extends far beyond what is usually published in scholarly editions. Not only would this reveal more variety and flexibility than is apparent from Kersken's study, as shown in the case of Skene's edition of Fordun's *Chronica Gentis Scotorum*; it would also, for example, allow short chronicles to be included (such as those edited by Dan Embree, Edward Donald Kennedy and Kathleen Daly),[77] and even the minimal treatments of the kingdom's past in king-lists and other similarly schematic texts, as found in the commonplace book of John Gray, secretary to William Schevez, archbishop of St Andrews (1479–97).[78] By considering manuscripts like these alongside the more typical codices of Fordun's and Bower's works, a more complete understanding of what 'national' history might have meant in a medieval context can begin to be developed.

76 Tucker, 'Understanding Scotland's Medieval Cartularies', p. 161.

77 Dan Embree, Edward Donald Kennedy and Kathleen Daly (eds), *Short Scottish Prose Chronicles* (Woodbridge, 2012).

78 Edinburgh, NLS, Adv. MS 34.7.3: only the second gathering (ff. 17–28) has texts relating to the kingdom's history (I use here the most recent foliation in pencil, rather than the ink foliation used by Marjorie Ogilvie Anderson, *Kings and Kingship in Early Scotland*, 2nd edn (Edinburgh, 1980), pp. 64–65, where she discusses this material).

# 3

# 'A traitor to the kingdom': Robert Bruce and the Use of Treason in Fourteenth-Century Scotland

Michael H. Brown

IN early August 1320, in a meeting of the Scottish parliament, a group of nobles was condemned for conspiring against their king, Robert Bruce. According to a near-contemporary chronicle, their actions were judged to be lese majesty, 'the crime which surpasses all other crimes,' plotting the death or downfall of one's own king.[1] By conspiring against King Robert, these nobles had committed high treason and now faced the full penalty of the horrific death reserved for traitors. However, 14 years earlier in the late summer of 1306 it had been Bruce who was denounced as a traitor. Robert's seizure of the Scottish throne and the killing of his rival, John Comyn, which preceded it, were widely condemned as unforgiveable betrayals of both earthly laws and moral precepts. 'The guilt of homicide and the stain of treason' justified the brutal treatment of Bruce's family and followers by Edward I of England, a fate which Robert himself would have shared had he been captured.[2] The wars over Scotland between 1296 and 1357 were struggles to claim and exercise authority over the kingdom. Charges of treason provided a way of signalling the illegitimacy of resistance to a ruler, stigmatising opposition, and providing the means to dispossess and eliminate those who acted against their royal lord. Their effectiveness was bound up with prevailing political conditions as much as fixed legal principles. Once he had secured control of the kingdom, the man accused of treason could bring the same charge against his own opponents. Moreover, from the late thirteenth century, treason law developed as a way of framing sovereignty. It defined the scope of royal authority by criminalising those accused of harming it within the territory and legal framework of the realm. In a struggle which centred on the status of Scotland and its rulers, treason was a central issue and a legal weapon.

1 *John of Fordun's Chronicle of the Scottish Nation*, ed. W. Skene, 2 vols (Edinburgh, 1872), ii, p. 341; Henry Bracton, *De Legibus et Consuetudinibus Angliae*, ed. G. Woodbine, 2 vols (New Haven, CT, 1922), ii, p. 334

2 *Vita Edwardi Secundi*, ed. W. Childs (Oxford, 2005), pp. 24–25.

If treason represented an element in the struggle to control Scotland, over a longer period and more widely it was a measure of relations between rulers and subjects and the right of the latter to resist their prince. In Scottish historiography there is an ongoing debate about the nature of this relationship during the fourteenth and fifteenth centuries. As it relates to Robert Bruce, the terms of the debate were set over 50 years ago by Geoffrey Barrow's magisterial study of the king and his times. Barrow consciously presented Robert as a monarch who ruled in partnership with the 'community of the realm'.[3] This contemporary term was interpreted to indicate a body which played an active role in government and politics, even making the king, to use Norman Reid's phrase, 'one to whom the community delegated its authority'.[4] Several historians have identified the clearest expression of this relationship as deriving from the Declaration of Arbroath, the letter sent in May 1320 on behalf of the barons and community of Scotland to Pope John XXII in the context of papal hostility to Bruce. The letter's statement that should Robert fail to defend the liberties of his kingdom against the English king he would suffer deposition by the community seems revolutionary. To Ted Cowan, Susan Reynolds and others this passage has suggested that a contractual approach to the rights of the monarch relative to the community in Scotland emerged far earlier than can be identified in other medieval realms.[5]

However, doubts have been expressed as to whether Robert should be regarded as a king whose authority was so intertwined with the active participation of the community of his subjects. The perceptive analysis of Bruce's early parliaments undertaken by Roland Tanner instead builds a picture of a king who, like Edward I in England, was 'only interested in concepts of collective decision making and the community of the realm in so far as they could be exploited for the ruthless enforcement of his wishes'.[6] Alice Taylor's 2012 work similarly argued that the use of communal language in legislation and legal texts associated with the reign of Robert I should 'not be seen as a form of early constitutional tradition rather a legitimising rhetoric used by Robert in order to justify and create a veneer of common support for his actions'.[7] For an insecure king beset by challenges

[3] G.W.S. Barrow, *Robert Bruce and the Community of the Realm of Scotland*, 1st edn (London, 1965).

[4] N. Reid, 'Crown and Community in the Reign of Robert I', in A. Grant and K. Stringer (eds), *Medieval Scotland: Crown, Lordship, Community: Essays presented to G.W.S. Barrow* (Edinburgh, 1993), pp. 202–22, at p. 221.

[5] E. Cowan, *The Declaration of Arbroath: For Freedom Alone* (East Linton, 1998), pp. 51–62; S. Reynolds, *Kingdoms and Communities in Western Europe 900–1300* (Oxford, 1997), pp. 273–76.

[6] R. Tanner, 'Cowing the Community: Coercion and Falsification in Robert Bruce's Parliaments', in Keith M. Brown and Roland Tanner (eds), *Parliament and Politics in Scotland, 1235–1560* (Edinburgh, 2004), pp. 50–73, at p. 72.

[7] A. Taylor, 'The Assizes of David I King of Scots, 1124–1153', *SHR* 91 (2012), 197–238 (quote at p. 229).

to his authority, claims of communal support and ancient pedigrees for his laws represented a 'legitimating force' which bolstered his rule.[8] However, Michael Penman in his extensive account of Robert's reign speaks of the king's 'personal style and cautious acceptance of, and sensitivity to counsel, petition and dialogue' providing a 'comfortable working relationship' with the community. He rejects the idea of the king using communal ideas as 'merely' a legitimising tool.[9]

Roger Mason's own work has cast convincing doubts on the significance of the Declaration of Arbroath as an influential constitutional document. Taking a later perspective, he has pointed out the lack of any evidence that the declaration shaped subsequent patterns of thought or action in Scotland. While the tradition of 'aristocratic conciliarism' which Mason identifies in Scotland (as in other realms) could be connected to the idea of the community of the realm as it was expressed from 1286 to 1329, he also observes the lack of later expressions of subjects' formal rights to counsel and consent, let alone depose, their rulers. Instead, he has consistently demonstrated that a monarchic view of politics predominated in political writings produced in Scotland.[10]

There is clearly now an active debate about the character of Robert I's kingship and, more broadly, about the legacy of the era of war and dislocation on Scotland's political culture. By focussing on the way in which charges of treason were developed and deployed by Bruce and his successors, this chapter will add to the reappraisal of Robert as a king whose contested position made him more ready to assert the full powers of his office, rather than accept a more limited authority. It will suggest too that his actions were driven directly by specific challenges rather than abstract concepts of kingship. The discussion will conclude by showing that Robert's approach to treason was not followed in the decades after his death, when changing political conditions meant the charge was deployed more sparingly in his realm.

The Scottish wars occurred as part of an era in which royal authority was heightened by the application of Roman legal precepts. The definition and use of treason charges against the enemies of the crown were an element in this development.[11] As in much else, the reign of Edward I has been seen as

[8] Taylor, 'The Assizes of David I King of Scots', pp. 232–4. See also A. Taylor, 'What Does *Regiam maiestatem* Actually Say (and What Does It Mean)?', in W. Eves, J. Hudson, I. Iversen and S. White (eds), *Common Law, Civil Law, Colonial Law: Essays in Comparative Legal History from the Twelfth to the Twentieth Centuries* (Cambridge, 2021), pp. 47–85.

[9] M. Penman, *Robert the Bruce King of the Scots* (New Haven, CT, 2014), p. 324.

[10] R. Mason, 'Beyond the Declaration of Arbroath: Kingship, Counsel and Consent in Late Medieval and Early Modern Scotland', in Boardman and Goodare (eds), *Kings, Lords and Men*, pp. 265–82; R. Mason, 'Kingship, Tyranny and the Right to Resist in Fifteenth-Century Scotland', *SHR* 66 (1987), 125–51.

[11] Walter Ullman, 'The Development of the Medieval Idea of Sovereignty', *English Historical Review* 250 (1949), 1–33; Sarah Tebbit, 'Papal Pronouncements on Legitimate Lordship and the Formulation of Nationhood in Early Fourteenth-Century Scottish Writings', *Journal of Medieval History* 40 (2014), 44–62; Joseph Canning, 'Law,

a watershed in the British Isles for the way in which treason was deployed. Before 1300 there was certainly no automatic assumption that nobles who opposed their king in arms were committing treason. Such actions did carry the risk of fines, forfeiture, banishment, or imprisonment, but in England between the aftermath of the Norman Conquest and the last year of Edward I's reign no great noble had been tried and executed as a traitor.[12] In these centuries, there was no clear or single definition of treason as a crime. Instead treason could be a general act of betrayal, the breaking of an oath of fealty to one's lord, or could encompass the Roman legal concept of *lèse-majesté*, the attempt to harm the royal person or power.[13] These overlapping but distinct concepts were stated but rarely deployed before 1300 despite numerous acts of armed opposition experienced by English kings in the preceding century.[14] This reluctance to equate resistance with treason changed fundamentally during the opening decades of the fourteenth century. The almost constant tensions and conflicts of Edward II's reign created an atmosphere in which charges of treason were deployed as political weapons. An imposing list of earls and barons in the English realm were executed as traitors between 1322 and 1330. The crimes for which they were executed included riding against the king with banners displayed in open war, seducing the king's subjects to turn against him, plundering the church, and even of using the royal power against the law of Magna Carta.[15]

The readiness to use treason to bring about the death of political opponents reflected the toxic personalities and politics of Edward II's reign. However, it has been argued that the key precedents for this shift in the crown's treatment of aristocratic resistance derived from the Welsh

---

Sovereignty and Corporation Theory 1300–1450', in J.H. Burns (ed.), *The Cambridge History of Medieval Political Thought* (Cambridge, 1988), pp. 454–76; J.G. Bellamy, *The Law of Treason in England in the Later Middle Ages* (Cambridge, 1970).

[12] M. Strickland, 'Treason, Feud and the Growth of State Violence: Edward I and the "War of the Earl of Carrick", 1306–7', in C. Given-Wilson, A. Kettle and L. Scales (eds), *War, Government and Aristocracy in the British Isles, c. 1150–1500* (Woodbridge, 2008), pp. 84–113, at pp. 88–9.

[13] Stephen D. White, 'Alternative Constructions of Treason in the Angevin Political World: Traïson in the History of William Marshal', *e-Spania* (online) 4 (2007), 3–4, DOI: https://doi.org/10.4000/e-spania.2233.

[14] Bellamy, *The Law of Treason*, pp. 1–14; J. Gillingham, 'Killing and Mutilating Political Enemies in the British Isles from the Late Twelfth to the Early Fourteenth Century: A Comparative Study', in B. Smith (ed), *Britain and Ireland, 900–1300: Insular Responses to Medieval European Change* (Cambridge, 1999), pp. 114–34, at pp. 131–32.

[15] Bellamy, *Law of Treason*, pp. 46–53, 64–66; D. Westerhof, 'Deconstructing Identities on the Scaffold: The Execution of Hugh Despenser the Younger, 1326', *Journal of Medieval History* 33 (2007), 87–106; J. Taylor, 'The Judgement of Hugh Despenser the Younger', *Medievalia et Humanistica* 12 (1958), 70–77; N. Fryde, *The Tyranny and Fall of Edward II, 1321–1326* (Cambridge, 1979), pp. 58–68; J. Gillingham, 'Enforcing Old Law in New Ways: Professional Lawyers and Treason in Early Fourteenth Century England and France', in P. Andersen, Mia Münster-Swendsen, and H. Voght (eds), *Law and Power in the Middle Ages: Proceedings of the Fourth Carlsberg Academy Conference on Medieval Legal History* (Copenhagen, 2008), pp. 187–206.

and Scottish wars of Edward I. John Gillingham and Matthew Strickland suggest that the king's treatment of opponents from these lands as not just rebels, but traitors for their resistance to his authority changed the rules of political behaviour. Strickland points specifically to the events of 1306 in Scotland as representing 'the fundamental watershed' in this process.[16] As Strickland has shown, in the first war, between 1296 and 1304, Edward did not bring charges of treason against his noble opponents, although he regarded them as rebelling against his legitimate authority and in breach of their sworn homage.[17] This was a pragmatic decision as much as one based on wider precepts. However, Edward's response to Robert Bruce's seizure of the Scottish throne in 1306 represented a major change. The public and degrading execution of members of 'Anglo-Norman chivalric society', like Edward's own cousin, John earl of Atholl, and Bruce's brothers did mark a significant shift in the treatment of the crown's enemies, one which, Strickland argues, provided a crucial precedent for the cycle of similar executions in England in the next two decades.[18]

However, the intended audience for Edward I's acts of judicial violence was not the English nobility but the Scots. The events of 1306 were designed to shock the nobility and community of Scotland and to indicate the utter illegality of adherence to Bruce's cause. From the outset, support for Robert was regarded by the English crown as different from recognition of John Balliol's kingship. Balliol had been accepted as king, and although Edward I regarded him as having forfeited his crown, his supporters could claim to be supporting a legally constituted ruler.[19] Having broken faith with Edward, usurped the royal title, and committed homicide on sacred ground when he murdered John Comyn, Robert's position was far worse. As we will see, Christians were obliged to withhold their support from an excommunicated criminal, and Edward regarded those who persisted in their rebellion as meriting the harshest penalties. This was clear from the ordinance issued by Edward from Lanercost Priory in late 1306 to be proclaimed at burghs and fairs across Scotland. The ordinance instructed that all those who counselled the death of Comyn or who 'received it with favour' be drawn

16 Strickland, 'Treason, Feud', p. 89; Gillingham, 'Killing', pp. 131–32. Gillingham has also identified the development of a professional judiciary in England (and France) as offering kings 'a new instrument of power'. Professional judges could provide rulers with the judicial arguments and mechanisms to condemn even their greatest subjects as traitors (Gillingham, 'Enforcing Old Laws', pp. 203–6).

17 For Edward's more lenient treatment of Scottish enemies in the war from 1296 to 1304 see M. Strickland, 'A Law of Arms or a Law of Treason? Conduct of War in Edward I's Campaigns in Scotland, 1296–1307', in R.W. Kaeuper (ed.), *Violence in Medieval Society* (Woodbridge, 2000), pp. 39–77.

18 Strickland, 'Treason, Feud,' pp. 89, 113.

19 M. Strickland, '"All Brought to Nought and Thy State Undone": Treason, Disinvestiture and the Disgracing of Arms under Edward II', in P. Coss and C. Tyerman (eds), *Soldiers, Nobles and Gentlemen: Essays in Honour of Maurice Keen* (Woodbridge, 2009), pp. 279–304; Strickland, 'Treason, Feud', pp. 110, 111.

and hanged. Those who were taken in war were to be hanged or beheaded. Notorious rebels and those who opposed the king before the defeat of Bruce at Methven were to be imprisoned at the king's will.[20] The executions of nobles, as well as the treatment of normally protected individuals, clergy and noblewomen, all reflect the application of this ordinance.[21] Though, even in 1306, such measures were not applied with consistent ferocity, the ordinance set the tone for the language of English royal records. This stressed the illegality of continued Scottish resistance. In particular, Robert Bruce continued to be identified as an 'enemy and traitor' who had 'treasonably' seized the throne.[22] By waging war against their rightful lord, his followers were 'enemies and rebels'.[23]

Though these descriptions continued to be used in the renewed warfare of the 1330s, when the 'continual and tortuous rebellion of many people of the kingdom' against both Edward III and Edward Balliol was criticised, there was a tendency to treat Scots captured in warfare as legitimate enemies to be held until ransomed.[24] As early as 1334, the two most effective Scottish leaders of the decade, Andrew Murray and William Douglas of Lothian, were (rather foolishly) released from captivity for ransom by Edward III.[25] In 1346 David II himself was dealt with as an honourable prisoner after his capture at Neville's Cross. However, two other captives from this battle were treated differently. John Graham earl of Menteith and Duncan earl of Fife were condemned as 'notorious traitors'. They were prosecuted for having broken oaths of homage to Edward III and Balliol.[26] Fife was spared execution but Menteith suffered a traitor's death, his quartered body being sent north for public display.[27]

The condemnation of the earls as traitors reminded the Scots that, since 1306, armed resistance to the English king in breach of a previous oath of fealty could be treated as not just rebellion but be punished as treason. This knowledge exerted a natural influence on the way in which the Scottish political class regarded the act of treason. Once again, 1306 marked a crucial year in this process. This was not just because of Edward I's punishment of his enemies. The survival of Robert Bruce and his successes in war created

20 F. Palgrave (ed.), *Documents and Records Illustrating the History of Scotland* (London, 1837), pp. 361–62.

21 For the details of Edward I's actions in 1306 see Strickland, 'Treason, Feud', pp. 92–104.

22 *Foedera*, ii, part 1, p. 114.

23 See for example *Foedera*, ii, part 1, pp. 116, 150–51, 246; *Rot. Scot.*, i, pp. 55, 61, 67, 86.

24 *Rot. Scot.*, i, p. 799.

25 *The Chronicle of Lanercost*, ed. H. Maxwell (Glasgow, 1913), pp. 274, 278, 286; *Fordun's Chronicle*, ed. Skene, i, p. 357; ii, p. 349; Nicholson, *Edward III*, pp. 166, 168–69.

26 *Foedera*, iii, part 1, p. 108.

27 *Rot. Scot.*, i, p. 689. In 1402 the Scottish knight, William Stewart of Jedforest, was condemned as a traitor after his capture at Homildon. According to Walter Bower the English justified their action by claiming that he had been born in Teviotdale under the English king's allegiance. Bower chose to present their motives as vindictiveness against a skilful enemy (*Scotichronicon by Walter Bower*, ed. Watt, viii, pp. 46–49).

another king who needed to represent resistance to him from within Scotland as illegitimate. During the years which followed 1306, a significant group of Scottish landowners refused to accept Bruce's position as king. The earlier rejection of the Bruce family's claim to the throne and Robert's killing of Comyn convinced many to see his actions as illegitimate. As these nobles had never sworn homage to him, it would be hard for Robert to treat them as traitors. Nevertheless, Robert did assert his right to treat opposition as illegal defiance of the rightful ruler of the realm. The earldom of Moray which Robert created for Thomas Randolph in 1312 included the lordships of Badenoch and Lochaber, indicating the disinheritance of John Comyn's son (who was in England).[28] Though the nature of this disinheritance is not mentioned in the charter, the enmity of the heir and his failure to perform homage would have provided justifications for it. More overtly, in 1310 Robert recorded the dispossession of a minor landowner, John Pollok, who would later serve in Edward II's garrisons in Dundee and Berwick. In a grant of Pollok's lands and goods to the monks of Arbroath, Bruce explained that,

> Because John de Pollok stands against our faith and fidelity and is adhering to our enemy and, as is well known, is plotting with his whole strength to the damage of our royal majesty (*lesione nostre regie magestatis*), for his deeds we take possession of all his goods, moveable and immoveable, wherever they can be found in our kingdom ... for our use.[29]

The use of the term lese majesty (*lesione ... magestatis*) must be treated as significant. It represented the deployment of a Roman legal phrase which English legal writers like Glanville and Bracton regarded as synonymous with treason.[30] The Scottish legal collection known as *Regiam Maiestatem*, which was produced during Robert's reign, followed these English texts in using lese majesty in this way to denote causing the death of the king or betrayal of the kingdom or army by a liegeman.[31] However, as understood by French jurists in the thirteenth century, lese majesty extended beyond the personal act of betrayal to encompass an action which caused harm to the sovereignty of the ruler and of his realm. The use of the charge against an individual who had probably never sworn homage to Robert may indicate the king's need to extend the legal boundaries of treason to provide him with the proper basis to act against his Scottish opponents.[32] If so, it would represent the shape of things to come in Robert's realm.

[28] *Regesta Regum Scotorum*, *v*, *The Acts of Robert I*, ed. A.A.M. Duncan (Edinburgh, 1988), no. 389.

[29] *Regesta Regum Scotorum*, *v*, ed. Duncan, no. 13.

[30] In a report by an English official written to Edward I in 1299, John Comyn was said to have accused Robert Bruce of plotting lese majesty against King John Balliol (*Facsimiles of the National Manuscripts of Scotland*, 3 vols [Southampton, 1867–71], ii, no. 8).

[31] *Regiam Majestatem and Quoniam Attachiamenta* (Edinburgh, 1947), p. 259.

[32] S.H. Cuttler, *The Law of Treason and Treason Trials in Later Medieval France* (Cambridge, 1981), pp. 8–15.

On one level, Robert's victory at Bannockburn should have resolved the issue. It allowed him to proceed against his remaining enemies within Scotland. In November 1314 the Scottish parliament held at Cambuskenneth Abbey duly issued a statute which sentenced 'all who died outside the faith and peace of the said lord king in the war or otherwise, or who had not come to his peace and faith on the said day' to be 'disinherited perpetually' and that they 'should be considered as the king and kingdom's enemies henceforth, perpetually deprived of any further claim of right'.[33] The statute was not explicitly about treason. Instead it stressed that homage was due to Robert and that those who, 'although they had been often summoned and lawfully expected', had failed to swear fealty were excluded from the realm.

The king would only be forced to produce an explicit statement about the crime of treason by the events of the years after Bannockburn. The context and language of this statement would indicate an effort to define treason as something beyond individual acts of disloyalty in war and politics. The first parliamentary statute which specified the extent of treason as an offence in Scotland was produced in response to the problems which faced Robert I during the late 1310s. In early December 1318 a parliament assembled at Scone in response to a summons which had probably been sent six weeks earlier. It was almost certainly prompted by news of the death of the king's brother, Edward Bruce, on 14 October.[34] Edward had been named as heir to Robert's throne in an assembly in April 1315 'as an energetic man abundantly experienced in deeds of war for the defence of the right and liberty of the realm of Scotland'.[35] Robert and his daughter, Marjory, had consented to this tailzie or entail which placed Edward above Marjory and her heirs in the line of succession. However, Edward's death in battle in Ireland, which had been preceded by Marjory's demise, left Robert without an adult heir.[36] In late 1318 a new statute was issued which specified that if the king had no legitimate son, 'the nearest and legitimate heir' was to be the king's infant grandson, Robert Stewart, the child of Marjory and Walter Steward of Scotland. The tailzie also specified the way in which the succession would be decided in the absence of a clear heir.[37]

Anxiety about the succession to the throne was heightened by the king's disputed status. As in the tailzie of 1315, the 1318 statute was preceded by an ordinance binding the community to obey King Robert. However, the language and scope of these ordinances differed greatly. In 1315 it was simply said that it was:

[33] *RPS*, 1314/1.

[34] *RPS*, 1318/1, 30; M. Penman, *Robert the Bruce King of the Scots* (New Haven, CT, 2014), p. 190–202.

[35] *RPS*, 1315/1.

[36] Michael Penman, '*Diffinicione successionis* as *regnum Scottorum*: Royal Succession in Scotland in the Later Middle Ages', in F. Lachaud and M. Penman (eds), *Making and Breaking the Rules: Succession in Medieval Europe* (Turnhout, 2008), pp. 43–60, at pp. 50–2.

[37] *RPS*, 1318/30.

> unanimously agreed and ordained in the form which follows. Namely that they, all and singular, both clerics and laymen, will obey and faithfully defend in all ways the magnificent prince and lord their liege lord Robert by the grace of God illustrious king of Scots ...[38]

However, three and half years later, while an ordinance was placed similarly in relation to the tailzie, its terms read very differently:

> Namely that in person all and singular people, both clerics and laymen, will obey the aforesaid lord king and his heirs as their king and liege lord in every way, each according to his estate and condition, and the same people should faithfully support the same as far as they are able for the protection and defence of the rights and the liberties of the aforesaid kingdom against all mortals, however powerful, who may be pre-eminent by reason of whatever power, authority or position. And that if anyone henceforth, which God forbid, shall be a violator of this ordinance, as a result he shall be considered as a traitor to the kingdom and guilty of the crime of lese majesty in perpetuity.[39]

Failure to support King Robert 'in every way' was unequivocally identified as treason and lese majesty. This change in content must partly reflect the increased sense of vulnerability felt by Robert in relation to the succession. However, by binding his subjects to obey Robert as king and to support the defence of 'the rights and liberties of the ... kingdom ... against all mortals, however powerful, who may be pre-eminent' due to their 'power, authority or position', the ordinance indicated a concern with specific individuals.

The mortals in question could have been Edward II of England or even Edward Balliol, son of the ousted King John. However, it is hardly likely that statutes issued under Bruce's auspices would ever suggest that these opponents 'may be pre-eminent'. Instead, the obvious candidate, as a mortal who could claim pre-eminence in Scotland on the basis of his authority and position, was a very different prince. In December 1318, Robert Bruce was the subject of papal censure. Eighteen months earlier Pope John XXII had written from Avignon to the rulers and prelates of England and Scotland announcing his intention of removing 'the horrible seed of dissension blown abroad by Satan's pestiferous breath'.[40] This would be achieved by the proclamation of a two-year truce which would aid the unity of Christendom and increase support for an expedition to recover the Holy Land.[41] In the Summer of 1317 two Cardinals arrived from the Papal Curia to proclaim the truce in both English and Scottish kingdoms. For Robert, the Pope's

38 *RPS*, 1315/1.

39 *RPS*, 1318/30.

40 R. Hill, 'Belief and Practice as Illustrated by John XXII's Excommunication of Robert Bruce', *Studies in Church History* 8 (1972), 135–38, at 136.

41 *Historical Papers and Letters from the Northern Registers*, ed. J.M. Raine (Rolls Series, 1873), no. 163.

action was unwelcome and appeared to represent a partisan intervention. Edward II had taken the cross in 1313 and reaffirmed his promise to join the crusade in June 1317. By contrast, Robert, who had already suffered excommunication for the killing of his rival, John Comyn, in a church, was of no such value in Pope John's plans.[42] The *Vita Edwardi Secundi* reported that in Spring 1317 the English king had sent envoys to the Curia asking for John XXII to excommunicate Bruce and place Scotland under an interdict until Robert abandoned his claims to be king. Though John rejected this request, its coincidence with his call for a truce may not have escaped the attention of Robert's adherents.[43] The proclamation of a truce would also hamper Robert's sustained efforts to capture Berwick, the last English-held burgh in Scotland, which reached their climax in the winter of 1317–18.[44] Against this background, Robert refused to receive the Pope's letters, either from the Cardinals in September or from the Franciscan friar from Berwick who was sent to proclaim the truce in December. Instead Robert's forces persisted with attacks on Berwick, which was captured in April 1318. A foray into northern England was launched the following month (probably to supply the continuing siege of Berwick Castle).[45]

For refusing to heed papal instructions like 'a deaf adder', John placed Robert under sentence of excommunication in June 1318.[46] The letters were sent to the Cardinals in England and proclaimed in St Paul's Cathedral in London in September.[47] According to a near-contemporary chronicle the sentence was also pronounced in the cathedrals of France.[48] Whilst he would remain excommunicated until the last year of his life, ruling his realm in the interim, the implications of the sentence for Robert should not be underestimated. In the initial letters proclaiming the truce, John had stressed to both Edward and Robert that if they suffered excommunication for continuing the war:

> we absolve the vassals and subjects of the king and of him who is bearing (the royal title) from their oaths of fealty, by which they would otherwise be held strictly to them or of them, during war and dissensions of this type, while they ought not to obey them in illicit actions for this time.[49]

42 S. Menache, *Clement V* (Cambridge, 1998), pp. 269–75; S. Menache, 'The Failure of John XXII's Policy toward France and England: Reasons and Outcomes, 1316–1334', *Church History* 55 (1986), 423–37; S. Phillips, *Edward II* (New Haven, CT, 2010), p. 210.

43 *Vita Edwardi Secundi*, ed. Childs, p. 135.

44 *Foedera*, ii, part 1, p. 351; *Regesta Regum Scotorum*, *v*, ed. Duncan, pp. 140–45.

45 *Chronicle of Lanercost*, ed. Maxwell, pp. 219–21; Colm McNamee, *The Wars of the Bruces: Scotland, England and Ireland 1306–1328* (East Linton, 1997), pp. 178–85.

46 *Foedera*, ii, part 1, p. 364.

47 *Annales Paulini* in *Chronicles of the Reigns of Edward I and Edward II*, ed. W. Stubbs (London, 1882), i, pp. 283–84.

48 *Chronique Parisienne anonyme du XIVe siècle*, ed. A. Hellot (Nogent-le-Rotrou, 1884), p. 34.

49 *Northern Registers*, ed. Raine, no. 163.

In addition, as this extract shows, Pope John was reluctant to accord Robert the royal title in his instructions and correspondence, referring to him as 'bearing himself as king of Scotland' or elsewhere as 'governor'.[50] In 1317 Robert and his close adherents had cited this incorrect form of address as a reason for refusing to receive the Pope's letters.[51] This may have been in part a pretext to allow Robert to continue the war without formally ignoring the papal orders, but the denial of his royal rank also constituted a real and worrying challenge. Pope John responded to the complaints on this score by citing the practice of his predecessors of not recognising titles which were in dispute.[52] He argued that he had made no reference to Edward II as king of Scotland either (though since the English kings had never employed the royal title of Scotland this was probably not a winning argument). Nevertheless, responding to the hostility of Robert and his subjects in this matter, in November 1317 Pope John wrote to Bruce according him the royal title, warning him that this was to help the ending of the bloodshed and took nothing away from Edward II's rights.[53] If his words provided a temporary resolution of the issue, Robert's excommunication reopened it. In the papal bull which carried the sentence, John addressed his words to 'Robert de Brus, detaining the realm of Scotland'.[54] Though this form was moderated to refer to Robert as 'ruling' or 'governing' Scotland or 'bearing himself as king', from summer 1318 onwards, Pope John withheld any acknowledgement of Robert's royal status.[55]

As a result, in December 1318 the Pope's letters no longer acknowledged Bruce's right to the title of King of Scotland. Moreover, by excommunicating him, John XXII was inviting, even expecting, that Robert's subjects would withhold their support for his warlike behaviour. Robert had only secured the homage of a number of his barons as a result of his successes in warfare during the previous five years. He could hardly have been sanguine about the effects of the Pope's absolution of these vassals from their oaths of allegiance. In a different way, Bruce would have been concerned about the pressure which the Pope's actions placed upon the Scottish clergy who John was demanding should enforce his sentences on the king and his realm. In such circumstances, to interpret the injunction in the parliamentary ordinance issued in December 1318 as referring directly to papal sentences would correspond to the timing and implications of John's recent actions. Robert and his councillors went beyond mere exhortations to obedience and loyalty to the king. The ordinance made clear that acting against Robert,

[50] *Foedera*, ii, part 1, p. 407.

[51] *Foedera*, ii, part 1, p. 340.

[52] S. Layfield, 'The Pope, the Scots, and their "Self-Styled" King: John XXII's Anglo-Scottish Policy, 1316–1334', in A. King and M. Penman (eds), *England and Scotland in the Fourteenth Century: New Perspectives* (Woodbridge, 2007), pp. 157–71, at pp. 162–63.

[53] *Calendar of Entries in the Papal Registers Relating to Great Britain and Ireland. Papal Letters*, ed. W.H. Bliss (London, 1895), ii, p. 419.

[54] *Foedera*, ii, part 1, p. 364.

[55] *Vetera Monumenta Hibernorum et Scotorum Historiam Illustrantia*, ed. A. Theiner (Rome, 1864), nos. 426, 427.

even if in line with the Pope's sanctions, would be condemned as treason. Pope John's right to intervene as the spiritual and moral, as well as ecclesiastical, head of Latin Christendom was effectively being denied.

The actions of both John and Robert were informed by clashes between royal and papal power during the previous two decades. Robert's position, as a king under papal displeasure and sanctions, was far from unique. In writing to the two Cardinals in England in November 1317 John even cited a parallel case as an example of what might be achieved to bring peace between warring parties.[56] He informed them of the recent settlement between the rival claimants to the Kingdom of Sicily. This conflict between the houses of Aragon and Anjou had been running since the 1280s and represented a much more direct challenge to the papacy's hopes for a crusade and territorial position than the Scottish wars. In this conflict the papacy had favoured the Angevins, who held the mainland part of the kingdom centred on Naples, while Frederick of Aragon suffered spells of excommunication with his lands in Sicily itself under an interdict.[57] In 1317 John had brought the two sides to an agreement. However, the peace rapidly collapsed and in 1321 Frederick was again excommunicated and the interdict on Sicily re-imposed.[58]

Though Robert was presumably aware of these events, more immediate influences on his reaction to papal hostility were provided by the clashes between Pope Boniface VIII and the kings of England and France during the 1290s. Robert himself, but more significantly many of his clerical supporters, had witnessed the diplomatic exchanges of this era at first hand. At that time the Scots had been actively and successfully seeking the advocacy of the Pope in their conflict with Edward I. In 1299 Boniface had issued a bull, entitled *Scimus Fili*, which ordered Edward to put his claims to Scotland to the judgement of the Holy See.[59] The English response, written in the name of the English barons, asserted that:

> the kings and kingdom of the Scots have never been under … anyone other than the kings of England; neither have the kings of England answered or had a duty to answer over their rights in the said kingdom or their other temporalities before any ecclesiastical or secular judge, such is the pre-eminence of the status of their royal rank and the custom inviolably observed at all times.[60]

[56] *Calendar of Entries in the Papal Registers*, ed. Bliss, ii, p. 419; S. Layfield, 'The Papacy and the Nations of Christendom: A Study with Particular Focus on the Pontificate of John XXII (1316–1334)' (unpublished PhD thesis, University of Durham, 2008), pp. 203–4.

[57] Pope John's compromise settlement in Sicily bears comparison with the plan brokered by his successor Benedict XII in 1335–36 to resolve the conflict in Scotland (Clifford Rogers, *War, Cruel and Sharp: English Strategy under Edward III* [Woodbridge, 2000], pp. 110–11; Michael Penman, *David II* [East Linton, 2004], p. 63).

[58] For the background to this conflict and the attempts to resolve it see D. Abulafia, *The Western Mediterranean Kingdoms 1200–1500* (Harlow, 1997), pp. 107–54; C.R. Backman, *The Decline and Fall of Medieval Sicily* (Cambridge, 1995).

[59] E.L.G. Stones, *Anglo-Scottish Relations* (Oxford, 1965), no. 28.

[60] *Foedera*, i, part 2, pp. 926–27.

While in the 1290s the Scots were arguing against this premise of English royal pre-eminence over temporal issues which included the subjection of their kingdom, this text, which was known in Scotland, may have informed Robert's response to papal pressure in 1318.[61]

The parallel and contemporary conflict between Boniface and Philip IV of France was more prolonged and bitter. It also went much further in producing statements concerning rival papal and royal authority within a kingdom. In the final phase of the dispute after 1302, Boniface asserted his primacy over the king's actions not just with regard to the French church but in all spheres of his rule. This assertion rested on the pope's duty to rebuke sins committed by any Christian, and in the bull *Unam Sanctam* it was stated that 'it is absolutely necessary for every human being to be subject to the Roman pontiff to attain salvation'.[62] Philip's refusal to abide by papal demands led to his excommunication and to the French bishops being summoned to Rome to answer for their obedience to their earthly lord. The French king and his councillors argued that such demands were the work of a pope who sought to subject the king and the kingdom to himself in temporal affairs. They resorted to the principle, expressed through the thirteenth century, 'that the king of France is a *princeps* in his own kingdom, since he does not recognize a superior in temporal matters'.[63] Texts produced in France during the dispute stressed the lack of any legal basis for papal efforts to interfere with the authority of King Philip in his realm.[64] They also championed the king's sovereign rights over the clergy in the kingdom. One text stated, 'the king, in right of his royal power, is supreme over the laws, customs and liberties granted to you clergy and ... he may add to them or take away from them or amend them'.[65]

Robert's position in 1318 was much weaker than those of Edward I and Philip IV. His ability to proclaim his sovereignty against papal interference

[61] This letter and another accompanying it from King Edward were copied down in Scotland and included alongside chronicle material about the events of this period. See *Scotichronicon by Walter Bower*, ed. Watt, vi, pp. 110–11. For its influence in Scotland see G. Simpson, 'The Declaration of Arbroath Revitalised', in *SHR* 56 (1977), 11–33, at p. 23. See also Scott Dempsey, 'The Evolution of Edward I's "Historical" Claim to Overlordship of Scotland, 1291–1301', in Chris Given-Wilson and David Green (eds), *Fourteenth Century England* XI (Woodbridge, 2019), pp. 1–33.

[62] J.A. Watt, 'Spiritual and Temporal Powers', in J.H. Burns (ed.), *The Cambridge History of Medieval Political Thought* (Cambridge, 1988), pp. 367–423; J. Strayer, *The Reign of Philip the Fair* (Princeton, 1980), pp. 271–74; Ullman, 'The Development of the Medieval Idea of Sovereignty'; Joseph Canning, *Ideas of Power in the Late Middle Ages, 1296–1417* (Cambridge, 2011), pp. 11–59.

[63] Strayer, *Philip the Fair*, pp. 269–74; Cuttler, *Law of Treason*, pp. 10–13. The quotation is from Guilelmus Durandus, *Speculum Juris* (Frankfurt, 1592), quoted at p. 12.

[64] John of Paris, *On Royal and Papal Power*, ed. A.P. Monaghan (New York, 1974); N.N. Erickson, 'A Dispute between a Priest and a Knight', *Proceedings of the American Philosophical Society* 111 (1967), 288–309; *Three Royalist Tracts 1296–1302*, ed. R.W. Dyson (London, 1999).

[65] Erickson, 'Dispute', p. 300.

cannot have been helped by the readiness of the Scottish leadership in 1299 to recognise 'the Roman church … both in temporal and spiritual matters as their lord'.[66] This precedent, designed to secure Pope Boniface's support, was not raised by John XXII as it would have antagonised the English, but it was still an awkward statement. More damagingly, Robert's own right to wield royal authority remained contested, and the actions taken by John against him were much more justifiable than Boniface's attacks on Philip IV. John was certainly not claiming the right of the papacy to exercise authority over a king in his realm. Instead his position was closer to that enunciated by the moderate royalist, John of Paris, in his work, *On Royal and Papal Power*. This stated that with a prince who proved 'incorrigible and contemptuous of ecclesiastical censure, the pope can do something among the people to have the man deprived of secular honour and deposed by the people'. Furthermore, if a king 'sins in temporal matters' his barons should correct him, but, if they could not or dared not, they might call on ecclesiastical aid to admonish or depose the ruler'.[67]

Charged for his refusal to answer papal censure and of thwarting efforts to heal the temporal schisms within Christendom, by these definitions Robert may well have had reason to fear the reach of John's condemnation. The Scottish king's defence against attempts to undermine his legitimacy and authority in his realm was, like Philip IV, to demonstrate the effectiveness of his sovereignty over the Scottish kingdom and its clergy. In part this was achieved by proclaiming the support he enjoyed from the people of Scotland. When he met the papal envoys in 1317, Robert stressed that he had 'obtained possession of the kingdom and the title of king in the whole kingdom'.[68] Seven years earlier, letters had been sent to the council of the church meeting at Vienne in the name of 'the Bishops, Abbots, Priors and the rest of the clergy in the kingdom of Scotland' declaring their recognition of Bruce's rights as king and recording their fealty to him.[69] The consecration of St Andrews Cathedral in July 1318 was timed to make a similar point. The reported presence at the ceremony of eight bishops, 15 abbots and many nobles was a display of the support Robert enjoyed from the Scottish clergy and laity as well as showing the king's concern for the health of the church.[70] As would be potently reiterated in the letter written in the name of the Scottish barons and community to Pope John in May 1320 and known as the Declaration of Arbroath, Robert could claim the adherence of his people 'both upon the account of his right and his own merit, as being the person who has restored the people's safety in defence of their liberties'.[71]

66 *Scotichronicon by Walter Bower*, ed. Watt, vi, pp. 102–3, 172–73.

67 John of Paris, *On Royal and Papal Power*, p. 66; Canning, *Ideas of Power*, pp. 49–59.

68 *Foedera*, ii, part 1, p. 340.

69 A.A.M. Duncan, 'The Declarations of the Clergy 1309–10', in G. Barrow (ed.), *The Declaration of Arbroath* (Edinburgh, 2003), pp. 32–49, at p. 44.

70 *Scotichronicon by Walter Bower*, ed. Watt, vi, pp. 412–15.

71 Barrow (ed.) *Declaration of Arbroath*, pp. xiii–xiv.

The ordinance attached to the tailzie of December 1318 represented the other side of King Robert's sovereignty. The 'great oath' demanded from all the people binding them to obey the king and support him in defence of the rights and liberties of the kingdom greatly extended the understanding of what constituted treason. In these terms the crime went far beyond a personal act of betrayal against the king. It could include a range of more limited actions, such as the refusal to serve the king in war, contribute financially to his efforts or withhold counsel from him. More pointedly, it meant any acceptance of the pope's censure could be regarded as treasonous. As in the disputes between Pope Boniface and the French and English kings, the most direct implications of this fell upon the Scottish clergy. They were forced to choose between enforcing the sentence of their spiritual father and ecclesiastical superior, and recognising the authority of their secular lord. A year later, in December 1319, four of the Scottish bishops were summoned to the Curia to answer for Robert's contempt for papal censure, and in July 1320 they were excommunicated for their failure to appear. Nevertheless the bishops continued firmly in their king's allegiance, apparently ignoring the interdict placed upon their church.[72]

However, a broader sense of lese majesty as denoting actions which harmed the state was explicit within the language of the oath. Its acceptance allowed the king to act against any whose loyalty he had reason to suspect. Even before 1318 Robert showed signs of being ready to act in this way. In March 1316 Robert made a grant to Robert Lauder of an estate which had been forfeited by Peter or Piers Lubaud. Lubaud was a Gascon knight who as keeper of Edinburgh Castle for Edward II had helped betray the stronghold to Thomas Randolph in early 1314. The charter stated that Lubaud had recently been convicted in the king's court of 'treason against us and our realm'.[73] One well-informed English account stated that Robert 'suspected him of treason because he was too open' and had been 'always English at heart and was waiting for the best chance to betray him'.[74] This suggests that, rather than waiting for Lubaud to commit treason, Robert had him condemned before he could do so. As an outsider, Lubaud could be executed as a warning to those Scottish lords who had also only recently accepted Bruce as their king.

The way in which Robert was prepared to bring charges of treason was shown most clearly at the so-called Black Parliament of August 1320. The arrest and trial of a group of Scottish nobles headed by William Soules of Liddesdale was an unprecedented act. No formal records of the charges or judgement survive, and any sense of these derives from fourteenth-century narratives. Both English and Scottish chronicles concur that Robert arrested

[72] *Calendar of Entries in the Papal Registers*, ed. Bliss, ii, pp. 191, 192, 199. Pope John never sought to depose the Scottish bishops for their actions (Layfield, 'The Papacy and the Nations of Christendom', pp. 211–12).

[73] *Regesta Regum Scotorum*, *v*, ed. Duncan, no. 84.

[74] Sir Thomas Gray, *Scalacronica*, ed. A. King, Surtees Society, 209 (Woodbridge, 2005), p. 73.

Soules and several other lords for conspiring against him.[75] The nature of this conspiracy was not explained, but as the earliest Scottish account affirms, they were charged with the crime of lese majesty. The broad definition of this provided in 1318 may have allowed Robert to act without clear evidence of the nature or scale of the crimes committed or intended. That Soules was spared execution and several of the others 'were not found guilty in any way' may suggest that, as with Lubaud, the king had acted on suspicion rather than in reaction to strong evidence. The acquittals may also suggest some reluctance on the part of the wider nobility to condemn those accused at the king's word. Those executed were three relatively minor figures and an experienced baron, David lord of Brechin.[76] According to the later account of John Barbour's poem *The Brus*, which unlike earlier narratives stated that Soules planned to replace Robert as king, Brechin was condemned because he knew of the conspiracy but, despite his oath of fealty to Robert, did not reveal this to his king. In the English legal text by Bracton (which was well-known in Scotland), failure to divulge such knowledge to the king within two days was regarded as treasonable.[77]

As Michael Penman has demonstrated, charges against Brechin, Soules and others reflected Robert's suspicions about the group of nobles who had supported Edward II until the period between 1312 and 1314 and who had connections to his enemies, the Comyn and Balliol families.[78] However, Robert's suspicions concerning these lords were also motivated by the predicament created by papal censure of himself and his realm. As we have seen, these were not distinct problems for Robert. To illustrate this, the English *Anonimalle Chronicle* stated that in 1319 the English assembled an army 'to destroy Robert Bruce at the pope's order for the devastation by which he had infringed the truce which the aforesaid pope had established …'.[79] More directly, in November 1320, Edward II wrote to his Scottish supporter, David earl of Atholl, permitting him to receive those Scottish lords who 'desire to come to his peace because their conscience is hurt by the sentence of excommunication in which they are involved by papal authority'.[80] These lords may well have been fleeing due to fear of King Robert's hostility after the Black Parliament, but concern over their spiritual wellbeing should not be written off as a mere pretext. To paraphrase John of Paris, Bruce's contempt for the sentence passed upon him by the church may have

[75] Ibid., p. 79; *Fordun's Chronicle*, ed. Skene, ii, p. 341; *Illustrations of Scottish History: From the Twelfth to the Sixteenth Century / Selected from Unpublished Manuscripts in the British Museum, and the Tower of London*, ed. J. Stevenson (Glasgow, 1834), pp. 9–10.

[76] Another baron, Roger Mowbray, died before his trial (*Fordun's Chronicle*, ed. Skene, ii, p. 341).

[77] Bracton, ed. Woodbine, ii, p. 335.

[78] M. Penman, 'A Fell Coniuration agayn Robert the Doughty King: The Soules Conspiracy of 1318–20', *IR* 50 (1999), 25–57.

[79] *The Anonimalle Chronicle 1307 to 1334*, ed. W. Childs and J. Taylor (Cambridge, 1991), p. 95.

[80] *Calendar of Close Rolls: Edward II, 1318–23* (London 1895), p. 280.

encouraged some of his subjects to seek the pope's help to have him 'deprived of secular honour'.[81] Archie Duncan suggested that Bruce's suspicions of a conspiracy were prompted by information received from the envoys who had carried diplomatic messages from the Scottish king and community to the Papal Curia in the summer of 1320.[82] If true, this could suggest that Robert's concern over the challenge to his legitimate authority presented by papal condemnation had been heightened by information gleaned at Avignon. From this perspective the charges of treason brought against Soules, Brechin and others were directly linked back to the ordinance of 1318 and the dispute with Pope John. The proceedings of the Black Parliament concerned not just a conflict over possession of the crown. They were also a statement of the primacy of the Scottish king's sovereign authority against all external claims on the faith of his subjects.

The need to define and express the legal status of Robert as King of Scots between 1314 and 1320 was not confined to the treason ordinance. Alice Taylor has recently argued that *Regiam Maiestatem* and the text known as 'The Assizes and Statutes of David King of Scotland' were compiled during the same period. Both texts were produced to provide Robert with 'well-needed bolsters for his kingship'.[83] As its title indicates, *Regiam Maiestatem* stressed the 'singular legal authority residing in the king alone' and presented the King of Scots 'as one without any superior'. Taylor also shows that the authors of *Regiam Maiestatem* deliberately downplayed concepts of counsel and consent which appeared in the English texts upon which it was based.[84] In these terms *Regiam Maiestatem* stated Robert's legal authority and autonomy as king in the face of the challenges to both represented by papal sanctions. Taylor and Duncan both identified the composition of *Regiam* with the December 1318 parliament.[85] Far from representing another expression of the comfortable partnership between king and community therefore, the assembly provided the setting for a statement of royal majesty which would have direct implications for any who witheld their support for Robert in the events of the Black Parliament.[86]

Eighteen months after the Black Parliament, Edward II executed a group of English nobles headed by his cousin, Thomas earl of Lancaster. This event, without parallel in England for 250 years, appalled English chroniclers, who saw it as a mark of the king's 'excessive cruelty' or a 'calamity' for the land

[81] John of Paris, *On Royal and Papal Power*, p. 66.

[82] A.A.M. Duncan, 'The War of the Scots, 1306–1323', *Transactions of the Royal Historical Society* 6th series, ii (1992), 125–51, at pp. 129–31.

[83] Taylor, 'The Assizes of David I', pp. 233–35; Taylor, 'What Does *Regiam maiestatem* Actually Say?', p. 77.

[84] Taylor, 'What Does *Regiam maiestatem* Actually Say?', p. 82.

[85] Ibid., p. 77; A.A.M. Duncan, 'Regiam Majestatem: A Reconsideration', *Juridical Review* (New Series) 6 (1961), 199–217.

[86] Taylor is right to question whether undue weight has been placed on the idea of *communitas* as the defining characteristic of Robert I's approach to rule. Taylor, 'What Does *Regiam maiestatem* Actually Say?', p. 82.

born from Lancaster's disloyalty.[87] Yet it was hard to dispute the justice of the king's court. Lancaster and his allies had been captured in open war against their lord and in alliance with his Scottish enemies after a decade of opposition and violence against Edward's friends. By comparison there is less evidence for the justice of King Robert's actions in 1320 which primarily reflected his continuing sense of insecurity. However, the real difference between these English and Scottish events lay in their aftermath. In England, the traitor's death suffered by Lancaster and eight other barons marked the start of a decade of such judicial killings. Moreover, despite the more limited definition of the crime placed on statute in 1352, charges of treason would re-emerge as a political weapon used frequently in the political disturbances of the reigns of Richard II and Henry IV between the 1380s and 1410s.[88] By contrast, in Scotland the Black Parliament was to remain an exceptional occasion. It was over a century, until 1425, before a Scottish king brought charges of treason against such an important group of nobles.[89] The intervening century was hardly free from breaches of sworn allegiance and acts of political defiance. The renewed conflict of the 1330s created fresh issues of conflicting and changing loyalties between the Bruce dynasty and its opponents, which now included both Edward Balliol and the English king together. The execution of the earls of Fife and Menteith as traitors in 1347 demonstrated how treason charges could be brought against those Scots who broke their allegiance to the two King Edwards.

However, there were no parallel examples from the Bruce side. The one parliamentary trial for treason in Scotland during David II's reign instead points to different attitudes at work. In June 1344 Malise earl of Strathearn was accused before parliament of committing 'felony and treason'. The treason charge was related specifically to the accusation that Malise had resigned his earldom to Edward Balliol as part of a contract with 'the lord king's mortal enemy', the English noble, John earl Warenne. The case was tried before an assize of 19 nobles which decided that he 'was found faithful in respect of the felony and treason'. It was, though, judged that he had resigned the earldom to Edward Balliol, and thus David II took Strathearn into his hands as king.[90] The politics of these events probably did much to shape

[87] *Chronicle of Lanercost*, ed. Maxwell, p. 235; *Vita Edwardi Secundi*, ed. Childs, pp. 212–13.

[88] The extension of the definition of treason was evident in Richard II's Questions to the Judges in 1387 and the response of his opponents after the brief civil war which followed (A.K. McHardy, *The Reign of Richard II: From Minority to Tyranny 1377–1397* [Manchester, 2012], nos. 91, 107). For the 1352 statute see Bellamy, *Law of Treason*, pp. 59–101.

[89] M. Brown, 'Public Authority and Factional Conflict', in Keith M. Brown and Roland Tanner (eds), *Parliament and Politics in Scotland, 1235–1560* (Edinburgh, 2004), pp. 123–44.

[90] J. Maitland Thomson, 'A Roll of the Scottish Parliament, 1344', *SHR* 9 (1912), 235–40; *RPS*, 1344/2–4.

the character of the trial.[91] The king was clearly seeking a legal basis for his annexation of Strathearn. Even allowing for this, the trial provides unique evidence about perceptions of treason in fourteenth-century Scotland. It indicates that David II regarded dealings with his mortal enemies as potential grounds for a charge of treason. However, the outcome suggests that, although the members of the assize accepted that Malise had performed homage to Balliol and resigned his earldom to be assigned to an English noble, they were not prepared to judge these actions as treasonous. Their reasons for this may be related to the jurors' own experiences. On the assize were the earls of Fife and Menteith, who would find themselves convicted in England for breaching oaths of loyalty to Edward III and Balliol, and at least four others who had probably sworn fealty to Balliol at some point.[92] For them and for other major nobles at the parliament like Robert Stewart and Patrick earl of March there was a personal interest in preventing a close alignment between the past performance of homage to rival royal claimants and the charge of treason. What the treatment of Strathearn suggests is not a change in the concept of treason from the reign of Robert I but its application. As the Black Parliament had shown to a degree, there was a reluctance to condemn as traitors those who had not openly sought the king's destruction.[93] Such reticence about treason charges would seem to represent a prevailing view within the Scottish polity which would endure for the rest of the fourteenth century.[94] The need to conserve and rebuild the unity of the kingdom after the renewed divisions of the 1330s outweighed concerns over the political records of some of its members as long as they were willing to affirm their loyalty to the king and crown.

The definition of treason in the 1318 ordinance and its use as a charge in 1320 were exceptional events in the context of fourteenth-century Scotland. They can be regarded as a response to exceptional circumstances. In part

[91] M. Penman, *David II* (East Linton, 2004), pp. 106–8.

[92] David Wemyss and Michael Scott had done homage to Edward Balliol with the earl of Fife in 1332. John Maxwell's family had served Edward III in the south-west. Alexander Craigie had served in the Edinburgh Castle garrison in 1335 (*Calendar of Documents Relating to Scotland*, ed. J. Bain, 4 vols [Edinburgh, 1881–88], iii, nos. 1143, 1184, 1186; *Chronicle of Lanercost*, ed. Maxwell, p. 272).

[93] Thus, during the early 1340s, numerous royal charters record the forfeiture of landholders as King David's enemies and rebels but these were individuals who had suffered exile or death in opposition to him (see for example *Regesta Regum Scotorum, vi, The Acts of David II*, ed. B. Webster [Edinburgh, 1982], nos. 14, 31, 36, 43, 52, 54, 80).

[94] For example, no charges of treason were brought against the earls who rebelled against David II in 1363 (although Robert Stewart was threatened with dishonour and disinheritance should he break the terms of his submission). Although George Dunbar earl of March was condemned, presumably for treason, in 1400 after he had defected to England, contemporary chronicles were sympathetic to his plight. In 1409 the earl was able to secure the restoration of his lands when he returned to Scottish allegiance, suggesting a very different landscape to contemporary English politics (*Scotichronicon by Walter Bower*, ed. Watt, vii, pp. 330–33; viii, pp. 31–33, 73–75; *Chron. Wyntoun*, ed. F.J. Amours [Edinburgh, 1908], vi, pp. 393–94).

these involved Robert's problems in securing recognition of his authority as king from his subjects. However, the statute of Cambuskenneth in 1314 provided a clear legal basis for proceeding against continued failure to swear homage to him as king. The real reason for a definition of treason which included any lack of support for the king, even if justified by claims to pre-eminence by another authority, was the pressure placed on Robert, and on his clerical and lay subjects, by papal censure. From summer 1318, Pope John was no longer neutral in his treatment of the Scottish kingdom and Robert Bruce. The latter reacted by asserting his full sovereignty over his realm. As Philip IV and Edward I had done in the previous decade, Robert did this by forbidding his subjects from obeying the terms of the pope's sentences of excommunication and interdict and making such an action an infringement of his royal majesty.

However, the reaction of Robert and his councillors to the situation raises wider questions about the character of his kingship more broadly. The treason ordinance was part of an approach to the royal office which stressed the fullest extent of the king's authority over his subjects and his freedom from external superiors. This approach suggests that Robert expected a very different relationship with his kingdom from the one which has been accepted previously. Rather than a king who regarded his role as ruling in partnership with the community of the realm and holding office as the defender of collective liberties, Robert's understanding of his office was as the divinely ordained sovereign whose defence of the 'liberties of the kingdom' was his right as well as his duty. Just as papal pressure produced an articulate assertion of Scotland's right to exist as a sovereign realm with Robert as its king in the Declaration of Arbroath, so it produced the treason ordinance of 1318. As a demand for support and service which presented a choice between death as a traitor or as an unshriven excommunicant, this was the declaration's sinister twin.

# 4

## *James and John: James I (1406–37), Monastic Reform, Kingship, and the Cult of John the Baptist*

Stephen Boardman

ONE of the defining features of the work of Roger Mason is a concern with the way in which political ideologies informed the political expectations and actions of the secular and ecclesiastical elites of late medieval and early modern Scotland. Mason's approach has never been an exercise in abstract intellectual history, but rather an attempt to understand how the views, arguments and writings of medieval thinkers, scholars and moralists might have shaped the way individuals and groups conceived of their role, duties, and obligations within the social and political structures of the realm. A persistent theme in Mason's work has been the relationship between kingship and royal government on the one hand, and the rights and beliefs of those subject to the authority of the crown on the other. The starting point for a series of thought-provoking and elegant 'Masonic' studies is the presumption that medieval kings and their administrators did indeed *have* ideas about the nature and reach of monarchical powers and rights and looked to find persuasive ways to articulate and promote these concepts in the public sphere to their own subjects. In this regard Mason has embraced 'Renaissance Kingship' as a useful umbrella term, denoting a royal lineage and establishment that consciously sought to enhance its status and the fullness of its authority through a variety of means. Renaissance monarchy was distinguished by a sustained emphasis on the supremacy of the king's legal authority within and throughout the realm. The (theoretically) unassailable nature of the monarch's power was promoted through the patronage of architectural, literary, and artistic works that stressed the elevated nature of royal 'majesty' and encouraged automatic deference to the king. The Renaissance court manipulated chivalric and religious sentiment and symbols to focus loyalty on the crown and used ceremony and ritual to stress formal hierarchy and the king's place as the font of social distinction and honour. Chronologically, the advent of Renaissance kingship in Scotland is usually placed, by Mason and others, in the reign of James III (1460–88).[1] However, another reign that has been proposed as marking a significant change in the articulation and assertion of royal rights and ambition within Scotland is that of James I (1406–37). It has been argued that the 18 years James spent as a prisoner of the English kings Henry IV (1399–1413) and Henry V (1413–22) between 1406 and 1424 meant that he necessarily absorbed ideas about the operation and projection of royal power from his captors. A.A. MacDonald, for example, suggested that:

> Few Scottish kings before James had been so exposed to such strong foreign cultural influences: the effective personal reign of James I (1424–37) may therefore be said to inaugurate a new kind of princely culture in Scotland.[2]

The present study seeks to explore some of the ways in which this 'new … princely culture' manifested itself in James I's reign, concentrating on the king's deployment of religious imagery and associations to bolster his rule and to assert his right and capacity to regulate the spiritual, ecclesiastical, political, and legal life of the realm.[3] The bulk of what follows looks at the evidence for James' interest in the figure and cult of John the Baptist. The cult of the Baptist in late medieval Europe was complex and multi-faceted. As with all popular devotions, John's widespread appeal lay in a general belief that he was a powerful and effective personal intercessor. John's reputation in this regard rested partly on literal Biblical exegesis that suggested he was a member of the extended Holy Family, a kinsman of Christ and the Virgin Mary, through the identification of John's mother Elizabeth as Mary's cousin. Aspects of John's Biblical story also, however, made the saint especially resonant for certain groups of devotees who saw him as an exemplar for their own role in society. John was frequently positioned as a divinely ordained forerunner of Christ – a model for, and an active agent of, the reform of religious and lay society. John's role as an interpreter and upholder of holy law, sent ahead to prepare the world for the coming of the Messiah and to facilitate the salvation of mankind, made him an ideal archetype for late medieval churchmen. His severe asceticism and eremitical life also ensured that he was particularly appealing to the most austere and reform minded medieval monastic orders.[4] It was, however, not only clerics who responded

[1] See, most recently, Roger Mason, 'Renaissance Monarchy? Stewart Kingship (1469–1542)', in Brown and Tanner (eds), *Scottish Kingship*, pp. 255–78.

[2] Alasdair A. MacDonald, 'Princely Culture in Scotland under James III and James IV', in M. Gosman, A. MacDonald and A. Vanderjagt (eds), *Princes and Princely Culture 1450–1650 Volume 1* (Leiden, 2003), pp. 147–72, at p. 147.

[3] Evaluation of the practical effectiveness of James I's various campaigns in securing the support of his subjects for his kingship has deliberately been left to one side, not least because it has already been expertly discussed. See M. Brown, *James I* (Edinburgh, 1994).

[4] Lynn Staley Johnson, 'St John the Baptist and Medieval English Ideology', *The American Benedictine Review* (1976), 105–25; Milton T. Walsh (ed. and trans.), *Ludolph of*

to the biblically attested role of John as the precursor of Christ the Saviour. Pious kings interested in the spiritual renewal of their realms (as all kings were supposed to be) could also view John as a resonant figure. The rights and duties of Christian monarchs could be construed as analogous to the role played by the Baptist in terms of inspiring and confirming the adherence of their subjects to the faith through the defence of church doctrine and teaching and the vigorous enforcement of God's law. It is argued below that James I's veneration of St John was openly linked to a wider initiative aimed ostensibly at monastic reform, and that James' assumption of the leading role in that programme of renewal was also intended to carry messages about the nature of royal power and the place of the king at the centre of the religious and spiritual life of the kingdom and his responsibility to ensure the salvation of his subjects. As part of this development James also sought to enhance liturgical provision in and around the royal court and secure the king and dynasty as a focus for quasi-religious veneration in churches and chapels across the kingdom. That James believed that kingship was an elevated and sacral office, and that he looked to convince his Scottish subjects of this through a campaign that employed architecture, ceremony, and liturgy, has considerable significance for discussion of the development of 'Renaissance' kingship in fifteenth-century Scotland. The surfacing of explicitly royalist ideologies in the reign of James III's grandfather certainly brings into question the idea that a radical break in the way Scottish kings thought about and justified their role in the realm occurred in the years around and after 1460.

James I returned to Scotland in April 1424 after 18 years as a reluctant guest of the English kings Henry IV and Henry V. These years in enforced exile have been seen as critical in shaping James' approach to ruling his own kingdom after 1424, with particular emphasis given to the potential impact of Henry V's kingship as a model that King James sought to recreate in the northern realm.[5] One area that has often been highlighted in this regard is James' approach to the exercise of justice. Henry V enjoyed and cultivated a contemporary reputation as a stern but scrupulous upholder of royal justice,

---

Saxony, *The Life of Jesus Christ: Part One, Volume 1, Chapters 1–40* (Collegeville, 2018), ch. 6. Ludolph was a fourteenth-century Carthusian cleric, but his emphasis on the importance of the Baptist reflected a widespread understanding of the critical role accorded to John by Biblical exegesis rather than a partisan attachment to his order's patron. The thirteenth-century *Legenda Aurea* (*Golden Legends*), summarising for an educated lay audience the significance assigned to saints and Biblical figures by earlier Christian theologians, also stressed the importance of the Baptist and the varied roles he played in the narrative of Christ and mankind's salvation. See William Granger Ryan (trans.), *Jacobus de Voragine, The Golden Legend*, 2 vols (Princeton, 1993), i, pp. 328–36.

[5] See Gordon MacKelvie, 'The Royal Prisoner of Henry IV and Henry V: James I of Scotland', in Matthew Bennett and Katherine Weikert (eds), *Medieval Hostageship: Hostage, Captive, Prisoner of War, Guarantee, Peacemaker* (London and New York, 2017), pp. 158–73; Michael Brown, 'James I (1406–1437)', in Brown and Tanner (eds), *Scottish Kingship*, pp. 155–78, at pp. 158–59.

and James' personal rule after 1424 was similarly distinguished by a stress on the king's rights and authority as a lawgiver and his willingness to enforce justice in an occasionally brutal, but essentially even-handed way.[6]

Henry was also noted as a ruler interested in augmenting the religious life of his realm, and the prestige of his own kingship, through the foundation of new monastic houses and by providing support for a large and impressive chapel royal that included skilled composers and liturgical specialists who attended the king even on his overseas expeditions.[7] In Henry's reign, the English royal court (indeed the realm in general) gained recognition for the excellence and sophistication of its liturgical and musical life, and the king himself may have been responsible for the composition of several liturgical pieces.[8] The fascination with liturgical performance was shared by the king's younger brother and heir presumptive Thomas, duke of Clarence (d. 1421). Around the time of the completion of his marriage to Margaret Holland, the widow of John Beaufort (d. 1410), in 1412, Thomas created a large household chapel, in line with late fourteenth- and early fifteenth-century trends, that included the prominent composer Lionel Power.[9] It is of some interest to note that one of the Beaufort step-children acquired by Clarence through his match with Margaret Holland was Joan, the future bride and queen of James I.[10] The Scottish king seems to have followed the example of Henry, his brother, and the wider English courtly elite in the development of a musical establishment attached to his own court after 1424. The contemporary chronicler Walter Bower, abbot of Inchcolm, who completed his *Scotichronicon* in 1445, noted in relation to James that the:

> degree of his interest in spiritual matters is evidenced by the way the service of the latter in his royal chapel was organised in a quite heavenly manner, with a large group of singers who travelled around as part of his court at very great and kingly expense, and who produced the sweetest of music in singing praise to the Lord.[11]

[6] Brown, *James I*, passim; Brown, 'James I', pp. 162–64; Edward Powell, 'The Restoration of Law and Order', in G.L. Harriss (ed.), *Henry V: The Practice of Kingship* (Oxford, 1985), pp. 53–74; Henry's reputation as a 'king under whose rule justice flourished' has been challenged by recent studies. See Christopher Allmand, 'Introduction', in Gwilym Dodd (ed.), *Henry V: New Interpretations* (York, 2013), pp. 1–10, at p. 5.

[7] Alison K. McHardy, 'Religion, Court Culture and Propaganda: The Chapel Royal in the Reign of Henry V', in Dodd (ed.), *Henry V: New Interpretations*, pp. 131–56.

[8] Ibid., pp. 138–42, and 139 for possible references to compositions by the king.

[9] Roger Bowers, 'Some Observations on the Life and Career of Lionel Power', *Proceedings of the Royal Musical Association* 102 (1975–76), 103–27; George R. Keiser, 'Patronage and Piety in Fifteenth-Century England: Margaret, Duchess of Clarence, Symon Wynter and Beinecke MS 317', *The Yale University Library Gazette* 60.1 (1985), 32–46.

[10] James seems to have been on good terms with his notably pious mother-in-law Margaret, sending her (styled as duchess of Clarence) barrelled salmon on several occasions in the 1430s. *ER*, iv, 536, 567, 569, cxlvi.

[11] *Scotichronicon by Walter Bower*, ed. Watt, viii, pp. 332–33.

The heavy investment in liturgical provision was not the only pious concern that James brought back with him in 1424. In the seven years after his return to Scotland James and his queen Joan Beaufort were responsible for initiatives at three different ecclesiastical sites with dedications, or intended dedications, to St John the Baptist. In chronological terms the earliest example of royal patronage directed towards the celebration of the Baptist was the establishment, around or shortly before May 1425, of three royal-funded chaplains to serve in a chapel dedicated to St John beside the parish kirk of Corstorphine.[12] The chapel had been founded by Sir Adam Forrester of Corstorphine (d. before November 1405), a burgess of Edinburgh and a 'man of business' around the early Stewart court, onetime chamberlain of James' mother Queen Annabella Drummond and a member of the council of 21 'wyse men and lele' who had been assigned to James' ill-fated elder brother David, duke of Rothesay, in 1399.[13] By 1425 the church's principal patrons were Adam's widow and the couple's eldest son Sir John Forrester. Sir John had served as an administrator in the Albany government during James' exile, but he was also appointed as master of the king's household before 10 July 1424 and later appeared as the king's chamberlain, showing that he was a trusted royal bureaucrat and councillor.[14] The royal endowment was augmented in 1429 by a grant from Sir John and his widowed mother of the revenues from Forrester family properties in the burgh of Edinburgh to support two further priests.[15] After 1429 Sir John campaigned to elevate the chapel of St John to collegiate status, and this was achieved before June 1436.[16] At that point the college still consisted of five priests (one of them functioning as prior), three of whom were presumably maintained by the royal gift made c. 1425. We can thus, perhaps, view the emergence of Corstorphine as a collegiate foundation as essentially a joint enterprise between the king and a well-favoured royal administrator.

In the year after James' investment in St John's chapel at Corstorphine, the king moved on to a much grander royal ecclesiastical project with links to the Baptist. The preparations for the foundation of a Carthusian priory near Perth commenced in 1426 although the physical construction of the monastery did not begin until 1429.[17] The choice of Perth as the location

[12] The chaplains were supported by a £20-pound annuity from the customs of Edinburgh. Their prayers were specifically stated to be for the salvation of the souls of the royal couple: *ER*, iv, 425, 455, 495, 521, 584, 638.

[13] *St Giles Reg.*, pp. 41–42 (for death of Adam by November 1405); *RPS*, 1399/1/3.

[14] *RMS*, ii, no.4; *ER*, iv, 379; Brown, *James I*, pp. 27, 51, 195.

[15] *RMS*, ii, no. 121.

[16] *CSSR*, iv, no. 305. Sir John sought first to increase the number of priests attached to the college by applying to annexe the revenues of the church of Ratho. Then, in May 1437, to further the physical rebuilding of the kirk, he sought the right to offer indulgences to visitors to the kirk on the feast of the Nativity and the beheading of St John (29 August). Ibid., no. 372.

[17] NRS, Records of the King James VI Hospital Perth, GD 79/2/1; Brown, *James I*,

for the monastery may well have been influenced by the burgh's already long-established association with the saint. Perth's alternative name of 'St John's town' was well attested in late medieval record. The burgh church was dedicated to St John and the communal seal of the town, attached to documents dating to 1296 and 1423, featured on its obverse a depiction of the saint holding the lamb of God (*Agnus Dei*). The legend of the seal proudly proclaimed that it was 'The town seal of the community of St John the Baptist of Perth'.[18] The reverse of the seal depicted St John's martyrdom. The Carthusians openly embraced, and sought to embody, the simple and devout lifestyle of John the Baptist, a saint typically portrayed in late medieval artistic representations as a proto-monastic desert hermit, exiled in a hostile wilderness, clothed in a rough camel skin.[19] Carthusian houses, like those of the Carmelite friars who also declared a spiritual affinity with early hermits and Biblical prophets, were designed as collections of independent hermit-cells. The Baptist was, alongside the Virgin Mary, the main patron of the Carthusian order and was indeed the dedicatee of the new Perth house. In an age where the venality, luxury and worldly corruption of the clergy had become the target of sustained criticism, it was perhaps no surprise that the Carthusian enthusiasm for eremitical poverty and self-denial drew a positive response from the secular elite across Europe. Patronage of the ascetic order became something of a fashion amongst high-ranking noblemen in late fourteenth- and early fifteenth-century Europe.[20] In 1383 Philip the Bold, duke of Burgundy, had commenced the building of a monastery at Champmol near Dijon which was also intended to act as a mausoleum for the Valois-Burgundian lineage.[21] In the English realm, many members of the court and

---

pp. 116–17; Joseph A. Gribbin, 'James I, the Stewart Dynasty and the Charterhouse of Perth', in Concepció Baucà de Mirabó Gralla (ed.), *Prínceps i Reis. Promotors de l'orde cartoixà* (Palma, 2003), pp. 467–79; Robert Scott Fittis, *Ecclesiastical Annals of Perth: To the Period of the Reformation* (Edinburgh, 1885), pp. 216–17; Richard Fawcett and Derek Hall, 'The Perth Charterhouse', *Tayside and Fife Archaeology Journal* (2005), 46–53.

[18] Henry Laing, *Supplemental Descriptive Catalogue of Ancient Scottish Seals* (Edinburgh, 1866), p. 221 (nos. 1247, 1248).

[19] Ibid.; Julian M. Luxford, 'Out of the Wilderness: A Fourteenth-Century English Drawing of John the Baptist', *Gesta* 49 (2010), 137–50. Ibid., 148 for the observation that 'during the fourteenth century … the English branch of the Benedictine order began in earnest to defend the prerogatives of monasticism by, among other things, asserting protomonastic status for John himself, a claim also made by other orders such as the Augustinian friars and the Carthusians'; W.A. Pantin, 'Some Medieval English Treatises on the Origins of Monasticism', in V. Ruffer and A.J. Taylor (eds), *Medieval Studies Presented to Rose Graham* (Oxford, 1950), pp. 189–215.

[20] M. Aston, 'The Development of the Carthusian Order in Europe and Britain: A Preliminary Survey', in M.O.H. Carver (ed.), *In Search of Cult: Essays in Honour of Philip Ratz* (Woodbridge, 1993), pp. 139–51.

[21] Christian de Mérindol, 'Nouvelles observations sur la symbolique royale à la fin du Moyen Age. Le couple de saint Jean-Baptiste et de sainte Catherine au portail de l'église de la chartreuse de Champmol', *Bulletin de la Société Nationale des Antiquaires de France* (1990), 288–302.

affinity of King Richard II (1377–99) displayed Carthusian sympathies, and some of the wealthiest invested in the construction of new Charterhouses.[22] King Richard, although not directly responsible for the foundation of a Charterhouse, exhibited a deep personal identification with the order's principal patron, St John. The most famous extant expression of Richard's connection to the saint is the Wilton Diptych, in which St John appeared as the most important of three saints (the others being St Edmund and Edward the Confessor) presenting the king to the Virgin Mary and infant Christ.[23] Alongside Richard's patronage of devotional art focused on the Baptist the king favoured liturgical ceremonies in which St John played a central part. He also acquired relics connected to the saint, and most strikingly, the Baptist was invoked in the inscription on the king's tomb in Westminster Abbey. Richard's obvious pious interest in St John has been interpreted as proof of the king's adoption of the Baptist as 'a personal patron saint who was integral to messianic kingship'.[24] The prominence of the Baptist in the king's devotional life has certainly been linked to Richard's espousing of an elevated view of kingship as a sacral, quasi-religious office. Richard's most recent biographer, Nigel Saul, has suggested that the king's engagement with the Baptist was part of a wider programme in which the monarch, seeking to compensate for weaknesses in his political position and personal authority, looked to present himself as a Christ-like figure in visual representations and, through the promotion of new forms of address, to 'draw attention to the "distance" that separated the king from his subjects. People were encouraged to see Richard as a supra-mortal, even a God-like, being.'[25]

[22] Nigel Saul, *Richard II* (New Haven, CT and London, 1997), pp. 322, 324; Jeremy Catto, 'Religion and the English Nobility in the Later Fourteenth Century', in H. Lloyd-Jones, V. Pearl and B. Worden (eds), *History and Imagination* (London, 1981), pp. 43–55; Anthony Tuck, 'Carthusian Monks and Lollard Knights: Religious Attitude at the Court of Richard II', in P. Strohm and T.J. Heffernan (eds), *Studies in the Age of Chaucer Proceedings, No. 1, 1984: Reconstructing Chaucer* (Knoxville, 1986), pp. 149–61.

[23] Dillian Gordon, *Making and Meaning: The Wilton Diptych* (London, 1993), pp. 55–57, 61–2; Saul, *Richard II*, p. 309; Shelagh Mitchell, 'Richard II: Kingship and the Cult of Saints', in Dillian Gordon, Lisa Monnas and Caroline Elam (eds), *The Regal Image of Richard II and the Wilton Dyptych* (London, 1997), pp. 115–24, at pp. 119–21.

[24] Saul, *Richard II*, p. 309; Mitchell, 'Richard II', pp. 119–21, quotation at p. 120. It was, in fact, Henry V who arranged for Richard's Westminster burial. On Richard's death in 1399 Henry IV did not allow the deposed king to be interred in the tomb he had already commissioned in Westminster Abbey and Richard was instead laid to rest in the Dominican Friary of King's Langley. When Henry V succeeded his father in 1413 Richard's body was exhumed and reinterred in the abbey, a gesture of reconciliation and atonement but also a means of ending speculation that Richard had not died in 1399. Saul, *Richard II*, pp. 428–29. It has been argued that the Westminster tomb sat amidst a network of chapels (dedicated to St John, St Edmund and Edward the Confessor) that reflected the saints and themes depicted on the Wilton Diptych: 'a visual expression of a complex intermingling of the sacred and the secular, of religious devotion and the idea of kingship'. Gordon, *Making and Meaning*, pp. 61–62.

[25] Nigel Saul, 'Richard II and the Vocabulary of Kingship', *English Historical Review* 110 (1995), 854–77, at p. 862.

The political rupture represented by Richard's deposition in 1399 and the establishment of the Lancastrian regime of Henry IV (1399–1413) did little to dent the popularity of the Carthusians and their reform agenda in and around English courtly circles. Most famously, Henry V established a great Charterhouse at Sheen in Surrey in 1414 as part of a complex that included a rebuilt royal palace.[26] While James' interest in the Carthusians and John the Baptist may certainly have been heightened by an awareness of Henry's initiative at Sheen, this was by no means the only route by which the king might have developed an attachment to the order, its saintly patron, and its programme of ecclesiastical reform. James' queen, Joan Beaufort, had close links to other individuals with a demonstrable record of promoting the Carthusians. Joan's maternal uncle Thomas Holland (ex. 1400), sixth earl of Kent and duke of Surrey, had founded a Carthusian priory at Mount Grace in Yorkshire in 1398, two years before he was executed for the support he had given to the deposed Richard II. With its patron removed, the fledgling priory at Mount Grace had teetered on the edge of dissolution before it was effectively re-founded by Thomas Beaufort, duke of Exeter, Joan Beaufort's paternal uncle.[27]

It is, of course, worth pointing out that engagement with the Carthusians and other ascetic religious orders with anchorite and puritan tendencies, such as the Carmelites, was not a uniquely English phenomenon. Interest in these orders was by no means unknown in Scotland both before and during James' period of exile. The much reported, although likely spurious, self-epitaph assigned to James' father Robert III, as reported (and perhaps invented) by Walter Bower, articulated sentiments on humility, the rejection of worldly display, and the inevitability of bodily corruption that were entirely in keeping with the austere religiosity associated with lay devotees of the Carthusians and Carmelites.[28] In c. 1401 James Douglas of Dalkeith moved to found a Carmelite friary at Linlithgow, while in 1419 Archibald, fourth earl of Douglas, petitioned the papacy to allow him to establish a Carthusian house in Scotland. Earl Archibald's scheme was never carried through, but the abandoned plan illustrated an awareness within Scotland of the merits and virtues of the Carthusians that pre-dated the return of James I to the realm.[29] Despite these caveats, however, it seems clear that the creation of the house of the 'Vale of Virtue' (as the Perth house was called) owed much

[26] Anthony Emery, *Greater Medieval Houses of England and Wales, 1300–1500*, 3 vols (Cambridge, 2006), iii, pp. 93, 155, 166, 218 n.1, 228, 244, 246–48, 262, 281, 283, 353, 407.

[27] Michael G. Sargent, 'Nicholas Love as an Ecclesiastical Reformer', *Church History and Religious Culture* 96 (2016), 40–64, at pp. 40–4; Glyn Coppack and Jackie Hall, 'The Church of Mount Grace Priory: Its Development and Origins', in Julian M. Luxford (ed.), *Studies in Carthusian Monasticism in the Late Middle Ages* (Turnhout, 2008), pp. 299–322; Glyn Coppack and Mick Aston, *Christ's Poor Men: The Carthusians in Britain* (Stroud, 2002).

[28] *Scotichronicon by Walter Bower*, ed. Watt, viii, pp. 64–65.

[29] Ian B. Cowan and David E. Easson, *Medieval Religious Houses: Scotland*, 2nd edn (London, 1976), p. 137; *CSSR*, i, p. 68; Brown, *Black Douglases*, pp. 113, 192.

to James' immersion in the culture of devotional piety of late fourteenth- and early fifteenth-century English aristocratic society.

That impression is deepened when we consider the third ecclesiastical initiative focused on John the Baptist planned by James and Joan. Alongside the Carthusian priory at Perth the other great building project of James' reign was the construction of a new and sophisticated royal palace at Linlithgow, where the previous royal castle/palace had been destroyed in an accidental fire in 1424.[30] The importance of the palace as a statement of royal ambition has long been acknowledged.[31] The eventually abortive royal plans for the neighbouring parish kirk of Linlithgow, dedicated to St Michael, are equally revealing, confirming both the importance of the Baptist to the royal couple and the king's desire to enhance liturgical provision for the royal household and court. The nave of St Michael's had reputedly been destroyed in the same 1424 fire that had ruined the then royal residence.[32] In October 1430 James supplicated the pope asking for permission to reconstitute the allegedly badly damaged parish kirk as a collegiate foundation 'for the augmentation of divine worship and honour of church, palace and town'.[33] In the following year a more ambitious and detailed proposal was submitted for papal approval. On 14 April 1431 the king and Queen Joan, 'bearing special devotion to St John the Baptist', asked that they be allowed to establish a collegiate church dedicated to the 'glory of God Omnipotent and of the Blessed Virgin Mary and of St John and all the choir of Heaven', with a provost and 12 perpetual chaplains.[34] The invocation of the 'choir of Heaven' may well have been a deliberate nod to the idea that the new church, with its well-endowed college of chaplains, was expected to provide musical excellence in liturgical performance. The old parish church, with its dedication to the long-time parochial saint, St Michael, was to be relocated elsewhere in the burgh. The envisaged end result of these plans would have been a well-staffed royal chantry chapel, dedicated to St John, that was adjacent to the king's new palace and equipped to deliver impressive liturgical celebrations.[35] In combination with the Carthusian house in Perth and the royal support for the collegiate kirk dedicated to John at Corstorphine, the unfulfilled plans for Linlithgow suggest a sustained royal commitment to the cult of the Baptist.

A more tenuous link between James and ecclesiastical institutions and orders dedicated to St John emerged after the king's assassination in February

30 *Scotichronicon by Walter Bower*, ed. Watt, viii, pp. 242–43.

31 Richard Fawcett, *The Architectural History of Scotland: From the Accession of the Stewarts to the Reformation, 1371–1560* (Edinburgh, 1994), pp. 301–3; Brown, *James I*, pp. 114–15.

32 Fawcett points out that the church seems to have been in use in the late 1420s and questions the extent of the damage to its fabric. *Architectural History*, p. 198.

33 *CSSR*, iii, p. 140.

34 *CSSR*, iii, pp. 131–32, 140, 145.

35 See Clive Burgess, '"For the Increase of Divine Service": Chantries in the Parish in Late Medieval Bristol', *Journal of Ecclesiastical History* 36 (1985), 46–65, for the stress laid on the desirability of having many priests and choristers available to deliver appropriately inspiring services.

1437. In the wake of this event James' heart was removed from his body and taken on a rather mysterious pilgrimage/crusade. How, precisely where, and by whom it was conveyed remains unknown, but the posthumous itinerary certainly involved travel in the eastern Mediterranean (and probably the Holy Land and Jerusalem) given that the heart was returned to Scotland in 1444–45 by a knight of the order of the Hospital of St John of Jerusalem on Rhodes and presented to the monks of the Carthusian house at Perth (to be interred with the rest of the king's remains).[36] That the post-obit travels of James I's heart involved the Hospitallers, an order dedicated to John the Baptist, is intriguing, but since the Knights of St John played a role in facilitating a high percentage of journeys to the Holy Land from elsewhere in Christian Europe the connection may be largely coincidental.

James' association with the Baptist cult hints at a view of, and a statement about, royal status and power that chimed with James' wider reputation and conduct as a 'lawgiver' king, determined to amend the failings of secular and ecclesiastical leaders and institutions. The Baptist could be seen to reflect the king's own obligations, duties, and rights as an agent of divine salvation, charged with making his realm ready for the arrival of Christ. This was a mission that confirmed the exercise of kingship as a sacred office and gave added weight to a monarch's claim to oversee, direct, reform and judge the lives and conduct of his subjects, both lay and clerical. The veneration of the Baptist would have been entirely consistent with other indications from the early years of James I's personal reign that he regarded (or at least presented) himself as not just a defender of the church, but as a leader responsible for the revival of religious life (particularly monastic observance) and the salvation of his people.

Attempts to place the monarch at the centre of both religious reform and the liturgical cycles of the Scottish kirk began almost as soon as the king returned to Scotland.[37] James' promotion of the Baptist and the Carthusian order provided a model for the revival and improvement of Scottish monastic life and devotional observance more widely. The king's investment in the exemplary self-discipline of the Carthusians should thus be viewed in the

[36] *ER*, v, preface, pp. 43, 44, 156, 179. Alan Denis Macquarrie, 'The Impact of the Crusading Movement in Scotland, 1095–c. 1560', 2 vols (unpublished University of Edinburgh PhD thesis, 1982), i, pp. 219–20; A.I. Dunlop, *The Life and Times of James Kennedy, Bishop of St Andrews* (Edinburgh, 1950), pp. 31 n. 6, 390, for the suggestion that the bearer of the heart on the outward leg of its journey was Sir Alexander Seton of Gordon. Seton deposited various golden coins, collars, jewels and other goods with a merchant in Bruges as collateral for a loan to allow a journey to the Holy Sepulchre. Seton apparently died on Rhodes and may have left his worldly goods to the Hospitallers, given that on 30 December 1440 the order's representative attempted to reclaim the items Seton had lodged in Bruges. L. Gilliodts-van Severen, *Mémoriaux de Bruges: recueil de textes et analyses de documents inédits ou peu connus concernant l'état social de cette ville, du quinzième au dix-neuvième siècle* (Bruges, 1913), no. 7.

[37] It is unclear whether the fact that James crossed the border into his kingdom on a date close to Easter Sunday 1424 (9 April) was mere happenstance or deliberately planned. *Scotichronicon by Walter Bower*, ed. Watt, viii, pp. 220–21 and notes on pp. 343–44.

context of a broader societal concern with the reform and reinvigoration of monastic ideals and lifestyles in longer-established Scottish monasteries. In this enterprise the Scottish king was clearly heavily influenced by his experiences in the southern realm before 1424. In England (and Europe more widely) the Carthusians were not only at the forefront of anti-heretical proselytising but also played a prominent role in attempts to enact ecclesiastical reform in the late fourteenth and early fifteenth centuries. Nicholas Love, the prior (1410–23) of the Carthusian house of Mount Grace – an institution, as noted above, founded and then re-founded by Joan Beaufort's maternal and paternal uncles – was a major figure in this movement. In 1421 Love persuaded Henry V to launch a royal-led attempt to reform the English Benedictine province through the summoning of an 'extraordinary chapter' to address 'excesses and abuses'. This chapter assembled on 7 May 1421 and ran alongside a parliament that opened at Westminster on 2 May.[38] King Henry's address to the Benedictines, as related by the chronicler Thomas Walsingham, highlighted

> the former religion of the monks, and ... the devotion of his [the king's] predecessors and others in the foundation and endowment of the monasteries, and of the negligence and lack of devotion in the modern houses ... He humbly entreated them to return to their former religious life, and to pray without ceasing for himself and for the good estate of the realm and the Church.[39]

Henry then handed over to the assembly a set of written articles outlining the reforms required. In practical terms the putative programme of monastic reform did not survive Henry's death in 1422, but the events of 1421 clearly made an impression on James I. In May 1421 James was high in Henry's favour. He had served in the English king's armies in France in the previous year and in February 1421 had been given a place of honour in the celebrations surrounding the coronation of Henry's new wife Catherine of Valois. On St George's Day 1421, barely a fortnight before Henry's meeting with the Benedictine chapter, James had been knighted by the English king. James may not have personally attended or observed the 7 May meeting, but he could hardly have been unaware of Henry's plans and motivations.[40]

The Carthusian-inspired attempt at monastic reform in England in 1421 may have foundered, but the sentiments and ideas underpinning it travelled north with James I and Joan Beaufort in 1424. On 17 March 1425, while his parliament sat in the burgh of Perth, James I wrote an open 'letter' to the abbots and priors of the Benedictine and Augustinian houses in Scotland that condemned the failings of the orders in trenchant terms echoing the tenor of

[38] Sargent, 'Nicholas Love', pp. 49–51.
[39] John Taylor, Wendy R. Childs, and Leslie Watkiss (eds), *The St Albans Chronicle: The Chronica Maiora of Thomas Walsingham, Vol. 2: 1394–1422* (Oxford, 2003), pp. 756–59.
[40] Brown, *James I*, p. 23.

Henry V's reported declaration to the Benedictine assembly in Westminster in May 1421.[41] The document, as preserved in Walter Bower's *Scotichronicon*, was said to have been issued under the privy seal *in parliamento nostro*, which may suggest that the text reflected a public declaration made by the king in the parliament chamber. The letter lamented:

> The downhill condition and threatening ruin of the holy religious life, which is now declining from day to day from the original practices of its foundation … It is appropriate accordingly to stir you up and to bring to mind how in our realm the decline of the monastic religious life, everywhere defamed and reduced to contempt, particularly through the laxity of the prelates, is leading to destruction (even as in former times Mother Jerusalem was despised by degenerate sons and repudiated by ignoble fathers).

James' claimed commitment to the preservation of the spiritual health of his realm and the salvation of his people gave him the authority to call on the abbots and priors to bring about the necessary reforms. The king's right to judge and lead in these matters was also based, as Henry V had similarly implied in 1421, on his place as the living representative of those monarchs who had patronised and endowed monastic foundations in the past. James urged action:

> lest through your negligence and idleness the kings who formerly for their own preservation and the salvation of their subjects splendidly endowed your monasteries in times past and nobly enriched them, may repent their munificence in erecting walls of marble when they consider how shamelessly you have abandoned the practices of your orders.[42]

Whether the vision of royal regret at the misuse of earlier gifts carried with it an implicit threat that the largesse of his ancestors might be revisited if the Augustinian and Benedictine monasteries did not reform themselves to the king's liking is unclear. It is likely that the pressure for reform remained an essentially moral argument and that the existing property and financial

41 *Scotichronicon by Walter Bower*, ed. Watt, viii, pp. 316–17. Bower, abbot of the Augustinian house at Inchcolm from 1417, would have been a recipient of any missive directed to the heads of Augustinian and Benedictine houses. Bower was not averse to updating documentary sources to suit his own needs so the text given in the *Scotichronicon* should be treated with some caution.

42 *Scotichronicon by Walter Bower*, ed. Watt, viii, pp. 316–17. The preservation of the text of James' criticism of the Augustinian and Benedictine houses in Bower's chronicle may explain why the king was remembered in early sixteenth-century works as a figure who had articulated concerns about the lands and resources previous kings, and especially David I (1124–53), had gifted to the church. John Major, *A History of Greater Britain* (Edinburgh, 1892), ed. A. Constable, pp. 135–36. In David Lindsay's *Satyre of the three estates*, the character known as John Commonweal famously noted that James had described David I as 'ane sair Sanct to the croun'. D. Hamer (ed.), *The Works of Sir David Lindsay of the Mount 1490–1555* (Edinburgh, 1930–36).

rights of the realm's monastic communities were not in real jeopardy. There were, nevertheless, some aspects of the legislation passed in the March 1425 parliament in relation to the realm's hospitals that displayed the crown's practical desire for enhanced supervision of ecclesiastical institutions. The stated purpose of the legislation was to ensure that clerical establishments fulfilled the purposes for which they had originally been founded and adhered to the terms of earlier gifts and grants made to them. Hospitals established 'for almouse deidis throu kingis' for the 'uphaldin of pure folk' were to receive visitations from the king's chancellor 'as has bene done in the kingis progenituris tymys of before' while those founded by bishops and secular lords were to receive visitations from the appropriate bishops or ecclesiastical ordinaries. The purpose of these visits was to 'reduce ande reforme' the various institutions 'to the effect of the fyrst fundatioune'.[43]

James I's scheme, underway before the end of 1426, to bring the Carthusians to Scotland should also be viewed in the context of his criticisms of the 'decline of the monastic religious life' in 1425. The arrival of the Carthusians was surely designed to promote the Reformation of the regular clergy by providing them with a model based on a revival of the virtues, poverty, and eremitical lifestyle of the early church. That the intended role of the Carthusians as a 'mirror' for long-established monastic communities was both understood, and perhaps resented, by other orders is suggested by the account of the king's foundation of the Charterhouse provided by Walter Bower. Bower, writing after James I's assassination in 1437, included a laudatory reflection on the holiness and austerity of the Carthusian monks that was partly framed as a defence against observations by unnamed critics that the order had, in comparison with others, produced few saints.[44]

There was a further feature of the legislation of the March 1425 parliament of interest in terms of James I's dealings with the Scottish church. One of the acts passed by the assembly ordained that every bishop was to order the clergymen in his diocese to 'mak processiounes and speciale preris for the weilfare and hailefull estaite of oure lord the king and oure lady the qweyne and thar barnetyme'.[45] The nature of these prayers and processions is not specified, but the clear intention was to make the royal family the focus of dedicated commemoration in prayer and processional celebrations in the liturgical cycle of churches throughout the realm. In a parliament held a year later in March 1426 James returned to this issue with a further act concerned with the *orationibus et processionibus pro rege fiendis*. The act noted that the clerical estate had already agreed (in the previous March) that 'certane orisonis' should be said for 'oure lorde the king, oure lady the queyn ande the childir cumande of thaim', and the king now looked to find means to implement the commitment. It was stipulated that every bishop

43 *RPS*, 1425/3/2 and 3.
44 *Scotichronicon by Walter Bower*, ed. Watt, viii, pp. 268–75.
45 *RPS*, 1425/3/19.

of the realm would, in their next diocesan council, insist that all priests within their diocese, whether regular or secular, 'say a certane collectis for the prospirite of oure said lorde the king, oure lady the queyn and thare childir' at every mass they conducted. This statute was to be enforced 'under certane payn pecuniare and censure of halykirk' and at the next meeting of the General Council of the Scottish clergy a universal statute enshrining this practice would be formalised.[46] By March 1426 the repeated call to organise compulsory prayers for the 'prosperity' of the king, queen and their offspring had acquired a new political significance. The intervening parliament of May 1425 had seen the arrest and execution of James' main political and dynastic rivals, the Albany Stewarts, most notably James' cousin Murdoch Stewart, duke of Albany and onetime guardian of the realm. James' actions had generated intense controversy and an armed rebellion against the crown that had been successfully suppressed. However, the principal leader of that rebellion, Murdoch's grandson James Stewart, had escaped to Ireland and, as the king's nearest adult male kinsman, continued to pose an existential threat to James I's hold on the throne.[47] The short- and long-term impacts and effectiveness of the legislation are difficult to judge, but its aim was clear enough. Royal attempts to use the ecclesiastical hierarchy to launch campaigns of prayers, sermons, and processions to inculcate loyalty, or to promote and justify specific royal policies, such as wars overseas or in the British Isles, were well-attested in fourteenth- and fifteenth-century England.[48] The proposed processions and prayers focused on the king, queen and their offspring as envisaged by the 1425 and 1426 acts theoretically ensuring that a collective concern with, and commitment to, the prosperity and well-being of the royal house would be expressed across the kingdom on a regular basis.[49] In the context of James' clash with the Albany Stewarts

[46] *RPS*, 1426/15.

[47] Brown, *James I*, pp. 60–75.

[48] McHardy, 'The Chapel Royal', p. 154, notes that 'to reach the wider public Henry V could employ well-established machinery for enlisting support for royal policies. Prayers and processions, organized through the archbishops and bishops, had been used in this way since the thirteenth century, so it is surprising that Henry V's first campaign in France was not preceded by any national call to prayer for its success. Later in the reign the king adopted this traditional practice.' David S. Bachrach, 'The *Ecclesia Anglicana* Goes to War: Prayers, Propaganda, and Conquest during the Reign of Edward I of England, 1272–1307', *Albion* 36.3 (2004), 393–406; A.K. McHardy, 'Some Reflections on Edward III's Use of Propaganda', in J. S. Bothwell (ed.), *The Age of Edward III* (York, 2001), pp. 171–89; Andrea Ruddock, 'National Sentiment and Religious Vocabulary in Fourteenth-Century England', *Journal of Ecclesiastical History* 60 (2009), 1–18. We may suspect that earlier Scottish monarchs had utilised the ecclesiastical hierarchy of the realm to affect opinion and mobilise support through prayers and processions, but no direct evidence of any such co-ordinated campaign survives.

[49] Evaluating the extent to which prayers and processions focused on the royal couple and their offspring became a well-entrenched part of the liturgical cycle in Scottish churches, and how far this differed from established practice, lies beyond the scope of the present study. It is worth noting in passing that there were isolated examples from James' reign of grants establishing masses at individual altars or, on a grander scale, founding

and other domestic opponents, the articulation of the hope that God would secure the good fortune of James, his queen, and their children was clearly politically charged. Moreover, the processional element would seem to have moved beyond a simple remembrance of the royal family in the prayers of the kingdom to a more active celebration (and veneration) of the king and dynasty through explicit association with the rituals and objects (such as saintly relics) that usually provided the focus for these ceremonies.

Another suggestive link between the king, royal government and divine worship emerged from legislation passed in the first parliament of the reign that declared the king's intention to strike new Scottish coins matching the value and weight of English coinage.[50] The coins issued as part of this scheme included the so-called Golden 'Demies'. These Demies bore, on the reverse, the legend *Salvum fac populum tuum*, a phrase taken from Psalm 27:9 ('O lord save thy people and bless thy inheritance: and rule them and exalt them for ever').[51] The Psalm was especially well known in late medieval Europe because it had been incorporated, in the early medieval period, into the ubiquitous hymn of praise, *Te Deum Laudamus*, that played such a prominent role in major communal ecclesiastical, civic, and regnal/royal celebrations and processions. The full significance of the appearance of Psalm 27:9 on the royal coinage is elusive, although the celebratory and processional function of the *Te Deum* may indeed link its use to the legislation of March 1425 and 1426. The psalm's concern with the salvation of a devout and Godly people could also be seen as consistent with the king's identification with the 'messianic' figure of John the Baptist.

James I's engagement with the cult of St John displayed a devout but largely conventional piety on the part of the king and his queen that reflected the concerns of a broad ecclesiastical reform movement in late fourteenth- and early fifteenth-century Europe. The couple's genuine interest in the proper organisation of their devotional life was certainly clear from the remarkably wide-ranging papal supplication they made in 1430 looking for privileges and concessions in relation to their personal religious observance.[52] But the king's wider initiatives in encouraging divine worship, liturgy, and public piety and focusing religious devotion on the royal house also seem to have been designed to convey a message about the divinely ordained nature of royal power to his own subjects and to his successors. There were certainly indications that the self-promoted picture of James as a redeeming Christ-like figure sent as king to ensure the good rule and salvation of his people

collegiate kirks, that specified that prayers were to be said for the king, queen and their children (e.g. *RMS*, ii, no. 60) or, more commonly, for the king and queen. Later in the century (1447), when Alexander Hundby was engaged to say prayers at St Giles altar in Edinburgh it was stipulated that he should 'dayly say mes at the said altar for the prosperite of oure soveraine lorde the king'. *St Giles Reg.*, pp. 78–79 (no. 58).

[50] *RPS*, 1424/33.

[51] Edward Burns, *The Coinage of Scotland*, 3 vols (Edinburgh, 1887), ii, pp. 34–46.

[52] *CSSR*, iii, nos. 77–78.

was not wholly abandoned on his death in 1437. In February 1442 a papal supplication requesting an indulgence for those who visited the Carthusian monastery at Perth (to allow the completion of the building work on the monastery that had stalled on the king's death) claimed that many of the kingdom's inhabitants already made their way to the church 'during the ember days of Lent when the exequies and anniversary of the late king are annually venerated'.[53] The implication was that James' tomb was the focus of a nascent 'royalist' cult where supporters of the king and, by implication, of his living representatives, his widow Joan and his young heir James II, gathered annually on the anniversary of the king's death. The image of James I as a kingly martyr may have become more persuasive as memories of his political and personal failings faded from memory. By the mid-fifteenth century the Book of Pluscarden, thought to date from the opening years of James III's reign, could provide an account of James I's assassination that explicitly depicted James I's demise as a form of martyrdom, and the king himself as a Christ-like sacrificial lamb who died for the good of his people and kingdom. Surrounded by his remorseless foes the king was:

> like an innocent lamb led to the slaughter, he expired giving thanks and imploring mercy from the Most High, with his hands raised to heaven; and after his wounds were washed, eight and twenty stabs were found on his breast ... This persecution he suffered for righteousness' sake.[54]

Similarly, a papal legate who happened to be visiting the royal court at the time supposedly declared that 'he would stake his soul on ... [the king] having died in a state of grace, like a martyr, for his defence of the common weal and his administration of justice'.[55]

Any continuity or incremental development in overtly royalist ideas and iconography over the course of the fifteenth century is not easily traced given the obvious breaks in the exercise of power by adult kings in the period. James I's own experiment in kingship was, of course, cut short by his assassination in 1437, an event that ushered in the long minority of his son James II. The younger James assumed control of the government of the realm c. 1449, but his adult rule lasted little more than a decade, and his explosive death at the siege of Roxburgh in 1460 initiated another near decade-long minority that only ended when James III reached his majority c. 1469. Much of the political debate between 1437 and 1469 was, then, dominated by arguments over who had the right to exercise authority on behalf of the king, rather than the nature and extent of royal power itself. Nevertheless, reflection on the policies pursued and the iconography deployed by James does raise an interesting question about the characterisation and periodisation of the Stewart monarchy in the fifteenth century. Was James I, author of the *Kingis*

53 *CSSR*, iv, no. 852.

54 *Liber Pluscardensis*, ed. F. J. H. Skene, 2 vols (Edinburgh, 1877–80), i, p. 390; ii, p. 290.

55 Ibid. The implied 'papal' recognition of the king's status as a martyr is striking.

*Quair*, builder of Linlithgow Palace, patron of the Carthusians and reformer of the church, really any less a 'Renaissance' figure than his grandson James III in terms of his deliberate promotion through various media of an expansive vision of kingship as a God-given office that brought with it wide powers over the realm and the conduct of its inhabitants? At the least, James, like John the Baptist, could be regarded as the precursor of a coming transformation, a man who left a significant reservoir of royalist sentiment, ideology, and iconography upon which his Stewart successors drew, and whose own 'martyrdom' became part of that legacy.

# 5

# *Sent Abroad to Talk for Their Country: Two Examples of Early Scottish Humanist Diplomacy*[1]

Nicola Royan

On 12 September 1484, at Nottingham Castle, Archibald Whitelaw addressed Richard III and his selected council, in his best humanist Latin, as a spokesman and ambassador for James III. The occasion was a diplomatic mission from the Scots, offering a truce and a royal marriage; Whitelaw was the royal secretary and archdeacon of Lothian.[2] In 1522, at the Ascensian press in Paris, Hector Boece's first historiographical work was printed, *Vitae Episcoporum Aberdonensium et Murthlacensium*.[3] In this work, Boece attributes to William Elphinstone, bishop of Aberdeen and Boece's patron, another ambassadorial speech on behalf of James III, this time to Louis XI in c. 1479.[4] In both cases, humanist Latin is pressed into Scottish political service. The choice of approach reflects the interests and preferences of the men involved: from the evidence of their libraries, both

1 The research for this chapter was funded by the British Academy. I would also like to thank the editor for his comments and careful reading. Any inaccuracies, of course, are mine.

2 London, British Library, Cotton MS Vespasian C xvi, ff. 75r–79v; the final leaf is in London British Library, Cotton MS Caligula B v ff. 151–52v. The standard edition is in David Laing (ed.), *The Bannatyne Miscellany II* (Edinburgh, 1836), pp. 41–48. The most recent edition and translation is Livia Visser-Fuchs, 'Richard III, Tydeus of Calydon and Their Boars in the Latin Oration of Archibald Whitelaw, Archdeacon of St Andrews, at Nottingham on 12 September 1484', *The Ricardian: Journal of the Richard III Society* 17 (2007), 1–21, from which the quotations are taken; another translation, by David Shotter, can be found in A.J. Pollard (ed.), *The North of England in the Age of Richard III* (Stroud, 1996), pp. 193–200.

3 Hector Boece, *Vitae Episcoporum Murthlacensium et Aberdonensium* (Paris, 1522), most readily available as *The Lives of the Bishops of Mortlach and Aberdeen*, ed. and trans. J. Moir (Aberdeen, 1879), pp. 66–73.

4 Leslie J. Macfarlane. *William Elphinstone and the Kingdom of Scotland 1431–1513: The Struggle of Order* (Aberdeen, 1996), pp. 123–29; Norman MacDougall does not see the embassy as significant in *James III: A Political Study* (Edinburgh, 1982), pp. 143–44, and in fact in his revised edition redates the embassy to 1482 following Tanner (Macdougall, *James III* [Edinburgh, 2009], pp. 274–75). My thanks to Steve Boardman for pointing out the redating to me.

Whitelaw and Elphinstone were engaged with the intellectual developments related to the Renaissance in mainland Europe, while Boece, a generation younger, is even more deeply embedded in humanist learning and practice. Nevertheless, in these speeches, there is more than personal preference at stake: the deployment of humanist rhetoric in these diplomatic situations asserts the speakers' intentions that the views of the Scottish crown be taken seriously, by ally and by enemy. Through an examination of the rhetorical features of these speeches, particularly their references to Classical Latin literature, this essay will consider the nature of these examples as two of the earliest demonstrations of Scottish humanism, its uses and its significance.[5] In so doing, it will rely heavily upon Roger Mason's work on Scottish descriptions and definitions of national identity – indeed, the juxtaposition of speeches that is the core of this essay is suggested by his article '*Regnum et Imperium*: Humanism and the Political Culture of Early Renaissance Scotland'.[6] There Mason draws attention to the significance of Whitelaw and Elphinstone as 'early adopters', and outlines what humanism might have contributed to Scottish government through the centrality of those bureaucrats and their intellectual allegiances, and what they passed on to their successors. This essay looks specifically at the rhetorical productions attributed to Whitelaw and Elphinstone, with three particular questions in mind: firstly, in what ways might these speeches be defined as humanist; secondly, how do they display their knowledge of Classical material; and finally and most significantly, to what end? Understanding the function of Classical reference, whether to flatter, to assert authority, or to express power, will demonstrate the utility of Classical and humanist learning on the political stage, and reinforce Mason's arguments on its significance for the framing of Scottish government at the end of the fifteenth century and into the sixteenth.

Archibald Whitelaw and William Elphinstone lived just within a generation of each other. Whitelaw was born around 1415/16, a date derived from his self-description as being 60 in 1475. He was educated at the University of St Andrews and graduated as a licentiate in arts in 1439. He taught at Cologne for a time, before returning to teach at St Andrews in the 1450s. By 1459, he was in royal service, as a diplomat and tutor to the royal heir, Prince James. From 1462, he is found as royal secretary in the regency government of James II's widow, Mary of Gueldres, mother to the now-king James III. He held this post until Christmas 1493, into the rule of James IV,

5 For a briefer discussion of these speeches, together with one by Walter Ogilvie, see Thomas Rutledge, 'The Development of Humanism in Late-Fifteenth-Century Scotland', in David Rundle (ed.), *Humanism in Fifteenth-Century Europe* (Oxford, 2012), pp. 237–63, esp. pp. 242–46.

6 Roger A. Mason, '*Regnum et Imperium*: Humanism and the Political Culture of Early Renaissance Scotland' in Mason, *Kingship and the Commonweal*, pp. 104–38, esp. pp. 117–18 and 129–30.

who had deposed his father, James III, in 1488. He was rewarded with various significant church livings, including the archdeaconry of Lothian and the subdeanery of Glasgow. While his speech at Nottingham is the only one recorded, he had had experience of diplomacy before 1484, as one of the negotiators of treaties with England in 1459 (with Richard, duke of York, Richard III's father), and again in 1474. His survival in royal service until the age of 82, across three regime changes, is remarkable: at the very least, we must presume he was trustworthy, efficient and reasonably immune to faction and excessive greed.[7]

Through the uncritical account in Boece's *Vitae*, we have a little more sense of William Elphinstone as a man. He was born in 1431, a younger contemporary of Whitelaw's.[8] He was an early graduate of Glasgow University, and continued his studies in law in Paris (1465–70), first as student and then as teacher. In 1470 he went to study civil law at the University of Orléans, but returned to Glasgow in 1471, to serve the diocese as its chief legal officer, and also the University as dean of the Faculty of Arts and then as rector. This period saw his first direct involvement in parliament, first as a representative of the clergy and then as a lord of Council. He served James III as diplomat and ambassador, and his son James IV as Chancellor and Keeper of the Privy Seal. In the *Vitae*, Boece, his loyal biographer, asserts that Elphinstone's love of literature, including Classical literature, was evident during his studies in Paris;[9] certainly, Elphinstone remained committed to that other humanist cause, education, as evidenced by his founding of King's College in 1495. Even Erasmus seems to have considered employment at King's College; it is not impossible that Elphinstone, along with Patrick Paniter, was influential in his appointment as tutor for Alexander Stewart, James IV's illegitimate son.[10] Like Whitelaw, Elphinstone remained in harness into old age, dying in October 1514, still at that point Chancellor of the realm, and guardian of the very young James V.

The surviving volumes from both Elphinstone's and Whitelaw's libraries provide evidence of their mutual interest in new learning from the Continent. While Elphinstone's books are primarily professionally appropriate legal and theological texts, his library also contained Lorenzo Valla's *Elegantiae latinae linguae*.[11] Valla (c. 1407–57) was a major figure in Italian humanism, whose philological work had challenged the legitimacy of the Donation of Constantine through linguistic analysis.[12]

7 Norman Macdougall, 'Whitelaw, Archibald (1415/16–1498), Ecclesiastic and Administrator', *ODNB* [54336].

8 See Macfarlane, *William Elphinstone*, for a full account of Elphinstone's life and works.

9 Boece, *Vitae*, p. 63.

10 Ibid., p. 88. Paniter was also at Montaigu College with Erasmus and Boece. See also Mason, 'Humanism and Political Culture', pp. 119–20.

11 John Durkan and Anthony Ross, 'Early Scottish Libraries', *IR* 9.1 (1958), 31–34, esp. p. 32.

12 Peter Mack, *Renaissance Argument: Valla and Agricola in the Traditions of Rhetoric and*

The *Elegantiae* (1449) was influential all over Europe as a model of good Classical Latin style, and Elphinstone's possession of a copy, perhaps brought back from his visit to Rome, suggests at the very least an interest in the application of humanist approaches to expression.[13] Such a view is also attested by Boece's accounts of Elphinstone, and indeed by the early curriculum of King's College in Aberdeen.[14] Elphinstone's commitment to the use of new technology in the interests of the realm is evident from his championing of the Aberdeen Breviary;[15] that he might also have seen political benefits from the adoption of new rhetorical emphases is entirely probable.

Whitelaw's surviving library is more wide-ranging. Aberdeen University Library now holds at least one manuscript with his ownership marks, containing two histories: Paulus Orosius, *Historiae adversus paganos*, and Lucius Amneius Florus, *Epitome rerum Romanorum*, bound with *Historia de origine Troianorum* by Dares Phrygius (Aberdeen, Aberdeen University Library MS 214).[16] There are three further manuscripts which have Whitelaw's hand commenting on the contents, one in St Andrews University Library, a copy of Cicero's *Opera Philosophica*, and two in the National Library of Scotland, Suetonius' *Vitae Caesarum* and an index for the commentaries of *Caesar*.[17] In addition, Durkan and Ross identify six early prints with his ownership mark: Albertus Magnus, *De Animalibus* (Mantua, 1479), Lucan's *Pharsalia* (Louvain, c. 1475), the works of Horace, Appianus, and Sallust, and Asconius' commentaries on Cicero's speeches, all printed in Venice between 1478 and 1481.[18] Taken together, these volumes suggest a breadth of literary and intellectual interest, including medieval standards and Classical works in humanist editions. Such a range indicates the gradual absorption of humanist learning into Scotland, and the generational differences in experience. By the late 1470s, when the earliest surviving prints were made, Whitelaw was in his sixties, too late perhaps to absorb an entirely new humanist Latin

*Dialectic* (Leiden, 1993) discusses Valla's influence across Europe.

[13] The Scots were also aware of Valla as an antagonist of Poggio Braccolini, another distinguished Italian humanist: Gavin Douglas makes reference to their dispute in *The Palice of Honour*, while including both men in Calliope's train (Gavin Douglas, *The Palice of Honour*, in Priscilla Bawcutt [ed.], *The Shorter Poems of Gavin Douglas*, rev. edn [Edinburgh, 2003], ll. 1232–33).

[14] Macfarlane, *William Elphinstone*, pp. 390–91.

[15] For details on the *Aberdeen Breviary*, see Alan Macquarrie with Rachel Butter (eds), *Legends of Scottish Saints. Readings, Hymns and Prayers for the Commemorations of Scottish Saints in the Aberdeen Breviary* (Dublin, 2012).

[16] See Aberdeen University Library catalogue: http://calms.abdn.ac.uk/DServe/dserve.exe?dsqIni=Dserve.ini&dsqApp=Archive&dsqCmd=Show.tcl&dsqDb=Catalog&dsqSearch=(PersonCode==%27NA15900%27)&dsqPos=0.

[17] Marcus Tullius Cicero, *Opera Philosophica*, c. 1480, University of St Andrews, Special Collections, GB 227 MSPa6295, A2A00. For the NLS manuscripts, Adv MS 18.3.11 and 18.3.10, see John Higgitt (ed.), *Scottish Libraries* (London, 2006), p. 47.

[18] Durkan and Ross, 'Early Scottish Libraries', p. 159.

style, but not too late to engage with new texts in new formats and see their potential for political ends.

The account of these men's books is a pathway to the examination of their rhetorical productions, a small part of their endeavours. This essay is not concerned with the revisions to bureaucratic practice that Whitelaw might have introduced into the royal secretariat, nor with Elphinstone's attention to legal and educational reform, nor indeed with the wider narrative that Mason suggests. Rather, it concentrates on two diplomatic speeches, one for each man, in which the Scottish realm and its king are represented in humanist Latin, and with a consistent engagement with Classical texts. This essay argues that the style and the form of these speeches present Whitelaw and Elphinstone as asserting Scottish intellectual and diplomatic authority in order to address an unreliable ally (Louis XI) and an equally unreliable enemy (Richard III).

It is as well to begin by acknowledging the differences between these speeches, particularly in their transmission. Whitelaw's speech in Nottingham is included in notes recording the embassy: while the record of the embassy meeting is not complete, it looks to be near contemporary, and to have recorded Whitelaw's speech to the best of the English scribe's abilities in Latin.[19] The manuscript books in which these notes are bound are both concerned with Scottish affairs from an English perspective: this would suggest that all the materials, including the transcription of Whitelaw's speech, have an English origin. Notably, though, the record indicates that the speech was delivered pretty much in the form in which it survives. This contrasts strongly with the record of Elphinstone's speech in Boece's *Vitae*: this work was published some nine years after Elphinstone's death and 40 years after the speech's supposed delivery. The speech forms part of Boece's hagiography of his patron, certainly imbuing him with eloquence and Ciceronian style as well as a gift for confident quotation. Elphinstone's modern biographer, Leslie Macfarlane, argued that Boece's account preserved the substance of Elphinstone's speech;[20] given both Macfarlane's loyalty to his subject and the lack of more contemporary record, that view may not be entirely convincing. Both speeches are

[19] Establishing the precise nature of the witness in Cotton Caligula C xvii is difficult. The volume is a collection of all kinds of documents relating to the Anglo-Scottish relationship. The speech comes first in its booklet and is very neatly written and effectively double-spaced. It ends at the top third of a page, and on the rest of the pages and those that follow there are notes largely in English about the embassy, including lists of attenders and what might be a seating diagram for the English party. The notes are less formally and more closely written. It does not look to me as if the speech were recorded from dictation at the embassy, but rather made from a written copy. Visser-Fuchs, however ('Richard III', pp. 7–8), on the basis of the errors in the Latin comes to a different conclusion. It may be that rough copies were provided in advance, to avoid any undiplomatic surprises, but, as is the case with many witnesses of medieval texts, we must assume a couple of stages between the author's production and the text that survives.

[20] Macfarlane, *Elphinstone*, p. 123.

singular, in that no other speech of Whitelaw's survives, and Boece does not provide any further orations by Elphinstone.[21] Considered together, these speeches give us a unique insight into how humanist rhetoric was first deployed for political and national goals, and they provide some of the earliest evidence for the reception and practice of humanist writing in Scotland.

The speeches may be regarded as gifts from the Scottish embassy to the respective kings, perhaps on the same lines as speeches at a royal entry, and the choice of Latin as their medium is a part of their value. This is easier to illustrate with Whitelaw's speech, for correspondence between James III and Richard III, and the discussions at the embassy, seem to have been conducted in the vernacular. The choice of Latin, therefore, and Whitelaw's efforts towards a humanist style offer Richard the best in culture and learning that Scotland could offer, and in so doing assert the fashionable sophistication of Scottish learning and culture.[22] The same would be true of Elphinstone's speech to Louis XI. Whether the conception of either speech lay with the king is unattested. Roger Mason has noted James' deployment of the closed imperial crown on coinage and in architecture, and while Alasdair MacDonald has argued for James' more extended engagement with royal self-presentation, there is little evidence for literary patronage and investment.[23] Both Whitelaw and Elphinstone had learning and experience enough to devise the speeches to suit royal policy, to enhance their embassies, and to assert the voice of their king.

Because of its mode of transmission, we know more about the occasion of Whitelaw's speech. The embassy to Nottingham in 1484 came at a point where Richard III's approach to relations with Scotland seem to have been changing.[24] Having previously followed a more aggressive

[21] Boece does record Elphinstone on other embassies, one to the Emperor Maximilian, to ask for his daughter to be married to James IV (*Vitae*, pp. 80–81), and another as a representative at a peace conference in 1497. In neither case is a speech provided.

[22] Douglas Gray notes that a royal entry contains 'elements both of panegyric and instruction': the same applies to diplomatic speeches. See 'The Royal Entry in Sixteenth-Century Scotland', in Sally Mapstone and Juliette Wood (eds), *The Rose and the Thistle: Essays on the Culture of Late Medieval and Renaissance Scotland* (East Linton, 1998), pp. 10–37, esp. pp. 14–15. For a more general account of ambassadorial practice, see Donald E. Queller, *The Office of the Ambassador in the Middle Ages* (Princeton, 1967), pp. 196–201.

[23] Roger A. Mason, 'Chivalry and Citizenship: Aspects of National Identity in Renaissance Scotland', in Mason, *Kingship and the Commonweal*, pp. 78–103, esp. pp. 93–94, and 'Humanism and Political Culture', pp. 129–31. In both cases, Elphinstone is part of Mason's discussion. MacDonald offers a more generous picture of James III in Alasdair A. MacDonald, 'James III: Kingship and Contested Reputation', in Boardman and Goodare (eds), *Kings, Lords and Men*, pp. 246–64, although not directly as a literary patron.

[24] The account of this embassy follows the presentation of Alexander Grant, 'Richard III and Scotland', in Pollard (ed.), *The North of England in the Age of Richard III*, pp. 115–48.

policy towards the Scots, despite continuing war at sea, by the time of the embassy, he was more interested in agreeing a truce than in previous years. He was even at the point of withdrawing support for James III's rebellious brother, Alexander, duke of Albany and his ally, James Douglas. A letter from James III in late July 1484 suggests that Richard was seeking both a truce and a marriage alliance, and that James, whose 'most consistent policy was peace with England', was happy to pursue this through the embassy.[25]

Whitelaw's speech is directed primarily towards the virtues of peace and the dangers of war. It is not a preview of the terms of any treaties or the finer points of negotiation, but rather designed to present peace as the only reasonable outcome, based on shared interests between the kings and their peoples. There is no direct reference to Richard's policies, or to the particular circumstances of 1484. Recent estimates suggest that it would have taken about half an hour to deliver, enough to focus attention, not enough to get in the way of discussion. Most comment on the speech refers to it as 'humanist'. It certainly aims for grandiloquence, but it is not a perfect example of Ciceronian style. David Shotter notes at the conclusion of his translation that 'the Latin is *studiedly* correct, but [...] lacks the impact of one with an essential *feel* for the language', and suggests that Whitelaw's style is 'more reminiscent of Cicero's philosophical and rhetorical treatises'.[26] The speech's most recent editor, Livia Visser-Fuchs, argues that Whitelaw was not well served by the scribe: it may be that the speech as delivered was better than the record suggests.[27]

Whitelaw must have used Latin as a working language for much of his life, and it is impossible to know at what point he might have chosen to develop a humanist style. Humanist style in the fifteenth and early sixteenth centuries tended to take Cicero as a rhetorical model, imitating his grammatical structures, his vocabulary, and his linguistic patterns, such as *tricola*, the pattern of three parallel phrases; at the very least, the expectation was that grammar, syntax and lexis would be derived from Classical Latin, rather than more recent habits.[28] Overall, Whitelaw's speech corresponds to those expectations, although there are some errors and confusions, as its most recent editors and translators note. There are also other features in the speech that now look curious, or rather, appear to be not best Ciceronian Latin. At the level of lexis, for instance, Whitelaw uses *guerra* instead of *bellum* for 'war':

[25] Grant, 'Richard III and Scotland', pp. 119, 134–37.

[26] Shotter, in Pollard (ed.), *The North of England in the Age of Richard III*, p. 200.

[27] Visser-Fuchs, 'Richard III', p. 8.

[28] For a discussion of the place of rhetoric, see Peter Mack, 'Humanist Rhetoric and Dialectic', in Jill Kraye (ed.), *The Cambridge Companion to Renaissance Humanism* (Cambridge, 1996), pp. 82–99.

> Tui enim subditi, serenissime princeps, in regni tui limitibus commorantes, qui dudum sua insolencia bellum paci pretulerant, nunc sua guerris inculta videntes agrorum iugera, pacem laudant, guerras et prelia damnant, et te ad fraternam cum nostro inclitissimo principe invitant caritatem, quam tui regni nobles prudentes et virtuosi deposcunt[.][29]

> Your subjects, most serene prince, who dwell at the borders of your kingdom have for a long time known no better than to prefer war to peace, but now, seeing their acres of land uncultivated because of war, they praise peace, and condemn war and battles, and ask you to feel brotherly love towards our famous king, a love also urgently demanded by the nobles of your kingdom, prudent and good as they are.[30]

*Guerra* is not a form found in Classical Latin, and here, particularly in parallel with *praelia*, it looks out of place. It does appear in the *Revised Medieval Latin Word List from British and Irish Sources*, with associations of feud or retaliation in the fourteenth century, but there is no reference at all from the fifteenth.[31] However, *guerra* is used in the title of the previous item of Cotton MS Vespasian C xvi, an account of Scoto-English border skirmishes in 1489. A definition of 'guerra guerrata' from Du Cange *et al.*, suggests also that *guerra* is the kind of war *quae inferebatur hosti per velitationes, per insidias, infestando commeatus, aliisque artibus bellicis, sed abstinendo a proeliis* ('which is waged against the enemy through skirmishing, ambushes, pestering convoys and through other arts of war, but abstaining from battle').[32] Taking this admittedly limited linguistic evidence together, we might surmise that Whitelaw uses *guerra* purposefully, to represent the particular kinds of warfare common on the Anglo-Scottish border. At the very least, we can note that Whitelaw's Latin was a flexible instrument, and was designed for effective communication, a choice of which Erasmus at least would have approved.[33] Nevertheless, Whitelaw's aim is a humanist style, designed, on such a notable occasion, to impress, to demonstrate Scottish intellectual wealth, and to flatter and to warn.[34]

Whitelaw's aspiration to humanist rhetorical models is particularly evident in his use of quotation and citation. Whitelaw cites a variety of Classical writers, including Cicero, Virgil, Seneca, Sallust, Livy, Valerius

[29] Visser-Fuchs, 'Richard III', p. 12.

[30] Ibid., p. 19. This translation elides the criticism inherent in *sua insolencia.*

[31] 'Guerra', in R.E. Latham (ed.), *Revised Medieval Latin Word List from British and Irish Sources* (London, 1965).

[32] Charles Du Fresne, *Glossarium Mediæ et Infimæ Latinitatis* (Niort, 1883–87), found at https://logeion.uchicago.edu/guerra.

[33] For *Ciceronianus*, where Erasmus discusses his view of humanist style, see H.C. Gotoff, 'Stylistic Criticism in Erasmus' *Ciceronianus*', *Illinois Classical Studies* 7.2 (1982), 359–70.

[34] For a very brief and slightly dated account of the history of Latin use at this period, see Mason Hammond, *Latin: A Historical and Linguistic Handbook* (Cambridge, MA and London, 1976), pp. 243–45.

Maximus, and Statius. In most cases, these references are singular – there is one quotation each from Seneca, from Sallust, and from Valerius Maximus. Cicero is quoted three times. Two of these are short quotations about the values of peace, one from *Pro Milone*, the other from *De Officiis*. The longer quotation is a patchwork from Cicero's speech *Pro Lege Manilia* in support of Gnaeus Pompey, Julius Caesar's main rival.[35] The patchwork is an articulation of the qualities of a great general and statesman, and placed to flatter Richard.[36] There is a shrewd omission of luck (*felicitas*) in a list derived from section 28 of Cicero's speech, but otherwise these quotations are very close to the Ciceronian text. Whitelaw draws on the literary authority of Cicero to outline the ideal general, and to compare Richard to Pompey. However, in the light of other quotations, particularly those from the epic poets, and in the light of one of the more curious arguments of the speech, Pompey's association with civil war seems more pointed. This is true of most of Whitelaw's quotations, which are superficially flattering, but carry an undertow of criticism, only evident to those who knew the broader context of the quotations.

Whitelaw's epic quotations are from Virgil and from Statius. From Virgil he draws lines from the *Eclogues*, *Georgics* and the *Aeneid*; the *Thebaid* is his source for Statius. The *Aeneid* is concerned with nation-building and constructing peace after civil war, the *Thebaid* with fraternal conflict and tragic doom. Of this pair, most quotations are drawn from Virgil. This most probably reflects Virgil's centrality as an *auctor* (authority) in the later Middle Ages, but his appearance in a speech about peace may also allude to his equivocal attitude to the glories of war.[37] Some of the Virgilian quotations, like those from Cicero, may be treated as tags: for instance, the use of a line from *Aeneid* IV, describing Carthage's reaction to Dido's suicide, to augment Whitelaw's account of the horrors of war does not seem to carry additional meaning, not least because Whitelaw does not signal its presence.[38] Other quotations suggest a more conscious use. For instance, in the first quotation from Virgil, Whitelaw melds together lines from *Eclogues* V and *Aeneid* I. As with the first quotation from Cicero, this blended quotation is designed to underline his praise of Richard III, and to imply that his reputation will be everlasting.[39] The comparison

[35] Cicero, *Pro Lege Manilia* 12 in Cicero, *Pro Lege Manilia. Pro Caecina. Pro Cluentio. Pro Rabirio Perduellionis Reo*, trans. H. Grose Hodge, Loeb Classical Library 198 (Cambridge, MA, 1927), pp. 2–85, sections 29 (pp. 40–43), 36 and 38 (pp. 48–51).

[36] For Richard III's own bookish interests, see Anne F. Sutton and Livia Visser-Fuchs, *Richard III's Books: Ideal and Reality in the Life and Library of a Medieval Prince* (Stroud, 1997).

[37] For ambivalent readings of the *Aeneid*, including some contemporaneous with Whitelaw, see Craig Kallendorf, *The Other Virgil: 'Pessimistic' Readings of the* Aeneid *in Early Modern Culture* (Oxford, 2007).

[38] Visser-Fuchs, 'Richard III', p. 13.

[39] Ibid., pp. 11 and 18; for the Virgilian texts, see Virgil, *Eclogues* 5: 76–77, and *Aeneid* 1: 607–9 in Virgil, *Eclogues. Georgics. Aeneid: Books 1–6*, trans. H. Rushton Fairclough

here is less Pompey and more Augustus, Virgil's patron – a more successful general, since after his successes he managed to impose peace. However, the quotations from Virgil are not all straightforward flattery. Whitelaw also draws on Anchises' speech in support of peace and just and kindly imperial rule when Aeneas meets him in the underworld in book 6:

> Hae tibi erunt artes, pacique imponere morem,
> Parcere subiectis, et debellare superbos. (*Aen.* 6: 851–53)
> These will be your skills: to crown peace with law.
> To spare the humble and subdue the proud.[40]

In the *Aeneid*, Anchises' speech is a prophecy about Rome's imperial success, and yet it is also a sad commentary on the civil wars that have preceded Augustus' rise to emperor. This quotation carries a broader allusion about the impact of war alongside its apparent celebration of good government.

Whitelaw's use of Statius' *Thebaid* has received considerable comment, mostly because of what it suggests about Richard III's height. The *Thebaid* relates the conflict between Polyneices and Eteocles, the sons of Oedipus and Jocasta: after their father's death, it had been agreed that they would hold power in Thebes in alternate years, with Eteocles taking the throne first. Predictably, the arrangement breaks down almost immediately, and Polyneices is forced into exile. He marries one of the daughters of Adrastus; her sister marries another exile, Tydeus, and together the brothers-in-law collect an army to assert Polyneices' rights at Thebes. The brothers die fighting one another, and neither wins the power they wanted: at its heart, the poem raises questions about the benefits of war even for those with most to gain, and so offers apposite lessons for an embassy in quest of a peace treaty. Although less familiar today than the *Aeneid*, the *Thebaid* was a common text in late medieval schoolrooms and was a common source of grammatical and poetic florilegia; rather like the *Aeneid*, it also had English vernacular versions, a summary by Chaucer in *Troilus and Criseyde* and a retelling by John Lydgate in *The Siege of Thebes* (c. 1421–22). The story of the *Thebaid* was thus available in both English and Latin, so it is reasonable to surmise that Whitelaw's listeners had a narrative context for his quotations, and that the Latin readers in his audience would have had some familiarity with the poem, although Whitelaw's use might have been a little more startling.

The *Thebaid* is the first Classical text from which Whitelaw quotes directly – ahead of both Cicero and Virgil. The opening quotations are applied to Richard III, to describe and to praise him through comparison to Tydeus. Tydeus, Polynices' ally and brother-in-law, is a doughty fighter with a short temper who endures a terrible end, when he is abandoned by his

(rev. G.P. Goold), Loeb Classical Library 63 (Cambridge, MA, 1916), pp. 58–59 and pp. 305–6.

[40] Quotation and translation from Visser-Fuchs, 'Richard III', pp. 13 and 19.

championing goddess, Athena, and reduced to cannibalism. The quotations describe Richard thus:

> verum nunc primum tuam faciem summo imperio et principatu dignam inspicio, quam moralis et heroica virtus illustrat. De te dici predicarique potuerit quod Thideo principi inclitissimo Stacius poeta hijs verbis contulit:
>
> numquam tam animi natura minori
> Corpori, nec tantas ausa est includere vires.[41]
>
> Et quid
>
> Maior in exiguo regnabat corpore virtus.[42]
>
> Truly, now for the first time do I behold your face, which is worthy of the highest authority and kingship and illuminated by moral and chivalric virtue. About you can be said what the poet Statius ascribed to the famous prince Tydeus:
>
> Never did Nature venture to enclose in such a small body
> Such a great spirit and such strength.
>
> And
>
> Very great prowess controlled his small body.[43]

Both of these excerpts stress height and prowess: Whitelaw's speech has been taken as evidence from an eyewitness that Richard's height was well-known and readily commented upon.[44] Visser-Fuchs has explored the link between Tydeus and Richard further, noting that they share the boar as their symbol (Tydeus wears a boar skin).[45] However, these comments do not exhaust the allusiveness of the quotations. That these should be explored is suggested by Whitelaw's direct references to Tydeus and the *Thebaid*, and might be approached by two routes. Firstly, there is more to consider in the direct comparison between Richard and Tydeus, and secondly, it is also fair to ask whether there are connections between the quotations Whitelaw uses, and

41 Statius, *Volume I: Thebaid: Books 1–7*, ed. and trans. D.R. Shackleton-Bailey, Loeb Classical Library 207 (Cambridge MA, 2004), pp. 388–89: *nunquam hunc animam Nature minori corpore nec tantas ausa est includere vires*. The differences between Whitelaw's quotation and the modern edition may result from any number of factors, including scribal mistakes and different lines of transmission.

42 Statius, *Thebaid* 1: 417, Loeb pp. 70–71.

43 Text and translation taken from Visser-Fuchs, 'Richard III', pp. 9–10 and 17.

44 Sarah Knight and Mary Ann Lund, 'Richard Crookback', *Times Literary Supplement* 6 February 2013, at www.the-tls.co.uk/articles/public/richard-crookback.

45 Visser-Fuchs, 'Richard III', pp. 5–6.

if so, if they hint at Scottish – or rather royal – political thinking behind the request for a treaty.

As mentioned, Whitelaw refers directly to Statius' poem in framing his quotations. At the very least, he is expecting his audience, including Richard himself, to be able to provide some contextualisation of the figure of Tydeus, even if not the exact lines. Statius' Tydeus is a hero of war, advocating it regularly, and pre-eminent in its conduct, defeating a large army by himself on his first journey to Thebes. Notwithstanding Richard's reputation on the battlefield, and the appropriateness of the comparison on grounds of height alone, it is perhaps an unusual comparison to use when arguing for peace. The first quotation Whitelaw uses occurs at *Thebaid* VI: 863–64, where it describes Tydeus' success in a wrestling competition, resulting from a combination of craft and strength. He wins the contest against Agylleus, a descendant of Hercules, and physically much larger, if much less strategic in his strength than Tydeus. The second quotation comes from the first book of the *Thebaid*, and is part of Tydeus' introduction to the narrative, where he fights his fellow fugitive Polynices for shelter. At that point, Tydeus is also a refugee, fleeing from Calydon *fraterni sanguinis illum conscius horror agit* ('driven by the guilty terror of a brother's blood').[46] Tydeus may be a heroic warrior in a small body, but his broader associations – as fratricidal, as usurping an inherited position, and as being a consistent advocate for war – are potentially provocative.

Tydeus' association with the symbol of the boar first comes into focus when Adrastus sees him and Polynices together at *Thebaid* I: 482–92, and realises that they are the sons-in-law foretold to him in a dream. The identification of the boar, as Visser-Fuchs argues, confirms the association between Richard and Tydeus. However, she does not comment on Polynices' symbol, the lion. Given the parties involved in the embassy, the lion is surely as broad in its range of significations as the boar. At the very least, the lion evokes the Scottish royal arms, and if the references to the *Thebaid* did not extend beyond Book 1, then the transformation of Polynices and Tydeus from combatants into brothers-in-law and comrades in arms would be easy to fit into an embassy of peace. However, Whitelaw begins with a quotation from Book 6, projecting into the longer narrative of Statius' poem, towards the feud between Polynices and his brother Eteocles, and towards the disastrous conclusion. Such a continuation suggests more fugitive associations: for instance, the alliance of Tydeus and Polynices against Eteocles might evoke Richard's support of the duke of Albany in his rebellions against James III. Such an evocation would not withstand extended consideration, but it foregrounds the catastrophic results of the fraternal war over the kingdom of Thebes. The significance of these references is unstable, since they have the potential to evoke different associations; one aspect is consistent, however, namely, the benefits of peace over war.

46 Statius, *Thebaid* 1: 417, Loeb, pp. 70–71.

At the heart of the *Thebaid* is a civil war, and the consequences of that. Civil war also plays its part in the quotations from Cicero's *De imperio Gn Pompeii* (otherwise *Pro Lege Manilia*) and from Virgil's works. While not known to Cicero at the point of the speech, Pompey's end of course was very well known in the fifteenth century, as a story of over-reaching military might. Virgil's ambivalence to war is evident in both the *Aeneid* and the *Eclogues*: the quotation from book 6, from Anchises' prophecy on the future of Rome, not only draws attention to the Roman mission, but also laments the breakdown of civil society before Augustus made himself emperor. While this focus on civil war sits oddly with an embassy between two kings, it does fit with Whitelaw's later reflection on the peoples of Britain:

> Innaturale enim est, inter nos bellum geri quos brevis occidui maris insula nectit, quos eadem celi influencia et loci vicinitas, similium corporum, voce, vultu, colore et complexione compaginat. Quinymo pocius animi virtus, Dei amor, et proximi timor, uno nos fonte benignitatis conglutinaret.[47]

> It is unnatural, indeed, for us to wage war, who are so closely held by a little island in the western sea, and joined together by the same influence of the sky and close proximity, of similar physique, language, facial appearance, colouring and complexion. May our courage, our love of God and fear of our neighbour bind us together even more in one well of goodwill.[48]

Here the idea of war between the Scots and the English is presented as foolish, because the peoples are so similar: *similium corporum, voce, vultu, colore et complexione*. Similarity in body is matched in mind: *animi virtus, Dei amor, et proximi timor* (even if it is not quite clear who the *proximus* in this context would be). Whitelaw does not go so far as to suggest that the peoples are so similar that they might as well be united under one ruler, but he does conclude with reference to one key part of the negotiations, the possibility of a marriage between James' son and an English royal kinswoman, already suggested by the alliance of Tydeus and Polynices. That suggestion underlies the references to *union, dulce connubium,* and *affinitas* in the speech. James III had sought marriage alliances throughout his rule, no matter who held the English crown; that the plan only came to fruition in 1503 was not for want of discussion.

Whitelaw's intertextual references serve several functions. They demonstrate a humanist knowledge of Classical texts beyond the commonplace. They are designed to flatter, both by comparison and by assumption of equal literary knowledge among his audience. At the same time, however, the allusions add bite: Tydeus may be a great warrior but he is certainly not without flaw; the success of Augustus is built on foundations of civil war; even Pompey

47 Visser-Fuchs, 'Richard III', p. 15.
48 Ibid., p. 21.

the Great is assassinated. Once recognised, they point out the reasons that Richard should listen to the Scots' requests and accept the benefits of peace, as much for his own benefit (and that of his realm) as for James and his. The argument in the middle of the speech, where Augustus' settlement of the Roman Empire and embrace of peace enabled the birth of the Saviour, also holds out the promise of other positive outcomes for any peace brokered between the Scots and the English. Overall, it is not a deferential speech, but one that asserts the importance of the voice and the perspective of the Scots. While its Classical comparisons may be flattering, they also allude to potential threats to Richard's power and his success as a king of England, without being embarrassingly direct. A similar message is conveyed by the speech attributed to Elphinstone, which also asserts the need for a rival king to pay attention to the Scots, and to what they bring to the table.

The function of Elphinstone's speech in the *Vitae* is to demonstrate Elphinstone's mastery of diplomatic and humanist rhetoric, equal to that of the best rhetoricians in Louis XI's court; its precise diplomatic function is less significant to Boece's narrative. Nevertheless, it shares many of the qualities and features of Whitelaw's speech and, assuming Macfarlane is correct, is probably representative of the version delivered.[49] It is slightly shorter, about 1200 words in Boece's text, suggesting a delivery time of about 15 minutes, possibly slightly longer, compared to Whitelaw's half an hour. And whereas Whitelaw's speech takes peace as its theme, Elphinstone focuses on friendship: taken together and noting the length of both speeches, these broad topics suggest that both would have had a similar purpose, as an introductory gift before any hard and practical bargaining took place. Elphinstone's speech fits an embassy drawing on a history of alliances. Friendship is here presented in moral terms, as a duty of mutual support as well as benefit, and again the structure of the speech is designed to elaborate on the theme, rather than to offer specific negotiating points. Indeed, the speech ends with the statement *caetera nostri principis postulata his ex ... viris et oratoribus quibus secretiora credidit consilia ... accipies* ('You will hear the other requests from our prince from the men and orators to whom he has entrusted his more confidential plans').[50] While, on the one hand, this has the inadvertent effect of implying that Elphinstone is only there for decoration and is not a central figure of the embassy, on the other, it also underlines the value attributed to exceptional rhetoric and its function as a gift.

To develop his theme, Elphinstone also uses appropriate Classical quotations, although not as many as Whitelaw. He has two main authorities: Cicero's *De Amicitia* and Aristotle's *Nicomachean Ethics*, both of which are deployed at the very beginning of the speech. Since there is no evidence that Elphinstone or indeed Boece read Greek, it seems probable that they knew

[49] Macfarlane, *Elphinstone*, p. 123; James Moir, the New Spalding Club editor and translator, expresses more scepticism in his notes: *Vitae*, pp. 151–52, notes to p. 67, l. 4 and p. 68, l. 1.

[50] Boece, *Vitae*, p. 74.

Aristotle's work through the Latin translations of the medieval university curriculum.[51] From the evidence of surviving manuscripts and its early *editio princeps* (Cologne, c. 1467), *De amicitia* was well-known in the fifteenth century, often circulating with *De Senectute*.[52] Both texts deal with the benefits of friendship primarily on a personal level, but given that this speech imagines an alliance and friendship between kings, albeit as representatives of their people, there is a thread of the political too. In conjunction with Aristotle, Cicero is presented as a philosopher, one expounding friendship as a divine gift.[53] The context from which the quotation is drawn is one discussing obligation, as opposed to being free from care, and the need to offer service. This is an appropriate message for an embassy where reciprocity in support from the host to the visiting party has been seen to be failing, a message probably not lost on the speech's audience, even if Cicero is primarily discussing personal rather than political friendship. The quotation from Aristotle is more substantive and equally pointed, also discussing friendship as a reciprocal relationship, where only friends can be relied upon to relieve catastrophe. In particular it notes that the powerful are in most need of friends: *nam et locupletes et in principatu potestateque constituti plurimum amicis indigere videntur* ('for those that are rich and those that are placed in a position of authority and power seem most of all to require friends').[54] As with *De amicitia*, this quotation's context emphasises the duties of friendship, even for the rich and powerful. At one and the same time these quotations both acknowledge the Scots' relative poverty compared to the French and assert an entitlement to respect, fair treatment and recognition of centuries of alliance and friendship.

There are also phrases that may be borrowed from Classical historians. One, *amicitia ea est concordia, qua stante, parvae res crescent, qua amota, res magnae dilabuntur* ('friendship is that harmony by whose existence small affairs grow to greatness, by whose removal great affairs gradually suffer decay') looks to be a direct evocation of Sallust's *The War with Jugurtha*, *Nam concordia parvae res crescunt, discordia maxumae dilabuntur* ('For harmony makes small states great, while the mightiest are undone by discord').[55] Another, *socium et amicum*

51 Macfarlane, *Elphinstone*, pp. 366–72.

52 See J.G.F. Powell, 'Cicero, Philosophical Works: *Cato Maior de senectute* and *Laelius de amicitia*', in Leighton D. Reynolds (ed.), *Texts and Transmission: A Survey of the Latin Classics* (Oxford, 1983), pp. 116–24.

53 Cicero, *Laelius de amicitia*, in Cicero, *On Old Age. On Friendship. On Divination*, trans. W.A. Falconer, Loeb Classical Library 154 (Cambridge, MA, 1923), pp. 103–212, esp. 13.47, pp. 158–59: *O praeclaram sapientiam! Solem enim e mundo tollere videntur ei, qui amicitiam e vita tollunt, qua nihil a dis immortalibus melius habemus, nihil iucundius*. Boece, *Vitae*, p. 68. Boece's quotation is very close, with only one change in word order, the omission of *ei*, and *de* instead of *e*.

54 Aristotle, *Nicomachean Ethics*, trans. H. Rackham, Loeb Classical Library 73 (Cambridge, MA, 1926), book 8.1–2, pp. 450–51. It is not possible to identify which Latin translation of Aristotle is likely to have been to hand, but Boece's version is in close keeping to the Loeb translation.

55 Sallust, *The War with Jugurtha*, 10.6, in Sallust, *The War with Catiline. The War with*

('allied and friendly people') can be found in this form and in variations in Livy and in Cicero, suggesting that it is less likely to be a direct quotation and more part of a lexical set in Classical writing. Both cases thus demonstrate an underpinning of humanist rhetoric with authentically Classical phrasing.

This is further underlined by the deployment of a range of rhetorical devices. After the requisite flattery of Louis XI, without any potential ambivalence, it begins with a list of the key qualities of friendship and common interest:

> Haec [amicitia] regum delectabile vinculum, haec stabilimentum regnorum, haec pacis et tranquillitatis mater, justitiae cultrix, misericordiae clementiaeque parens; sine quibus nec reges regnant, nec stabiliuntur imperia, nec civitates consistunt, nullus demum publicus aut privatus sibi patriaeve aut vivere aut prodesse potest, quod nullum bonum sit in vita quod amicitia non sit, aut amicitiae conjunctum.

> Friendship is the pleasing bond that unites kings. Friendship is the stay of kingdoms, the mother of peace and tranquillity, the patron of justice, the parent of pity and mercy. Without these fruits of friendship kings cannot reign, nor government be established. Communities cannot exist, nor can anyone in a public or a private capacity live for or benefit his country; for there is no good thing in life apart from friendship, or which is not connected in some degree with friendship.[56]

There is patterned asyndeton (*haec* … *haec* … *haec*), beginning with the oxymoron *delectabile vinculum*. The third clause has three personifications, two of which are female (*mater*, *cultrix*), and which, together with the third (*parens*), evoke three of the Four Daughters of God (peace, justice, mercy).[57] Only truth is missing, perhaps to be understood as encoded in the speech as a whole. Despite the discussion of more private friendship in *De amicitia*, here Elphinstone is clear about its political significance, not least its role in ensuring stable rule (*nullus* … *potest*). Such concerns are general features of advice to princes: there seems to be nothing deliberately pointed here, perhaps because the Scots were looking for support, and were less sure of success. Nevertheless, there is a careful mix of pragmatism – alliances assist in maintaining power, not least because there are fewer places for would-be insurgents to hide – and aspirations towards good kingship, measured by justice, mercy and peace. The rhetorical patterning makes it hard to resist the drive of the argument, and the

Jugurtha, ed. John T. Ramsey, trans. J.C. Rolfe, Loeb Classical Library 116 (Cambridge, MA, 2013), pp. 184–85.

[56] Boece, *Vitae*, p. 68.

[57] See Sally Mapstone, 'A Mirror for a Divine Prince: John Ireland and the Four Daughters of God', in J. Derrick McClure and Michael R.G. Spiller (eds), *Bryght Lanternis: Essays on the Language and Literature of Medieval and Renaissance Scotland* (Aberdeen, 1989), pp. 308–23. Ireland was also a member of James III's court. The interaction between Latin and vernacular literature is often ignored, but both audiences and writers overlap.

assessment of the value of friendship in general, before Elphinstone moves on to the benefit of friendship with the Scots in particular.

In addition to the political arguments, Elphinstone goes on to draw from natural law, and from incidences of friendship from the animal kingdom.

> Videmus et animantium quibusdam absque rationis usu, his praesertim quibus mansuetum miteque ingenium, equis, bobus, ovibus, reliquis quoque simili praeditis natura, suo more amicitiam inesse: aliis feroci, crudeli, immansuetoque ingenio natura procreatis, quae in suum et in alienum genus saeviunt, perpetuam contentionem. Haec tametsi ob ineptiam ad humanum usum, raro mactata, aeris autem inclementia absumpta nunquam, exiguo tamen semper et pene eodem persistere numero: illa vero, quotidie et humana gula populata et saevientius feris, coeli quoque injuriae semper obnoxia, abundare, in majoremque indies excrescere numerum. Indicium profecto amicitiam ad rerum omnium incrementa in vita summe necessariam.

> We see, too, friendship of its own kind existing even in certain animals devoid of reason, especially those possessed of a tame and gentle spirit, such as horses, cattle, sheep and other creatures of like nature. On the other hand, we see that creatures born with a ferocious, cruel and untamed nature, which wreak their fury on their own and other species, live in continual warfare. Yet these latter, though from being of no use to man, they are rarely slain, and though they are never swept away by the inclemency of the weather, yet continue to exist only in the same limited numbers; whereas the former, though daily sacrificed to the human appetite, preyed on by wild beasts, and ever exposed to the extremities of climate, abound in ever-increasing numbers. Here, surely, is a proof that friendship is in an eminent degree necessary for the advancement of all living creatures.[58]

The argument suggests that placid prey animals enjoy friendship in herds and flocks because they survive and flourish when living in large numbers, whereas savage predators are far rarer. At first sight, the association of friendship with sheep does not seem an obvious winner: sheep and other domesticated animals are vulnerable, often powerless, and subject to ill treatment and injustice.[59] Their only benefit from friendship is survival, but survival as a group rather than as individuals. Sheep particularly, however, are biblically innocent, closer to God, and their survival in greater numbers bodes well for their owners (implied in *ad humanum usum*). The complex metaphor here seems to work best allegorically, where the English, savage, predatory and perhaps without friends, are threatening to both the Scots and

[58] Boece, *Vitae*, p. 69.

[59] See for instance, the representation of sheep in the roughly contemporary *Moral Fabillis* of Robert Henryson, where being part of a flock is certainly not a guarantee of safety: Denton Fox (ed.), *The Poems of Robert Henryson* (Oxford, 1981), especially 'The Sheep and the Dog', 'The Wolf and the Wether' and 'The Wolf and the Lamb'.

the French. Their threat can be mitigated, and this would result in a mutual growth and natural flourishing through friendship between Louis and James.

Such a reading is supported by the development of the speech, where friendship becomes an active support for shared interests:

> Cognosce idcirco, Lodovice, rex optime, quo animo Scoti in te tuamque hanc gentem semper fuere, qui, spretis Anglorum armis, marisque periculis posthabitis, huc ad tuum hoc regnum accessere; cum inimica gente conseruere manus in exitium usque, ut socium et amicum populum periculo (cui proximus erat) omni atque hostili metu liberarent. Adeo sacra foederis jura semper coluere. Verum sancitum foedus, tot regibus per tot secula excultum et conservatum, uti inclytus princeps noster accepit, nixi sunt impuri quidam (quantum per eos fieri potuit) violare, sinistra partim insinuatione, partim commentis fictis, frivolis quoque occasionibus adinventis, unde inter socios et amicos adeo populos dissidio pararent damnum utrisque perpetuum atque perniciosum, communibus vero hostibus commodum et delectamentum.
>
> Recognise, then, Louis, most excellent prince, what the feelings of the Scots have ever been towards you and your people, seeing that, disregarding the English arms and perils of the deep, they have come to this realm of yours. They have fought even to death with their ancient enemies, in order to deliver from all danger (to which they were very nigh) and from fear of their enemies, ancient allies and friends. So sacred has been their observance of the treaties between them. This sacred league, cherished and maintained by so many kings for so many ages, certain vile men, as our illustrious prince has heard, have endeavoured so far as in them lay, to destroy partly by wicked insinuations, partly by fabricated falsehoods, and partly even by devising wretched excuses for breaking the treaty. Their object has been, by creating a quarrel between close allies and friends, to bring perpetual and fatal disaster on both nations, and advantage and delight to their common enemies.[60]

By this point in the speech, the relationship between the Scots and the French has been characterised as one where the Scots pay their dues but the French do not reciprocate. The dangers of such negligence have been implied in the choice of quotations at the very beginning – if not in the quotations themselves, then certainly in their contexts. Although the approach here is quite direct in contrasting Scots and French behaviour, what Moir suggests would be too forthright for an embassy to Louis, at the very end it swerves away from direct accusation of the king to the *impuri*, 'the vile men', who are seeking to disrupt this alliance.[61] It is not clear who these men are or what benefit would fall to them from a breakdown in the Franco-Scottish alliance,

[60] Boece, *Vitae*, pp. 71–72.

[61] Moir, notes to Boece, *Vitae*, p. 152, n. to p. 68, line 1.

but such a device is face-saving: like evil counsellors in many types of political literature, they deflect responsibility from the sovereign to disposable others. It also aligns the speaker with truth, as he opposes three kinds of liars (a proper *tricolon*), with evidence of the Scots' faithful adherence to their promises. Whether this represents what actually happened is of course irrelevant: what matters is the careful positioning of the speaker and those he represents.

The peroration is a series of instructions based on ensuring reciprocity between the Scots and the French. The kings are presented as equivalent: for Louis's ability to heal scrofula, and for *liliis caelesti munere insigni* ('lilies, the gift of heaven') on his arms, James is able to offer a realm at peace, with Highland insurrections suppressed in his youth.[62] As a result, therefore, the French are honour-bound to reciprocate Scottish support and loyalty. At the very end, the speech alludes to the quotations at the beginning, promising that a proper display of friendship will grant the French realm prosperity, and maintain the realm from external assault. The quotations therefore become more than additional decoration. Rather, they are an integral structural device, which prevent any challenge to those base assumptions. For who could go against the views of Aristotle and Cicero?

While the tone may have shocked Moir, this speech is still designed to flatter Louis as something of a scholar, as an honourable king with a concern for keeping his word and keeping his treaties, and as a pragmatist, able to recognise the benefits of maintaining a friendly alliance with the Scots in the teeth of English aggression. Its transmission through the *Vitae* may have enhanced its performative aspects, as Moir suspects, and made Elphinstone a sharper speaker than might originally have been the case. It may also have embedded more deeply some aspects of humanist style, such as the use of such a regular idiom as *socius et amicus*. The structure, however, arising from self-evident truths expressed by the authoritative Aristotle and Cicero, suggests an early engagement with humanist rhetoric.

At the beginning of this chapter, I noted the different methods and contexts of transmission of these speeches. It is hard to determine precisely the effects that they have on the texts that survive for us, since the variables include the Latin competency of the embassy scribe compared to that of Boece's secretaries and Ascensius' type setters, whether or not we believe Macfarlane's view of Boece's mediation, and indeed what role speeches such as these played in diplomacy. It is certainly true that Elphinstone's speech demonstrates a smoother humanist idiom, in terms of phrasing and syntax, and its style is certainly not markedly different from the rest of Boece's narrative. But then, deliberate stylistic anachronism is not a feature of Boece's historiographical writing at any point. Despite such difficulties, however, there are points of comparison, suggesting that, at the very least, Whitelaw

62 Boece, *Vitae*, p. 73. Macdougall, *James III* (1982), pp. 89–90, offers a much less dramatic account of James III's tours of the north and west.

and Elphinstone (in whatever form his speech was available to Boece) shared an understanding of some humanist tendencies.

The most obvious of these is the benefit of using Classical quotation to flatter and also to allude to less comfortable truths. Whitelaw's weighting towards narrative and epic, against Elphinstone's philosophy, may well reflect the interests of the king he was addressing; his allusions are certainly much more pointed in their application. The choice of Aristotle in particular in Elphinstone might locate the origins of the speech Boece records in the fifteenth century, before fluency in Greek is clearly evident in Scottish practice, but when Aristotle was well known in university curricula. Elphinstone's quotations provide the structural foundation for the speech, whereas Whitelaw's gives his a warning edge, almost needling. In both cases, however, the main quotations are carefully chosen. In Whitelaw's case, the sheer number of references and allusions seems designed to signal a broad Classical reading; in the case of Elphinstone, the apposite quotation is matched by the Classically idiomatic language, so there is less need for direct and marked quotation. For both speakers, the quotations implicitly reflect the education and cultural experience of the audience they were addressing.

Both speeches deploy humanist rhetoric patterns, familiar from the works of Cicero – repetitions, *tricola*, contrast – to the point where it is difficult to resist the direction of the argument. Both take a fairly self-evident general position – peace is good, friendship is good, both need attention – and work it towards specific advice for the purpose of the embassy. The base assertions, rooted in Classical authority, are what allow for the hectoring of both Richard and Louis, with the kind of direct instruction that might seem odd for a negotiating embassy. Their tones, however, also portray a self-confidence in the Scottish position (whether or not that was reflected in the actual political circumstances). The adoption of humanist style and practices allowed Whitelaw and Elphinstone access to intellectual authority, displaying the renewed knowledge of authoritative old texts, and an ability to present their concerns, or rather their monarch's, with all the gravitas of Cicero. Both speeches are performances of authority rather than power, but they nonetheless assert a Scottish intention to be heard and to be recognised in the political decisions of the realm's nearest neighbours.

# 6

# 'O wretched king!': Ireland, Denmark–Norway, and Kingship in the Reign of James V[1]

Alison Cathcart

It was in a chapter published in 1999 that Roger Mason outlined, with characteristic lucidity and cogency, the iconography utilised in the reigns of James III, James IV, and James V as a means of conveying the concept of imperial monarchy.[2] In producing such visual propaganda these Scottish monarchs projected an idea of themselves as rulers – emperors within their own kingdoms – who possessed full jurisdictional authority over their realm. No doubt James V was influenced by events of the 1530s in England where Henry VIII – even if he did not become a Protestant – did go so far as to break with Rome on the grounds that England was an empire and he himself an emperor.[3] Even before his personal rule began, however, in November 1526, the Scottish parliament had claimed such jurisdiction on James' behalf, asserting that he 'and his maist noble progenitouris has evire bene fre and emperouris within thame self, nocht subject to na erdlie creature undir God in thar temporalite'.[4] It was Mason's contention that James V was equally

1 Earlier versions of this chapter were presented to the Scottish History seminar series, University of St Andrews (November 2020), Research Institute of Irish Scottish Studies / Centre for Early Modern Studies seminar series (February 2021), and Institute of Northern Studies seminar series (November 2022). I am grateful to all who attended and asked questions or made comments. In addition, I would like to express my thanks to both Amy Blakeway and Aonghas MacCoinnich who read drafts of this chapter and made helpful comments on it; my thanks also to Robert Frost for discussing ideas of elective and hereditary kingship with me on a number of occasions.

2 In relation to James V such views have been further developed and reinforced by Andrea Thomas, *Princelie Majestie: The Court of James V of Scotland, 1528–1542* (Edinburgh, 2005).

3 The preamble to the Act in Restraint of Appeals to Rome (1533) stated that 'this realm of England is an empire, and so hath been accepted in the world, governed by one supreme head and king having the dignity and royal estate of the imperial crown of the same'. For these developments in England, see J. Guy, 'Thomas Cromwell and the Intellectual Origins of the Henrician Reformation', in A. Fox and J.A. Guy (eds), *Reassessing the Henrician Age: Humanism, Politics and Reform, 1500–1550* (Oxford, 1986), pp. 151–78.

4 *RPS*, 1526/11/53. I am grateful to Dr Amy Blakeway for drawing this to my attention

conscious of his imperial status, and that, if he did not need or want to challenge the pope's supremacy over the church, he did set about enforcing the crown's supremacy over temporal lords and lordships within his kingdom. A symbol of this assertion of his *imperium*, argued Mason, was his 'virtual circumnavigation of the kingdom' as the king led 'a heavily armed, seaborne expedition' to Orkney and the Western Isles in 1540.[5] This expedition resulted in a number of interventions in the peripheries beyond the usual warding of Hebridean chiefs and included: the 1540 Act of Annexation which saw the North and South Isles, Kintyre, and Orkney and Shetland now firmly in crown hands;[6] the commencement of a survey of these newly acquired crown lands in the west and a subsequent significant increase in returns to the crown;[7] the granting of a new tack of crown lands in Orkney and Shetland to Oliver Sinclair (who was said to be a favourite of the king at that time) which also saw significantly increased rentals;[8] and James' nomination of Robert Reid, abbot of Kinloss, as successor to Robert Maxwell as bishop of Orkney.[9] Taken together this all chimes well with Mason's view that the 1540 expedition aimed at 'ensuring the submission of the outlying regions of his realm'.[10]

Mason also argued that the closed imperial crown, so evident during the later years of James V's reign, and especially so after his sojourn in France over

and for so generously sharing her detailed knowledge of James V with me.

5 Roger A. Mason, 'This Realm of Scotland Is an Empire? Imperial Ideas and Iconography in Early Renaissance Scotland', in B.E. Crawford (ed.), *Church, Chronicle and Learning in Medieval and Early Renaissance Scotland* (Edinburgh, 1999), pp. 73–91, at pp. 80–81; Roger A. Mason, 'Renaissance Monarchy? Stewart Kingship (1469–1542)', in Brown and Tanner (eds), *Scottish Kingship*, pp. 255–78, at pp. 272–73.

6 *RPS*, 1540/12/26. The Act of Annexation extended to the 'landis and lordschipis of all his [the king's] Ilis, south and north; the tua Kintyris' and 'the landis and lordschip of Orkney and Yetland and the ilis pertening thereto and thare pertinentis'. For the significance of the 1540 parliament and the rest of the lands that came into crown hands at this time, see Jamie Cameron, *James V: The Personal Rule 1528–1542* (Edinburgh, 1998), pp. 213–14, 271–72.

7 *ER*, xvii, pp. 611–50.

8 In April 1541 Oliver Sinclair was granted commission as sheriff along with the tack of the crown rights in Orkney and Shetland (formerly leased by Lady Sinclair), in short, making Oliver and his male heirs 'justices, shereffis, admirallis, and baillies of all and sindry the forsaidis landis and lordschippis, baith by sey and land' with all associated rights and pertinents for three years (later extended to five), for the payment of 3000 merks yearly. This was a significant increase on previous rental payments, which at best had been slightly under £400. See J. Storer Clouston (ed.), *Records of the Earldom of Orkney 1299–1614* (Edinburgh, 1914), no. xxvii (pp. 61–63). Peter Anderson, *The Stewart Earls of Orkney* (Edinburgh, 2012), p. 10, suggests Oliver Sinclair was a favourite of the king at court. See also nn. 45 and 79 below.

9 D. Hay and R.K. Hannay (eds), *Letters of James V* (Edinburgh, 1954), p. 423. James highlighted to the pope that Reid was well known, had performed good service, and thus was the ideal fit to ensure both religious development and 'the improvement of manners'.

10 Mason, 'This Realm of Scotland Is an Empire?', p. 81.

the winter of 1536–37, also symbolised 'freedom from external jurisdiction'.[11] Beyond a reference to English claims to lordship over Scotland, however, Mason left this 'external jurisdiction' largely unexplored. Similarly, the possibility that James V, like his grandson James VI and I, might have laid claim to an empire in the more familiar sense of an 'aggregation of dominions' was given no consideration.[12] In this context, it is surely significant that in 1540 James was offered the kingship of Ireland.[13] Indeed, the 1540 voyage of circumnavigation, when looked at in more depth, reveals a king juggling these ideas of empire along with a much more complex set of diplomatic concerns and opportunities than is commonly allowed. This chapter, therefore, seeks to explore other factors that prompted James to embark on the 1540 expedition, during which he sought to exercise his authority, both on land and sea, and to both his own subjects and external observers. In doing so it will move beyond the all-too-familiar stomping ground of Scotland's relations with England and France, to the neighbouring realms of Ireland and Denmark–Norway, while also suggesting that however tempted James may have been to expand his empire, by interfering in a kingdom under another monarch's jurisdiction, he neither wanted to set a precedent nor to tempt fate.[14]

## Denmark–Norway, the Lübeckers, and the Nature of Kingship

The betrothal and marriage of James III to Margaret, daughter of Christian I of Denmark–Norway, over 1468–69 saw the cancelling of the debt of taxation that Scotland owed Denmark for the Hebrides and the Isle of Man, but also saw the islands of Orkney and Shetland mortgaged to the Scottish crown.[15] It is generally regarded as the decisive incorporation of the Northern

[11] Ibid., p. 83.

[12] Brian P. Levack, *The Formation of the British State. England, Scotland and the Union 1603–1707* (Oxford, 1987), p. 2.

[13] For the offer of the kingship to Ireland within its wider context see Alison Cathcart, 'James V, King of Scotland – and Ireland?', in Seán Duffy (ed.), *The World of the Galloglass. Kings, Warlords and Warriors in Ireland and Scotland, 1200–1600* (Dublin, 2007), pp. 124–43.

[14] Although the main focus was relations with France, a study that discussed Scottish affairs in relation to events both in Ireland and Denmark–Norway can be found in Norman Macdougall, '"The greattest scheip that ewer saillit in Ingland or France": James IV's "Great Michael"', in Norman Macdougall (ed.), *Scotland and War AD 79–1918* (Edinburgh, 1991), pp. 36–60.

[15] *RPS*, 1472/14. In 1489 Henry, Lord Sinclair, received a tack of the lands and lordships of Orkney and Shetland for 13 years along with the office of justiciary and bailliary of the said lands; see *RMS*, ii, nos. 1842, 1844. James III further asserted his rights over Orkney in 1470, by requiring William, 1st Earl of Caithness, to resign his earldom of Orkney, then held from the Norwegian crown, in exchange for Ravenscraig Castle, before annexing and uniting Orkney and Shetland to the crown in 1472 'not to be given away in the future to any person or persons except to one of the king's legitimate sons only'.

Isles into the Scottish kingdom, but that was very far from the case.[16] The crown of Denmark–Norway was both elective and hereditary – following their election all monarchs had to agree to certain conditions before their coronation – and monarchs were bound by the conditions of their election charters and ruled alongside a council. The Norwegian council of the realm was far from happy that the islands had been pledged to Scotland and believed Christian I of Denmark–Norway had no such right to do so. Indeed, one of the conditions of his election was that he would not

> pledge or alienate the kingdom's castles, fiefs or rents unless there be a demand and necessity, and only according to the advice of Norway's council of the realm ....[17]

The council of the realm clearly understood the islands to have been in, and therefore should return to, Norwegian hands. Nonetheless, in both documents concerning the mortgaging of Orkney and Shetland, Christian I asserted his right to redeem the islands 'until the whole and full payment' was made by his 'heirs and successors, kings of Norway, to the foresaid James ... his heirs and successors'.[18] Little more than a decade later, in 1482, the Norwegian council began demanding that Orkney and Shetland should be redeemed, and at his coronation in 1483, King Hans swore an oath that he would take steps to do so.[19] In fact, the election charters of Hans (1493), Christian II (1513), Frederick I (1523), and Christian III (1534) all included the obligation to 'reclaim Orkney and Shetland for the crown'; such a clause continued to appear in election charters until the later seventeenth century.

Alongside the issue of Orkney and Shetland, the 1469 marriage treaty had also included a mutual defence alliance between Christian I and James III which compelled both the Oldenburg and Stewart houses to provide 'mutual friendship and the maintenance of the new alliance, help, aid and assistance, each in his turn, at the request of the other, against whatsoever prince or princes, nation or people ... and by the tenor of the presents assuredly to

[16] Ian Peter Grohse, 'The Lost Cause. Kings, the Council, and the Question of Orkney and Shetland, 1468–1536', *Scandinavian Journal of History* 43.3 (2020), 286–308.

[17] Ibid., pp. 290–91. Although often styled king of Denmark, Christian was also king of Norway, and his pledging of the isles was 'an affront to Norway'. A treaty concluded in Bergen in 1450 saw Norway and Denmark united; see Steinar Imsen, 'The Union of Calmar – Nordic Great Power or Northern German Outpost?', in Christopher Ocker, Michael Printy, Peter Starenko, and Peter Wallace (eds), *Politics and Reformations: Communities, Polities, Nations, and Empires: Essays in Honor of Thomas A. Brady Jr.* (Leiden, 2007), pp. 471–89, at p. 473.

[18] Grohse, 'The Lost Cause', p. 287.

[19] Ibid., pp. 291–92. In 1485 James III wrote to Hans that it was hoped Hans 'would not wish to take back or interfere with what was given to his sister, mother of three children, against law and good faith'; see Shetland Archives, D1/147. The original document can be found at Edinburgh University Library, Laing MSS, La. III.322, ff. 16–17. I am deeply indebted to John Ballantyne for sharing with me a great deal of information on Orkney and Shetland, including this reference.

maintain them, pledging hereto ourselves and our heirs and successors'.[20] The alliance was renewed on a number of occasions by Hans of Denmark–Norway and James IV, but the obligations of this treaty came into play more fully during the minority and personal rule of James V.[21] In seeking support from Christian II in 1514, John Stewart, duke of Albany, and regent during James' minority, offered to return the islands in exchange for 6000 armed men.[22] In February 1523–24 Albany again was requesting aid, this time from Frederick I, in response to English hostility; Albany made it clear that if money was provided, repayment would be 'secured on Orkney and Shetland'.[23] Although nothing ever came of these negotiations, it was less to do with any Norwegian lack of desire to redeem Orkney and Shetland, and more to do with the internal situation in Denmark–Norway, that prevented such a course of action.

From 1523 through to 1536 Denmark–Norway was experiencing significant political turmoil, which explains why Frederick I was in no position to take up Albany's offer. On his death in 1513 King Hans was succeeded by his son, Christian II, but Christian's reign was far from successful – especially in Sweden where he tried, forcibly, to revive the Kalmar Union.[24] In 1522 Sweden left the Kalmar Union and the following year Christian II was deposed when a gathering of the Danish parliament offered the Danish crown to his uncle, the duke of Holstein – who then became Frederick I – and Christian fled into exile.[25] He was later captured and imprisoned by his uncle in the castles of Sønderborg and Kalundborg where he would remain until his death in 1559. Christian's existence, however, whether in exile or in prison, meant that Frederick faced ongoing opposition and, from the time of his accession in 1523, Denmark–Norway faced nothing short of civil war for the next 13 years.[26] This internal unrest was exacerbated by the wider

[20] Gordon Donaldson (ed.), *Scottish Historical Documents* (Glasgow, 1974), pp. 86–87, at p. 87; allies before the date of the treaty were to be excepted.

[21] On Hans and James IV, see R.L. Mackie (ed.), *The Letters of James the Fourth 1505–1513* (Edinburgh, 1953), nos. 286, 453, 455.

[22] Grohse, 'The Lost Cause', p. 295. Following this 'Christian II addressed "all good men who toil and reside in Orkney" explaining that "we will as soon as possible redeem you to Norway's crown, to remain under us and Norway's king as it should rightfully be"' (Ibid., p. 295). This explains Albany's letter of 16 June 1515 in which he states 'the Orkney islands … according to Christian's letters, are to be deemed in the very near future'; see Hay and Hannay (eds), *Letters of James V*, pp. 24–25.

[23] Hay and Hannay (eds), *Letters of James V*, p. 98.

[24] The Kalmar Union was the union of the monarchies of Norway, Sweden, and Denmark, and lasted from 1397 to 1523, albeit not without a few interruptions; see Imsen, 'The Union of Calmar'.

[25] Frederick was the younger brother of Hans, son of Christian I, and elected co-duke of Schleswig and Holstein in 1482. For more on Christian II's reign see Paul Douglas Lockhart, *Denmark, 1513–1660: The Rise and Decline of a Renaissance Monarchy* (Oxford, 2007), pp. 11–28; Michael Roberts, *The Early Vasas. A History of Sweden, 1523–1611* (Cambridge, 1968), pp. 1–24.

[26] Lockhart, *Denmark, 1513–1660*, pp. 11–28, but the introduction also provides a useful and concise overview.

Reformation context and the issue of succession, an issue which came to the fore when Frederick died in 1533. The council postponed an election, ruling during the interregnum of the next year itself, before offering the crown to the Lutheran Christian, duke of Holstein, son of the deceased Frederick, although this decision was far from unanimous.[27] Remaining supporters of Christian II had allied with the Lübeckers and together were opposing the new king, Christian III.[28] After Christian III had been proclaimed king of Demark, ambassadors from Lübeck and Hamburg arrived at the English court in late June 1534. The Lübeckers had long-standing grievances against Denmark–Norway – during the previous decades they had lost a number of traditional trading privileges –but they sought to exploit both the situation there and the wider Reformation context to achieve their own ends by opening negotiations with Henry VIII and casting him as their ally.[29]

They praised Henry for his break with Rome and began discussions concerning doctrinal issues including 'the question of the Sacrament'.[30] While they may have exploited wider confessional issues to gain access to Henry VIII, it is clear the agenda of the Lübeckers was political. Although their overarching aim was the restoration of trading and other privileges they had previously enjoyed, they sought to 'elect a king of Denmark' who would be 'wholly at their devotion' and offered Henry the 'quiet possession of Denmark'.[31] Henry was

[27] Count Christopher of Oldenburg, second cousin of both Christian II and Christian III, and descended from a brother of Christian I, was proclaimed regent in various provinces at the same time, ensuring opposition to Christian III's rule from the outset. While Frederick had been Catholic, Christian was openly Lutheran and the opposing sides in a two-year war from 1534–36, known as the Count's Feud, was largely, but not exclusively, drawn along religious lines; see Lockhart, *Denmark, 1513–1660*, pp. 24–28.

[28] From the mid-fourteenth century Danish kings had come head-to-head with the economic strength of the Hanse; by the early sixteenth century west European merchants were challenging the commercial dominance of the Hanse. While some Hanse towns benefitted from trade with the Dutch and the English, others sided with Lübeck in their efforts to maintain commercial dominance and its monopoly on trade between east and west. Previous kings of Denmark had sought to undermine Hanse dominance in order to secure Denmark's position as the leading maritime power; both Christian I and Hans of Denmark had forbidden Sweden to trade with Lübeck. Thus, when Christian II, as part of his efforts to revive the Kalmar Union, imposed an embargo on trade between Sweden and the Lübeckers, it was met with significant hostility. By this stage, enemies of Denmark would become allies of Lübeck. For a more detailed discussion of the relationship between Denmark, Sweden, and Lübeck, see Roberts, *The Early Vasas*, pp. 12–14, 19–24; Lockhart, *Denmark, 1513–1660*, p. 18.

[29] Lockhart, *Denmark, 1513–1660*, pp. 17–18; Roberts, *The Early Vasas*, pp. 19–20, 21–24, 33–35, 91–101. Indeed, as early as 1509 King Hans of Denmark–Norway had been writing to James IV regarding the Lübeckers; see Mackie (ed.), *Letters of James the Fourth*, no. 283.

[30] *L&P Henry VIII*, VII, no. 1141, dated 10 September 1534.

[31] Ibid., VII, nos. 957–58. Ibid., VIII, nos. 1159, 1163; Hay and Hannay (eds), *Letters of James V*, p. 290 note. In Germany the Lübeckers published terms of a treaty agreed with Henry, although this was later claimed to be a forgery. It was reported that Henry gave them 20,000 gold pieces in return. Roberts, *The Early Vasas*, p. 100, does mention the overtures of the Lübeckers to Henry VIII but simply states they approached him 'for aid';

intrigued and engaged them in negotiations over the winter of 1534–35.[32] But between February and June 1535, Peter Severinus, secretary to Christian III, was in England negotiating for a peace treaty between the English, Denmark, and the Lübeckers.[33] As Severinus was acting on behalf of Christian III, the crown of Denmark was not on offer but, it was argued, if Henry paid the sum required to redeem Orkney and Shetland, 'the islands would … be handed over … on the same conditions', adding that 'Iceland … perhaps' could be 'pledged' to Henry also. At this point in the discussions Henry appears to have stalled: while he 'extolled' Christian III, he was concerned about going back on his 'promises'. In reality, it is likely that Henry began to be become concerned about what he was getting into, thinking, as he argued to Severinus, that Christian II 'had the greatest right to recover Denmark'. Severinus disagreed and sought to emphasise the real agenda of the Lübeckers; at the same time he explained that the council of Denmark 'had not driven' Christian II 'from the kingdom without the best reasons' because:

> Danish kings were created with certain conditions; if they did not keep what they swore to, the people were free to revolt from them; nor did they do fealty to their King except on these conditions.[34]

Henry had not fully appreciated the hereditary and elective nature of the kings of Denmark–Norway. When he did, and when the reality of what that offer of kingship entailed, and the fact it was conditional, dawned on him, his response was: 'O wretched king!' Henry uttered these words in relation to Christian II, and following this conversation, Henry appears to have lost interest and began actively to work towards peace, offering friendship to 'the duke of Holstein' (and thus not recognising 'the duke' as Christian III).

In response to requests from Christian III and Peter Severinus James said he would duly advise his uncle to 'divert his mind from Danish ambitions … and cease to favour the men of Lübeck against Christian'.[35] This he did, but in truth

---

in return Henry 'offered ships'.

32 *L&P Henry VIII*, VII, no. 955; VIII, no. 1159.

33 Ibid., VIII, no. 1160 (pp. 456–57). Severinus' proposals for peace included agreement that Christian III 'should be allowed to hold Denmark and Norway' in the same way as previous kings had 'without any derogation from the rights of the King or the councillors' while also obtaining for the Lübeckers 'the enjoyment of their ancient privileges in Denmark and Norway'. Christian also needed assistance in the form of money, men, and ships, emphasising that Henry ought to be supporting the son of 'his deceased friend' (Frederick I). Severinus suggested that in return Henry might be granted privileges in Denmark, such as the use of the island of Barnholm, which Frederick previously had granted to the Lübeckers. But Severinus went further; while the Lübeckers might have offered Denmark, Christian III could supply Henry with 'at least' 8000 German infantry when matters were 'settled'.

34 *L&P Henry VIII*, VIII, no. 1178 (p. 466).

35 Hay and Hannay (eds), *Letters of James V*, p. 291. Indeed Severinus requested that James 'dissuade Henry from assisting Lübeck' on the grounds that neither James nor Christian, 'would … wish to see an Englishman king of Denmark'; see Ibid., VIII, no. 1159.

James' behaviour was no better than that of his uncle. For sure, James would not want to see Henry redeem Orkney and Shetland and, while in confessional terms James would be more likely to support the Catholic Christian II, he was not prepared to back the losing side.[36] Thus he offered little more than platitudes and empty gestures to both men. No doubt James would have been concerned by the suggestion that, if Henry were to redeem Orkney and Shetland, he would hold them and perhaps Iceland too. The rumours of Henry becoming king of Denmark, however unlikely that may have been, would hardly have been welcome news. But the immediacy of the situation was resolved in early 1536 when the Lübeckers formally withdrew support for Christian II, while Christian III finally defeated his opponents in July of the same year.[37] By this time, Christian III's resources were spent, having only won the war on account of his alliance with Gustav Vasa of Sweden.[38] Thus, regardless of the obligation in his election charter to 'reclaim Orkney and Shetland for the crown', this was highly unlikely for Christian now.[39] Consequently, James was relatively unconcerned enough to be distracted by a nine-month sojourn in France, during which time he married Madeleine de Valois, daughter of Francis I – who unfortunately died a few months later – followed shortly by his marriage to Marie de Guise-Lorraine. Soon, however, he started to pay attention to domestic matters once more.

## The Kingship of Ireland

THE refocusing of James' attention to domestic matters has been attributed to the outbreak of rebellion in the Western Isles in 1539.[40] Instigated by Donald Gruamach MacDonald of Sleat, who proclaimed restoration of the forfeited Lordship of the Isles as an aim, the rebellion was in reality about settling personal grievances, as MacDonald wasted the lands of Trotternish in Skye before making his way to Ross (thus also exploiting the absence of MacKenzie of Kintail from his lands at that time) and harrying Kinlochewe. The rebellion petered out quickly after MacDonald of Sleat was killed during his efforts to take Eilean Donan castle.[41] While this unrest may have

36 Ibid., VIII, no. 1178 (pp. 469–73); Hay and Hannay (eds), *Letters of James V*, pp. 291, 297, 301–02. Christian did convert to Lutheranism briefly during a stay in Wittenberg; see Lockhart, *Denmark, 1513–1660*, p. 20.

37 While Severinus gave James a full account of his time at Henry's court, it is likely that James would have had 'advertisement' of such affairs anyway; see Amy Blakeway, 'Spies and Intelligence in Scotland, c. 1530–1550', in Sara M. Butler and Krista J. Kesselring (eds), *Crossing Borders: Boundaries and Margins in Medieval and Early Modern Britain. Essays in Honour of Cynthia J. Neville* (Leiden, 2018), pp. 83–104.

38 Lockhart, *Denmark, 1513–1660*, p. 28; Roberts, *The Early Vasas*, pp. 101–07.

39 Although see Grohse, 'The Lost Cause', pp. 297–98.

40 Donald Gregory, *The History of the Western Highlands and Isles of Scotland, 1493–1625*, reprinted edn with an introduction by Martin MacGregor (Edinburgh, 2008), pp. 145–46.

41 Alison Cathcart, 'A Spent Force?', in Richard D. Oram (ed.), *The Lordship of the Isles*

prompted James to plan a voyage to the west as a means of asserting his royal authority in the region, a closer look at James' interest would suggest the 1540 expedition was far from a knee-jerk reaction to these events, no matter how unsettling the rebellion may have been for the king.[42] It is more likely that the expedition was a long-term plan to shore up his influence in the west, an influence that had been diminishing since the death of Alexander MacDonald of Dunivaig and the Glens in 1536.

Meanwhile, the situation in Orkney had been something of a concern since 1536 and the death of James Sinclair of Brecks. Sinclair had been in charge following the Battle of Summerdale in the summer of 1529.[43] Although largely a family dispute over control of Orkney it was not welcomed by James, who, following the end of his minority and the beginning of his personal rule, was still trying to assert his royal authority within Scotland.[44] But little change was effected in Orkney, and Sinclair remained in charge, albeit without any formal position. This was rectified when James officially acknowledged the status quo in Orkney in 1535 by granting Sinclair a knighthood and lands, a move described as 'a deliberate policy on the part of the king to bring the "usurper" into royal favour'.[45] But if the king hoped this would ensure ongoing stability he was wrong, as Sinclair committed suicide the following year.[46] James sought to de-escalate the situation by granting a respite to those involved in the battle of 1529 ahead of his plans to visit the islands himself.[47] Taken together, James' actions reinforce the view that the 1540 expedition was being planned and prepared for well in advance, rather than being a rushed reaction to another island rebellion.

The arrival of '8 gentlemen of Ierlande' at court during Lent 1540, a couple of months ahead of the expedition, was coincidental. How much they were welcomed by the Scottish king is questionable. No doubt James had involved himself in Irish affairs during the 1530s but, following his uncle's firm handling of the Kildare rebellion and the execution, in 1537, of all but one of the male members of the FitzGerald family, James sought to distance himself from the

(Leiden, 2015), pp. 254–70, at p. 260. However, other historians interpret the rebellion as more than a personal grievance, a view which holds some merit; see Wilson McLeod, '*Rí Innsi Gall, Rí Fionnghall, Ceannas nan Gàidheal*: Sovereignty and Rhetoric in the Late Medieval Hebrides', *Cambrian Medieval Celtic Studies* 43 (2002), 25–48, at p. 37.

42 Cameron, *James V*, pp. 228–54.

43 John H. Ballantye and Brian Smith (eds), *Shetland Documents: 1195–1579* (Lerwick, 1999), no. 51 is a copy of William, Lord Sinclair's account of what happened in 1529.

44 Anderson, *Stewart Earls of Orkney*, p. 9, refers to it as a 'family quarrel', while Cameron, *James V*, p. 243, describes it as a 'family feud'.

45 Cameron, *James V*, p. 244; Anderson, *Stewart Earls of Orkney*, pp. 9–10. Oliver Sinclair of Pitcairn was cousin of both the late John Sinclair, earl of Caithness, and James Sinclair of Brecks himself.

46 Cameron, *James V*, p. 244; Anderson, *Stewart Earls of Orkney*, pp. 9–11.

47 There was also reconciliation between the two sides of the Sinclair family when, on 6 September 1539, William, Lord Sinclair, and Edward Sinclair of Strom contracted a bond of manrent and maintenance, signed at Falkland; see Ballantye and Smith (eds), *Shetland Documents*, no. 64.

situation. The emergence of the Geraldine League, galvanised around the figurehead of Gerald FitzGerald, the last surviving member of the family, saw ongoing resistance to Henry and attempts to introduce Protestantism to Ireland. For many of the Irish who joined, both the Kildare rebellion and the Geraldine League were vehicles for expression of resistance to the exercise of English authority in Ireland (politically, economically, and militarily) alongside local grievances, enabling them to capitalise on the momentum. But the League gradually petered out as Irish lords one-by-one made their peace. While Manus O'Donnell did not submit until May 1540 (after James V's refusal of the offer of kingship), others, such as Conor O'Brien, submitted much earlier.

Conor O'Brien of Thomond, described to Thomas Cromwell as 'the grettis … and the strongyst man … the chyf capten of all Eyyres men', had written to Charles V in 1534–35 during the Kildare rebellion.[48] He emphasised the Iberian origins of the Irish and argued that the claims of the English crown to sovereignty over Ireland were unfounded because the Irish had not 'yielded' their 'ancient rights and liberties'.[49] Admittedly in October 1535, just a few months after the submission of Thomas FitzGerald, Lord Offaly and the formal ending of the Kildare rebellion, the very same Conor wrote to Henry VIII promising his obedience and loyalty, and explaining his actions in the recent rebellion, adding that he had been 'counselled by light people':

> as for the receiving of Thomas Ffitzgerald into my country, I insure you that I never sent for him … but I could not for very shame refuse him of meat and drinke, for it hath been of old custom amonge Irish men to give meat and drinke, & such like goods as we have.[50]

Most interesting is the last section of this letter where once again O'Brien emphasised Irish custom. Having declared his own loyalty, adding that he, like his ancestors, had always 'done right good service' to the king's deputies in Ireland, he asked:

> if it would please your Grace to be soe good and gracious to this poor Land, and to us your poor subjects as to send some noble man to govern us, and in especially if it would please your highnesse to send your sonne the Duke of Richmond to this poor country. I insure your grace that I and my brother and all my kinsmen with all my friends shall doe him as lowly service and as trew as any men living, and I my kinsmen & friends shall right gladly receive him to our ffooster sonne after the custom of Ireland, and shall live and dye in his right & service for ever ….[51]

48 *SP Henry VIII*, no. CXX (p. 307).

49 Quoted in J.A. Froude, *History of England from the Fall of Wolsey to the Death of Elizabeth* (London, 1862), pp. 295–96, taken from Christopher Maginn, 'Whose Island?: Sovereignty in Late Medieval and Early Modern Ireland', *Éire–Ireland* 44.3&4 (2009), 229–47, at p. 237.

50 *SP Henry VIII*, no. CVIII (p. 287).

51 Ibid., no. CVIII (p. 288).

It is not clear what O'Brien's agenda was. It is possible the Irish lords looked to the duke of Richmond as someone who had wider experience of the Anglo-Scottish border and European diplomacy while also holding various posts including chamberlain of Chester and north Wales, Lord Warden of the Cinque Ports, constable of Dover Castle, and Lord Admiral of England. More importantly for O'Brien, perhaps, was Richmond's brief appointment as Lord Lieutenant of Ireland from 1529–30, and while Richmond presented an alternative to Henry VIII, he also had a direct blood connection to the king.[52] The Irish may have hoped for a monarch or overlord who lived in Ireland and to whom they could turn to settle disputes between warring Irish lords; or perhaps they wanted to be free from an English-born Lord Deputy unsympathetic to Irish customs and culture. The suggestion that they would accept Richmond as a foster-son perhaps speaks to that latter alternative, reviving his previous appointment as Lord Lieutenant but, as O'Brien asked Henry 'to send … Richmond to this poor country', it is clear the Irish wanted him to be resident in Ireland. Thus, O'Brien's communication suggests that while English rule was still acceptable, what was not acceptable was Thomas Cromwell's level of interference or the policies of either the new English-born Lord Deputy, William Skeffington, or Lord Leonard Grey, marshal of the English army in Ireland.[53] Fosterage was a custom prevalent in Ireland, but O'Brien's suggestion that the duke of Richmond be received as 'our ffooster sonne' turns the view of 'educating' the Irish in the ways of the English on its head. In this instance the duke of Richmond would be regarded as a foster-son and, by implication, would be brought up and educated by the Irish in their ways, customs, and laws.

Understandably nothing came of this suggestion as the duke died in the summer of 1536. There was little tangible support coming from Charles V, but the emperor was undoubtedly distracted by affairs elsewhere in Europe as the Reformation gathered full pace and alliances were continually being reshaped. Nonetheless, the interest in Ireland in the later 1530s shown by James V may have encouraged the Irish to look closer to home for an alternative to Henry, resulting in the offer to James of the kingship of Ireland in 1540.[54] Unfortunately for the Irish the timing could not have

[52] Beverley A. Murphy, 'Fitzroy, Henry, Duke of Richmond and Somerset (1519–1536), Royal Bastard', *ODNB* [9635].

[53] Lord Leonard Grey had been brother-in-law to the 9th earl of Kildare (Kildare's second wife was Elizabeth Grey, sister of Leonard). Grey had negotiated the surrender of Thomas FitzGerald, apparently on the 'false promise that his life would be spared'; see S.J. Connolly, *Contested Island. Ireland 1460–1630* (Oxford, 2007), p. 101; Mary Ann Lyons, 'Grey, Leonard [Known as Lord Leonard Grey], Viscount Graney (c. 1490–1541), Lord Deputy of Ireland', *ODNB* [11551]. In the following year, 1536, he was appointed Lord Deputy of Ireland.

[54] Rumours that Con O'Neill sought to claim the high kingship appear to have been started by the English; see Maginn, 'Whose Island?', p. 235.

been worse. James' extended stay in France during 1536–37 had enabled him to withdraw somewhat from Irish affairs. Although James had never gone to Ireland himself, he had been informed of events there regularly, largely through his communication with Alexander MacDonald of Dunivaig and the Glens. In 1535 James received Charles Reynalds, a servant of Kildare, at the Scottish court and provided 'commendatory letters' on account of 'his friendship with the earl' before Reynalds departed for Rome.[55] In 1536 James petitioned the papacy twice on behalf of Manus O'Donnell, one letter preferring O'Donnell's candidate for the see of Raphoe, the other concerning a dispensation for O'Donnell's second marriage to Eleanor MacCarthy, aunt of the young Gerald FitzGerald.[56] Although in 1538 James would again write to the papacy concerning the appointment to the see of Raphoe, the Scottish king would not be drawn into Irish politics any further.[57] It was not just the reaction of his uncle, Henry, that James had to consider, but also the recent events involving Denmark–Norway. The offer of the crown of Denmark to Henry hardly concerned James, but the possibility that Orkney and Shetland might be redeemed and thus lost from James' kingdom would be a blow to his prestige while also upsetting the balance of power across the North Sea.

## The Rights and Responsibilities of Kingship

As we have seen, the crown of Denmark–Norway was both elective and hereditary, as members of the Oldenburg family were fully aware, and Paul Douglas Lockhart has emphasised how keenly the Council understood their 'rights of resistance'.[58] But this was not a tradition in Scotland, England, or Ireland. Indeed, Henry could barely conceal his contempt for Christian II's position when he grasped the reality of it and immediately ceased harbouring any thoughts he might have entertained of accepting such an offer. Across the archipelago, however, the situation differed somewhat. While previous Scottish monarchs had been, in one way or another, removed from the throne, there had been no attempt to overthrow the Stewart monarchy; by contrast, England had fought long and bitter civil and dynastic wars over the throne, and rival claimants had even been crowned in Ireland. In Scotland, the fourteenth-century Wars of Independence had seen the crown settled in the Bruce-Stewart line, and succession by primogeniture was uncontested through to the accession of James V's baby daughter in 1542 and well beyond.

[55] Hay and Hannay (eds), *Letters of James V*, p. 284.

[56] Ibid., pp. 321–22. This marriage brought Manus to the forefront of the Geraldine League.

[57] Ibid., p. 348. For fuller discussion of James' involvement in Ireland during the 1530s see Cathcart, 'James V, King of Scotland – and Ireland?'.

[58] Lockhart, *Denmark, 1513–1660*, p. 19.

As Mason has argued, while ideas of contractual monarchy were certainly current in late medieval Scotland, particularly in academic circles, the idea of an elective Scottish monarchy, such as existed in Denmark–Norway, played no part in the kingdom's politics before the Reformation of 1560.[59]

Meanwhile in Ireland there had been the high-kingship but the last individual to hold that position was Rory O'Connor in the late twelfth century prior to the Norman arrival and subsequent take-over of Ireland.[60] To be sure, there were sporadic, and largely opportunistic, attempts to revive the position but no Irish chief could really hope to establish his authority over the entire island.[61] Brendan Kane has argued recently that in the 1590s O'Neill of Tyrone and O'Donnell of Tyrconnell sought to confer the position of the Irish kingship on another – again external – individual, but in so doing the Irish lords retained possession of '*flaitheas* (the capacity to determine who would rule and how)' ensuring 'they could tear them down and start again'. As such, he argues, 'their inspiration was always Warwick and not Brian Boru'.[62] Again, however, that is a later sixteenth-century example, and earlier evidence for elective kingship in Ireland is sparse – though not entirely absent. Like the Declaration of Arbroath, the 1317 Irish Remonstrance – while not exactly an expression of elective kingship as such – is rarely mentioned.[63] The Remonstrance referred to the papal bull *Laudabiliter*, granted to Henry II by Adrian IV, by which 'Henry entered Ireland promising to preserve the rights of the Irish church and improve the lives of the people, but … in fact did quite the opposite.'[64] While the author of the Declaration of Arbroath was able to 'depict Robert Bruce's kingship as a *fait accompli*', the Irish had more of an 'uphill battle' and asked the pope to approve their setting up of Edward

59 Roger A. Mason, 'Beyond the Declaration of Arbroath: Kingship, Counsel and Consent in Late Medieval and Early Modern Scotland', in Boardman and Goodare (eds), *Kings, Lords and Men*, pp. 265–82; Mason, *Kingship and the Commonweal*, chs. 2–3.

60 Katharine Simms, *From Kings to Warlords. The Changing Political Structure of Gaelic Ireland in the Later Middle Ages* (Woodbridge, 2000), pp. 10–15, 41–59, although see pp. 60–78 for the role of assemblies. For more reading on the high-kingship of Ireland see F.J. Byrne, *Irish Kings and High-Kings* (London, 1973; reprinted with author's additions and corrections, Dublin, 2000); F.J. Byrne, 'Ireland and Her Neighbours, *c.*1014–*c.*1072', in Dáibhí O Cróinín (ed.), *A New History of Ireland: volume I, Prehistoric and Early Ireland* (Oxford, 2005), pp. 862–98; Marie Therese Flanagan, 'High-Kings with Opposition, 1072–1166', in O Cróinín (ed.), *A New History of Ireland: volume I*, pp. 899–933.

61 Maginn, 'Whose Island?', p. 232.

62 Brendan Kane, 'The Nine Years' War in Ireland (1594–1603) as a Problem of Government', in William J. Bulman and Freddy C. Dominguez (eds), *Political and Religious Practice in the Early Modern British World* (Manchester, 2022), pp. 181–202, at pp. 196, 199.

63 Indeed, Mason has argued the Declaration of Arbroath is never mentioned at all; see Mason, 'Beyond the Declaration of Arbroath'.

64 Seán Duffy, 'The Irish Remonstrance and the Declaration of Arbroath', *SHR* 101.3 (2022), 395–428, at p. 415. See also 'The Remonstrance of the Irish princes to Pope John XXII, 1317', in Seán Duffy (ed.), *Robert the Bruce's Irish Wars. The Invasions of Ireland 1360–1329* (Stroud, 2002), pp. 179–86.

Bruce 'as king and lord' in Ireland.[65] Nonetheless, it was evidence of the Irish lords – or at least one Irish lord, Donald O'Neill – asserting their right to choose someone else as king. Nor is there much discussion in studies of the kingship of Ireland in the sixteenth century of the more contemporaneous late fifteenth- or early sixteenth-century 'Second Life of St Máedóc' that refers to the inauguration of the kings of Breifne. As Katherine Simms has noted, it suggests 'the conferring of kingship is conditional on his carrying out his undertakings' – although this could be interpreted in a purely judicial or spiritual context.[66]

There is, therefore, little evidence for a sustained tradition of elective kingship in either Scotland or Ireland, although this does not deny that there were those advocating for a more conciliar approach to government or for more accountability of the king to the people (or, rather, the political community). The offer of the crown of Ireland to James V, much like the offer of the crown of Denmark to Henry VIII, appears to have been opportunistic, though with much less precedent to warrant it. In both cases subsequent events changed the wider context significantly. The withdrawal of support for Christian II by the Lübeckers in 1536 and the victory of Christian III secured for him the kingdoms of Denmark and Norway, although whether this precluded any attempt by Henry to redeem Orkney and Shetland is unclear. Meanwhile in Ireland, no doubt there were other factors contributing to the move, but the offer of kingship to James must also have contributed to Henry's 1541 Act for the Kingly Title, which transformed the constitutional position of Ireland from that of lordship to kingdom.[67] Certainly this act would have thwarted any willingness on the part of James to take up such an offer. In February 1541, Pope Paul III encouraged James to consider 'the weal of Ireland which … has a claim upon James' loyalty and touches his reputation', but it is unlikely that James was tempted.[68] As with Henry, James' understanding of imperial monarchy made the offer of a kingship with strings attached far from appealing. If he shared Henry's view of Christian II as a 'wretched king', it is likely that the Irish lords' offer of the kingship of Ireland had the words of Peter Severinus ringing in his ears: they 'offered to give what they do not even hope to gain'.[69] By 1541, James had undertaken his expedition to the Isles and was putting in place various measures to exert his authority over the kingdom's island peripheries. From this perspective the expedition of 1540 and the circumnavigation of the realm

[65] Duffy, 'The Irish Remonstrance and the Declaration of Arbroath', pp. 422–23; 'The Remonstrance of the Irish princes to Pope John XXII, 1317', p. 186.

[66] Katherine Simms, *Gaelic Ulster in the Middle Ages: History, Culture and Society* (Dublin, 2020), pp. 251, 256.

[67] Brendan Bradshaw, *The Irish Constitutional Revolution of the Sixteenth Century* (Cambridge, 1979); Maginn, 'Whose Island?, pp. 235–36. The 1541 act was followed up by the policy of surrender and regrant which ensured the Irish lords accepted this new status.

[68] Hay and Hannay (eds), *Letters of James V*, p. 420.

[69] Ibid., pp. 310–11. Indeed, while Peter Severinus' words referred to the offer of the crown of Denmark to Henry VIII by the Lübeckers it could be applied to the Irish context too. My thanks to Professor Ciaran Brady for discussing this point with me.

begins to look like more of a defensive move on the part of James, an attempt to assert his royal authority across his kingdom both to pacify internal unrest and send a clear message to external observers. But to view the expedition purely in terms of projections of kingship is thus to overlook a crucial but largely ignored aspect of the voyage.

## James V and the 1540 Expedition

As previously noted, the planning for the expedition had been taking place for some time. In 1535 Alexander MacDonald of Dunivaig and the Glens was put to the horn as a rebel and died the following year, thus ending James' direct line of communication to the Western Isles; in Orkney the suicide of Sinclair of Brecks left something of a vacuum in terms of governance on the ground; and that year also saw the eventual triumph of Christian III.[70] Following his return from France, James sought to re-establish links between the houses of Oldenburg and Stewart and, now he was married into the house of Valois, proposed incorporating Christian into the alliance between James and Francis I.[71] Christian's response was rather lukewarm. While he was 'not disinclined' he wanted to 'know what the stipulations ought to be, and what aid is expected of each party in the other's need, lest a vague compact lead to a dispute about reciprocal obligations'.[72] Indeed, the rest of his letter to James was uncharacteristically frank and direct, devoid of the usual platitudes. Referring to the lack of support he received from other European powers, Christian wrote that he:

> marvels how it comes about that so many kings of wealth and power, on friendly terms too with his father in the days of his peace, could passively see the son and successor, duly elected by councillors, stand in danger of losing his right by succession and election, and nearly driven with his young brothers from their hereditary duchies.[73]

Christian also outlined to James the state of the country which was 'altered out of recognition by long warfare' and which had 'consumed all the valuables and treasures of the crown' to the extent that Denmark was now a place of 'want and dearth'. On account of this, and his need to settle Norway and take over the crown there 'with consent of the Norwegian council', he was in no position to respond to James' recent request for 'a ship well furnished with powder and guns'.[74]

70 Cameron, *James V*, p. 237.
71 James wrote to Christian III in July 1537, days before Madeleine died; see Hay and Hannay (eds), *Letters of James V*, pp. 333–34.
72 Hay and Hannay (eds), *Letters of James V*, pp. 336–37.
73 Ibid.
74 Ibid.

The precarious state of Denmark and the inability of an old, long-term ally of the house of Stewart to offer aid was not comforting for James. The internal unrest Denmark experienced, combined with wider religious schism, had shaped allegiances across Europe and, by the end of the 1530s, Henry was no longer quite so isolated and insecure as he had been a few years earlier. Neither the papacy nor the emperor had taken any direct action against Henry (each had urged the other to do so), and Henry himself had dealt harshly but firmly with internal political and religious unrest.[75] To that extent, he had ridden out the storm he created with his break from Rome, although Anglo-Scottish relations were increasingly antagonistic.[76] The wider European context of the 1530s, and his own diplomatic isolation, had caused Henry to take steps to secure his southern coastline and reinforce fortifications in the event of external threats.[77] James had not, and while gifts of favour from the pope and renewal of the Auld Alliance brought him prestige and allies, neither would secure his kingdom in the event of an English attack. James needed to build up the defences of his kingdom; after all, it was all very well to express ideas of his *imperium*, but he needed to be able to back that up with action if required. While James had been able to increase crown revenue through the usual measures of remissions, feuing of crown lands, forfeitures, and exploitation of the church, he had also spent lavishly on building projects and the College of Justice. Defence of the realm would require significant further funding, and James needed to increase crown income.[78]

Thus the 1540 expedition was stimulated by both financial and security concerns. It went far beyond the survey of crown lands in the Western Isles alongside increased rentals there and in the Northern Isles too; it also went further than the development of the first Scottish sailing rutter that was produced following the expedition, a move that also signalled his concern with the security of his kingdom.[79] Long before his grandson sought to

[75] Ibid., pp. 264–67. See, for example, *L&P Henry VIII*, VI, nos. 568, 570, 655, 699, 853, 854, 997, 1136; VII, 39, 185, 300, 311, 367, 484.

[76] For relations between James and Henry VIII see Amy Blakeway, 'The Privy Council of James V of Scotland, 1528–1542', *The Historical Journal* 59.1 (2016), 23–44; Blakeway, 'Spies and Intelligence in Scotland', pp. 83–104.

[77] British Library, Cotton MS Augustus I: Maps and Plans, I, 35, 36, 38, 39; see also the British Library online gallery at www.bl.uk/collection–items/henry–viii–coastal–defence–maps (accessed 31 December 2021); *L&P Henry VIII*, XIV (I), nos. 398, 399, 400; Alison Cathcart, *Plantations by Land and Sea. North Channel Communities of the Atlantic Archipelago, c.1550–1625* (Oxford, 2021), pp. 17–18.

[78] In December 1540 parliament sought to prevent James from feuing the lands mentioned in the Act of Annexation (*RPS*, 1540/12/26), while the College of Justice was funded by the 'Great Tax' granted by the pope (Cameron, *James V*, p. 135). Nonetheless, James' reign had seen 'considerable activity and development' in maritime matters and the king had 'issued … instructions for the fortification of coastal towns and castles during the hostilities with England of 1533' (Thomas, *Princelie Majestie*, pp. 155–64, at p. 164).

[79] A rutter was a set of sailing directions used by a pilot in coastal navigation. For the first Scottish rutter, see Alexander Lindsay, *A Rutter of the Scottish Seas (ca. 1540)*, ed. I.H. Adams and G. Fortune (Greenwich, 1980). It covered Scotland from Leith south to the

exploit the economic resources of his western and northern regions (what Mason called his 'Gaelic Eldorado'), James V was attempting a similar move.[80] Throughout his reign James had been encouraging the search for mineral wealth in Scotland by employing a number of individuals, largely from Denmark and Germany, to undertake this work. Between December 1525 and January 1526 he sent Gunther von Lauichz to 'that part of Scotland in which there is said to be much gold … to inspect the ground and the veins of metal'.[81] In 1532 a contract was made with men from Hamburg to mine for metals in Scotland while, after Marie de Guise arrived in Scotland, her familial contacts were asked to 'send experienced miners' to work in Scotland, specifically at the mine at Crawfordmuir.[82] No doubt James was influenced by Christian II whose, albeit unsuccessful, efforts to ensure Sweden remained within the Kalmar Union were in large part due to his desire to control Bergslag, a mining district in north Svealand that had been of importance throughout previous centuries.[83]

As well as exploiting the natural resources of his land, James also wanted to secure the resources of the sea. Throughout his reign James was in communication with other foreign powers regarding the fate of Scottish merchants, their ships and cargo, whether they were unfairly detained elsewhere or prevented from trading lawfully, or whether their ships had been attacked and goods taken; the problem of piracy and determining guilt in such cases was ubiquitous. In August 1540, however, James wrote to the authorities of Bremen and 'other imperial officers' and to Charles V concerning the fishing around Orkney and Shetland. He referred to an

Humber, and then from Leith north to Caithness and, via the north and west of Scotland, to the Mull of Galloway and the River Solway. Each section provided information on the direction of tidal streams, timings of ebb and flood tides, distances from one headland to the next, and details such as safe harbours, sea roads, and any dangers such as rocks; see David W. Waters, *The Art of Navigation in England in Elizabethan and Early Stuart Times* (London, 1958), pp. 11–14; Cathcart, *Plantations by Land and Sea*, pp. 11, 14–16. In 1532 Orkney and Shetland and the lordship of the Isles were valued at 10,000 francs yearly (approximately £4500 scots). The earldom of Orkney itself was valued at £1000. Anderson, *Stewart Earls of Orkney*, pp. 12–13, argues that James 'had been favourably impressed with Orkney' and its fertility so it is no surprise the rental for Orkney increased substantially. Pitcairn's first annual return in 1542 was for £960, a significant increase on previous rental payments, which at best had been slightly under £400; see Clouston (ed.), *Records of the Earldom of Orkney*, no. XXVII [pp. 61–63]; Cameron, *James V*, pp. 242–45.

80 Roger A. Mason, 'Civil Society and the Celts: Hector Boece, George Buchanan and the Ancient Scottish Past', in Edward J. Cowan and Richard J. Finlay (eds), *Scottish History. The Power of the Past* (Edinburgh, 2002), pp. 95–119, at p. 96.

81 Hay and Hannay (eds), *Letters of James V*, pp. 129, 136, 287–88. Gunther von Lauichz was a servant of Christian II.

82 Hay and Hannay (eds), *Letters of James V*, pp. 287–88; Thomas, *Princelie Majestie*, pp. 177–78. The goldmines at Crawfordmuir were first worked during the reign of James IV and by 1537–38 gold from these mines 'was being delivered to the royal treasury' (p. 178).

83 Roberts, *The Early Vasas*, pp. 15–16, 31–33. Meanwhile in October 1540 Christian III would write to James that 'Norway is rich in silver mines, and in mines of every sort of metal'; see Hay and Hannay (eds), *Letters of James V*, p. 415.

incident that had occurred in 1530 whereby a number of fishermen were 'run down and drowned while fishing in Orkney seas by certain Hollanders', apparently for 'no other reason than that they were Scots'.[84] Because the Scots had 'suffered so long and so much in their own waters' James had decided to take firm action. He asked the authorities to ensure their fishermen did not 'invade his waters and bounds with intent to deprive Scots by illegal methods of the fruit of their toil on the coasts', arguing that these regulations were necessary to 'preserve the immunity of the Scots by land and sea'.[85] James may well have been impressed by the fertility of Orkney during his visit there in 1540, but having been informed of the large numbers of Hollanders and Flemish fishing in Scottish waters, he took action to protect the fishing of his own subjects.[86] James' intervention at this stage may have been prompted by the 1539 publication of *Carta Marina* by Olaus Magnus, an exiled Swedish priest. This was a detailed map of Nordic countries from Iceland to Finland and included both the Orkney and Shetland islands as well as parts of the east coast of England and Scotland. Alongside various vessels, sea monsters, and ocean eddies, it depicted a sea-battle between 'Hamburgen' and 'Scott', said to be a reflection of 'commercial tensions'.[87] It has been argued that the geographic region encompassed in *Carta Marina* 'reflects both the political history and the political aspirations of the North in the late Middle Ages'.[88] That may be so, but the map clearly incorporates a number of fishing vessels, and fish, alongside a strategically placed crest of Norway in and around the Orkney islands. Whether this was deliberate aggravation of James V is unclear, although it sent a clear signal that the islands were still regarded as Norwegian – but these were lands, seas, and resources that James evidently regarded as Scottish and wanted to preserve for the enrichment of his own kingdom.[89]

[84] Hay and Hannay (eds), *Letters of James V*, p. 187; Pascual de Gayangos (ed.), *Calendar of Letters, Despatches and State Papers Relating to the Negotiations between England and Spain Preserved in the Archives of Simancas, Vienna, Brussels and Elsewhere*, vol. VI (I): Henry VIII, 1538–1542 (London, 1890), no. 148 (p. 305).

[85] Hay and Hannay (eds), *Letters of James V*, pp. 408–09.

[86] He gained this information from his admiral on his return from the isles. Indeed, as Rorke and MacCoinnich have argued, fishing from the Isles resulted in a significant increase in exports from Scotland during the 1540s; see Martin Rorke, 'The Scottish Herring Trade, 1470–1600', *SHR* 84.2 (2005), 149–65, at pp. 155–57, 159; Aonghas MacCoinnich, 'The Maritime Dimension to Scotland's "Highland Problem", ca.1540–1630', *Journal of the North Atlantic: special volume 12* (2019), 44–72.

[87] H. Thomas Rossby and Peter Miller, 'Ocean Eddies in the 1539 Carta Marina by Olaus Magnus', *Oceanography* 16.4 (2003), 77–88, at p. 81 (although the authors suggest the 'sea battle between *Hamburgen* and *Scott* may reflect the commercial tensions between the Hansa and England').

[88] John Granlund and G.R. Crone, 'The "Carta Marina" of Olaus Magnus', *Imago Mundi* 8 (1951), 35–43, at p. 40. See also Allan I. Macinnes, *The British Revolution, 1629–1660* (Basingstoke, 2005), pp. 20–21, 62.

[89] See Olaus Magnus, *Carta Marina*.

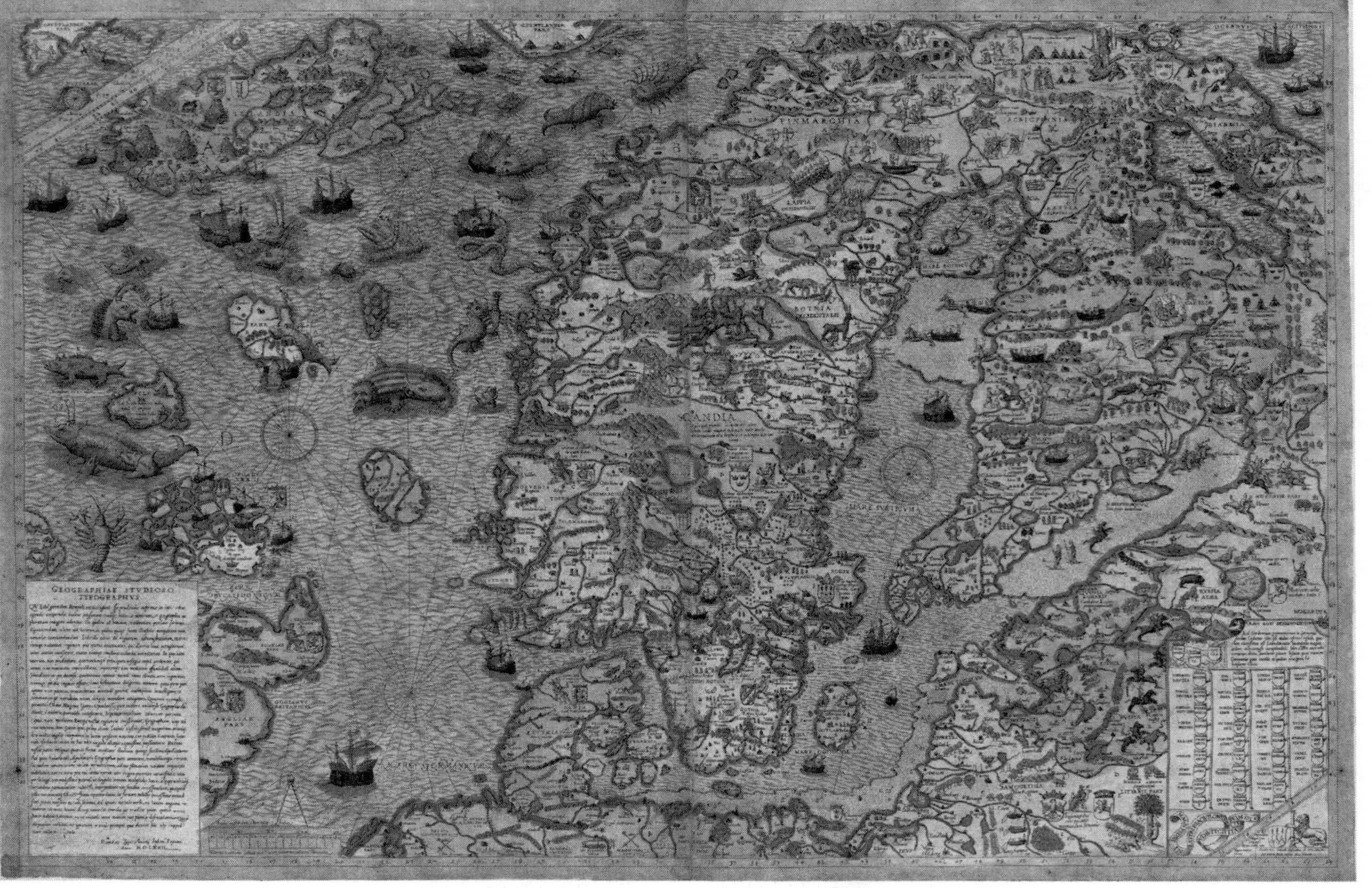


*Carta Marina* by Olaus Magnus, Kungliga Biblioteket / National Library of Sweden.

James' unexpected death in 1542 means that any further discussion of the review of his defences is largely speculative. Nonetheless, it is evident that James had quite an agenda as he embarked on the expedition of 1540. It was not just an outward show of royal authority; James used the voyage to progress his efforts to bring stability to the northern and western periphery, while also raising income from those regions and gaining greater knowledge of the waters surrounding his kingdom and how to navigate them. The subsequent increase in rentals in the western Isles and Orkney, as well as his efforts to protect the fishing around 'the Orkneys, the Shetlands, and the northern mainland', suggest a much earlier effort by the Stewart monarchy to exploit the economic resources of the region, while also seeking to develop mining industries elsewhere in his kingdom.[90] That James was already spending significant sums on building projects and the College of Justice, combined with a recognition that he could not rely on allies to come to his aid, suggests he had defence of his kingdom in mind, unsurprisingly perhaps in the light of increased tension in Anglo-Scottish relations.

## Conclusion

WHILE barely scratching the surface of James' governance of the Western and Northern Isles of Scotland, this discussion has sought to look deeper into James' reign and the importance of the outlying, peripheral regions of his kingdom.[91] In doing so, while focusing on the later 1530s, a wider geographic context has been invoked, taking into consideration events not only in England or France, but more specifically events in Ireland and Denmark–Norway. Such a perspective brings further nuance to arguments concerning elective monarchy or imperial kingship. Indeed, while James was content to interfere in his uncle's Irish kingdom and may well have relished the opportunity of extending his empire through an 'aggregation of dominions', events elsewhere resulted in his refusal of the offer of Irish kinship.[92] The possibility that his uncle might accept an offer of kingship from the Lübeckers, thus potentially enabling Henry to redeem Orkney and Shetland, had caused James to reconsider his imperial aims. James preferred to project an image of imperial kingship free from external jurisdiction; in turning down the offer of Irish kingship he consolidated his withdrawal from Irish affairs, consciously avoiding setting a precedent, and

[90] Hay and Hannay (eds), *Letters of James V*, p. 408.

[91] The voyage took in Orkney but not the Shetland islands. No doubt, Shetland was regarded as part of the lands and lordship of Orkney, but if the voyage was also about acquiring navigational knowledge and expertise, as well as increasing income from land and sea, it questions why Shetland was not included and leaves unanswered the status of the Shetland islands vis-à-vis Scotland and Denmark–Norway.

[92] Levack, *Formation of the British State*, p. 2.

focused his attention on his own realm. Meanwhile, however much Henry was attracted by the Lübeckers' offer, the reality of such an offer, and the conditions that may have come with it, was not something he was prepared to countenance. Although it is unclear whether any conditions were attached to the offer to James by the Irish lords, the tradition in Denmark–Norway was of hereditary and elective kinship. No doubt both James and Henry sought to extend their empire during the 1530s, but the means by which they might achieve that, conditional kingship, were not justified by the end. Notwithstanding the discussion of kingship, this chapter has argued that there is much more to James V than a king concerned with the symbols of empire; rather it suggests a king who was concerned with asserting his *imperium* on both land and sea. While Mason detailed the iconography utilised by James, this chapter has sought to outline the practical application of such ideals of imperial monarchy.[93] Not simply a symbolic circumnavigation of his realm, James' 1540 expedition to Orkney and the Western Isles had very real and tangible aims. The recent intrigue between Henry and the Lübeckers meant that James was determined to extend his royal authority throughout his *imperium*, but given the wider upheaval on the Continent, he also wanted to send a message to those abroad. At the same time, James was aware of the need to reinforce his kingdom's defences and establish maritime supremacy. The rutter that followed the 1540 expedition gave him vital knowledge of the Scottish seas at a time when his uncle, in the light of international affairs and notably the 1539 truce between France and Spain, was similarly concerned with the security of his southern coast. James needed to increase crown finances to facilitate additional expenditure on coastal fortifications and to further develop the kingdom's maritime power. The increased rentals from the Isles would be welcome, but James had long been seeking to develop the mineral wealth of Scotland too, and in this endeavour he had been influenced by Christian II. Alongside exploitation of the land James also looked to the 'riche fischeingis be sey'.[94] In doing so, he sought to ensure it was his kingdom that reaped the revenues of the fisheries off the west and north of Scotland – and did so decades before his grandson, James VI.[95] Indeed, while too often the comparison is made between James V and his father, James IV, this chapter suggests we should instead consider James V in relation to his grandson. Long before James VI looked to solve his economic woes through increased rents in the north and west, exploration of mineral wealth, and exploitation of fishing while also projecting an image of imperial monarchy

93 Mason, 'This Realm of Scotland Is an Empire?'.

94 *RPS*, 1597/11/40.

95 For the various attempts to exploit the fisheries of Scotland, see Aonghas MacCoinnich, *Plantation and Civility in the North Atlantic World: The Case of the Northern Hebrides, 1570–1636* (Leiden, 2015).

and sending a message to external observers regarding his royal authority, James V was doing much the same. Perhaps James V's efforts are overlooked because his reign was cut short by his untimely death, or perhaps because his actions did not result in such significant repercussions. Following his accession to the thrones of England and Ireland in 1603, James VI and I declared *mare clausum* around his island empire in an effort to prevent the Dutch from fishing in 'British' waters. The result was a seminal dispute with Hugo Grotius regarding the freedom of the seas that helped lay the foundations of international maritime law.[96] This should not diminish the achievements of James V, who chose not to extend the bounds of his empire, instead preferring to consolidate and strengthen his kingship throughout his realm, both symbolically and in practice, and by both land and sea.

[96] T.W. Fulton, *The Sovereignty of the Sea. An Historical Account of the Claims of England to the Dominion of the British Seas, and of the Evolution of the Territorial Waters: With Special Reference to the Rights of Fishing and the Naval Salute* (London, 1911), pp. 118–208.

# III

# Literature, Politics and Religion: Renaissance and Reformation

# 7

# 'The time of reformation': The Evolution of Early Modern Protestant Memories of the Scottish Reformation

Bess Rhodes

THE summer of 1579 saw the General Assembly of the Church of Scotland lamenting how little the Scottish Reformation had achieved. According to a petition despatched by the ministers of the Assembly to James VI, recent 'cruel and unnatural murders', the widespread 'contempt of the poor', a prevailing 'corruption of justice', and 'many other evils which overflow this commonwealth' all indicated 'how slender and small success hitherto followed the reformation of religion within this realm'.[1] Such a pessimistic outlook on the nature and legacy of the Scottish Reformation formed a notable departure from the attitudes of Protestant leaders 20 years earlier. The decade or so between the Reformation rising of the summer of 1559 and the murder of Regent Moray in January 1570 was characterised by a remarkable optimism in Protestant circles about the progress of religious reform in Scotland. In November 1559 the Genevan reformer John Calvin wrote to John Knox and his Scottish supporters congratulating them on 'success incredible in so short a time' and remarking on the 'abundant matter for confidence in [the] future'.[2] Protestant pronouncements became even more assured following the Reformation Parliament's rejection of papal authority and the Mass in August 1560. Indeed, by May 1564 it was possible for the elders of the St Andrews Kirk Session to boast that 'the face of a perfect reformed kirk has been seen within this city [for] the space of five years'.[3]

[1] Thomas Thomson (ed.), *Acts and Proceedings of the General Assemblies of the Kirk of Scotland*, 3 vols (Edinburgh, 1840), ii, pp. 446–47.

[2] Knox, *Works*, vi, p. 95.

[3] David Hay Fleming (ed.), *Register of the Minister, Elders and Deacons of the Christian Congregation of St Andrews, 1559–1600*, 2 vols (Edinburgh, 1889), p. 198. This quotation has previously been discussed by Jane Dawson in the context of St Andrews' (potentially exaggerated) identity as a beacon of reform. See Jane Dawson, '"The Face of Ane Perfyt Reformed Kyrk": St Andrews and the Early Scottish Reformation', in James Kirk (ed.), *Humanism and Reform: The Church in Europe, England, and Scotland, 1400–1643* (Oxford, 1991), pp. 413–35.

During the final decades of the sixteenth century a significant change emerged in how Protestants depicted the Scottish Reformation.[4] Texts written in the immediate aftermath of the events of 1559 and 1560 typically present Scotland's shift from Catholicism to Protestantism as a successful moment of conversion – an extraordinary achievement which took place within a short space of time. In contrast, Protestants writing in the 1570s, 1580s, and 1590s tended to be more negative, often portraying reform as a protracted and problematic process. This pattern can be seen across a range of genres including memoirs, sermons, and administrative records. The exact nature of the criticisms varied depending on the agenda of the author. Yet whether radical or reactionary, in favour of bishops or advocating for presbyteries, late sixteenth-century authors increasingly presented reform as an unfinished journey towards a better church. In the words of the General Assembly of 1579, Scots must not 'look how meekle is done, but rather how meekle resteth unreformed'.[5]

The late sixteenth-century reframing of Scotland's experience of religious change and the journey from optimism to pessimism regarding the legacy of 1560 have received limited attention from modern scholars. Despite pioneering work by Roger Mason on how Renaissance Scots used history for political purposes, research into memory and the Scottish Reformation is still quite restricted.[6] (In this respect Scottish historiography lags behind that of England, where there have been several recent publications on how the Reformation was reinterpreted and remembered.)[7] The causes of this oversight are no doubt complex, but the tendency of researchers to focus on questions of nationhood and identity has perhaps overshadowed other themes in early modern writing about Scotland's past.[8]

[4] It should be noted that this is a study specifically of Protestant depictions of religious reform. There are also interesting questions to be asked about Catholic understandings of the Reformation era. However, they will not form a part of this study, where the shifting attitudes of different sections of the Church of Scotland already provide considerable complexity. 'Protestant' is here being used as a catch-all for anyone who broadly accepted the Church of Scotland (in its many variant forms) during the late sixteenth and early seventeenth centuries. Although there has been some criticism (particularly from scholars of the Continental and English Reformations) regarding the use of the word Protestant, it provides a more satisfactory general categorisation than terms such as 'evangelical' for the Scots who rejected Catholicism from the late 1550s onwards. Late sixteenth-century Scots often described themselves as Protestants and the phrase is used in the Confession of Faith of 1560. See *RPS*, A1560/8/3.

[5] Thomson (ed.), *Acts and Proceedings of the General Assemblies*, ii, p. 448.

[6] For publications by Roger Mason on the writing of history in early modern Scotland see the select bibliography at the end of this book.

[7] In England this area of research has been significantly shaped by Alexandra Walsham's work as an author and editor. Alexandra Walsham, 'History, Memory, and the English Reformation', *The Historical Journal* 55.4 (2012), 899–938; Alexandra Walsham, Bronwyn Wallace, Ceri Law, and Brian Cummings (eds), *Memory and the English Reformation* (Cambridge, 2020).

[8] It is striking how many of the (often ground-breaking and insightful) studies of history writing in the era of the Scottish Reformation have focused on questions of identity, such

The types of sources commonly examined by intellectual historians may have also contributed to a lack of awareness regarding shifts in late sixteenth-century attitudes to the Scottish Reformation. Research into how early modern Scots wrote about the origins of the Church of Scotland has been dominated by a small number of sixteenth-century histories and political works. Although books such as John Knox's *History of the Reformation of Religion within the Realm of Scotland* or George Buchanan's *Rerum Scoticarum Historia* shaped the views of later generations, they are not necessarily representative of ideas circulating in wider Scottish society during the 1560s, 1570s, and 1580s.[9] The details of elite negotiations about ecclesiastical policy that feature in both histories (and are presented as undermining God's work) reflect the experiences of two difficult men who were deeply involved in politics and religious affairs, rather than definitively recording how reform was remembered by Protestant Scots. A focus on explicitly historical narratives limits the quantity of available sources and disproportionately privileges a few voices. Furthermore, it can obscure alterations in outlook over short time frames. In this context, it is perhaps worthwhile noting that neither Buchanan's *Historia* nor Knox's *History* were published in any form until the 1580s, and the exact date when many passages in these works were composed is uncertain.[10]

Yet history books were just one of many ways in which sixteenth-century Scots recorded and recalled the events of the Reformation. For many Scots the pronouncements of ministers, kirk sessions, and burgh councils were probably far more influential in shaping their perspectives on the significance and legacy of religious change. Sources such as kirk session registers and burgh council records survive in moderately large numbers, and should be an integral part of our efforts to unpick early modern memories of reform.[11]

as: Roger A. Mason, 'Usable Pasts: History and Identity in Reformation Scotland', *SHR* 76 (1997), 54–68; Roger A. Mason, 'Chivalry and Citizenship: Aspects of National Identity in Renaissance Scotland', in Mason, *Kingship and the Commonweal*, pp. 78–103; Michael Lynch, 'A Nation Born Again? Scottish Identity in the Sixteenth and Seventeenth Centuries', in Dauvit Broun *et al.* (eds), *Image and Identity: The Making and Re-making of Scotland through the Ages* (Edinburgh, 1998), pp. 82–104; Arthur Williamson, *Scottish National Consciousness in the Age of James VI: The Apocalypse, the Union and the Shaping of Scotland's Public Culture* (Edinburgh, 1979).

[9] George Buchanan, *Rerum Scoticarum Historia* (Edinburgh, 1582); John Knox, *History of the Reformation of Religion within the Realm of Scotland* (London, 1587).

[10] Buchanan seems to have mainly worked on his *Historia* during the 1570s while teaching the young James VI. Knox appears to have begun gathering material for a history of the Reformation in Scotland as early as 1559, although much of the writing took place in the mid-1560s (during a period of considerable personal discontent towards the end of Mary Queen of Scots' rule). Roger A. Mason, 'How Andrew Melville Read His George Buchanan', in Mason and Reid (eds), *Andrew Melville*, pp. 11–45, at p. 14. Jane Dawson, *John Knox* (New Haven, CT and London, 2015), pp. 251–57.

[11] Kirk session records and burgh council minutes are often examined by modern historians. However, for many years these sources were primarily quarries for social histories. The considerable potential of such texts as an insight into the intellectual assumptions of local authorities has only begun to be investigated. The possibilities of urban civic

What is more, the date at which many of these sources were created can often be established relatively precisely. For obvious reasons the compilers of official records were usually careful to ensure that the date on which decisions and announcements were made was noted. When these additional genres are compared with memoirs and chronicles, overlooked aspects of the interaction between sixteenth-century Scots and their recent past are revealed – not least the increasing negativity of Protestant elites towards the events which established their Church.

So how did early modern Scots, and specifically those of a Protestant bent, depict the religious changes of the mid-sixteenth century? Why might those portrayals have altered over time? The first point to be emphasised is the speed with which religious change came to be regarded as a historical event, a decisive moment in local and national life which was now complete. As early as December 1561 the Superintendent of Fife, John Winram, spoke of 'the reformed city of St Andrews' and noted that an illegal divorce had taken place 'long after the said city was reformed by sincere preaching and hearing of God's true Word'.[12] Winram was not alone in St Andrews in his perception that the Reformation was a particular moment which passed quite quickly. Around 1570 the St Andrews burgh council prefaced an inventory of charters from the local Dominican friary with the statement that the documents were handed over 'after the time of reformation of religion when all friars was discharged out of this realm'.[13] Similar statements can be found further afield. In March 1568, when John Hamilton was presented to the vicarage pensionary of Bothwell, it was noted that he was entitled to payments formerly spent on bread, wax, and wine for the local collegiate church, but which had not been put to 'any other good use ... since the time of reformation of religion'.[14] During the 1560s and 1570s both the Privy Council and Parliament likewise employed phrases such as 'since the reformation of religion in this realm', and 'before the said Reformation'.[15] Indeed, some sixteenth-century Scots appear to have used the change in religion as a chronological marker, a point in their lives by which other events could be measured. For example, Thomas Wode's part books record that a version of the penitential song *Aspice Domine* was 'set in V parts by an Italian. Set three or four year before reformation'.[16]

records (admittedly from a slightly earlier period) as a window onto the wider thinking of burgh elites is impressively demonstrated in Claire Hawes' doctoral thesis. Claire Hawes, 'Community and Public Authority in Later Fifteenth-Century Scotland' (unpublished University of St Andrews PhD thesis, 2015).

12 Hay Fleming (ed.), *Register*, i, p. 134.

13 St Andrews University Library, B65/1/1, f. 52r.

14 *RSS*, vi, p. 51.

15 *RPC*, ii, pp. 263, 391, 490. *RPS*, 1567/12/35, 1571/8/7, 1578/7/20.

16 The religious changes of 1559 and 1560 probably had a particularly profound impact on Thomas Wode as he was originally a monk at Lindores Abbey before converting and becoming a Church of Scotland minister. Hilda Hutchinson, 'The St Andrews Psalter: Transcription and Critical Study' (unpublished University of Edinburgh Mus. Doc. thesis, 1957), vol. 1, p. 169A. James Ross, 'Wode [Wood], Thomas (d. 1592), Church of Scotland

The conceptualising of the Reformation as a specific moment in time probably arose from a range of factors. On a basic level, it reflects the scale of upheaval which accompanied the rebellion of the Lords of the Congregation. Although there had for some years been murmurings of religious discontent (and even occasional acts of iconoclasm), the extent of disruption in 1559 and 1560 was unprecedented. Within a matter of months a large swathe of Lowland Scotland saw statues smashed, churches whitewashed, and religious observance transformed. On 1 July 1559 Sir William Kirkcaldy wrote that Protestant campaigners:

> Pull down all manner of friaries, and some abbeys, which willingly receive not their reformation. As to parish churches, they cleanse them of images and all other monuments of idolatry, and command that no masses be said in them; in place thereof, the book set forth by Godly King Edward is read in the same churches.[17]

For people who lived through these changes it must have been a truly memorable experience, an astonishing break in the rhythm of their daily lives.[18] Such a time of disruption almost certainly formed a major mental marker, and particularly so in a pre-industrial society rooted in continuity and tradition.[19]

The desire to pinpoint the moment of reform also served practical legal and religious purposes. In many areas of administration there was a need to draw a line between the time of Catholic power and the establishment of new Reformed authorities. This problem arose in relation to issues as diverse as land transactions, marriage disputes, and local government. In this context, it is perhaps significant that one of the most specific dates provided for reform is a 1587 confirmation of property rights in the burgh of Perth which disregards any conflicting alienations since 'the time of the reformation of religion, which happened on 6 March in the year of the Lord 1558' (i.e. 1559 according to the modern calendar).[20]

Identifying reform as a specific and communal instant of conversion had a number of benefits for Scottish Protestants during the 1560s. At that time the majority of members of Reformed congregations had only recently become public supporters of Protestantism. Many of the men serving as ministers, sitting on kirk sessions, or holding office on burgh councils had a few years earlier been upholding Catholic traditions.[21] Rather than rejecting

---

Minister and Musician', *ODNB* [55931].

17 Knox, *Works*, vi, p. 34.

18 See Dawson, 'The Face of Ane Perfyt Reformed Kyrk'.

19 For a wider discussion of how people in a pre-industrial society used important events in their lives for constructing memories and providing a personal chronology, see John Bedell, 'Memory and Proof of Age in England 1272–1327', *Past and Present* 162 (1999), 3–27.

20 *RPS*, 1587/7/133.

21 For example, John Winram, the post-Reformation Superintendent of Fife quoted

these recent converts as ideologically unsound, it was far more satisfactory to put forward a narrative of a shared moment of revelation, a communal movement from darkness into light, from ignorance into knowledge. This convenient perspective on events is apparent in Edinburgh burgh council's decree of April 1561 regarding the abolition of the vintners' confraternity of St Anthony. According to the burgh council, the confraternity was founded 'in the time of blindness and misknowledge of the truth', but since 'it has pleased the Almighty to open the eyes of all people' it was now 'known that all such confraternities, bands, and promises (invented by ungodly sort of papists for filling of their bellies) are contrary to the will and glory of God'.[22] The councillors drew a clear distinction between their own enlightened times and the period 'heretofore in time of ignorance' – a concept which surfaces repeatedly in the Edinburgh records from the early 1560s.

The characterisation of reform as a particular moment of conversion did more, though, than simply assuage the consciences of officials with a problematic past. It also provided a justification for prosecuting recalcitrant individuals who insisted on clinging to Catholic customs. When the head of the Dominican order in Scotland, Friar John Grierson, joined the Reformed Church in March 1560, his recantation conceded that 'in time bypast' he had upheld 'diverse kinds of superstition' and (significantly) 'remained over long at the opinion and defence of such things'.[23] Similar admissions are to be found in the confessions of other Catholic churchmen from the early 1560s. Their offence was not that they were ever Catholic (that was true of most adults in Scotland at the time), but that they continued to be so after the acceptable cut-off point of the conversion of their local community.

Stating that a community was reformed and that 'the multitude of the inhabitants' were now 'by profession and protestation adjoined into a Christian congregation' served a clear polemical purpose.[24] However, we should not discount the genuine jubilation that probably lay behind many early statements of Protestant success. When, in 1564, the St Andrews Kirk Session rejoiced in their liberation from 'the bondage and yoke of Antichrist' and proclaimed their deliverance by 'the light of the Evangel of Jesus Christ' its members would have known that only six years earlier people were being burnt for propounding Reformist views.[25] There is even less reason to doubt the sincerity of William Douglas (later 6th earl of Morton) when in the late 1560s he wrote in his private memoir that he praised God for 'the planting of this thy kirk newly reformed within this country from ignorance and idolatry,

above, was a former Augustinian canon, and had previously been actively involved in Catholic heresy trials. For a relatively sympathetic discussion of Winram's complicated religious loyalties see Linda Dunbar, *Reforming the Scottish Church: John Winram (c. 1492–1582) and the Example of Fife* (Aldershot, 2002).

[22] J.D. Marwick (ed.), *Extracts from the Records of the Burgh of Edinburgh, volume 3* (Edinburgh, 1875), p. 111.

[23] Hay Fleming (ed.), *Register*, i, pp. 16–17.

[24] Ibid., i, p. 134.

[25] Ibid., i, p. 198.

whereof thy whole kirk of Scotland, and I as a poor member thereof, does render thy most humble and hearty thanks'.[26] The religious transformation (particularly in urban areas of Lowland Scotland) undertaken in the years around 1560 was remarkable, and, from a Protestant perspective, given by God. In such a context it is perhaps unsurprising that even John Knox felt that 'the trumpet soundeth overall' and 'the long thirst of my wretched heart is satisfied in abundance'.[27]

For much of the 1560s, Scottish Protestants usually perceived the Reformation as a success story, the sudden triumph of a righteous cause. However, as James VI's reign (1567–1625) went on members of the Church of Scotland increasingly abandoned the depiction of reform as a rapid and effective conversion, in favour of a concept of a flawed and unfinished struggle. When, and why, did this shift in opinion take place?

Although the 1560s were not without difficulties for the Reformed Church, an optimistic spirit seems to have persisted for much of Mary, Queen of Scots' personal rule (1561–67). Protestant confidence in the achievements of the recent past, and hope for the future, survived (and was perhaps reinforced by) Mary's deposition, and the establishment of the regency of the earl of Moray in the summer of 1567. In January 1568 the General Assembly of the Church of Scotland rejoiced that:

> The Lord our God hath at all times been from the beginning of this his work of reformation … most beneficial and bountiful toward this realm, so that he now by this last, but most miraculous victory and overthrow, poured forth the riches of his mercies … as now we may think well our ship is received, and placed in a most happy and blessed port; our enemies, praised be God, are dashed; religion established; sufficient provision made for ministers … and above all, a godly magistrate, whom God of his eternal and heavenly Providence hath reserved to this age …[28]

However, the murder of Regent Moray (the so-called 'godly magistrate') in January 1570 seems to have been followed by a shift in Calvinist attitudes towards the extent of their success in Scotland. The anonymous (though apparently anti-Marian) author of the *Diurnal of Remarkable Occurrents* remarked that 'the death of my lord regent was the cause of great dolour to all them of Christ's religion'.[29] Meanwhile, the notes made by John Knox's secretary Richard Bannatyne on the early months of 1570 implore God to

[26] NRS, GD150/2234. I am grateful to Jane Dawson for bringing this document to my attention.

[27] It must be admitted that Knox's views did fluctuate over time. However, his letters often reveal high elation at the progress of reform – though he does also express fear and frustration at moments of crisis. Knox, *Works*, vi, pp. 21, 78.

[28] Thomson (ed.), *Acts and Proceedings of the General Assemblies*, i, p. 120.

[29] *Diurnal*, p. 156.

show mercy 'upon thy poor kirk, and upon me that sobs for resolution, at thy good pleasure!'.[30]

The succeeding decade saw major divisions within the Church of Scotland, and growing criticism of the nature and legacy of the Reformation of 1560. Critiques came from a variety of factions within the Reformed Kirk. Increasingly, those of a less radical frame of mind voiced reservations about the unruly and destructive nature of religious change. When John Maxwell, 4th Lord Herries, compiled his memoirs in the 1570s (and perhaps early 1580s), he was highly critical of the Reformers' attacks on religious sites. Describing the early phases of the Reformation campaign, Herries stated:

> Now arises tumults upon tumults, killing of priests, sacking and pulling down of churches, ruining of stately abbacies, and other glorious buildings, dissolving hospitals; all in confusion. In a word, these ancient buildings and brave fabrics, monuments of antiquity and marks of piety ... shall, in few months be destroyed and razed to the ground! The ornaments and riches of the churches fell to the share of the common rabble; the estates and lands were divided amongst the great men, by themselves, without any right or law ...[31]

Such comments are striking coming from a man who for much of 1559 was imprisoned by the Crown for his Protestant views.[32] Herries' concerns about the violence and disorderliness of the Reformation arguably indicate how alarmed conservative nobles were by ongoing political disruption. The instability of the late 1560s and early 1570s seems to have led some sections of Scottish society to re-evaluate their perceptions of previous religious upheavals.

Lord Herries was of course one of the nobles who opposed the deposition of Mary, Queen of Scots, an experience which probably shaped his views on rebellions. Yet during the childhood of James VI doubts about the events of 1559 and 1560 also spread among members of the king's government. James Melville (admittedly, hardly an impartial commentator) claimed that in the 1570s the regent, James Douglas, 4th earl of Morton, criticised the Reformation of Perth by saying 'tauntingly, "Read ye ever of such an act as we did at St Johnston?"'[33] To which provocation James' uncle Andrew Melville supposedly replied 'If ye be ashamed of that act, Christ will be ashamed of you!' Regent Morton's doubts about what had happened at Perth in 1559 were perhaps influenced by the challenge to royal authority

[30] Robert Pitcairn (ed.), *Memorials of Transactions in Scotland, A.D. MDLXIX – A.D. MDLXXIII. By Richard Bannatyne, Secretary to John Knox* (Edinburgh, 1836), p. 18.
[31] Robert Pitcairn (ed.), *Historical Memoirs of the Reign of Mary Queen of Scots and a Portion of the Reign of James the Sixth. By Lord Herries* (Edinburgh, 1836), p. 38.
[32] G.R. Hewitt, 'Maxwell, John, Fourth Lord Herries of Terregles (c.1512–1583)', *ODNB* [18403].
[33] Robert Pitcairn (ed.), *The Autobiography and Diary of Mr James Melvill* (Edinburgh, 1842), p. 68.

posed by hardline Protestants such as Andrew Melville in the 1570s.[34] Yet the damage to religious buildings during the Reformation rising may have also been a concern. In 1573 Regent Morton backed taxes to repair parish churches. Significantly, the legislation in support of the taxation sadly noted that 'there have been diverse parish kirks within this realm demolished, cast down and destroyed for the most part'.[35] Such reservations persisted in government circles after Morton's execution. When, in November 1581, the Scottish Parliament established a commission to reorganise hospitals and alms houses it was noted that 'under colour of reformation of the religion' significant funds had been diverted to other purposes and 'the godly houses that were appointed for receiving and lodging of the poor' had been 'demolished'.[36] The resulting lack of provision for the impoverished was described as 'a deed that in no part of Christendom, yea, not amongst the very Turks, would be suffered'.

The increasing negativity regarding the rising of 1559 and 1560 was initially controversial – as indicated by a disagreement about remarks supposedly made by John Rutherford, Provost of St Salvator's College in St Andrews around 1572. In a letter to John Knox, Rutherford stated concern about reports that he had said 'Cupar in Fife and St Johnston were ever authors of sedition!'[37] Instead Rutherford claimed his actual words were 'in Cupar and in St Johnston was oft sedition, and so the persons of these towns should beware withal', and therefore he beseeched Knox 'I would ye meddled nothing in the matter, as it appertains nothing to you; and I assure you we have as good zeal in this college towards God's word … as any other.'[38]

While in the early 1570s John Rutherford was clearly worried by suggestions that he had criticised Knox's reforming actions, as James VI grew to adulthood the belief that the Reformation of 1560 was alarmingly turbulent became entrenched in court circles – not least because of the opinions of the young king. During the early 1580s (and in particular after the Ruthven Raid of 1582 when James was imprisoned for ten months), relations between the monarch and many supporters of Presbyterian church government deteriorated.[39] Against a background of tensions between crown and kirk the events of 1559 and 1560 were reinterpreted. In his memoirs James Melville regretfully observed that the teenage James VI began 'to think worst of the best men that ever served in this kirk and country; to think the whole manner of reformation of religion to have been done by

[34] Andrew Melville's attitudes to royal authority were complex and arguably evolved during his lifetime. He generally appears to have regarded monarchy as integral to good governance, but rejected royal interference in church affairs. For discussion of Andrew Melville's attitudes to James VI and monarchy see Steven Reid, 'Andrew Melville and the Law of Kingship', in Mason and Reid (eds), *Andrew Melville*, pp. 47–74.

[35] *RPS*, A1573/1/13.

[36] *RPS*, 1581/10/36.

[37] Pitcairn (ed.), *Historical Memoirs*, p. 257.

[38] Ibid., pp. 257–58.

[39] Reid, 'Andrew Melville and the Law of Kingship', pp. 51–52.

a privy faction, turbulently and treasonably'.[40] This accusation was not without foundation, as the king's adult writings demonstrate. In *Basilicon Doron* James VI complained that 'the reformation of religion in Scotland' was 'extraordinarily wrought' and that 'many things were inordinately done by a popular tumult and rebellion … and not proceeding from the Prince's order, as it did in our neighbour country of England'.[41] For the king (and other advocates of increased deference and religious hierarchy), the rising of the Lords of the Congregation came to symbolise what had gone wrong with the implementation of reform in Scotland.

Yet interestingly, criticism of the events and achievements of 1560 was not confined to the most ardent supporters of James VI's religious policies. By the later decades of the sixteenth century many who backed Presbyterian church government were also voicing reservations about the Reformation and its legacy. In January 1572, David Ferguson (who participated in the rising of 1559, and subsequently became moderator of the General Assembly of the Church of Scotland) delivered a sermon at Leith condemning the destruction and disrepair of church buildings. Ferguson claimed that Scottish churches 'where the word of God should be preached and the sacraments ministered' had descended into 'ruin and decay'.[42] In Ferguson's eyes the kirks were 'so profaned' that had he been a visitor from Germany (or 'any other country where Christ is truly preached, and all things done decently') and travelled to Scotland, 'the foul deformity and desolation' of religious buildings would have led him to doubt whether 'there had been any fear of God or right religion in the most part of this realm'.[43] Similar concerns about damage to churches were raised by the anonymous author of *The Lamentation of Lady Scotland*, probably printed in March 1573 and dedicated to that veteran of reform (and Superintendent of Angus and the Mearns) John Erskine of Dun.[44] According to *The Lamentation*:

> The rooms appointed people to consider,
> To hear God's word, where they should pray together,
> Are now converted in sheep-cots and folds,
> Or else are fallen, because none them upholds;
> The parish kirks, I mean, they so misguide
> That none for wind and rain therein may bide …[45]

[40] Pitcairn (ed.), *Autobiography and Diary of Mr James Melvill*, p. 119.

[41] James Craigie (ed.), *The Basilicon Doron of James VI*, 2 vols (Edinburgh, 1944), i, p. 75. Roger Mason has of course previously discussed this passage and its connection to James' views on church governance. Roger Mason, 'George Buchanan, James VI and the Presbyterians', in Mason, *Kingship and the Commonweal*, pp. 196–200.

[42] John Lee (ed.), *Tracts by David Fergusson, Minister of Dunfermline* (Edinburgh, 1860), p. 73.

[43] Ibid., p. 73.

[44] James Cranstoun (ed.), *Satirical Poems of the Time of the Reformation*, 2 vols (Edinburgh, 1891), i, pp. 226–39.

[45] Ibid., i, p. 232.

Comparable criticisms are made of the state of university buildings, where:

> I see your temples casten down and riven:
> The most part are but thatched with the heaven ...[46]

As the century wore on, the ruinous buildings and poor funding of the Reformed Kirk were increasingly ascribed by Presbyterian writers to the events of 1559 and 1560. In the late 1590s Robert Pont (who served six times as moderator of the General Assembly of the Church of Scotland) bemoaned that:

> At the first reformation of religion amongst us ... a great many ... joined themselves with the congregation of the reformers, not so much for zeal of religion, as to reap some earthly commodity, and to be enriched by the spoil of the kirks and abbey places. And when the preachers told them that such places of idolatry should be pulled down, they accepted gladly the enterprise; and rudely passing to work, pulled down all, both idols and places where they were found. Not making difference between these places of idolatry and many parish kirks where God's word should have been preached ...[47]

The lived reality of roofless choirs and decaying naves seems to have caused some (even quite radical) members of the Church of Scotland to rethink the Reformers' enthusiastic iconoclasm. Yet these criticisms contrast with the delight in destruction recorded in Protestant writings from 1559. In June of that year, Knox gleefully informed his friend Anne Locke that Lindores Abbey 'was reformed, their altars overthrown, their idols, vestments of idolatry, and mass books were burnt' before exclaiming 'thus far hath God advanced the glory of his dear Son amongst us'.[48]

While ministers such as Ferguson and Pont regretted the material destruction of reform, other advocates of Presbyterian government felt the settlement of 1560 failed to bring about the moral transformation of the people of Scotland. The 1570s and 1580s saw many Protestants (especially those of a radical persuasion) profoundly depressed about the state of religion in Scotland, and by extension the inheritance of the Reformation. There was in some quarters concern that reform had not fulfilled its early promise. In August 1589, the ministers of Dundee complained to the burgh council about poor church attendance, 'delating the coldness and lack of the former zeal which was in the hearts of all persons at the beginning and opening up of the evangel now preached and taught among us'.[49] Similar worries

[46] Ibid., i, p. 233.
[47] Robert Pont, *Against Sacrilege: Three Sermons Preached by Maister Robert Pont* (Edinburgh, 1599), f. 14r.
[48] Knox, *Works*, vi, p. 26.
[49] Alex J. Warden (ed.), *Burgh Laws of Dundee, with the History, Statutes, & Proceedings of the Guild of Merchants and Fraternities of Craftsmen* (London, 1872), pp. 126–27.

afflicted the elders of Perth's kirk session, a little further up the River Tay. In November 1587 the Perth Kirk Session forbade any interaction with papists, complaining that some local residents had 'been keeping familiar society with them, contrary to God's command, and to the great slander and infection of this congregation where the truth first began in this kingdom to be published'.[50] As the sixteenth century progressed there seems to have been a feeling that the 'godly enterprise of bringing the spiritual building of the house of God to perfection' was facing 'many and great impediments'.[51]

It was against this discontented background that the idea of a 'first' and 'second' Reformation began to develop. Today the phrase 'the Second Reformation' is often applied to the Covenanting movement (an association it had already gained by the mid-seventeenth century).[52] However, the concept of multiple periods of reform predates the events of 1638. When, in the autumn of 1585, a group of banished nobles petitioned James VI against taking advice from 'persons of no desert or worthiness', they protested against religious policies which undermined 'laudable custom permitted ever since the first reformation of religion'.[53] The phrase 'the first reformation of religion' was of course also used by Robert Pont in the passage quoted above, and repeatedly employed by James Melville.[54] By the early seventeenth century the concept of a 'first reformation' seems to have been relatively established. For instance, in the 1622 treatise *The Course of Conformitie* (probably written by the minister of Cupar, William Scott) the imaginary character Epaphras states: 'To begin then with your first demand, the length thereof reaching from the first reformation, through manifold alterations, to the last Parliament.'[55] Arguably, the notion of a 'first' Reformation was more than a mere chronological description. It implied that the initial era of reform was incomplete or insufficient – an inference drawn by the English Puritan author Oliver Pigg who in 1591 described how the Biblical King Josiah 'twice in his days reformed religion, the first reformation not being perfect enough'.[56]

The concept of an imperfect Reformation obviously had a particular relevance to Godly English audiences. Yet it also fitted with perceptions among Protestant Scots that the work of reform was still ongoing. The Church of Scotland's *Second Book of Discipline* (completed in 1578) carefully listed 'the present abuses remaining in the Kirk' and described the reorganisation of

50 Margo Todd (ed.), *The Perth Kirk Session Books, 1577–1590* (Woodbridge, 2012), p. 383.

51 Thomson (ed.), *Acts and Proceedings of the General Assemblies*, ii, p. 446.

52 See, for instance, George Gillespie, *A Treatise of Miscellany Questions Wherein Many Usefull Questions and Cases of Conscience are Resolved* (Edinburgh, 1649), p. 22.

53 British Library, Cotton MS Caligula C/VII, ff. 358r–359r.

54 Pitcairn (ed.), *Autobiography and Diary of Mr James Melvill*, pp. 14, 78, 561, 591.

55 William Scott, *The Course of Conformitie as it hath Proceeded, is Concluded, Should be Refused* (Amsterdam, 1622), p. 3.

56 Oliver Pigg, *Sermons Upon the 101 Psalm* (London, 1591), p. 93.

church funding as 'the right reformation which God craves'.[57] The reception of *The Second Book of Discipline* was mixed. While most ministers in the General Assembly adopted its policies without 'any argument in the contrary', many figures in the Scottish government had significant reservations.[58] The rejection of bishops, the limiting of royal interference in religious matters, and the economic reforms proposed in *The Second Book of Discipline* caused concern to Regent Morton and the Privy Council – who for some months tried to ignore the recommendations because of 'urgent affairs' before eventually requesting a committee 'to review the ... book ... and to confer thereupon and upon all other things ... that may be profitable to setting forth of the said policy to the quietness of the whole kirk'.[59] Against this background of delays, prevarication, and occasional obstruction, Presbyterian clergy sought to enlist the support of the adolescent king (who at this point they still thought might be sympathetic to their cause). In July 1579 the ministers of the General Assembly wrote to James VI urging him:

> To pass forward in this great work of reformation of religion, and building of the spiritual temple of the Lord, the foundation whereof being already laid by public and universal preaching ... It resteth, that the work may be prosecute, and the building brought to a good perfection, by establishing of discipline, and meet policy in the Kirk of God ... which thing wisely begun in your Highness name, by your first Regent of godly memory, and ordained by act of Parliament to be followed forth, hath been diligently pressed for from time to time ...[60]

According to the General Assembly, the Scottish Church was a half-built edifice, with the Reformation of 1560 merely having laid the foundation for future 'travails' in the cause of 'true religion'.[61] This perspective was partly attributable to the contemporary arguments about ecclesiastical government and secular influence. However, the belief in stricter Protestant circles that reform was incomplete may have also arisen from the inherent challenge of improving the morality of a whole country.

The 1570s, 1580s, and 1590s saw repeated complaints by ministers in the General Assembly regarding the 'great coldness and slackness of religion' prevailing in Scotland and the 'licentious and godless living of the multitude'.[62] Unsurprisingly, the establishment of kirk sessions did not automatically create a kingdom of perfect Protestants; immorality and indifference persisted in some quarters.[63] What is striking, though, is the way

[57] James Kirk (ed.), *The Second Book of Discipline* (Edinburgh, 1980), pp. 217, 230.
[58] Thomson (ed.), *Acts and Proceedings of the General Assemblies*, ii, p. 408.
[59] Ibid., ii, p. 404; *RPS*, 1578/7/19.
[60] Thomson (ed.), *Acts and Proceedings of the General Assemblies*, ii, p. 445.
[61] Ibid., ii, p. 442.
[62] Ibid., ii, pp. 409–10, 446.
[63] The challenges of imposing moral discipline and creating Protestant communities are discussed in some detail in John McCallum's case study of Fife. John McCallum, *Reforming*

in which authorities in the later decades of the sixteenth century seemed to feel this inadequacy even more keenly than many Reformers in the early 1560s. According to the ministers attending the General Assembly of 1596, Scotland 'overflowed with atheism and all kind of vice' and 'sacrilege in all estates without any conscience' was 'growing continually more and more, to the utter undoing of the Kirk, and staying of the planting of the gospel'.[64] Such concerns were not confined to the ministry. In 1588 the burgh council of Edinburgh complained that 'all kind of vice is appearing to abound', and that many houses in the burgh were occupied by a range of wrongdoers, including 'papists', persons who led 'a wicked and licentious life in harlotry and theft', and 'blasphemers of God's name' (a problem the council attributed to outsiders 'flocking in' and landlords letting property without checking 'the religion or conversation of their tenants').[65] In the same year, even councillors in supposedly conservative Aberdeen were worrying about 'the coldness entered in practice within this burgh' and the 'great number of the inhabitants' who rather than attending daily sermons were 'passing to taverns and alehouses'.[66] Lapses in the morality of many Scots were linked by some members of the ministry to a failure to properly implement reform in the parishes. In 1587, the General Assembly complained about 'all kind of sin lying in every nook and part of this land', and bemoaned a range of problems including 'profaning of the Sabbath day ... gluttony, drunkenness, fighting, playing [and] dancing'.[67] Unhappy with this state of affairs the ministers advised that 'the only way to plant and continue true religion in this country, is to repair universally all ruinous kirks', before going on to stress the particular 'necessity' of establishing 'kirks with qualified ministers' in 'the North and South' and doing 'all other things that are necessary for the reformation of the saids [*sic*] bounds and reducing them to a good order, establishing of the Evangel, and good discipline of the Kirk'.[68]

The growing pessimism about the extent and success of reform are perhaps indicative of rising Protestant expectations. Although the Confession of Faith passed by Parliament in 1560 proudly likened Scottish Protestant churches to 'the true kirk of Christ ... such as was in Corinth, Galatia, Ephesus, and other places, in which the ministry was planted by Paul', the actual criteria by which it measured a Reformed congregation were relatively modest.[69] According to the Confession, the signs of a true kirk were 'preaching of the word of God', 'the right administration of the sacraments', and 'ecclesiastical discipline administered uprightly'.[70] It is perhaps significant that the Confession also had

*the Scottish Parish: The Reformation in Fife, 1560–1640* (Farnham, 2010).

64 Thomson (ed.), *Acts and Proceedings of the General Assemblies*, iii, pp. 874, 876.

65 Marwick (ed.), *Extracts from the Records of the Burgh of Edinburgh*, iv, p. 516.

66 John Stuart (ed.), *Extracts from the Council Register of the Burgh of Aberdeen*, 2 vols (Aberdeen, 1848), ii, p. 62.

67 Thomson (ed.), *Acts and Proceedings of the General Assemblies*, ii, p. 724.

68 Ibid., ii, pp. 723–24.

69 *RPS*, A1560/8/3.

70 Ibid.

an urban focus, noting how 'we, the inhabitants of the realm of Scotland … profess ourselves to have reformed [kirks] in our cities, towns, and places'.[71] Similarly, when in 1564 the St Andrews Kirk Session praised the perfection of their reformed church they concentrated on 'the city' and noted that within this space the 'sacraments' were 'duly ministered', 'all things done in the kirk by comely order established', and 'discipline used and received without contempt'.[72] In contrast, late sixteenth-century Protestant expectations of a Reformed nation were more ambitious. Increasingly, church leaders were attempting to transform religious provision across the entire country (rather than focusing on lowland burghs), while the standards of behaviour they were asking of individuals and communities were significantly stricter. By the 1590s the General Assembly of the Church of Scotland was fretting about the infrequency of 'religious exercises' in families and regretting that dinner table conversation was often 'of profane, wanton, and worldly matters'.[73]

The goalposts for successful reform shifted during the late sixteenth century. This alteration in objectives is key to understanding how and why Presbyterian attitudes towards the completeness (or otherwise) of the 'first' Reformation also changed. In the 1560s Scottish Protestants were delighted just to have established Reformed ministry in their major burghs (no mean feat considering the situation only a few years earlier). However, by the 1580s practices such as 'setting of bonfires' and 'singing of carols within and about kirks at certain seasons' were causing alarm that 'dregs of idolatry yet remain in diverse parts of the realm'.[74] The generation of Protestants living in the immediate aftermath of 1560 were amazed by recent changes. For them, 'purified' church buildings, regular preaching, and opportunities to read the Bible in the vernacular were signs of incredible progress. In contrast, Scots who had been living with such things for many years regarded these achievements as normal, and were turning their attention to problems like foul language at the royal court, and the prevalence of 'balling' and night-time entertainment amongst Anna of Denmark's 'gentlewomen'.[75] The gains of the earlier generation of Reformers had become assumed, while the moral problems which persisted seemed of grave concern. As the ministers of the General Assembly explained, it was no longer sufficient that 'the truth of the Evangel' be 'truly and sincerely preached … the next care and study ought to be, how this divine work may more and more be furthered and performed'.[76]

By the time of James VI's departure to England in 1603 many of the parameters for seventeenth-century debate about the nature and legacy of the Scottish Reformation had already been defined. When in 1639 the General Assembly declared that 'after the reformation of this Kingdom, the Kirk was

71 Ibid.
72 Hay Fleming (ed.), *Register*, i, p. 198.
73 Thomson (ed.), *Acts and Proceedings of the General Assemblies*, iii, pp. 873–74.
74 *RPS*, 1581/10/25.
75 Thomson (ed.), *Acts and Proceedings of the General Assemblies*, iii, p. 873.
76 Ibid., ii, p. 444.

still wrestling against all corruptions' and that 'the power of the enemies of reformation withstood them long', they were echoing a narrative conceived of by their radical predecessors in the Assembly during the final decades of the sixteenth century.[77] Similarly, when Archbishop John Spottiswoode bemoaned how, during the early years of reform, churches were 'either defaced, or pulled to the ground' and 'all was ruined' in 'barbarous proceedings', he was repeating a version of events outlined by men such as Lord Herries (and even perhaps Robert Pont) during the minority and young adulthood of James VI.

It has been suggested that by the seventeenth century Protestant Scots had acquired a 'mentality of continuous Reformation'.[78] However, scholars should not assume that such an attitude to reform was typical in the immediate aftermath of 1560. The ongoing religious divisions which afflicted Scotland during the late sixteenth and seventeenth centuries meant the story of the Reformation became contested and reinterpreted. While a nascent Episcopal tradition portrayed religious change in Scotland as unnecessarily turbulent, a more radical Presbyterian discourse regretted the impediments which hindered the delivery of a fully Reformed church. Yet, amidst the later doom, gloom, and recrimination, it is important not to forget the upbeat assessments of the early 1560s. According to this older generation the events of 1559 and 1560 were a transformative moment, a time when it 'pleased' God to 'illuminate the hearts of a great part ... of this realm'.[79] While this portrayal served a propagandistic purpose, it perhaps also reflected many Protestants' contemporary feelings about the righteousness and rapidity of religious change. The story of how sixteenth-century Protestants remembered the Scottish Reformation is a microcosm of how later concerns and experiences can alter perceptions of the past, reshaping an apparently successful moment of conversion into a problematic and protracted struggle. The lens of the 1590s was surprisingly different from the Protestant viewpoints recorded in the aftermath of the Rising of the Lords of the Congregation. For a period in the 1560s a vocal section of Protestant Scots seem to have been confident in the present, and thankful for the recent past. It was when 'happy beginnings' seemed not to deliver the 'success as apparently might have followed' that reservations about the nature and achievements of the Reformation arose – a pattern perhaps discernible in more places and times than sixteenth-century Scotland.[80]

[77] General Assembly of the Church of Scotland, *An Answer to the Profession and Declaration Made by James Marques of Hammilton, His Maiesties High Commissioner* (Edinburgh, 1639), p. 27.

[78] Alasdair Raffe, 'Confessions, Covenants and Continuous Reformation in Early Modern Scotland', *Études Épistémè* 32 (2017), available at https://doi.org/10.4000/episteme.1836.

[79] Hay Fleming (ed.), *Register*, i, p. 73.

[80] It should perhaps be noted that this remark by the General Assembly about 'happy beginnings' not delivering the expected 'success' is not actually a judgment about what had happened in Scotland, but a statement about the sad state of affairs in other countries (which the Assembly regards as a cautionary tale for James VI and the Scots). Thomson (ed.), *Acts and Proceedings of the General Assemblies*, ii, p. 444.

# 8

# *James and John: The Stormy Relationship between James Stewart, Regent Moray and John Knox*[1]

Jane E.A. Dawson

IN 1881 George Stuart, 14th earl of Moray, commemorated his ancestor, James Stewart, Regent Moray, by erecting a memorial stained-glass window in St Giles' Church in Edinburgh.[2] Its top panel dramatically illustrated the Regent's assassination in Linlithgow in 1570, portraying him as dying for his country, then riven by civil war. The bottom panel depicted John Knox, the Scottish Reformer, in full preaching flow delivering the funeral sermon. In Victorian Scotland it was taken as axiomatic that Moray and Knox belonged together as heroes of the Scottish Protestant Reformation. Many Scots of that period assumed Protestantism had moulded their national identity and that its providential outlook and mission was actively shaping the British Empire.[3] The sixteenth-century labels of Knox as an Old Testament prophet and Moray as a captain of Israel continued to resonate in Scotland and Britain in subsequent centuries, but their first names suggest additional New Testament parallels.[4] The apostles James and John, sons of Zebedee, had been nicknamed 'Sons of Thunder' by Jesus because they had wanted to send a fiery vengeance upon a Samaritan village that had failed to welcome him.[5] Like the first sons of thunder, James Stewart and John Knox shared a desire for

1 My grateful thanks to the two anonymous readers and the editor for helping improve an earlier rough-hewn draft of this essay and to Timothy Duffy for reading the second draft for me.

2 This was at the time of the Chambers restoration completed in 1883 that envisioned St Giles' becoming Scotland's Westminster Abbey: https://stgilescathedral.org.uk/nineteenth-century-restorations/.

3 As Stewart J. Brown commented, in Victorian Britain 'there also remained for many a strong sense of Britain as a fundamentally Christian nation, with a collective responsibility before God. This was especially true as British Christians contemplated their power and influence in the wider world'; *Providence and Empire: Religion, Politics and Society in the United Kingdom, 1815–1914* (Harlow, 2008), p. 286.

4 The term 'captain of Israel' was based on Sir Nicholas Throckmorton's report; see below. Knox believed he was a prophet like Elijah or Jeremiah: Jane Dawson, *John Knox* (New Haven, CT and London, 2015), pp. 267, 292, 297.

5 Mark 3:17; Luke 9:51–56.

vengeance against those they labelled enemies of God. They were prepared with all their might to wield the civil and the spiritual swords against their opponents. The Biblical account also related how Simon Peter, James and John were the three disciples present at Jesus' Transfiguration. Not long after that indication of their special status, their mother, Salome, had asked Jesus to, when he came to glory, place James and John on his right- and left-hand sides. This provoked indignation from their fellow disciples and a rebuke from Jesus that explained the meaning of true discipleship.[6] Moray's mother, the formidable Margaret Erskine, Lady Lochleven, was similarly ambitious for her eldest son. She did not forget that his father, King James V, had sought a papal annulment to separate her from her husband, Sir William Douglas of Lochleven, so he could marry her instead.[7] With royal blood flowing in his veins and a close facial resemblance to his father, Moray was proud of his status as 'the Queen's brother' and later as the Regent for James VI.[8] Knox was equally defensive about his divine vocation to be a prophet, leading his contemporaries to make jokes that this John was a member of God's privy council.[9] Both James and John also stirred up indignation and opposition among their fellows. Even among the honour-sensitive Scottish nobility, Moray was frequently at feud and turned former friends and allies into opponents.[10] Thinking he was surrounded by enemies, Knox often assumed that anyone who was not for him was against him. Even in their own stormy relationship, the sixteenth-century James and John fell out, refusing to speak for 18 months during 1563 and 1564.

[6] Transfiguration: Matthew 17:1–9; Mark 9:2–8; Luke 9:28–36. Salome was found in Matthew's account; Matthew 20:20–28; Mark 10:35–45.

[7] Mark Loughlin, 'James Stewart, First Earl of Moray', *ODNB* [26479]. Margaret Erskine was probably the model for Dame Sensuality in David Lyndsay's *Satire of the Three Estates*: Peter D. Anderson, 'James V, Mistresses and Children of (Act. c. 1529–1592)', *ODNB* [69935].

[8] Queen Mary spoke and wrote of her brother, for e.g. Queen Mary to Archibald Campbell, earl of Argyll, sending commendations to 'our brother' (Moray was also Argyll's brother-in law), 31 March 1566, in A. MacDonald (ed.), *Letters to the Argyll Family* (Edinburgh, 1839), pp. 5–6. When Moray was regent, he enjoyed the status of a duke and one of Melville of Halhill's criticisms was that he was surrounded by flatterers and relished being called 'your grace'. *Memoirs of his own life by Sir James Melville of Halhill* (Edinburgh, 1827), p. 261.

[9] The joke seemed to have originated with Thomas Randolph, the English ambassador, but Knox became very upset in 1571 when it was recycled by the Queen's Party: Knox, *Works*, vi, pp. 146, 592; Dawson, *Knox*, p. 291.

[10] Bishop John Leslie later asserted that Moray deliberately undermined the ancient nobility: John Leslie, *The History of Scotland* (Edinburgh, 1830), p. 300. Moray had serious feuds with James Hepburn, earl of Bothwell; George Gordon, earl of Huntly; and John Hamilton, archbishop of St Andrews. He quarrelled with his friends, Archibald Campbell, earl of Argyll; William Maitland of Lethington; William Kirkcaldy of Grange; and Robert Melville of Murdocairnie and his brothers James of Halhill and Walter, one of Moray's gentlemen.

Down the centuries the reputations of James and John have been deeply influenced by the narrators' attitudes towards Mary, Queen of Scots. Based on the famous 'interviews' between Queen Mary and Knox, those two protagonists have become characterised as the Scottish version of the 'wrong and wromantic (sic)' Cavalier monarch versus the 'right and repulsive' Puritan.[11] Similarly, Moray has been cast as the scheming half-brother who betrayed and ruined his Queen. By contrast, in George Buchanan's version, as Professor Mason has explained, the Regent was a model just ruler and the polar opposite of his half-sister.[12] Since both men have been pigeonholed as Mary's opponents, the importance of their own fundamental disagreement about the Queen has been overlooked.

When writing the chronicle of his own times, Knox was aware of his part in the making or marring of the Regent's good name. Moray's Secretary, John Wood, had repeatedly pressed for the publication of the *History of the Reformation in Scotland*. Knox kept refusing his friend and 'beloved in the Lord', and finally told Wood that he would not allow the *History* to be published during his own lifetime.[13] Knox was well aware his chronicle might compromise Moray's godly reputation, but he would not modify his account of 1561–64 with its 'prophecies' about the Queen and his serious quarrel with Moray. He chose to end the *History*'s Book IV with a final sentence blaming Moray for the rift: 'In all that time the Earl of Moray was so formed to John Knox, that neither by word nor writ was there any communication between them.'[14] Once it had been published, the *History* became an extremely influential source, as Professor Mason has demonstrated in his discussions of early modern Scottish historical writing.[15] Knox's *History* has dominated assumptions made about the relationship between James and

[11] The humorous descriptions used about King Charles I and the Puritan opposition he faced during the English Civil Wars found in W.C. Sellar & R.J. Yateman, *1066 and All That* (1st edn, London, 1930), ch. 35. The Queen Mary–Knox interviews suffer from the same one-sidedness as the Moray–Knox relationship, because the details can only be found in John Knox, *History of the Reformation in Scotland*, ed. W. C. Dickinson, 2 vols (London, 1949), ii, pp. 13–20, 43–46, 71–78, 81–84. They have been brilliantly discussed by Jenny Wormald, 'Godly Reformer, Godless Monarch: John Knox and Mary, Queen of Scots', in Roger A. Mason (ed.), *John Knox and the British Reformations* (Aldershot, 1998), pp. 220–41.

[12] Professor Mason summed it up succinctly: 'There is no doubt that Moray is the real hero of the later books of the *History*, his "austerity" and "integrity" constantly contrasted with Mary's "licentiousness".' Mason and Smith, p. lxviii; Roger A. Mason, 'George Buchanan and Mary, Queen of Scots', *RSCHS* 30 (2000), 1–23.

[13] Knox told Wood, 'My purpose (not to publish) … frome which I can not be moved'. 14 February 1568, Laing (ed.), *Works of John Knox*, vi, p. 558. For historical writing in this period, see Roger Mason, 'Usable Pasts: History and Identity in Reformation Scotland', in Mason, *Kingship and the Commonweal*, pp. 165–86.

[14] Knox, *History*, ii. p. 134 and n. 4. As the textual note explains, 'This word is clearly written *formed*, but is equally intended to be *fremmed*, that is, *strange*, *foreign*, *alien*.' Book IV was the last section written by Knox with Book V composed by a continuator, probably his secretary, Richard Bannatyne: Dawson, *Knox*, pp. 256–57.

[15] See the select bibliography at the end of the book.

John, and because other sources contain little regarding Moray's point of view, it has been harder to counter-balance Knox's one-sided version of what happened.[16]

This study of Moray and Knox will start by placing the two men in their personal social contexts and then concentrate upon the period from 1558, rather than offering a blow-by-blow account of their entire relationship. It will examine how the Scottish Protestant Reformation Crisis (1559–60) threw the two men together and how they helped bring about the victory of the summer of 1560 that signalled a new Anglo-Scottish friendship and the official endorsement of a Protestant Confession of Faith. The relative harmony of that partnership did not survive the return of Queen Mary to her native land in 1561, with the following years bringing a serious rupture where they stopped speaking to each other for 18 months. The prospect of the Scottish Queen's marriage to Henry, Lord Darnley, horrified both men. Though it brought them into alliance once more, Moray's disastrous rebellion forced him into a humiliating exile in England. Following the murder of Riccio, Moray was restored to the Queen's favour, but during the crisis-ridden final period of Mary's personal rule (1566–67), both James and John appeared to step away from the limelight, with Knox withdrawing for over a year from the capital. After the murder of Darnley and the rise to pre-eminence of the earl of Bothwell, Moray obtained royal permission to leave Scotland in the spring of 1567. New evidence suggests that when passing through England to France, Moray might have met Knox in London when the preacher was on an extended visit through that kingdom. The relationship between the two men entered a new phase when Moray returned in August 1567 to accept the Regency for the child King James VI. Knox gave his full support to the new Regent and to the King's Party in the subsequent civil wars. Moray's assassination in January 1570 had a profound impact upon Knox, who spent the remaining two years of his own life bent on vengeance upon the Hamilton kindred and the entire Queen's Party whom he held responsible for the murder. Alongside the political writings of George Buchanan,[17] Knox

16 Knox has attracted far more biographical interest than Moray. From Thomas McCrie's ground-breaking *Life of John Knox* (Edinburgh, 1812) and especially after David Laing's six volume edition of Knox's *Works*, there has been no shortage of biographies. More recently, scholarly examination was boosted by the 'John Knox and the British Reformations' conference and essays organised by Professor Mason, and aided by his encouragement and help, this led to my own biography (see above). The standard treatment of Moray's life has been Maurice Lee Jnr, *James Stewart Earl of Moray* (Westport, CT, 1953), with an excellent summary by Mark Loughlin in the *Oxford Dictionary of National Biography*. The regency has been covered by Claire L. Webb: 'The "Gude Regent"? A Diplomatic Perspective upon the Earl of Moray, Mary, Queen of Scots, and the Scottish Regency, 1567–1570' (unpublished University of St Andrews PhD thesis, 2008), and Amy Blakeway's perceptive analysis, *Regency in Sixteenth-Century Scotland* (Woodbridge, 2015).

17 Professor Mason, in his edition of Buchanan's *De Iure Regni* and his numerous essays, has dominated the recent study of Buchanan.

helped develop the abiding image of Moray as a Godly Regent who had died serving his country and his Protestant faith.

## James Stewart and John Knox

GIVEN the social structure of early modern Scotland, the relationship between James and John was framed by their different social positions. John Knox was born around 1515 into a Haddington family from the higher reaches of the burgh's merchant community, which had international trading connections. He had taken priestly orders in the Catholic Church and become a notary apostolic before his conversion to Protestantism and later calling to the Reformed ministry. Knox married 'above his station', first to the Englishwoman, Marjorie Bowes, from a family of landed gentry in royal service in the north-east of England. His second marriage in 1564 was to the young Margaret Stewart, daughter of Andrew, Lord Ochiltree. The identity of Knox's bride infuriated his monarch, 'whear at the Quene stormethe wonderfullye, for that she [Margaret] is of the bludde and name'.[18] Moray's reaction to becoming Knox's distant relative by marriage was not recorded. As Edinburgh's leading Reformed cleric, Knox ranked alongside the Superintendents of the new kirk in terms of his status and salary. Like medieval 'holy men', his self-adopted role as the kingdom's 'prophet' placed him outside the conventional social hierarchy.

That did not alter the fact that John was manifestly the social inferior of James, the King's son born in 1531 or 1532. James V had acknowledged and provided for his nine illegitimate offspring, and after his death, his widow, Mary of Guise, with considerable generosity of spirit increased their involvement at court. Two of the king's illegitimate sons were named after him, but the elder, who had been made commendator abbot of both Melrose and Kelso, died in 1557.[19] This left James, the future earl of Moray, as the eldest among his father's children. Taking this responsibility seriously, he assumed he had the right to criticise his siblings and act as their representative. In 1538 James was made commendator prior of St Andrews, one of the richest of Scotland's monasteries, where he was supervised by John Winram, the sub-prior, who became his mentor and father-figure.[20] Though not making monasticism his profession nor taking full sacramental orders, Lord James was educated to become a high-ranking ecclesiastic.[21] Alongside his book learning at the

[18] Randolph to Cecil, 18 March 1564, *CSP Scot.*, ii, no. 67.

[19] The seal matrix for the elder James Stewart, purchased recently by the National Museum of Scotland, demonstrates the full status his royal father wanted for his sons. See www.nms.ac.uk/about-us/press-office/james-stewart-seal-matrix/.

[20] Linda J Dunbar, *Reforming the Scottish Church: John Winram (c. 1492–1582) and the Example of Fife* (Aldershot, 2002) pp. 8–10, 163–66.

[21] Lord James donated books from this period to his alma mater, St Leonard's College; D.W. Doughty, 'The Library of James Stewart, Earl of Moray, 1531–70', *IR* 21 (1970), 17–29.

priory's St Leonard's College, he was trained in noble pursuits and took an active part in military engagements in Fife during the Rough Wooing.[22] Throughout the 1550s James' lay or clerical status remained unresolved, though no one lost sight of the fact that he was the Queen's brother.[23]

John Winram was thus the first link between his protege and John Knox. The teenage commendator first encountered Knox, the schoolmaster turned Protestant preacher, in St Andrews. In 1547 during the siege of the Castle that followed the murder of Cardinal Beaton, Winram arranged a disputation in St Leonard's College Yards. The Protestant preachers Knox and John Rough debated with the Franciscan Friar Alexander Arbuckle, who might have been one of Lord James' teachers.[24] James was merely an interested observer and did not have a proper conversation with Knox until they met in London in 1552, possibly at Winram's suggestion.[25] Four years later Lord James was part of a religious discussion at Calder House in Lothian during Knox's brief clandestine preaching tour in Scotland. When Knox returned to Geneva, letters were exchanged between him and the Scottish Protestant nobles.[26] During 1558 and 1559 Scotland and Europe experienced a series of events that dramatically shifted their political alignments. At Easter 1558, Mary, Queen of Scots, married Francis, the Dauphin of France, thereby cementing the Franco-Scottish dynastic union. The death in the following November of Queen Mary Tudor of England and succession of her half-sister, Queen Elizabeth, made the young Scottish Queen the 'true heir' to the English throne in Roman Catholic eyes. The change of English monarch had also made it easier to conclude the long-running European wars between the Habsburg and Valois dynasties in the Peace of Câteau-Cambrésis of April 1559. As a consequence, the Scottish political landscape appeared very different in the spring of 1559 from the start of 1558, and this had a direct impact upon both James and John and upon their relationship. It changed from a nodding acquaintance into a close alliance that transformed their lives.

[22] *The Historie and Cronicles … by Robert Lindesay of Pitscottie*, ed. A.J.G. Mackay, 3 vols (Edinburgh, 1899–1911), ii, pp. 104, 108–9.

[23] Lady Lochleven appeared to be contemplating a sideways move for Lord James into the secular nobility. Pre-nuptial negotiations were completed in 1550 regarding James and Christina Stewart, the young heiress of the Buchan earldom who was in her care. Dunbar, *Winram*, pp. 163–64.

[24] Knox, *History*, i, pp. 90–92.

[25] Knox recalled these initial encounters in his 'discharge' letter to Moray (see below): Knox, *History*, ii, p. 78.

[26] Lord James signed earlier letters to Knox but did not sign the 'First Band' of December 1557 that marked those nobles willing openly to defend Protestant worship and its ministers. Jane E.A. Dawson, 'Bonding, Religious Allegiance and Covenanting', in Boardman and Goodare (eds), *Kings, Lords and Men*, pp. 155–72, at pp. 155–60; Dawson, *Knox*, pp. 128–36.

## Miraculous Transformations

BETWEEN March 1559 and August 1560, Scotland experienced a successful rebellion that catapulted Lord James and John Knox into national prominence and power in political and religious affairs. During that time they worked together in pursuit of their shared goals of establishing Protestantism in Scotland and creating a permanent friendship with England. In July 1560 Knox preached a stirring sermon in Edinburgh in which he thanked God for blessing the kingdom with two miracles. The first was the victory of the Lords of the Congregation over their enemies, the Roman Catholic hierarchy and the forces of French hegemony led by the late Regent, Mary of Guise. With divine aid the Lords had 'suppressed idolatry and taken from above our heads the devouring sword of merciless strangers'.[27] The second miracle was the aid received from England enabling that victory and changing the English from old enemies into new friends. The resulting amity would rest firmly on a shared Protestantism that would bind together the island of Britain.[28]

Knox's first dramatic intervention in the Reformation Crisis was his sermon in Perth on 11 May 1559, which provoked a major iconoclastic riot throughout the burgh and which has traditionally been viewed as the start of the Scottish Protestant Reformation. Having only returned to Scotland ten days earlier, Knox was not in step with the strategy of the noble Protestant leadership. The violent consequences of his sermon caught by surprise Lord James and his close friend, Archibald Campbell, earl of Argyll, at a time when they were committed to supporting the Regent. However, Mary of Guise's uncharacteristically clumsy and aggressive dealings with Perth permitted the friends to change sides and join the 'Lords of the Congregation' in open rebellion.[29] They moved directly onto the offensive in St Andrews, Scotland's ecclesiastical capital, where Lord James and Winram had already worked behind-the-scenes to gain the support or acquiescence of the university, the burgh council and the St Andrews' guilds. Knox's oratory was deliberately employed to provoke a transition from Catholic to Protestant worship and Lord James and Argyll had sufficient armed supporters to dissuade the Archbishop's men from carrying out the threat to shoot Knox as he preached. In the parish church of Holy Trinity between 11 and 14 June

[27] Knox, *History*, i, p. 333.

[28] Roger A Mason, 'Scotland, Elizabethan England and the Idea of Britain', in *Transactions of the Royal Historical Society* 14 (2004), 279–93; 'The Scottish Reformation and the Origins of Anglo-British Imperialism', in Mason, *Kingship and the Commonweal*, pp. 242–69.

[29] For the various bonds made by the Lords of the Congregation, see Dawson, 'Bonding', pp. 160–64. Once Lord James had emerged as one of the main Congregation leaders he was accused by Mary of Guise of aiming for the throne. James Melville of Halhill was sent by his then master, the Constable of France, to check on Lord James: *Memoirs*, pp. 78–79. Predictably, the accusation re-emerged during Moray's regency and was central to Thomas Maitland's and Nicol Burne's accusations: Blakeway, *Regency*, pp. 35–36, and see below.

Knox expounded the New Testament story of Christ cleansing the Temple and, unlike at Perth, an orderly 'cleansing' of the church followed.[30]

In fear of his life Archbishop John Hamilton left St Andrews to meet up with the regent based at Falkland Palace, and she dispatched troops hoping to crush the rebellion before it spread. In response Lord James gambled by marching to meet the Regent's forces before they reached the recently reformed burgh of Cupar. In what was to prove a major turning-point in the Wars of the Congregation, instead of fighting a battle at Cuparmuir, a temporary truce was negotiated. Knox hailed the timely arrival of Protestant reinforcements as miraculous: 'God did so multiply our number, that it appeared as [if] men had rained from the clouds.'[31] As an army chaplain accompanying the Congregation's troops, Knox's ability to interpret such 'miracles' and his biblically inspired vision of ultimate victory proved invaluable for troop morale.[32] When the Congregation faced defeat, Knox's preaching helped hold the troops together and motivate them to fight again; in one vivid recollection, the sermons were better than having 500 trumpets blowing in one's ears.[33] Some of Knox's hard-hitting sermons were critical of the Congregation's leaders, and his attack upon the military leadership of James Hamilton, the young earl of Arran, was deemed 'too extream'. At the start of 1560 Knox thus found himself limited to St Andrews, away 'from all public assemblies to my privat study': it was a portent of the splits to come between James and John.[34]

The second 'miraculous' transformation needed for the Protestant rebellion to succeed was diplomatic and military: gaining substantial assistance from England. From the end of June 1559, Lord James was in contact with English officials via William Kirkcaldy of Grange, his military lieutenant.[35] Grange, Knox's friend from their days in the St Andrews Castle siege, was a leading figure among the Anglophile and Protestant group within Fife who encouraged Lord James to adopt their strong commitment to an English alliance. Having spent the previous decade in exile among the

30 For the inter-relationships within St Andrews, see Roger A. Mason, 'University, City and Society', in M. Brown and K. Stevenson (eds), *Medieval St Andrews: Church, Cult, City* (Woodbridge, 2017), pp. 268–97. For the latest and best analysis of the effect upon St Andrews of the Reformation, see Bess Rhodes, *Riches and Reform: Ecclesiastical Wealth in St Andrews, c. 1520–1580* (Leiden, 2019).

31 Knox, *History*, i, p. 183. *Pitscottie*, ii, pp. 152–59 provides the most detailed account of Cuparmuir.

32 As Thomas Wode recorded in his Tenor Part-Book written in St Andrews, 'Albeit maister Knox for the maist part maid his residence heir (as the cheiff lords of the congregation often did) he read and preachit quhair the lordis wes.' Edinburgh University Library, Laing MS III 483.2, p. 137.

33 E.g. the Stirling sermon, Nov 1559, Knox, *History*, i, pp. 265–71; and Knox reminded, 'I promised unto you victory', ii, p. 80. Randolph in his letter to Cecil recalled the trumpet's effect: 7 Sept. 1561; *CSP Scot.*, i, no. 2017.

34 Knox, *Works*, vi, p. 105.

35 As it was denied at the time, Knox disguised how early contact with the English had been made: Knox, *History*, i, p. 229 n. 2; Knox and Grange's letters to Sir Henry Percy, 1 July 1559: Knox, *Works*, vi, pp. 33–36.

English, Knox possessed an extensive network of contacts, especially with his former Genevan congregation. They proved crucial in gathering support and finance in England for the Lords of the Congregation.[36] Knox could also write directly to William Cecil, Queen Elizabeth's secretary, whom he had known since King Edward VI's reign. Being the 'odious' author of the *First Blast of the Trumpet*, a denunciation of female rule that had enraged Queen Elizabeth, Knox needed to maintain a low profile in the protracted Anglo-Scottish negotiations.[37] For Lord James and the Congregation the military turning-point arrived when an English fleet was sighted off the Isle of May in the Firth of Forth in January 1560. Moray's teenage half-brother, William Douglas, who was fighting with Lord James in the rear-guard action, saw the English ships and was sure God had rescued the Congregation from certain disaster. He wrote, 'Surely it may be called thy (God's) wark for it wes thy hand that wrocht the same, for we wer na company.'[38]

During the following months Lord James negotiated the Treaty of Berwick with Queen Elizabeth's commissioners that led to the unprecedented event of an English army being welcomed into Scotland. The Congregation's victory was secured by the international pressure on France from the Habsburgs, English military assistance and Mary of Guise's death in May 1560, all of which encouraged the conclusion of a peace settlement. The negotiations brought William Cecil to Edinburgh as head of the English delegation, and Lord James formed a personal acquaintance with him that reinforced links with the English government. Over the summer of 1560 the Congregation morphed into a provisional government led by Lord James, Argyll, Arran and William Maitland of Lethington as its influential Secretary. In August the 'Reformation Parliament' accepted the *Scots Confession of Faith* and banned papal jurisdiction and Roman Catholic worship.[39] The miraculous transformations Knox had celebrated in his Thanksgiving Prayer now existed; an officially Protestant Scotland was in alliance with England, and James and John appeared to be working in harmony.

## Thunderous Clashes

THE Wars of the Congregation resulted in Lord James sitting at the centre of the Scottish government. When Queen Mary returned to rule her kingdom in August 1561, he skilfully managed to maintain and enhance that

[36] Knox's letters to Anne Locke, July 1559 to Nov. 1560: Knox, *Works*, vi, pp. 21–27, 30, 77–79, 83–85, 100–1, 103–4, 107–9.
[37] For the *First Blast*, see *Knox: On Rebellion*, pp. 3–47. Knox to Cecil, 19 July 1559: Knox, *Works*, vi, pp. 45–47; Dawson, *Knox*, pp. 143, 184–86.
[38] Cited in 'Sir William Douglas', in M.H.B. Sanderson, *Mary Stewart's People* (Edinburgh, 1987), p. 56. Michael Pearce's transcription of Douglas' memoir from NRS GD150/2234: www.academia.edu/37574010/Memoir_of_Sir_William_Douglas_of_Lochleven_c_1585_text.
[39] RPS, A1560/8/3–6.

position. In the following year Lord James achieved his personal desire of marrying his 'long love', Annas Keith, eldest daughter of the earl Marischal.[40] The wedding on 8 February 1562 'was public in the church of Edinburgh' with John Knox preaching and giving an admonition to the couple 'to behave themselves moderately in all things'. Addressing Lord James, Knox added, 'For, unto this day the Kirk of God hath received comfort by you, and by your labours; in the which, if hereafter ye shall be found fainter than that ye were before, it will be said that your wife hath changed your nature.'[41] Such a misogynistic observation offering gratuitous offence to the bride suggested that at this point Knox knew little of Annas and her Protestant piety. However, the real target of Knox's barbed remark was her husband. While a few months earlier Knox had told John Calvin that Lord James 'alone among those that frequent the Court opposes himself to ungodliness', he was now afraid the Queen and Court were working a change.[42] Queen Mary, an enthusiastic matchmaker and wedding organiser, had seized upon this royal family event to create her first major spectacle for the Scottish court. No expense was spared for the three days of wedding banqueting and elaborate festivities at Holyrood Palace.[43] The Queen showered favours upon James, creating him earl of Mar in public, and secretly also earl of Moray. She knighted ten men, six of whom were Moray's personal clients, with the special honour of becoming a 'golden knight' bestowed upon Grange.[44] A grumpy Knox was left criticising court extravagance and fearful that his ally was deserting the Protestant cause.

The previous year Lord James, with his naturally blunt and no-nonsense approach, had achieved a diplomatic triumph by travelling to France and securing an agreement with the newly widowed Queen Mary concerning her return to Scotland.[45] She would be permitted her private Catholic worship provided she recognised the current government and Protestant status quo. Knox was convinced he was about to witness a repetition of the reign of England's Queen Mary, when a female Catholic monarch rejected her kingdom's commitment to true religion and its covenant with God

[40] Randolph to Cecil, 24 Oct. 1561: *CSP Scot.*, i, no. 1035. Amy Blakeway, 'Annas [Agnes] Keith, Countess of Moray and Argyll (c. 1540–1588)', *ODNB* [70476].

[41] Knox, *History*, ii, p. 32.

[42] Knox to Calvin, 24 Oct. 1561: Knox, *Works*, vi, p. 135.

[43] The special nature of the wedding caused comment: *Diurnal*, pp. 70–71. Queen Mary's uncle said 'he never saw such a bridal in France, not (even) the king's own bridal'; *Pitscottie*, ii, p. 17 and n. 7. Expensive wedding portraits were also commissioned from Hans Eworth, a renowned Flemish painter active in England.

[44] These golden knights are discussed by Alex Maxwell Findlater, *Sir David Lyndsay's Armorial*, 2 vols (Edinburgh, 2018), i, pp. 3–4. Kirkcaldy was called 'equiti aurato' in a confirmation charter, 5 Oct. 1564: *RMS*, iv, no. 1553 (p. 360 and note). I am grateful to Alex Maxwell Findlater for clarification on these points.

[45] Mary rejected offers of Catholic support made by George Gordon, earl of Huntly. Randolph later described to Cecil how Lord James dealt with Mary according to his nature, 'rudely, homelye and bluntlye' (n. 39 above).

and persecuted Protestants.[46] In Scotland Mary of Guise had opposed the Protestants, and Knox was sure her daughter wanted to do likewise. For him, all Queen Marys would follow that agenda openly or secretly, and Lord James' agreement offered no guarantees for a Protestant Scotland. Worse in Knox's eyes, since Roman Catholic worship was 'idolatry', permitting its practice even in private breached God's covenant and would inevitably bring divine plagues upon the realm. On the first Sunday after the Queen's return, Knox's supporters put Lord James' agreement to the test by attempting to storm the Chapel Royal to stop Mass. They failed because Lord James stood protecting the chapel doors at Holyrood and ensured the priests left safely. Being proud and stubborn men, James and John were each convinced they were in the right and neither was open to compromise. The 'great familiarity' they had previously enjoyed dwindled, and Knox became increasingly suspicious of the influence upon Moray of Secretary Lethington and other 'placeboes' or 'yes-men' of the court.[47]

During the initial years of Mary's personal rule, James believed he was serving the Protestant cause domestically and internationally and that John ought to be grateful for his successes. Amity with England seemed secure as Queen Mary had been persuaded that a close friendship with her royal 'sister' was the surest route to being recognised as Queen Elizabeth's heir. Within Scottish politics the greatest Catholic magnate, George Gordon, earl of Huntly, had been removed. He had found so little favour with the Queen that he had stumbled into rebellion in the summer of 1562. At the Battle of Corrichie Lord James defeated the Gordons himself, and he and his clients benefitted from their forfeiture. The new Reformed Kirk continued to enjoy the exclusive use of the kingdom's parish churches, and a public celebration of Mass by the Archbishop of St Andrews had been prosecuted as an illegal act. Despite Knox's carping, the 'thirds of benefices' tax on the resources of the Catholic Church had been authorised and provided an income stream from which ministers could be paid.[48] Mary's government under Moray's aegis proceeded to uphold Protestant morality – laws were passed against adultery and witchcraft, and legislation concerning manses, glebes and church repairs gave the Kirk additional control over the parish system.

Moray also attempted to draw Knox into a more cordial relationship with the Queen through a series of personal meetings. He was usually present

[46] Knox was radicalised by Mary Tudor's persecution of English Protestants and had created a composite character in his mind, encompassing three Marys; Mary, Queen of England, Mary of Guise, and Mary, Queen of Scots. He assumed that, whatever the individual's personality, the same stereotypical behaviour would result: Dawson, *Knox*, pp. 317–18.

[47] Knox, *History*, ii, pp. 79, 81, 94. Knox was constantly clashing with Lethington: Mark Loughlin, 'The Career of Maitland of Lethington, c.1526–1573' (unpublished University of Edinburgh PhD thesis, 1991) and his *ODNB* article: 'William Maitland of Lethington, (1525x30–73)' [17838].

[48] Knox had quipped that two thirds remained with the Devil and the final third was split between the Devil and the Kirk, but some of his own salary and benefits were provided by the scheme: Knox, *History*, ii, p. 29; Dawson, *Knox*, p. 222.

during these private discussions but rarely intervened.[49] These encounters only served to confirm Knox's pre-existing opinion of his sovereign and underscored how different his approach was, with its aggressive and disdainful interrogation of Mary that frequently reduced her to tears, from Moray's careful handling of his sister.

The calling of the first parliament of Mary's personal rule in 1563 brought matters to a head between James and John, and it produced a blinding row between them: 'The matter fell so hot betwixt the Earl of Moray and some others of the Court, and John Knox, that familiarly after that time they spake not together more than a year and a half.' To confirm the break, Knox sent a 'letter of discharge' containing a providential chronology of their relationship, tracing its inception to the current breakdown. He drew particular attention to the divine intervention that had secured Moray's rise in political fortune, 'above man's judgement'.[50] John declared to James that henceforth he would abstain from 'all further intromission or care with his affairs'. Believing the warning delivered at Moray's wedding had been ignored, Knox condemned Moray's lack of religious zeal and the pursuit of his personal advancement:

> But seeing that I perceive myself frustrate of my expectation, which was, that ye should ever have preferred God to your own affection, and the advancement of his truth to your singular commodity, I commit you to your own wit, and to the conducting of those who better can please you.

Donning his prophetic hat, Knox added a final barb:

> I praise my God, I this day leave you victor of your enemies, promoted to great honours, and in credit and authority with your Sovereign. If so ye long continue, none within this realm shall be more glad than I shall be: but if that after this ye shall decay (as I fear that ye shall), then call to mind by what means God exalted you; which was neither by bearing with impiety, neither yet by maintaining of pestilent Papists.[51]

Knox's prediction of James' future 'decay' proved only too accurate when Moray's policy of amity between the English and Scottish Queens was wrecked on the rock of the English succession. Moray's political power was destroyed by the return of Matthew Stewart, earl of Lennox, and of his son, Henry Stewart, Lord Darnley, whom the Queen chose as her second husband.

49 As Wormald noted, one of Moray's remarks revealed how different his views were from Knox's concerning the right of resistance: 'Godly Reformer, Godless Monarch', pp. 224–25.

50 Knox, *History*, ii, p. 78. Unfortunately, Knox in his *History* only included the text of his concluding discharge and not the entire letter.

51 Knox noted that some of Moray's supporters were happy for the split to continue and poured oil on the flames of the quarrel: Knox, *History*, ii, pp. 78–79.

## Trust in God

In the winter of 1565–66 Moray's fortunes were at their lowest ebb: his rebellion against Queen Mary and King Henry had been a disaster, and the promised help had not been forthcoming from England. He was profoundly shaken by the loss of status and power he had enjoyed as the Queen's pre-eminent adviser and trusted brother, and his fall revealed his vulnerability because his power-base could not weather royal disfavour.[52] In exile Moray continued to rely upon his English friends, despite being subjected to Queen Elizabeth's harangue on the wickedness of rebelling against his monarch that was staged to impress the London diplomatic corps. From Newcastle, where he spent most of his exile, Moray wrote to his wife, Annas, on 17 February 1566, 'I pray zow be blyth and prayse God for all that he sendis for it is he only that gevis and takis and it is he only that may and will restoyr agayne.' He closed, 'with my commendatious to all freyndis that ar freyndis in deid, the number quhairof is growen merwelous skant, praysed be God quha met preserve zou .... Zouris as ze knaw.'[53] During this time of trouble, James relied upon his wife to manage affairs in Scotland and clung fast to his personal faith and Protestant devotions.[54] Moray had long been drawn to the story of Abraham's faith as related in Romans 4:18 and used the phrase 'In spe contra spem' (hoping against hope) as the motto he placed inside some of his own books.[55] He and his household were renowned for their Reformed piety with a Biblical chapter read at mealtimes often accompanied by discussion on its interpretation with the 'learned' at his table.[56] In 1562 Moray had commissioned the setting for four parts of the new Psalm book, producing

[52] When outlawed, his fellow rebel, Argyll, was able to retreat to the West Highlands, but Moray's base in St Andrews Priory was sequestrated and his Fife clients were specifically targeted by Queen Mary and King Henry. Archbishop Hamilton invoked his regality powers to take possession of the Priory's assets, and a legal battle was required to regain them for the crown. The harassment and dispossession of Countess Annas, who was pregnant, added to Moray's bitterness. Dunbar, *Winram*, pp. 140–42.

[53] Edinburgh, NLS, MS 73, f. 13r, printed in T. Thomson *et al.* (eds), *Registrum honoris de Morton*, 2 vols (Edinburgh, 1853), i, pp. 14–15. The English attempt in October 1565 to rescue Annas had failed: Francis Russell, earl of Bedford to English Privy Council, 12 Nov. 1565; TNA SP59/10, f. 186v.

[54] Knox's best friend, Christopher Goodman, had been the minister at St Andrews, and in November 1565 he came from Countess Annas to join Moray in Newcastle. Moray wrote to the earl of Leicester to help secure for Goodman, 'my verrye good freynd', a licence to preach in England: 7 Dec. 1565, BL Egerton MS 1818, f. 39.

[55] Doughty referred to it as a stoical motto and missed the additional reference to Romans: 'The Library of James Stewart, Earl of Moray', pp. 22, 27–29. Another motto was displayed on Moray's wedding portrait: 'Recte (faciendo) securus' ('Safe by doing right or acting justly').

[56] Dana Sutton, Hypertext critical edition of George Buchanan's *Rerum Scoticarum Historia* (Philological Museum, 2009), www.philological.bham.ac.uk/scothist/, Book 19, para. 52; Calderwood, *History*, ii, p. 511.

what is now known as the Wode Psalter.[57] A keen sermon attender, Moray stopped political business to go to the preaching and, even though his Edinburgh lodging was a good distance from St Giles', returned for Sunday afternoon sermons. [58] While aware of Moray's piety, Knox had been unable to comprehend how anyone who possessed 'true' Protestant zeal would fail to follow the unequivocal divine commands that he had been proclaiming in his sermons.

As Moray had remarked to his wife, it was easy to recognise those few friends and supporters who had remained loyal. Possibly brokered by Christopher Goodman, their mutual friend, Moray's stand-off with Knox had been resolved at the end of 1564. What had not been mended was the unified Protestant party of 1559–60 that Knox had done so much to break after the Queen's return. During the 1565 rebellion, Moray's cry of 'the Kirk in danger' fell on deaf ears as many Scottish allies and co-religionists backed Queen Mary. In the event, Moray's exile in England only lasted an uncomfortable and penniless few months.[59] The experience did not alter James' belief in the worth of an English alliance.[60] The prospect of parliamentary forfeitures mobilised domestic opposition, and a coup was planned to alter Queen Mary's 'Catholic' policies and remove her favourite, David Riccio.[61] Having a remission for their rebellion signed by King Henry (Darnley), Moray and his fellow exiles waited close to Edinburgh on 9 March 1566. That night, when Riccio was murdered in front of the Queen, they benefitted greatly by not being present in the Palace of Holyrood. The Queen countered the coup, regaining control by manipulating Darnley. She then pardoned Moray and turned her fury upon Riccio's murderers, who, with the exception of her husband, were driven into exile. Having been party to the Riccio plot, Knox quit the capital, giving up his St Giles' ministry and retreating to the safety of Ayrshire. Refusing to return to his Edinburgh ministry, Knox remained in Ayr, and in December 1566 the General Assembly granted him leave of absence to visit his sons in England. Around the end of March 1567 Knox

[57] See 'Museums, Archives, and Libraries Scheme: The World of Reformation Britain: Seen and Heard in the Wode Psalter', at www.research.ed.ac.uk/en/projects/museums-archives-and-libraries-scheme-the-world-of-rformation-bri.

[58] E.g., Moray had told Throckmorton, 'We must now serve God, for the preacher tarrieth for us.' Throckmorton to Queen Elizabeth, 20 Aug. 1567, in R. Keith, *History of the Affairs of Church and State in Scotland from the Beginning of the Reformation to the Year 1568*, eds J.P. Lawson and C. J. Lyon, 3 vols (Edinburgh, 1844–50), ii, p. 740.

[59] Moray had been 'comfortless and in great misery' and even approached David Riccio, 'more humbly than any man would have believed': Melville, *Memoirs*, pp. 135, 147.

[60] This was different from the reaction of his friend and fellow rebel, the earl of Argyll, who had been able to remain in his own 'country' after the rebellion, but had become disillusioned with the English alliance: Jane E.A. Dawson, *The Politics of Religion in the Age of Mary, Queen of Scots: The Earl of Argyll and the Struggle for Britain and Ireland* (Cambridge, 2002), pp. 137–42.

[61] Julian Goodare, 'Queen Mary's Catholic Interlude', in M. Lynch (ed.), *Mary Stewart: Queen in Three Kingdoms* (Oxford, 1988), pp. 154–70.

left on his secretive English tour.[62] He visited his sons and Bowes relatives in the north-east, and his friend Goodman in Chester, and he reconnected in London with other members of their former exile congregation and with 'zealous' Protestant supporters. For the remainder of his life Knox remained in close touch with his extensive network of English friends. He shared their hope in further reformation for the Church of England and amity between the two Protestant kingdoms in the island of Britain that might even spread to Ireland.[63]

For the key episodes in 1566 and 1567 that transformed the Queen's position, James and John shared a knack for not being present either in Edinburgh or the realm. In the long run this permitted Moray to emerge as a 'blameless' regent for King James VI and Knox to return to a position of prominence in the national kirk. After his pardon in the spring of 1566 Moray returned to a close relationship with his royal sister, though not to the dominant political position he had previously enjoyed. Whatever he knew about the plot to assassinate Darnley, Moray was not in Edinburgh on the night of 9 February 1567 when the murder occurred. He left the capital earlier that Sunday, rushing to attend his wife in St Andrews. Annas' life hung in the balance, having experienced a miscarriage complicated by smallpox.[64] Two months later Moray's absence from court and country was carefully pre-planned. Despite being strongly associated with Darnley's murder, James Hepburn, 4th earl of Bothwell, was high in royal favour, and his power continued to increase in the spring of 1567. A violent and dangerous enemy, those who crossed Bothwell feared for their lives.[65] The rumours that Bothwell was plotting his death enabled Moray to persuade the Queen to grant him leave of absence to visit Europe.[66] Departing in early April, the earl did not return to Scotland until 11 August, by which time the Queen had been deposed and her son crowned as James VI: the benefit of hindsight makes this appear like a carefully constructed strategy rather than a voluntary leaving to avoid the threat from Bothwell. Later, when the Confederate Lords had assembled against the Queen, those excellent tacticians, Lethington and Grange, recognised the advantages of Moray's absence and moved speedily to crown the young king before his return.

[62] Bedford, having received an unspecified urgent request from Knox, consulted Cecil: Bedford to Cecil, 11 March 1567, TNA SP59/12, f. 220.

[63] Details of Knox's 1567 visit to England have been difficult to establish as he kept a very low profile, probably because he remained *persona non grata* with Queen Elizabeth: Dawson, *Knox*, pp. 250, 257–66.

[64] As reported by Buchanan: see *The Tyrannous Reign of Mary Stewart*, ed. W. Gatherer (Edinburgh, 1958), pp. 112, 114. Buchanan had earlier related the curious story of Queen Mary asking Annas to fake illness when they were in Jedburgh in Oct. 1566 so that the Queen could refuse to let Darnley stay overnight: *The Tyrannous Reign*, p. 107.

[65] E.g., when threatened by Bothwell, Sir Robert Melville and his brother James left court: Melville, *Memoirs*, pp. xxv, 176–78.

[66] *Pitscottie*, ii, p. 193. The Queen was well aware of the long-running feud between the two men.

In the last week of April Moray passed through London on his way to France. There is a reasonable possibility that he met Knox in the English capital, though it was never mentioned by either of them.[67] In a later tract the Catholic polemicist, Nicol Burne, described a meeting between the two men, probably in 'Paul's Walk' (the central nave of the medieval St Paul's Cathedral), which was the hub of London news and gossip.[68] Burne wrote of the beguiling promises Knox made to Moray:

> quhom he deceauit in S. Paulis kirk in Londone, bringand him in consait, that God had chosin him extraordinarlie as Iosias to be king of Scotland, to ruit out Idolatrie, and to plant the licht of his neu Euangel, quhair they conuenit in this maner, that the Prior of Sanct Androis Erl of Murray sould mentene the neu Elias aganis the Preistis of Baal, (for sua blasphemouslie he namit the preistis of Christ Iesus) and the new Elias, sould fortifie the new Iosias, be procuring the fauor of the people againis Iezebel, blasphem-ing maist impudentlie the Quenis M[ajesty].[69]

Whatever might have happened in London, when Knox arrived back in Edinburgh at the end of June 1567 his attitude had completely changed following his own withdrawal from the political limelight. He willingly embraced his national, prophetic role once again, preaching to 'unthankfull, yea alace miserable, Scotland'.[70] His sermons to the Confederate Lords and at the hastily arranged coronation of James VI on 29 July had one unmistakeable message. He thundered that the adulterous Queen Mary had been involved in the murder of her husband. Employing Old Testament examples, he demanded she should be punished with death for those sinful

67 Having recently re-examined the 1567 visit to England, it seems highly likely that Knox was in London at that time. Both Knox and Moray remained in close contact with their English supporters enabling them to exploit the speed of the English government's postal service and keep open communications with their Scottish friends. News of Scottish events, of Mary's possible links to the Darnley murder, and of the formation of the Confederate Lords were being secretly fed into those English networks that were also in contact with Knox and Moray, e.g., Grange's three letters to Bedford (that went on to Cecil) in April 1567: TNA SP/52/13, ff. 35, 37, 40. Also communications in (the inadequately calendared) SP 59.

68 For Paul's Walk, see https://en.wikipedia.org/wiki/Paul%27s_walk.

69 Nicol Burne's 'The Disputation Concerning the Controversit Heddis of Religion (1581)', in T. Law (ed.), *Catholic Tractates of the Sixteenth Century* (Edinburgh, 1901), pp. 107–72, at p. 163, within a section addressing the obedience due to the pope (and temporal authority). J.H. Burns, 'Nicol Burne (fl. 1574–1598)', *ODNB* [4049]. Historians have previously ignored Burne's account, assuming it was invented because it appeared to describe the 1552 London meeting between James and John mentioned in Knox's 1563 discharge letter (n. 49 above). Since a 1567 London meeting now appears possible, the Biblical allusions make more sense and match the rhetoric of Moray's regency.

70 Knox to Goodman, 18 Feb. 1567: Jane Dawson and Lionel Glassey, 'Some Unpublished Letters from John Knox to Christopher Goodman', *SHR* 84 (2005), 116–201, at pp. 190–91.

crimes to remove the country's blood guilt and prove it was upholding its covenant with God.[71]

By the time Moray returned to Scotland on 11 August, he was also convinced he had a new role in Scotland as the leader of the people of God. Sir Nicholas Throckmorton, the perceptive English ambassador who knew Moray well, reported of the 'Regent to be' that he 'wyll goe more stowtlye to work than anye man hath done yet. For he sekes to imytate rather some which have led the people of Israel, than anye capytaynes of our age.' Moray's priority was to get obedience to James VI from all estates 'or yt shall cost hym hys lyffe'.[72] For a second time James and John had become allies, serving as the captain and the prophet of the people of God.

## 'The Godly Regent''

On 24 January 1570, the day after Regent Moray's assassination in Linlithgow, Knox 'poured forth the grief and sorrow of his soule' after the sermon. In characteristic fashion this was 'a fervent supplication before the Lord' in which he reminded God and his audience of the blessings bestowed upon Scotland since 1559.[73] Moray was placed as a chief actor in the providential plan as the Scots were delivered from 'the tyrannie of merciless strangers, next from the bondage of idolatry, and last the yoak of that wretched Woman, the mother of all mischief'. To uphold the young King's authority, God 'didst appoynt a Regent endued with such graces as the Divell himself cannot accuse or justly convict him'. Even though the divine image clearly shone through Moray, the sins and ingratitude of Scots who failed to appreciate 'so pretious a gift' meant he fell, 'to our great griefe, to cruell and traterous murtherers'. Scotland had been left 'as a flock without a pastor in civill policie, and as a shippe without a rudder

[71] He was influenced by John Craig, his co-minister, who had been in Edinburgh throughout the crisis months up to the Battle of Carberry, and possibly also by Grange. Knox preached the General Fast sermons in Edinburgh (19 and 20 July) on the fall of the House of Ahab and the fate of his descendants (2 Kings and 2 Chronicles). The theme continued in the Stirling sermon at James VI's coronation (29 July) on the execution of Queen Athaliah and the crowning of King Joash (2 Kings 11 and 2 Chronicles 23). He had previously used the Athaliah story in his *First Blast*: *Knox: On Rebellion*, pp. xv, 11, 31–32, 34, 44. A note in William Cecil's distinctive hand on his memo of Instructions to Throckmorton, 30 June 1567, reads 'Athalia interempta per Joas regem' (Athalia was killed so that Joash could be king): TNA SP 52/14/1. John Guy has cited this note as 'proof' the English Secretary already had in mind in 1567 the regicide of Mary, Queen of Scots: *My Heart Is My Own* (London, 2004), pp. 363, 539. However, the note's presence might suggest that when in London the previous month Knox had been in contact with Cecil and this Biblical precedent had been mentioned.

[72] Throckmorton to Cecil, 20 Aug 1567: *CSP Scot.*, ii, no. 605.

[73] Knox, *Works*, vi, pp. 568–70. Calderwood, *History*, ii, pp. 513–15 mentioned Knox also used this prayer after the thanksgiving for food.

in the midst of the storm'. Such shedding of innocent blood had always been odious to God and 'it defyleth the whole land where it is shed and not punished'. Knox coupled Moray's assassination with Darnley's murder and called for vengeance upon the murderers, especially Mary, 'that most wicked woman' and all 'her faction'.[74] Even while eulogising Moray, Knox did not pass over the Regent's one fault, 'that foolish pity did so farre prevail in him, concerning execution and punishment' of Queen Mary.[75] James and John had held different views about Queen Mary and how she should be treated. Knox believed a covenant obligation had been neglected and his prophetic voice had been ignored, and with the benefit of hindsight, he blamed Moray's 'foolish pity' for causing his murder.

On his return in August 1567 Moray had visited Mary in prison and as her elder brother had delivered an extended lecture in the manner of a spiritual director concerning her moral and political failings.[76] Moray then declared he had accepted the Regency because his sister had begged him to undertake it. When addressing his fellow nobles, Moray emphasised the traditional attributes of a Scottish ruler of 'planting the treu religion, justice and polytye within this miserable cuntrye'.[77] Moray carefully signalled his Reformed credentials when at his inauguration as Regent he chose to sing the Scottish metrical version of the 'royal psalm' (Ps. 72).[78] His first parliament at the end of 1567 saw legislation in favour of the Reformed Kirk and ministry, in particular the re-enactment of the laws passed in the Reformation Parliament of 1560, thereby giving them indisputable legal force.[79] Moray was a stern enforcer of justice who gained a reputation for personally attending the Court of Session and for championing the causes of the poor, widows and orphans, in line with the Biblical characteristics

74 The significance of the motif of spilt blood and revenge has been highlighted in Amy Blakeway's important article covering the assassination, the funeral and the polemic: 'The Response to the Regent Moray's Assassination', *SHR* 88 (2009), 9–33.

75 The phrase 'foolish pity' came from the Geneva Bible's side-note to 2 Chronicles 15:16 when King Asa had not executed his idolatrous mother Maachah, 'herein he shewed yt he lacked zeale: for she oght to have dyed bothe by the covenant, and by the Lawe of God; but he gave place to foolish pity'. This 'bitter note' greatly offended the adult James VI because of its significance in resistance theories. Professor Mason has written extensively on that subject: see 'Select Bibliography'.

76 Throckmorton's account to Queen Elizabeth (dated 20 Aug. 1567) spoke of Moray's tone being more like a 'ghostly father': Keith, *History*, ii, pp. 734–41. According to Melville, Moray's lack of gentleness at this juncture for ever 'cut the thread of love and credit' Mary had for him: *Memoirs*, p. 194.

77 Draft letter to John Maxwell, Lord Herries, *Historical Manuscripts Commission 6th Report* (Moray Manuscripts, London, 1877), p. 641.

78 For a full description of Moray's inauguration before the Estates assembled in the Tolbooth: Blakeway, *Regency*, pp. 62–64.

79 The legal profession had regarded the 1560 legislation as invalid. For the latest discussion of this complex issue, see Thomas M. Green, *The Spiritual Jurisdiction in Reformation Scotland: A Legal History* (Edinburgh, 2019), chapters 1 and 2.

of a just ruler.[80] Assessing how much Moray's short Regency contributed to the establishment of the Reformed Kirk has proved difficult, not least because his regime was consciously intent upon presenting him in the guise of the 'Gude Regent'.[81]

Knox was perfectly willing to promote Moray as a captain of Israel. Writing on behalf of the General Assembly to John Willock to urge his return to Scotland, Knox explained in fulsome terms how Scottish politics had been transformed. At the start of 1568 the kingdom was filled with divine blessings and above all possessed 'a godly magistrate, whom God of His eternal and heavenly providence has reserved to this age, to put into execution whatsoever He by His law commands'.[82] That optimistic tone was harder to sustain after Mary's escape from prison and repudiation of her abdication, thereby demolishing Moray's original justification for his regency. The Queen's proclamation before the Battle of Langside attacked Moray as a traitor, 'quhome we of an spurious bastard (althocht nameit our brother) promovit fra ane religious monke to Erle and Lord'.[83] Although Mary's forces lost the battle and she made the disastrous decision to flee to England, the extent of opposition to the Regent had been revealed. Moray subsequently found himself on the back foot, struggling to maintain authority and facing plots against his life from within his circle as well as the Queen's Party.[84]

Knox also found himself a target, with enemies intent upon his death or banishment.[85] It strengthened his view that Mary was the source of all Scotland's troubles, as he bitterly lamented: 'yf ever there was more wickenes in one woman then has burst furht (sic) hyr … let hyr lief speak'.[86] Knox wished to appear free from involvement in the regency government, remarking to John Wood, 'I live as a man alreadie deid from all affairs civill.'[87] This did not prevent Wood, Moray's secretary, keeping Knox fully informed of government policies and politics. In his memoirs, Melville of Halhill portrayed Wood as a ringleader of the 'precise' Protestants trying to push the Regent in a more radical direction. During Mary's 'first trial' at York and Westminster in 1568, they were responsible for placing in the

[80] *Pitscottie*, ii, p. 202; *Diurnal*, p. 156; Blakeway, 'Response', pp. 22–23.

[81] Dr Webb concludes that Moray made limited concessions to the Kirk and extensive use of Protestant propaganda: 'The "Gude Regent"?', pp. 201–2.

[82] D. Shaw (ed.), *The Acts and Proceedings of the General Assemblies of the Church of Scotland 1560 to 1618*, 3 vols (Edinburgh, 2004), i, pp. 153–54.

[83] William Fraser, *The Lennox* (Edinburgh, 1874), pp. 437–47, at p. 438.

[84] E.g., the mysterious plot of summer 1568 involving Moray's own client, the Lord Lyon, William Stewart of Luthrie, who was executed in St Andrews for necromancy a year later.

[85] Knox to Goodman, 3 Nov. 1568: Dawson and Glassey, 'Some Unpublished Letters', p. 196.

[86] Knox to Goodman, 20 May 1569: Dawson and Glassey, 'Some Unpublished Letters', pp. 197–98.

[87] Sept. 1568: Knox, *Works*, vi, p. 561.

public domain the charges of murder and adultery against the Queen and the 'proof' contained in the Casket Letters. Knox was probably cheering from Edinburgh when he heard of the deployment of the Letters. He continued to encourage the radicals to oppose Lethington and other moderates who counselled Moray to reach an inclusive settlement that brought in sections of the Queen's Party and provided a role for Mary herself.[88] The Queen's Party had no doubt Knox's hand was directing behind the scenes and included him in the satirical tract written by Lethington's brother at the end of 1569. Thomas Maitland manufactured a 'conference' about the long-term plans for the Regency, and his six pen portraits of Moray's counsellors were brilliantly written to show they intended to place Moray on the Scottish throne. Knox's character declared he had written a book in which he had proved 'that all kingis, princis and rewleris goes not be successione: and that birth hes no power to promote, nor bastardy to seclude men from government'.[89] A similar theme appeared in the second part of Burne's narration of the Knox–Moray London meeting, where it was asserted that to his death Knox had preached against Queen Mary and young James, her 'seed'. Since it was known that King James V had promised marriage to Moray's mother, Knox allegedly asserted that the couple had been lawfully married and Moray was therefore the 'reable heir to his father' and should not be blocked from promotion to rule the kingdom of Scotland.[90]

Moray's assassination plunged Knox into grief at the death of a godly ruler and deep gloom over Scotland's future. The final two years of his life were consumed by the 'afterlife' of his relationship with Moray, as he vented his anger against Archbishop Hamilton (who had organised the killing), his Hamilton kindred and the rest of the Queen's Party.[91] Lesser figures with far less culpability, such as Moray's namesake, James Stewart, Lord St Colm, also attracted Knox's wrath as being 'the shame of all Stewartis, and unworthie to be rekned amongis men, for that dowbill treasone that he committed against that puire man, the Regent James Stewart'.[92] The

[88] Melville, *Memoirs*, p. 204; Gordon Donaldson, *The First Trial of Mary, Queen of Scots* (London, 1969).

[89] 'An Account of a Pretended Conference', in W. Scott and D. Laing (eds), *Bannatyne Miscellany* (Edinburgh, 1827), i, pp. 37–50, at p. 42; Dawson, *Knox*, pp. 278–80. Like his brother, Thomas had started among the King's Men. Though no copy appears to have survived, Knox had written a tract after the Battle of Langside that was circulated among his supporters in the west, and a copy was sent to Goodman: Knox to Goodman, 3 Nov. 1568; Dawson and Glassey, 'Some Unpublished Letters', p. 196 and n. 47.

[90] As noted above, an annulment had been sought without success. The 'reable heir' was one who had been legitimised or rehabilitated. Burne, 'Disputation', p. 164. In the opening of his *Appellation* (*Knox: On Rebellion*, pp. 72–114), Knox had stretched a different legal argument far beyond its normal bounds. However, the 'reable heir' proposition appears far-fetched, even for Knox.

[91] The Archbishop's feud with Moray had been exacerbated after Langside, where two of his sons were killed and his ecclesiastical lands forfeited. J. Foggie, 'John Hamilton (1510/11–1571), Roman Catholic Archbishop of St Andrews', *ODNB* [12102].

[92] Robert Pitcairn (ed.), *Memorials of Transactions in Scotland, A.D. MDLXIX – A.D.*

different strands of the response to Moray's murder were drawn together by the blood motif combining the traditions of the Scottish bloodfeud with Old Testament strictures.[93] In ballads circulating on Edinburgh's streets, the call for vengeance was expressed in the opening words of the metrical version of Psalm 43, 'Judge and revenge my cause.'[94] During the civil wars, when Edinburgh was occupied by the Queen's Party and the Hamiltons issued death threats against him, Knox was forced to leave for St Andrews. Despite deteriorating health, Knox continued to preach in the burgh's parish church, attacking all Hamiltons without distinction, including Robert, the minister whose pulpit he occupied. When challenged by Archibald Hamilton, a regent at St Mary's College, Knox provoked an ugly wrangle, heightening existing tensions between St Mary's and St Leonard's Colleges. The preacher departed the burgh in September 1572 to return to Edinburgh to die, leaving a trail of enmity behind him.[95]

## Conclusion

On 14 February 1570 James Stewart, Regent Moray, was buried in St Anthony's chapel on the south aisle of St Giles', the Edinburgh parish church.[96] His funeral was setting a new Protestant norm, as the last 'state funeral' for a Scottish ruler had been when Moray's father, King James V, was laid to rest in 1542 in the chapel at Holyrood. A full heraldic procession led by Grange accompanied Moray's body from the palace of Holyrood up the Royal Mile to the Tolbooth and then St Giles' Kirk. Annas, Moray's widow, had organised the funeral and probably suggested her husband's resting place in the church where they were married: when she died in 1588 she chose to be buried alongside the Regent. Knox was involved in the arrangements as the minister of St Giles', and by preaching

*MDLXXIII. By Richard Bannatyne, Secretary to John Knox* (Edinburgh, 1836), p. 51. Countess Annas was more forgiving, and her eldest daughter Elizabeth later married St Colm's son who became the 2nd earl of Moray by right of his wife and was the famous 'Bonnie earl o' Moray', murdered in 1592.

93 For the wider context of feud and justice, see A. Mark Godfrey, 'Rethinking the Justice of the Feud in Sixteenth-Century Scotland', in Boardman and Goodare (eds), *Kings, Lords and Men*, pp. 136–54.

94 Blakeway, 'Response', pp. 26–30. For the use of the bloodfeud psalm against the Hamiltons, see Jamie Reid-Baxter, '"Judge and Revenge My Caus": The Earl of Morton, Robert Sempill and the Fall of the House of Hamilton, 1579', in S. Mapstone (ed.), *Older Scots Literature* (Edinburgh, 2005), pp. 467–92. The visual links between Moray's and Darnley's murder were seen in the production in 1570 of a similar banner to the ensign carried at Carberry by the Confederate Lords: Randolph to Cecil, 1 March 1570, TNA SP52/17, f. 67.

95 Dawson, *Knox*, pp. 301–4.

96 Blakeway, 'Response', pp. 14–17. *Pitscottie*, ii, p. 225 noted that Moray was buried in the 'paroche kirk'.

and permitting a burial inside the church he ignored some of the funeral guidelines laid down in the *First Book of Discipline* that he had helped write.[97] When the coffin arrived and had been positioned in front of the pulpit, John 'maid ane lamentable sermon' for James on the text, 'Blessed are those that die in the Lord.' John portrayed James' death from the assassin's bullet as giving his life for the Protestant cause and eulogised him as the epitome of godliness. In his *History* David Calderwood recorded that Knox moved three thousand 'to shedd teares for the losse of suche a good and godlie governour'. [98] The contemporary broadsheet *The Regentis Tragedie* assumed his Edinburgh audience knew the sermon's contents: 'Ze hard zour self quhat Knox spak at the preiching.'[99] Equally, George Buchanan immortalised the Regent as the perfect model of a just ruler in a Latin epitaph, inscribed on the bronze plaque above Moray's sober tomb, and in his later writings.[100] As Knox and Buchanan had intended, that image of Moray as the good and godly regent took root and flourished.[101] It remained a tribute to their rhetorical skills and their enduring impact upon the Scottish tradition of historical and political thought until the late twentieth century, topics that have been repeatedly revealed and neatly unpicked in Professor Mason's work.[102]

Given their differing social positions and ages, it was inherently unlikely that James and John would become close allies. The initial link between them was provided by their shared Protestant faith, which might subsequently have developed into a closer pastoral relationship. However, the unusual circumstances of the rebellion of 1559–60 thrust the two men into partnership as they worked to secure the victory of the Lords of the Congregation. That struggle produced the 'miracle' of a religious and diplomatic re-alignment for the kingdom with the realisation of their common aims of an official Reformed Kirk and amity with England. Knox assumed such a divine deliverance required in response a covenant commitment from a grateful Scottish people. By contrast, Lord James probably saw an excellent start to a process of political and religious reform that he hoped to guide from his newly

[97] Other noble funerals and burials also 'broke the rules': C. McMillan, 'Negotiating Burial in Early Modern Scotland', in Peter Jupp and Hilary Grainger (eds), *Death in Scotland: Chapters from the Twelfth Century to the Twenty-First* (Oxford, 2019), pp. 109–25.
[98] *Diurnal*, p. 158; Randolph to Cecil, 22 Feb. 1570, Knox, *Works*, vi, p. 571; Calderwood, *History*, ii, p. 525.
[99] Cranstoun (ed.), *Satirical Poems of the Reformation*, i, p. 103, line 90.
[100] The Latin epitaph is printed in *George Buchanan: The Political Poetry*, ed. and trans. P. McGinnis and A. Williamson (Edinburgh, 1995), pp. 162–63. Calderwood credits Buchanan with the tomb inscription: *History*, ii, p. 526. Thomas Craig also wrote two Latin elegies: Jamie Reid-Baxter, *Two Elegies for James Stewart, Earl of Moray and Regent of Scotland (ob. 1570): A Hypertext Critical Edition* (2014), www.philological.bham.ac.uk/craig/ (accessed 23 April 2021).
[101] Buchanan also employed the vernacular: Roger A. Mason, 'George Buchanan's Vernacular Polemics, 1570–1572', *IR* 54 (2003), 47–68.
[102] See 'Select Bibliography'.

found position of authority within the Scottish government. The unexpected death of King Francis II threatened that hope, but Lord James brokered an advantageous deal for the return to Scotland of the widowed Queen Mary. Her arrival in the summer of 1561 started the collapse of his partnership with Knox. The two men held completely different understandings of the Scottish monarch. To John, the Scottish Queen was another example of a Catholic Queen Mary who, given half a chance, would persecute Protestants. For James, his half-sister was a younger family member who could be persuaded and guided into following his policies. Within a couple of years, those two perspectives created a rift sufficiently deep that Moray and Knox no longer spoke to each other.

Moray's plans to continue as his sister's chief advisor were shattered in 1565. He fell completely out of royal favour when in his opposition to the Queen's marriage to Darnley he sought to defend both the Scottish Kirk and the amity with England. His failed rebellion and flight across the border made him determined in the future not to repeat the painful experience of an enforced exile. During their low points between 1565 and 1567 both James and John in their different ways clung to the rocks of their religious faith and their English friends. After Riccio's murder in 1566, Knox had withdrawn from his Edinburgh ministry to Ayrshire and showed no inclination to return. In 1567 he undertook an extended visit around England, during which he probably met Moray in London's St Paul's Cathedral. He might then have encouraged James to see a future role for himself as a leader of the covenanted kingdom of Scotland. By the time Knox re-entered that kingdom, he had rejected 'retirement', returning to his prophetic role in the capital city convinced of Queen Mary's guilt for Darnley's murder.

In April 1567, before Mary's marriage to Bothwell, Moray had secured royal permission for his withdrawal to France. With hindsight, his absence turned out to be a clever choice; it certainly allowed him to return with 'clean hands' after the Queen's deposition and accept the Regency for the young James VI. Whether by long-term strategy or seizing tactical advantages as they appeared, the summer of 1567 saw James and John emerge once more as allies at the centre of Scottish political life. During the Regency Knox did not waver from his total condemnation of that 'wicked woman' and continually called for her punishment. Though remaining a firm supporter of the Regent, his harsh line on Mary meant he did not march in perfect step with Moray. Her escape from Lochleven and flight into England severely weakened the Regent's position, despite his victory at Langside. After the 'first trial' of Queen Mary, he found himself the central target for the Queen's supporters and more dependent than ever upon his English allies. Following the Regent's assassination, alongside George Buchanan, Knox helped create the long-lasting image of the 'Gude Regent', though James' 'foolish pity' towards Queen Mary was the one fault John mentioned in his eulogies. Ironically, it was Mary's permanent and implacable enemy who died peacefully in his bed while the Regent was 'executed' by the Queen's supporters.[103] In death, like the 'brothers in the faith' and the allies they had sometimes been in life, James and John were buried relatively close to each other. Moray was placed in his noble tomb inside the church building, Knox outside in an unmarked grave within St Giles' churchyard.[104] The two men also lay far enough apart to demonstrate the social gap separating the Queen's brother from the preacher.

[103] Mirroring the traditional stories of the deaths of the apostles James, who was executed, and John, who died in his bed.

[104] Knox was buried in the churchyard of St Giles' that now forms the car park in front of the Scottish Court of Session. Tradition has placed the grave in one of the parking bays that is roughly opposite the wall of St Giles' forming the back of the side chapel in which Moray and Annas were buried.

# 9

# A Disciple of Buchanan in the Marian Civil War: Thomas Maitland's 'The Consecration of James VI, King of Scots' ('Jacobi VI, Scotorum Regis Inauguratio')

Steven J. Reid

ROGER Mason redefined how we think about the exercise of kingship amongst the monarchs of the Stewart dynasty, and led the way in re-interpreting and re-evaluating (and in several cases, evaluating for the first time) many of the major texts of the Renaissance and Reformation in Scotland, including the Latin histories of John Mair and Hector Boece, the *Complaynt of Scotland*, the *Trew Lawe*, and the *Basilikon Doron*.[1] Mason also spent much of his earlier career evaluating the political theology of John Knox within a British and covenanted context, which resulted in his critical edition of a wide range of the reformer's letters and tracts 'on rebellion'.[2] However, perhaps his greatest gift to Scottish History is the critical edition of George Buchanan's *De Iure Regni Apud Scotos Dialogus* ('A Dialogue on the Law of Kingship among the Scots'), edited with Martin Smith and first published in 2004, which gave scholars access for the first time to a clear and fully referenced translation of Buchanan's major ideological statement on the nature of kingship and how to deal with tyrants.[3] Buchanan's ideas had a broad and long cultural afterlife, influencing the thought of leading reformed intellectuals including Andrew Melville, and serving as a source of justification for radicals ranging from republicans in the seventeenth century through to the soldiers of the American Revolution.[4] Like Buchanan, Mason has had

1 Roger A. Mason, 'This Realm of Scotland is an Empire? Imperial Ideas and Iconography in Early Renaissance Scotland', in B.A. Crawford (ed.), *Church, Chronicle, and Learning in Medieval and Early Renaissance Scotland* (Edinburgh, 1999), pp. 73–91, at pp. 80–81; Roger A. Mason, 'Renaissance Monarchy? Stewart Kingship (1469–1542)', in Brown and Tanner (eds), *Scottish Kingship*, pp. 255–78, at pp. 272–73.

2 *Knox: On Rebellion.*

3 Mason and Smith.

4 Caroline Erskine, 'The Reputation of George Buchanan (1506–82) in the British Atlantic World before 1832' (unpublished University of Glasgow PhD thesis,

considerable intellectual influence on younger generations of scholars as a mentor, whether to the classes he taught for almost four decades at St Andrews, to the many colleagues he has offered a 'killer question' to in seminars and conferences or, above all, to his many PhD students. As one of those former students, it seems appropriate that this chapter focuses on Buchanan's relationship with his own supposed acolyte, Thomas Maitland. It is also appropriate, given Mason's interest in texts, that this relationship is revealed to us in a previously overlooked poem by Maitland, the 'Jacobi VI, Scotorum Regis inauguratio' ('On the Consecration of James VI, King of Scots'). This poem, like all Maitland's extant poetry, exists solely in Latin in a single witness – the *Delitiae Poetarum Scotorum*, the anthology of Scottish neo-Latin poetry edited by Arthur Johnstone and Sir John Scot of Scotstarvit and published at Amsterdam in 1637.[5] The 'inauguratio' is one of a handful of poems written by Maitland that are linked to the Marian Civil War, the six-year conflict that engulfed Scottish politics following the capture and abdication of Mary, Queen of Scots in the summer of 1567.[6] Of these, the 'inauguratio' is of major importance, as the only known poem associated with James' coronation, as an account of Maitland's view of Mary's deposition and the actions of James Hepburn, the fourth earl Bothwell, and as evidence of his own ideas on the punishments owed to tyrants and the nature of Scottish kingship.[7] As we shall see, this poem provides vital evidence of the reception of Buchanan's ideas at the very earliest moment of their dissemination

2004); Caroline Erskine and Roger A. Mason, *George Buchanan: Political Thought in Early Modern Britain and Europe* (Farnham, 2012); Roger A. Mason, 'How Andrew Melville Read His George Buchanan', and Steven J. Reid, 'Andrew Melville and the Law of Kingship', in Mason and Reid (eds), *Andrew Melville*, pp. 11–45 and 47–74, respectively.

[5] These are all available as an electronic edition, with full critical commentary at 'Bridging the Continental Divide: Neo-Latin and its Cultural Role in Jacobean Scotland, as Seen in the *Delitiae Poetarum Scotorum* (1637)', ed. Steven J. Reid and David McOmish: www.dps.gla.ac.uk/electronic-resource/poems/?aid=MaiT.

[6] These comprise two short pieces relating to James Stewart, the earl of Moray, Mary's half-brother and regent of Scotland between August 1567 and January 1570 (one criticising his destruction of Dunbar Castle in December 1567 and the other celebrating his return from the York–Westminster trial in early 1569); a piece addressed to Maitland's brother and Mary's former secretary William Maitland of Lethington, originally attached to a now lost text advising Scots to make war against the Turks instead of one another; and a short polemic against the radical preacher 'Janus Virbius', which may be a pseudonym for John Knox. See Maitland, 'Elegia VI: Deditio arcis Dumbarae ad Regem'; 'Sylva II: Jacobo Stuarto Scotiae Proregi, patriae sub Amaryllidos nomine, de reditu ex Anglia, Gratulatio'; 'Sylva IV: Ad Guilelmum fratrem, de bello in Turcas suscipiendo praefixa'; and 'In Ianum Virbium', in *DPS*, ii, pp. 151–52, 163–67, 171–73, 177.

[7] *DPS*, ii, pp. 154–63. The critical edition referred to here, and all translations and line numbers, are cited from Reid and McOmish (eds), *Corona Borealis*, pp. 67–95.

during the initial stages of the Marian conflict, at a point when Maitland, like the rest of his family, were still opposed to Mary's restoration.

## Thomas Maitland (c. 1545–72), His Family, and the Marian Civil War (1567–73)

THOMAS Maitland's biography and personal relationship with Buchanan have been examined at length elsewhere, but it is important to recount some of these key details.[8] Thomas was the youngest of the three sons of the poet, lawyer, and compiler of the Maitland Quarto and Folio, Richard Maitland of Lethington (1496–1586). His two older brothers, William ('of Lethington', 1528?–73) and John ('of Thirlestane', 1543–95), both served as secretaries to Mary and James VI respectively. All four men were impressive writers, but where Richard and William wrote predominantly in Scots, John's and Thomas' extant poetry is exclusively in Latin.[9] Thomas was born around 1545 and matriculated in St Mary's College St Andrews in 1559. He left Scotland in October 1563 to continue his studies in Paris, but the evidence of the 'inauguratio' and his poem on the surrender of one of Bothwell's main strongholds, Dunbar Castle, between October and December 1567 strongly suggests that he was back in Scotland by 1567.[10] In 1570 he was active as a courier of letters from the earl of Suffolk to his brother William, for which he was briefly imprisoned in May and June, and in August he travelled with Lord Seton to secure finance and troops from the duke of Alva to bolster the Marian-held castles of Dumbarton and Edinburgh. He was probably already unwell by the time of this expedition, and at the end of 1571 he travelled to Italy for unknown reasons, where he died in early 1572.

The evidence for Maitland's career and political convictions exists, as William McKechnie found in his attempt to reconstruct his biography, in a series of 'scattered references', and there are many questions that remain unanswerable.[11] One of the biggest is the exact nature of his relationship with George Buchanan. It is thanks to Buchanan's placing of Maitland as his 'interlocutor' in the pages of the *De Iure Regni* that Maitland is so well known to posterity. Maitland may have met Buchanan during the latter's brief return to France in 1566, and the wide variety of verse forms

[8] For the biographical detail which follows, see William S. McKechnie, 'Thomas Maitland', *SHR* 4 (1907), 274–93; Michael R.G. Spiller, 'Maitland, Sir Richard, of Lethington (1496–1586), Courtier and Writer', *ODNB* [17831]; Mark Loughlin, 'Maitland, William, of Lethington (1525x30–1573), Courtier and Diplomat', *ODNB* [17838]; Maurice Lee, 'Maitland, John, First Lord Maitland of Thirlestane (1543–1595), Lord Chancellor of Scotland', *ODNB* [17826].

[9] Loughlin, 'The Career of William Maitland of Lethington', p. 26.

[10] McKechnie, 'Thomas Maitland', pp. 276–77.

[11] Ibid., pp. 274–75.

he employed in his surviving Latin poetry – comprising seven elegies, four *sylvae* (or 'occasional poems') in hexameter, and 28 short poems and epigrams in a variety of lengths and meters – suggest that he may have been mentored by Buchanan. He certainly provided similar encouragement to both Andrew Melville and Patrick Adamson during their time with the elder humanist in Paris.[12] Like Buchanan, Maitland chose to write a variety of obscene and erotic Latin elegies, a choice of subject matter that was exceedingly rare amongst Scottish neo-Latin authors.[13] There is the merest hint of textual influence in his work from Buchanan's cycles of 'profane' poetry, in terms of themes, in the select use of some stylistic features (such as diminutives and alliteration) and in the deployment of rare obscene words such as *deglubere*. However, these links could also come from a shared knowledge of the poetic works of Catullus and other Roman authors of erotic poetry, such as Propertius and Tibullus.[14]

Whether or not Buchanan had a significant influence on Maitland's poetic style, and whether the two initially met in Paris or back in Scotland, the two had obviously developed some relationship by the time Buchanan drafted the *De Iure Regni*, which internal evidence suggests was completed in time for the meeting of the parliament in December 1567 that ratified Queen Mary's deposition.[15] The *De Iure Regni* attempted to justify the deposition of Mary, an act that shocked the other monarchies of Europe, by offering an explanation of what made a good king and what made a tyrant, and the rewards and punishments due to both.[16] For Buchanan, an ideal king would naturally command respect and following from his people, because he would be virtually flawless.[17] However, the rareness of such a model exemplar of humanity – if they could exist at all – meant that laws were needed to restrain human monarchs who were all too fallible and prone to poor judgment.[18] A good ruler was a moral figurehead and example for his people, who oversaw the enacting of the laws, but had no actual role

[12] I.D. McFarlane, *Buchanan* (London, 1981), pp. 256–57. Adamson contributed a prefatory verse to the first printed edition of Buchanan's *Franciscanus* (Paris, 1566), and helped secure the position of principal of St Leonard's College, St Andrews, for him on his return in 1570: *RPS*, A1570/3/1.

[13] The only other Scottish author of erotic elegy in the late sixteenth century was Mark Boyd, whose *Epistolae Quindecim* (Bourges, 1590) and *Heroides et Hymni* (La Rochelle, 1592) were responses to and a continuation of Ovid's *Heroides*. See Edward Paleit, 'Sexual and Political Liberty and Neo-Latin Poetics: The "Heroides" of Mark Alexander Boyd', *Renaissance Studies* 22 (2008), 351–67; Steven J. Reid, 'Classical Reception and Erotic Latin Poetry in Sixteenth-Century Scotland: The Case of Thomas Maitland (ca. 1548–1572)', in A. Petrina and I. Johnston (eds), *The Impact of Latin Culture on Medieval and Early Modern Scottish Writing* (Kalamazoo, MI, 2018), pp. 3–40, esp. pp. 10–11.

[14] Reid, 'Classical Reception and Erotic Latin Poetry in Sixteenth-Century Scotland', pp. 22–28.

[15] Mason and Smith, p. xxvii.

[16] Ibid., pp. 5–7.

[17] Ibid., p. 27.

[18] Ibid., p. 33.

in setting them. This was the preserve of the assembled people, a group that Buchanan left deliberately vague.[19] Buchanan argued that rulers in Scotland had, until the reign of Kenneth III, been approved on an elective basis to allow for their removal should they fail to act as servants of the people, with their coronation oath serving as the basis of a contract between ruler and subject.[20] If a king fell into tyranny, they could be restrained, punished and killed for their crimes in the same way as any subject, and a private individual could take the enacting of this final sanction into their own hands if necessary.[21]

T.D. Robb and William McKechnie both viewed Maitland uncritically as an ardent follower of Buchanan's views, with McKechnie suggesting his inclusion in the *De Iure Regni* 'witnesses to the existence of a spirit of the utmost friendship and cordiality between the two debaters', while Robb described Maitland's discussion of kingship in his 'inauguratio' as 'the plainest utterance of that democratic spirit to which George Buchanan gave expression'.[22] However, Maitland would later strongly deny any affiliation with Buchanan, and according to Father Thomas Innes he had written to Queen Mary on 1 December 1570 (in a now lost letter) to protest that 'his being brought as interlocutor into that dialogue, to say whatever *Buchanan* thought proper for his purpose, was wholly *Buchanan's* own invention; and that he, *Thomas Maitland*, had not the least hand in it' (original emphasis).[23]

The reason for these conflicting views is not hard to find. In the gap of three years between 1567 and 1570, the Maitland family radically shifted their view of the action taken against Mary, though we can only fully witness this shift by tracking the career of Thomas' eldest brother William. In 1567 Lethington backed the revolution due to his fear of Bothwell's usurpation of control over Scottish politics, and due to ongoing tensions between the two men over the rights to Haddington Abbey and other properties in the Lothian region.[24] It was for this reason that Lethington, who had been Mary's loyal secretary throughout her personal reign, deserted her on 5 June 1567, just prior to the events of Carberry Hill, and refused to countenance her restoration unless Bothwell was permanently separated from her by annulment, divorce, or death. While there has been considerable debate over whether he continued to act covertly in her interests during her captivity in Lochleven and at her 'trial' at York and Westminster following her flight to England, he did not return to a position of open support for the queen until the summer of 1569. At this time he was a leading advocate in

19 Ibid., pp. 55–57.
20 Ibid., p. 97.
21 See discussion below.
22 McKechnie, 'Thomas Maitland', p. 277; T.D. Robb, '*Delitiae Poetarum Scotorum*', *Proceedings of the Royal Philosophical Society of Glasgow* 39 (1907–8), pp. 97–120, at p. 105.
23 Thomas Innes, *A Critical Essay on the Ancient Inhabitants of the Northern Part of Britain or Scotland*, 2 vols (London, 1729), i, p. 359; McKechnie, 'Thomas Maitland', pp. 287–88.
24 Loughlin, 'Maitland of Lethington', pp. 251–52.

parliament for a motion to procure her divorce from Bothwell, which was defeated by 40 votes to nine.[25] This action was part of his plans to secure a fourth marriage for Mary with the duke of Norfolk, which he hoped would remove the last obstacle for many to Mary's restitution, or at least to her release from English confinement. In response Moray had him arrested for complicity in the murder of Lord Darnley, but in September 1569 Maitland was able to arrange his escape. He secured refuge in Edinburgh Castle, which became the last stronghold for Marian supporters thanks to the defection of its captain, Sir William Kirkcaldy of Grange, to the Queen's Party. By early 1570, Lethington's position had thus changed to one of support for Mary, and he had become the most politically active member of the Queen's Party.[26]

Firm evidence for Thomas' whereabouts only exists from 1569 onwards, but his strenuous denial of involvement in the writing of the *De Iure Regni* and the evidence of his activities on Mary's behalf in the last two years of his life suggest that his political allegiances shifted along with those of his brother. Both men, and their third brother John, were forfeited by the regency government led by Matthew Stewart, 4th earl of Lennox, at the 'Creeping Parliament' of May 1571 for their support of the queen.[27] Lethington would remain on Mary's side until his capture and subsequent death (possibly from illness or suicide) after the fall of Edinburgh Castle in May 1573.[28] John Maitland also maintained some form of dialogue with Mary long after the end of the civil war, as he was implicated in attempts to restore her to Scotland as part of a plan for joint rule with her son, known as the 'Association', in 1584.[29]

It was after this dramatic familial change in loyalties that Maitland achieved notoriety as the suspected author of a pasquinade, a satirical sketch of a purported conference held between the Regent Moray and six of his leading supporters (including John Knox).[30] This text was either written just prior to Moray's death or to mark it, and in one account was left in John Knox's pulpit for him to find with the injunction that he 'take up the man whom you accounted another god, and consider the end whereto

[25] Mark Loughlin and Clare Webb offer two very differing accounts of Maitland's attitude towards Mary in this crucial period: Loughlin, 'Maitland of Lethington', pp. 237, 246, 250–53, 257–60, 266–72; and Claire L. Webb: 'The "Gude Regent"? A Diplomatic Perspective upon the Earl of Moray, Mary, Queen of Scots, and the Scottish Regency, 1567–1570' (unpublished University of St Andrews PhD thesis, 2008), pp. 27–30, 34, 52–57, 68, 90–92, 96–97, 121, 143–50.

[26] Webb, 'Gude Regent?', pp. 168–74.

[27] McKechnie, 'Thomas Maitland', p. 289; Lee, *Maitland*, p. 33; *RPS*, A1570/10/2–5; Calderwood, *History*, iii, p.18; *Diurnal*, p.191.

[28] Lee, *Maitland*, p. 35.

[29] Ibid., pp. 62–63.

[30] For copies, see W. Scott and D. Laing (eds), *Bannatyne Miscellany* (Edinburgh, 1827), i, pp. 37–50; Robert Pitcairn (ed.), *Memorials of Transactions in Scotland, A.D. MDLXIX – A.D. MDLXXIII. By Richard Bannatyne, Secretary to John Knox* (Edinburgh, 1836), pp. 5–13; Calderwood, *History*, iii, pp. 515–25.

his ambition hath brought him'.[31] This caricature has been described as 'remarkable as perhaps the first example of its kind, not only in Scotland but in Christendom', and was seen as highly witty by contemporaries. Maitland is also believed to be the author of a long treatise or 'Letter' (*epistola*) to Queen Elizabeth which discusses Mary's situation, and which survives in a single unedited and untranslated manuscript in the Drummond Collection at the University of Edinburgh.[32] While most of Maitland's extant works are thus strongly pro-Marian in tone, the 'inauguratio' is notable for its contrasting strong endorsement of the events of Mary's deposition and James' coronation as king.

## Maitland, Mary, James, and Bothwell: The Consecration of James VI, King of Scots

MAITLAND was one of four Latin poets who wrote poems on the birth and infancy of the young king – the other three being Patrick Adamson, Thomas Craig, and George Buchanan – and the only one to write specifically in response to James' coronation. The three 'birth poems' (*genethliaca*) have some thematic overlap with the ideas on display both in Maitland's poem and in Buchanan's later writings on kingship.[33] All three *genethliaca* claim that James will usher in an age of long-awaited peace, though Buchanan avoids any specific reference to James inheriting both the Scottish and English thrones. Adamson and Craig both draw, to varying degrees, on a contemporary prophecy, first referenced by Alexander Scott in his poem 'Ane New Year's Gift' given to Mary in 1562, that the ninth generation descendant of Robert the Bruce would return from France and unite the British Isles under their rule.[34] Both men suggest that Mary is the foretold

[31] John Spottiswoode, *History of the Church of Scotland*, ed. M. Russell and M. Napier, 3 vols (Edinburgh, 1847–51), ii, p. 121; McKechnie, 'Thomas Maitland', p. 280.

[32] Edinburgh University Library, MS De.4.22. This work is currently being translated and edited by John-Mark Philo, whose edition we eagerly await.

[33] George Buchanan, 'Genethliacon Jacobi Sexti Regis Scotorum'; Patrick Adamson, 'Genethliacum Serenissimi Scotiae, Angliae, et Hiberniae Principis, Iacobi VI, Mariae Reginae Filii'; Thomas Craig, 'Iacobi Serenissimi Scotorum Principis Ducis Rothesaia Genethliacum, 1566'. For critical editions, see Reid and McOmish (eds), *Corona Borealis*, pp. 1–65.

[34] Alexander Scott, 'Ane new yeir gift to the Queen Mary', in *The Poems of Alexander Scott*, ed. Alexander Karley Donald (London, 1902), pp. 1–8, lines 193–200; see also Theo van Heijnsbergen, 'Advice to a Princess: The Literary Articulation of a Religious, Political and Cultural Programme for Mary Queen of Scots, 1562', in Julian Goodare and Alasdair A. MacDonald (eds), *Sixteenth-Century Scotland: Essays in Honour of Michael Lynch* (Leiden and Boston, MA, 2008), pp. 99–122. The prophecy apparently originated with the fourteenth-century Augustinian monk Saint John of Bridlington and was circulated heavily at the time of the Union of the Crowns. See [Anon.,] *The Whole Prophesie of Scotland, England, & some part of France, and Denmark, Prophesied bee mervellous Merling, Beid, Bertlingtoun, Thomas Rymour, Waldhave, Eltraine, Banester, and Sibbilla, all according in one. Containing many strange and mervelous things* (Edinburgh, 1603), sig. B5r. Facsimile

figure in that prophecy, though instead of being the monarch who would unite the realms she is in fact the vessel for her 'noble offspring', whom the whole of Britannia 'saves herself to be governed by'.[35] Adamson and Craig both also see James' rule as divinely mandated, in Craig's case because of James' long and distinguished dynasty, and in Adamson's case because he believes that James will be the first monarch of a Protestant British nation that will wage war against Catholic Europe and the Ottoman Empire.[36] Buchanan's *genethliacon* clearly presages his later ideas on the importance of the king's moral virtue as an example to his subjects, and suggests that any king who would act as a tyrant will find divine vengeance wrought upon them immediately. Buchanan cites as his evidence the examples of the Roman tyrants Nero, Domitian, Tarquinius Superbus and Catiline, who were driven to madness or death for not ruling in accordance with the wishes of their people or God.[37]

All three 'birth-poems' were published in Paris in 1566–67, and while Adamson's work was far more polemical than the other two in announcing the beginning of a Stewart empire, all three sought to use Latin poetry to communicate the news of a male heir to an international audience.[38] By contrast, the only known copy of Maitland's poem exists in the printed version in the *Delitiae*, and there is no evidence of its circulation in manuscript form. This prompts some necessary speculation – did Maitland write it simply to celebrate the coronation, or was it produced as a piece of propaganda in support of the early King's Party? It is certainly true that the King's Party made unprecedented use of texts to bolster their regime, ranging from Buchanan's own 'Detectioun' traducing Mary through to ballads lamenting the death of the Regent Moray in 1570. They also produced a wide range of visual propaganda on coins, collected acts of parliament, and banners, frequently showing James in his cradle crying out for vengeance for his murdered father.[39] If Maitland and Buchanan were friends and allies in the summer of 1567, and assuming that Maitland was present in the country, then he may have been encouraged to produce a poem that could bolster the view of the King's Party's actions

in David Laing (ed.), *A Collection of Ancient Scottish Prophecies, in alliterate verse: reprinted from the Waldegrave edition, M.DC.III.* (Edinburgh, 1833), p. 25; see also Alasdair A. MacDonald, 'Poetry, Propaganda and Political Culture: *The Whole Prophesie of Scotland* (1603)', in David Parkinson (ed.), *James VI and I, Literature and Scotland: Tides of Change, 1567–1625* (Leuven, 2013), pp. 209–32, and Michael Riordan, 'Mysticism and Prophecy in Scotland in the Long Eighteenth Century' (unpublished University of Cambridge PhD thesis, 2015), pp. 32–98.

[35] Craig, 'Genethliacum', lines 104–6; Adamson, 'Genethliacum', lines 39–46.

[36] Craig, 'Genethliacum', lines 148–52, 240–52, 316–44; Adamson, 'Genethliacum', lines 136–62.

[37] Buchanan, 'Genethliacon', lines 20–91.

[38] For further discussion, see Steven J. Reid, *The Early Life of James VI: A Long Apprenticeship, 1566–1585* (Edinburgh, 2023), chapter 1.

[39] For a full survey, see Reid, *The Early Life of James VI*, chapter 2.

internationally in the way that the vernacular outpourings from the press of Robert Lekprevik did locally. However, if this was the case, then like the *De Iure Regni* it seems never to have made it to print, as it is unlikely that a contemporary printed pamphlet commemorating such a significant event would be wholly lost.

Regardless of its early dissemination, Maitland's 'inauguratio' is of significant length at 363 lines, making it the equivalent of about three quarters of a book of the *Aeneid*, and one of the longest of any of the major neo-Latin poems associated with the events of James' personal reign in Scotland.[40] After a brief 14-line invocation to James, the 'greatest hope, long awaited' (*spes summa ... expectata diu*) for the nation, the poem explores three key themes, which are distributed across the poem.[41] Lines 14 to 127 recount the reasons for Mary's abdication in favour of James, and suggest reasons as to why the young prince is so suited to succeed his mother. Lines 128 to 176 and 221 to 276 discuss James Hepburn, the 4th earl of Bothwell, the divine vengeance he will receive for his crime at the hands of James, and his flight from Carberry Hill on 15 June 1567. Lines 177 to 220 and 276 to 363 recount the martial and chivalric virtues of the nation of the Scots, the role and responsibilities of a just and virtuous king, several examples of tyrants from Classical antiquity, and the punishments due to tyrants in general.

## Mary's Abdication and Elective Versus Divine Kingship among the Scots

The first major theme discussed by Maitland is the abdication of Mary, why she has demitted power, and conversely why James is so well-suited to rule, even though he is an infant. Within Scotland, a striking feature of James' coronation at the Kirk of the Haly Rude on 29 July 1567 was not only the modest setting – held in the parish church and not the Chapel Royal, with a handful of attendees and a sermon by John Knox – but the long recital of Mary's signed instruments of abdication.[42] These

[40] The three *genethliaca* range between 114 and 344 lines, and Maitland's piece is also longer than Andrew Melville's 'Stephaniskion' on the coronation of Queen Anna published in 1590 (215 lines) and his 'Principis Scoto-Britannorum Natalia' on the birth of Prince Henry in 1594 (92 lines). It is, however, far smaller than Hercules Rollock's account of James' proxy marriage to Anna of Denmark in 1589, which comprises 534 lines. See Hercules Rollock, 'De Augustissimo Iacobi VI Scotorum Regis, et Annae ... epithalamium'; Andrew Melville, 'ΣΤΕΦΑΝΙΣΚΙΟΝ ad Scotia Regem, habitum in coronatione reginae, 17 Maii, 1590'; and Andrew Melville, 'Principis Scoto-Britannorum Natalia', in Reid and McOmish (eds), *Corona Borealis*, pp. 167–243.

[41] Lines 1–2.

[42] On the coronation, see *RPC*, i, pp. 537–42; Michael Lynch, 'Scotland's First Protestant Coronation: Revolutionaries, Sovereignty and the Culture of Nostalgia', in L. Houwen (ed.), *Literature and Religion in Late Medieval and Early Modern Scotland* (Leuven, 2012), pp. 177–207; Lucinda H.S. Dean, 'Crowns, Wedding Rings, and Processions: Continuity

letters, signed by Mary five days earlier under the watchful eyes of Patrick Lord Lindsay of the Byres and William Lord Ruthven, underpinned the parliamentary acts approving Moray's regency and the formal demission of Mary in December 1567.[43] Mary's reasons for abdicating were clearly fabricated by her captors. Describing herself as so 'vexit, brokin, and unquietit' by the burden of rule, she indicated that she could no longer 'induir sa greit and tollerabill panis and travellis', and that James had been granted to her by God in case of her premature death. Fearing that he might face great 'resistence and troubill' in establishing his own rule, Mary could think of nothing more joyous than to see her son 'in oure awin lyftyme peciabillie placeit in that rowme and honorabill estait quhairto he justlie aucht and man succeed to'. But rather than have any role in guiding him through to adulthood, Mary demitted responsibility for James into the hands of Morton and the other leading confederate lords, and to Moray for leading his government.[44] Despite the inherent contradiction in these letters, it was on their basis that a wide cross-section of nobility duly signed a 'second band' swearing their loyalty to James and promising to carry Mary's wishes out.

Maitland also packages Mary's abdication as an act benefitting her and as a public service to the kingdom, exactly aligned with the content of the abdication documents. Maitland begins his discussion of Mary immediately after his first reference to Carberry Hill, obliquely described as a 'joyful triumph over a wicked enemy',[45] where he notes Mary's exhaustion and inability to continue as ruler after so many personal hardships:

> … your mother, the most beautiful amongst the shapely nymphs, exhausted by a labour greater than Hercules', gave over to you the rule of the nation, and the honours of the kingdom. As Atlas, stooped by the oppressive weight of the heavens, calls earnestly in his prayers for another to support the poles: and as an athlete, exhausted by his panting lap of the stadium, hands over the glowing torch and withdraws from the arena: so the queen, long buffeted by a multitude of storms, and looking for a port providing calm from a shipwrecking sea, divested herself of sovereignty, and handed over the burdens of rule and the reins of government to you.[46]

---

and Change in Representations of Scottish Royal Authority in State Ceremony, c.1214–c.1603' (unpublished Stirling PhD thesis, 2013), pp. 198–208; Lucinda H.S. Dean, 'Crowning the Child: Representing Authority in the Inaugurations and Coronations of Minors in Scotland, c.1214 to c.1567', in E. Woodacre and S. McGlyn (eds), *The Image and Perception of Monarchy in Medieval and Early Modern Europe* (Cambridge, 2014), pp. 254–80, esp. pp. 277–80.

[43] James Anderson (ed.), *Collections Relating to the History of Mary Queen of Scotland*, 4 vols (Edinburgh, 1727–28), ii, pp. 206, 215, 251, 254.

[44] *RPC*, i, 531–533.

[45] '… rettulerant laetum scelerato ex hoste triumphum', line 17.

[46] '… tibi formosas inter pulcherrima Nymphas,/ Herculeo plusquam genitrix defessa

Maitland also views the abdication through a patriarchal lens, and for him the demission of a female monarch for a male, even an infant male, is an entirely natural and right process. Just 'as the spouse yields to her husband' and 'lilies overshadow grass', so too does James naturally outshine his mother and command the awe and respect of the Scottish people.[47] Maitland offers little in the way of hard evidence to defend this assertion. Despite the fact that he had probably never seen James in person, Maitland first suggests that James' preternatural beauty – which apparently rivalled that of Narcissus, Ganymede and Adonis – was an externally visible symbol of his outstanding virtue.[48] Maitland follows this with a brief account of James' lineage, the 'continual chain' of ancestors back to Fergus I in 330 BC that includes luminaries such as Robert the Bruce and in turn links James to the sovereign authority of the kingdom.[49] Just as Maitland uses the opening of the poem to fit his view of Mary to the official abdication documents, so too does this sequence square – at least partially – with Buchanan's views on kingship, particularly the idea that an ideal king will be so naturally fitted to rule that his people will unquestioningly follow him. In Maitland's account of recent history leading up to this momentous event, the history of Mary's minority and personal reign is effectively erased. Instead, he suggests that an ill-defined period of massive disruption since the death of James V has now been brought to a close thanks to divine intervention:

> When our lands were given up to death (I still remember), after the father [James V] was incorporated among the stars and increased the number of heaven-dwellers, and the rule of the kingdom was given to a tender girl, there was always one alone in our prayers: all were chanting in unison: 'when will be that day, when a tiny boy with a charming face will call you mother, most beautiful of nymphs? When will be that day, when rule will be given to the Stewarts to enjoy, and a child will sit on the ancestral throne?' The almighty father, with a smile on his charming face, gave his assent when you were born, and passed his judgment on those responsible for the prayer as they rejoiced. And now a child more

labore,/ detulit imperium, patriique insignia regni./ Ut declivis Atlas onerosi pondere caeli,/ deposcit votis alium qui fulciat axem:/ utque pugil stadii cursu lassatus anhelo,/ lampada candentem tradens decedit arena:/ sic regina diu variis agitata procellis,/ navifrago placidum spectans ex aequore portum,/ exuit imperio sese, tibi pondera regni,/ et tibi fraenandas rerum transmittit habenas', lines 18–28.

[47] 'Quantum sponsa viro … quantum sole premunt exustum lilia gramen', lines 33–34.

[48] Lines 62–81. Given James' confinement in Edinburgh and then Stirling Castle for most of the first year of his life, it is highly unlikely that any of the poets who wrote about his birth and coronation had seen him. See Reid, *The Early Life of James VI*, chapter 1.

[49] 'perpetua serie': lines 82–97.

> beautiful than his beautiful mother holds the rule of the kingdom, and sits on the ancestral throne.[50]

In addition to skipping blithely over the events of the Rough Wooing and Mary's attempts to rule in her own name, Maitland partially engages with Buchanan's view of the ideal king and suggests that, even though an infant, he willingly receives the consent of his people to govern precisely because he also has divine assent:

> Now Mother Nature has produced so great a king born from so great a family tree: so that if the choice is freely ours, or if the highest power were to grant our prayer, the loyalty of the human mind does not demand another. Thus the nobility rejoices at a king who is not lacking divine approval … Undoubtedly all men freely accept your rule because they have not been forced to submit to it, for who would refuse to obey he who their own votes have given the deserved kingdom?[51]

Maitland also notes that nature itself could not overturn James' accession, and in a striking simile suggests that no sooner could a fish jump out of the Tay and eat the goats grazing on its banks than the people of Scotland could turn against him.[52] The resulting mix of ideas here is overall a strange one. On the one hand, Maitland is quite clear that James has come to the throne of Scotland with the willing consent of its people, but at the same time seems unwilling to relinquish the idea that divine providence has played a role in this process. While this providence confines itself largely to endowing the king with divine aesthetic qualities and a strong and enduring lineage, this is the only section of the poem where Maitland's conception of kingship deviates from that of Buchanan's, as there is considerable ambiguity over whether that providence is providing James with the virtues needed to win over his subjects naturally, or is compelling them to accept his rule.

[50] 'Semper (adhuc memini), terris in morte relictis,/ postquam caelicolum numerum pater insitus astris/ auxit, et imperii tenerae data sceptra puellae,/ unum erat in votis: omnes uno ore canebant:/ "quando erit ille dies, quo (te, pulcherrima) parvus/ nympharum blando matrem puer ore vocabit:/ quando erit ille dies, dabitur quo sceptra tueri/ Stuartis, infans solioque sedebit avito?"/ Annuit, et blando arridens pater optimus ore,/ te nascente reos voti damnavit ovantes./ Et jam formosae matris formosior infans/ regni sceptra tenet, solioque insedit avito', lines 98–109.

[51] 'Iam talem tali natum de stemmate regem/ produxit Natura parens: ut si optio nobis/ libera, vel voti fieret si summa potestas,/ non alium humanae poscat fiducia mentis/ Ergo tuae, proceres quem non sine numine regem/ esse jubent … Scilicet, imperium quod non subiere coacti,/ sponte ferunt omnes, nam quis parere recuset,/ cui sua detulerant meritum suffragia regnum?', lines 110–15, 125–27.

[52] Lines 120–21.

## 'Paris and his half-man retinue': The Presentation of Bothwell as Tyrant

WHILE the infant James is presented with some vagueness as an ideal king who appears to enjoy both divine mandate and the willing approval of his people, Maitland offers a clear and unambiguous model of a tyrant in his presentation of Bothwell. In Buchanan's discourse, a tyrant is a near-bestial figure who seizes rule without consent either by violence or deceit, and who aims at power only to enrich themselves and to feed their unnatural appetite for vice.[53] Even if tyrants prove ultimately to be benevolent rulers, for Buchanan the crime by which they achieved power can never be expiated. A tyrant's own moral deficiencies makes him wholly unsuited to the station of king, 'even if he goes about with a numerous train of attendants, flaunts himself in magnificent finery, inflicts summary punishments, [and] wins over the mob'.[54] Because tyrants can never command loyalty for themselves, the only followers they attract are mercenaries who can just as easily be turned from them for a higher price. As a result, tyrants spend their whole life in a state of perpetual terror of 'their enemies abroad and their subjects at home, and not just their subjects but their servants, kinsmen, brothers, wives, children and parents'.[55] The removal or execution of a tyrant is thus a blessing to the people, and Buchanan cites several examples of Scottish kings who faced imprisonment or death for such behaviour, including the ancient kings Culen and Evenus and the more contemporary examples of James I and III.[56]

Bothwell is presented in the 'inauguratio' very much as a tyrant fitting Buchanan's description, both in terms of his uncontrolled lust and his propensity for extreme violence, which hides an underlying cowardice. When he is first introduced into the poem at line 128, he is immediately denounced as an 'incendiary' (*fax*) and the 'foulest plague of our people' (*nostrae pestis teterrima gentis*) against whom the whole nation has united in arms, who has murdered Henry Stewart Lord Darnley, and who now looks 'to demand a similar outrage against the head of a tiny prince' after violently seizing his mother.[57] In a passage denouncing Bothwell's abandonment of his first wife Jean Gordon, Maitland narrates how his unbridled sexual appetites have led him into tyranny, and the resulting fear with which he must now contend for the rest of his days. Just like Buchanan's classic tyrant, Bothwell is haunted by nightmares and visions of betrayal from which he can never escape:

53 Mason and Smith, pp. 85–89.

54 Ibid., p. 89.

55 Ibid., pp. 85, 91.

56 Ibid., p. 97.

57 Lines 130, 133–35: 'Quidve caput sacro cinctum diademate parvi/ profuit ad patriae similem deposcere caedem/ principis, abductae vitiumque offerre parenti?'

> Ah, how much better would it have been to spend your life in private with your own wife? Then neither would the eyes of the mob or the terrifying wrath of the judge reserved for the guilty frighten you: a shifting apparition would not disturb peaceful sleep, or your mind conscious of its crimes quake at empty gusts of air: instead, an infamous adulterer has stolen the widowed queen to himself to share a marriage bed with deathly consequence for all.[58]

The idea of Bothwell's inherent cowardice and his need to pay for loyalty is also succinctly captured in Maitland's account of Carberry, where he describes Bothwell as 'that Paris … with a half-man retinue' who comes to the battlefield with Mary as a captive, 'vomiting out many terrifying words and gusts with no power'.[59] The identification of Bothwell with Paris, the son of King Priam and Queen Hecuba of Troy and one of the central characters of Homer's *Iliad*, is highly appropriate in the context of the poem. It is Paris' elopement with Helen, the wife of Menelaus of Sparta, that triggers the war which causes the destruction of Troy, and the description of Bothwell and his bodyguard is a direct quotation from the prayer of vengeance laid against Aeneas for seducing and abandoning Dido at Carthage, leading her to kill herself.[60] Both references would have been immediately obvious to a sixteenth-century reader, and compounded together succinctly convey Bothwell's effeminacy in his inability to master his appetites, and the wholesale destruction that he has caused as a result.

Though Bothwell offered a challenge of single combat at Carberry to anyone willing to fight him to settle the conflict, no formal fighting took place, and Mary gave herself up to the confederate forces while Bothwell fled.[61] In Maitland's version, in a passage also redolent of the language and tone of epic conflict in the *Aeneid*, it is the sight of the royal banners featuring the Lion Rampant and the image of James in his cradle, beseeching god to 'judge and revenge my cause o lord', that makes Bothwell's heart quail:

[58] 'Quam fuit ah satius propria cum conjuge vitam/ degere privatam? Tum te neque lumina vulgi/ nec metuenda reis terreret judicis ira:/ lubrica nec placidos somnos turbaret imago, aut/ conscia mens sceleris ventos horreret inanes:/ at sibi funestis viduam famosus adulter/ reginam omnibus thalamo sociare jugali/ legit …', lines 141–48.

[59] 'ille Paris cum semiviro comitatu', line 238; 'multa vomens et verba leves terrentia ventos', line 241.

[60] Virgil, *Aeneid* 4.215. Paris is briefly mentioned in the *De Iure Regni* when Buchanan recounts a theory that it was only a phantom version of Helen that had accompanied him and his crew back to Troy, while the real Helen remained in Egypt with Proteus: Mason and Smith, p. 79.

[61] Antonia Fraser, *Mary Queen of Scots* (2015 edn), pp. 409–11.

> The royal murderer himself, high among the chief men, exults while brandishing a spear with his unyielding arms: the battle-line advances, and the standard-bearer unfurls his sign right there: once the image of the weeping prince has made conspicuous the slaughter of his father, the murderer's breast freezes over with cold; he drops the weapon from his hands; he suddenly flees from the sloping mount as the incautious traveller, unaware that he has stood upon a snake concealed beneath his feet, stops and turns his feet and limbs in another direction. He did not stop until he had shut up his trembling body in the fortified tower, and had abandoned the wife he had ravished.[62]

Thus Bothwell is ultimately overcome by the cowardice and fear that is the natural disposition of every tyrant, despite his initial bravado on the battlefield. Bothwell also has a fate ordained for him by Maitland that is entirely in keeping with the divine punishments meted out to tyrants by God and exemplified in the many instances of wicked kings that Buchanan mentions both in the *De Iure Regni* and in his later history of Scotland. Recounting Darnley's savage murder by Bothwell under the cover of darkness 'with a troop of mercenaries' (*stipante … caterva*), Maitland declares that the young king will be the instrument of vengeance when his 'royal fire' (*regia … flamma*) will mirror the gunpowder used at Kirk O'Field and destroy Bothwell's residences.[63] Maitland uses this sequence to show again how much better suited to ruling the young James is than his mother, as he will naturally be inclined to take up arms to secure his vengeance:

> But see! A child more fiercely spirited by far than his mother takes a stand, remarkable in his sovereignty, and who stirred by righteous anger will lay waste to you and your house, torn up from its barren root … and will expiate murder with enemy murder. Because grief for the slaughtered king, and the tears of his son, and the betrothal of his abducted mother rouse the gods.[64]

[62] 'Regius ipse inter primos sicarius alte/ exultat quassans duris hastile lacertis:/ procedunt acies, vexillum signifer isthic/ explicat: ut patriam caedem deflentis imago/ principis effulsit, caesori frigore pectus/ congelat; a manibus telum excidit, ille repente/ ut fugit incautus declivi a monte viator,/ nescius abstrusum donec pede presserit anguem,/ consistit, retroque pedem et vestigia flectit./ Nec prius abstiterat, quam rapta uxore relicta,/ munita corpus trepidum conclusit in arce', lines 246–56.

[63] Lines 154, 168. The phrase 'stipante … caterva' describing the mercenaries is another direct borrowing from the *Aeneid*, used in books 1 (line 497) and 4 (line 136).

[64] 'En modo longe instat genitore ferocior infans/ insignis sceptro, justa qui percitus ira,/ teque, domumque tuam sterili a radice revulsam/ destruet … caedemque hostili caede piabit./ Quippe Deos movit caesi miseratio regis,/ et lachrymae pueri, et raptae sponsalia matris', lines 160–63, 165–67.

## 'The strength of this nation of axe-wielding Scots': Maitland on Scottish Kingship and Tyranny

MAITLAND'S description of Mary's abdication and the punishment owed to Bothwell closely reflects similar discourses in the propaganda surrounding Mary's removal and the sections of the *De Iure Regni* that discuss the nature and character of a tyrant in detail. However, Maitland also provides the reader with several passages on the history and constitution of Scotland, the character of its people, and the expectations on its monarchs which further reflect the tenor and ideas of Buchanan's work. It is here above all that Maitland comes closest to emulating his older counterpart. At lines 177 to 220, Maitland exhorts the infant James to be mindful of the great gifts God has given him in coming to rule at such a young age a nation rich in natural resources and livestock. Recalling earlier depictions of the Scottish people in histories by Hector Boece and echoed almost verbatim in the poems of Thomas Craig,[65] Maitland also celebrates the martial and almost 'spartan' nature of Scottish life, and a people who now make ready to put their considerable military power in the hands of their king:

> The strength of this nation of axe-wielding Scots is to lie at ease in encampments, to withstand famine and thirst, to lie in wait for the enemy, to laugh off cold and to suffer heat, to outrun stags in their course, and to overcome moats with a leap, and rivers with a stroke, to scale inaccessible crags, to jump over battlements, to cast around the deadly weights of sulphurous cannonballs: to twirl the swift arrow from taut string, to bend a horse to one's will, to fight fiercely with the pike at close quarters, and when a fiery force from a sword enters the breast, to fight foot to foot, to despise one's wounds, and to look for death and renown with no thought for one's life.[66]

With these skills, Maitland argues, the Scots have endured against all enemy invaders since records began, and with such a force James can conquer whatever land he wishes. However, the military might of the

[65] On Boece, see Roger A. Mason, 'Chivalry and Citizenship: Aspects of National Identity in Renaissance Scotland', in Roger A. Mason and Norman Macdougall (eds), *People and Power in Scotland: Essays in Honour of T.C. Smout* (Edinburgh, 1992), pp. 50–73 (repr. Mason, *Kingship and the Commonweal*, pp. 78–103). For a very similar passage in Craig, see 'Genethliacum', lines 292–309.

[66] 'Illa securigeris virtus est patria Scotis/ in castris recubare, famem perferre sitimque,/ insidias hosti componere, spernere frigus/ sudoremque pati, cursu praevertere cervos,/ et fossas saltu, et fluvios superare natatu,/ scandere inaccessos colles, transcendere muros,/ spargere sulphureas letalia pondera glandes:/ adducto celerem nervo torquere sagittam,/ flectere cornipedem, pugnare ferociter hasta/ cominus, et gladio cum vis subit ignea pectus,/ mox conferre pedem, contemnere vulnera, mortemque/ et celebrem vita neglecta quaerere famam', lines 190–201.

nation will not slavishly offer its obedience to James, and James must educate himself in 'the arts one should learn about of a prince who will be victorious' if he wishes to earn their enduring support.[67] Maitland's description of these arts in the concluding section of the poem (lines 276 to 363) is a direct repetition of Buchanan's views. A king must be pious, avoid lust, and comport himself to the laws of his people, for the king's greatest value (as Buchanan also notes) is as a moral figurehead and mirror for the society he rules:

> If you desire the voice of a gracious God to be favourable to you, let religion be your concern ... The people fashion themselves after the example of the king, and the wickedness of a ruler will make the mob think that every kind of crime is lawful. If uncontrollable lust seizes you unexpectedly, and if you desire to have plots arranged, to defile the beds of married men, and to have seized the riches of good men ... alas, what kind of madness, tell me, will seize the people, drawing a deadly poison from the example of their king? ... No worthier words (believe me) can be spoken by a noble prince, than surrounding himself of his own accord with the boundaries of the laws.[68]

The whole poem builds to an explosive final statement, when after discussing the violent deaths that befell the tyrants Dionysius II of Syracuse (a key example also cited in the *De Iure Regni*),[69] Tarquinius Superbus, and Julius Caesar, Maitland reminds the young king that the people of Scotland will just as easily turn their bodies, usually used to protect their monarch, to his imprisonment and destruction:

> Our celebrated race, the scions of Scota – which by its own will submits itself to you who bears the rule, and is accustomed to defending good kings using their bodies as a shield, and which will yield to no danger while it keeps the sword away from the holy body of the king – that same race, if at any time a fierce and blood-thirsty person rises up who wishes to conquer the brave senate along with the fearful people and to infringe upon the laws of the nation, does not suffer it, but instead rumour flies, and with sudden uproar the armed strength of the outraged people heroically seizes the power of rule, and shortly after bridles the tyrant

[67] 'discendas victuri principis artes', line 278.

[68] 'Si tibi propitii facilem vis Numinis auram,/ relligio tibi sit curae, ... Regis ad exemplum populus se format, et atrox/ principis omne scelus vulgus fas esse putabit./ Si te transversum rapiet vesana libido/ insidias ut si cupias struxisse, maritum/ incestare thoros, et opes rapuisse bonorum:/ ... heu quaenam capiet dementia plebem,/ principis exemplo virus lethale trahentem?/ ... Non vox (crede mihi) generoso principe dici/ dignior ulla potest, quam libertate fruendo/ sponte sua sibi cancellos circumdare legum', lines 301–2, 304–8, 310–11, 318–20.

[69] Mason and Smith, p. 91.

> thrown from his seat, sometimes with a harsh prison and sometimes with a horrible death.[70]

Despite his later protestations about his involvement in the production of the *De Iure Regni*, the stark warning inherent in this passage closely reflects the words of Maitland's own character in the dialogue: 'whoever kills them [tyrants] benefits not only himself but the whole community'.[71] It also recalls the motto inscribed on the first coin and one of the earliest forms of visual propaganda produced by the King's Party, the 'James Ryal' minted in August 1567, which showed a sword going through an imperial crown and the words: 'for me or against me if I deserve [it]'.[72] The strong thematic and intellectual links between these differing expressions of Buchananesque views of kingship, all of which were written in or around 1567, seem to make it inescapable that Maitland was, in fact, at that point in his short life a clear disciple of Buchanan's ideas on monarchy.

## Conclusion

Maitland's 'inauguratio' is one of a host of poems narrating key events during James VI's personal residence in Scotland, all of which provide important perspectives on these events but which have been overlooked or forgotten until recently because they are in Latin. We are slowly recovering these texts and adding them back to the canon of early modern Scottish literature, and as the 'inauguratio' shows they are clearly deserving of inclusion. Although we cannot confirm conclusively that it was written at the time of James' actual coronation, it must have been written at some point between that event and Maitland's own death in early 1572. The close parallels between Maitland's presentation of Mary's abdication and the official abdication letters provide one reason to believe that it was written very close to these events, as he must have been aware of their arguments. If we assume that the 'inauguratio' was in fact produced in the summer of 1567, then the poem provides important corroborative evidence

70 '… Gens inclyta Scotae/ progenies, quae sponte sua tibi jura ferenti/ obsequitur, consueata bonos defendere reges/ opposítu laterum, nullis cessura periclis,/ dum sancto regis depellat corpore ferrum,/ illa eadem, si quando ferox, sitiensque cruoris/ exurgat, fortem trepida cum plebe Senatum/ qui vincire velit, patriaeque infringere leges,/ non tolerat, sed fama volat, subitoque tumultu/ accensi heroes virtusque armata popelli/ sceptra rapit, mox dejectum de sede tyrannum/ nunc morte horrifica, saevo nunc carcere fraenat', lines 335–46.

71 Mason and Smith, p. 89.

72 'pro mi si merior in me'. For the coin, see Hunterian, GLAHM:39010; Ian Stewart, 'Coinage and Propaganda: An Interpretation of the Coin-Types of James VI', in Anne O'Connor and D.V. Clarke (eds), *From the Stone Age to the 'Forty-Five: Studies Presented to R.B.K. Stevenson* (Edinburgh, 1983), pp. 450–62, at pp. 453–54.

for the development of Buchanan's *De Iure Regni*. Given its close synergy with Maitland's description of the 'tyrannical' qualities of Bothwell's character and the resulting punishments due to him, and with Maitland's account of the nature of good kingship and of tyranny, we can further assume that Buchanan was actively discussing these ideas with Maitland close to or at the time of the coronation. As such, the 'inauguratio' provides further circumstantial evidence that the *De Iure Regni* was in fact composed prior to the December parliament of 1567 which approved the proceedings against Mary, or at least that its ideas were sufficiently well developed for Maitland to have accessed.

Why it was produced is a question that cannot be answered due to the lack of extant evidence surrounding its initial drafting and dissemination. However, the 'inauguratio' is also important as another example of 'hidden' propaganda produced by the competing factions during the Marian Civil War. It is known that the pro-Marian faction made use of ballads and other popular texts to encourage popular opinion to support the queen, though the Moray regime's widespread censorship and destruction of these texts has left almost no extant evidence.[73] Similarly, Mark Loughlin's discovery of the manuscript account of the anonymous 'Dialogue of the Twa Wyfeis' shows that other texts supportive of the King's Party did circulate in non-printed form, in much the same way that early drafts of Buchanan's texts did.[74] Mason has rightly cautioned against attributing this text, and other anonymous pieces of polemic in the vernacular, to Buchanan solely because they bear traces of his ideas.[75] However, the survival of the 'inauguratio' suggests that other texts beyond Buchanan's were drafted in Latin to provide positive accounts of the actions of the King's Party. Whether Maitland's text is a unique and spontaneous outpouring designed for private circulation, a draft of a text that was planned for print in 1567 and never sent to press, or a text that was printed and has now been lost, is now impossible to recover.

Finally, the poem itself is also important as a case study of the impact that Buchanan had upon the generation of intellectuals and poets coming to adulthood in the wake of the Protestant Reformation in Scotland. The contents of the 'inauguratio' versus that of Maitland's later poetry shows that this relationship was not always linear or easy. Maitland's poem condemning the destruction of Dunbar Castle in December 1567, his pasquinade and his 'letter' to Elizabeth I all show an increasing criticism of the Moray regime for the severity of its treatment of those merely guilty

[73] Reid, *The Early Life of James VI*, chapter 2.

[74] Mark Loughlin, '"The Dialogue of the Twa Wyfeis": Maitland, Machiavelli and the Propaganda of the Scottish Civil War', in A.A. MacDonald, Michael Lynch, and Ian B. Cowan (eds), *The Renaissance in Scotland: Studies in Literature, Religion, History and Culture Offered to John Durkan* (Leiden, 1994), pp. 226–45.

[75] Roger A. Mason, 'George Buchanan's Vernacular Polemics, 1570–1572', *IR* 54.1 (2003), 47–68.

of association with Bothwell, disenchantment with the prolonged violence of the Marian Civil War, and vocal support for Mary. These writings all reflect the familial shift away from support for the king's cause, a shift which was evident in the political career of Maitland of Lethington from the latter half of 1567 as well. Yet the 'inauguratio' does not betray any such sense of disenchantment. While it portrays some sympathy for Mary's plight and exhibits some latitude over whether a monarch is given power by the will of God or the will of the people, the contents of the 'inauguratio' overwhelmingly reflect the ideas put in the mouth of Maitland's 'interlocutor' in the *De Iure Regni*. While Maitland would later protest to Mary that he had never endorsed Buchanan's ideas, if this poem is taken as evidence of his views in the heady summer of 1567, then he truly was, at least for a short while, Buchanan's disciple.

# 10

# *'Long lyf and welth vith veilfair and great gloir'*: *New Year and the Giving of Advice at the Stewart Court*

Kate McClune

'Men may leif *with*out ane king / Ane king but men may beir no crowne'
('Princely Liberality', Maitland Folio MS).[1]

THIS rather blunt reminder to a ruler that the security of his crown is contingent upon the satisfaction of his subjects (a relationship which is here not necessarily figured as symbiotic) is one of two anonymous poems in the Maitland Folio manuscript addressed to kings at New Year. The stern tone reflects elements of sixteenth-century Scots political discourse in which the rights of subjects to resist and depose inadequate rulers were asserted, and the Scots tendency to direct often profoundly didactic literature to monarchs is well-attested.[2] However, this particular poem's temporal setting at New Year introduces another dimension to the familiar advisory tone. It is one of a group of Scots writings addressed to monarchs and presented as New Year poems (also known as 'strena' or 'étrenne').[3] These are part of a European tradition in which, as Heal puts it, New Year formed an 'opportunity for the gift of good advice, to friends and family, to readers and, taking advantage of the license of the festival, from counsellors to monarchs'.[4] Not all Scots New Year poems are written for monarchs, but those which are display a marked concern with 'correct' regal behaviour,

[1] See W.A. Craigie (ed.), *The Maitland Folio Manuscript*, 2 vols (Edinburgh and London, 1919–27), pp. 207–9, lines 41–42.

[2] See Matthew P. McDiarmid, 'The Kingship of the Scots in Their Writers', *Scottish Literary Journal* 6 (1979), 5–18; Roger A. Mason, 'Kingship, Tyranny and the Right to Resist in Fifteenth Century Scotland', *SHR* 66 (1987), 125–51, at p. 126; and his discussion of George Buchanan's *De Iure Regni* in 'Beyond the Declaration of Arbroath: Kingship, Counsel and Consent in Late Medieval and Early Modern Scotland', in Boardman and Goodare (eds), *Kings, Lords and Men*, pp. 265–82, at p. 277.

[3] I use 'Scots' here to refer to those poems written in Older Scots, as opposed to Scottish neo-Latin poems (which are briefly discussed below).

[4] See Felicity Heal, *The Power of Gifts: Gift Exchange in Early Modern England* (Oxford, 2014), p. 81.

and the sometimes tense relationship between ruler, nation, and subject.[5] This chapter examines a group of poems dating from c. 1500 to 1583, a period covering the reigns (and the minorities) of James IV, James V, Mary, Queen of Scots, and James VI. The anxiety generated by these repeated periods of minority rule is well attested in Scots literature, and Scots New Year poems are no outliers.[6] James IV was the oldest to be crowned, at just 15; James V was 18 months old, while his daughter Mary was only seven days. James VI was 12 months old when he became king. Their reigns were characterised by periods of regency interspersed with (initially) youthful rule, and the literature of the time reflects an associated unease at this frequent turn of circumstance, and a perception that greedy regents, young rulers, and over-powerful counsellors can make the nation vulnerable.[7]

The poems discussed below are directed in different ways. Some are explicitly addressed to named kings, or to the queen. Some are written during periods of monarchic youth or absence and engage with the anxieties that such a deficiency produces. But what they have in common, and what differentiates them from their European, English, and neo-Latin Scottish counterparts, is the extent to which, even in apparently ceremonial poems, the didactic tone dominates. The exploitation of New Year license in Scotland is significant because there is a long literary tradition in which Older Scots writings address

5 Among the New Year poems omitted from this analysis are seventeenth-century examples by Alexander Craig (?1567–1627) and Sir Robert Ayton (1570–1638). Craig's collection, *The Amorose Songes, Sonets, and Elegies: of* M. *Alexander Craige, Scoto-Britane* (London, 1606) contains two New Year's gift poems addressed to Penelope and Idea, two of eight mistresses, each representing a different element of love. The overall collection is dedicated to Queen Anne, whose 'munificens and frequent benefites' (p. 7) to the poet are cited, but the texts themselves are not advisory. See D. Laing (ed.), *The Poetical Works of Alexander Craig of Rose-Craig 1604–1631* (Glasgow, 1873). Ayton's 'To Queen Anne upone a New-year's-day 1604' (British Library Additional MS 28622) does not engage in political assumption and prediction, although it restates the link between regal generosity and moral worth. It was subsequently adapted by John Ayton in 1661 in his 'new year's Gift' to King Charles II. For the text, see Charles B. Gullans (ed.), *The English and Latin Poems of Sir Robert Ayton* (Edinburgh, 1963), p. 168. Both these poets are writing at a time of relative regal security when James had become the first king of a united British Isles, and had three surviving children (Henry, Elizabeth, and Charles), seemingly ensuring dynastic strength. As such, the tone of dramatic urgency of the sixteenth-century poems is absent. On Ayton, see Harriet Harvey Wood, 'Ayton, Sir Robert (1570–1638), Poet and Courtier', *ODNB* [958], and Helena Mennie Shire, *Song, Dance, and Poetry of the Court of Scotland under King James VI* (Cambridge, 1969), pp. 215–54, and at p. 226 on the New Year poem. For Craig, see Michael R.G. Spiller, 'Craig [Craige], Alexander, of Rosecraig (1567?–1627), Poet', *ODNB* [6569].

6 See Jenny Wormald, *Court, Kirk, and Community: Scotland 1470–1625* (Edinburgh, 1981), pp. 12–16; Amy Blakeway, *Regency in Sixteenth-Century Scotland* (Woodbridge, 2015); Kate McClune, '"He was but a Yong Man": Age, Kingship, and Arthur', in Joanna Martin and Emily Wingfield (eds), *Premodern Scotland: Literature and Governance 1420–1587: Essays for Sally Mapstone* (Oxford, 2017), pp. 85–98.

7 On literary depictions of emotionally vulnerable youthful kings, see Joanna M. Martin, *Kingship and Love in Scottish Poetry 1424–1540* (Aldershot, 2008).

the moral strengths – and weaknesses – of monarchs, regardless of season. In tracing the development of these Scots strena, and the ways in which they speak to monarchs, one can see how poets attempted to use their writing in order not just to negotiate with, but also to shape regal authority.

## History and Background: New Year Literary Gifts

THE Scots strena did not emerge *ex nihilo*. It was part of a seasonal rite of symbolic gift exchange at New Year, traceable to the Ancient Near East.[8] Courtly gift-exchange was an important – and performative – representation of both loyal service and regal generosity. As Heal comments: 'to give, and indeed to receive, properly, were … crucial attributes for Scots rulers'.[9] Records of James VI's spending at New Year indicate substantial (and expensive) commissions, from gold and bejewelled rings and bracelets to tablets (flat ornaments made of precious stones or metal), to the extent that in 1587 he could not pay for his purchases, and had to 'pledge a great tabled diamond'.[10] But while historical records provide details of what a gift was, and

8 For a broad history of gift-giving, see Marcel Mauss, *The Gift: The Form and Reason for Exchange in Archaic Societies* (English edition first published by Cohen & West, 1954; London and New York, 2006); Natalie Zemon Davis, *The Gift in Sixteenth-Century France* (Oxford, 2000). Brigitte Buettner discusses the history and background of the New Year tradition in 'Past Presents: New Year's Gifts at the Valois Courts, ca. 1400', in *The Art Bulletin* 83.4 (2001), 598–625. See also L.G. Black, 'Some Renaissance Children's Verse', *Review of English Studies* 24.93 (1973), 1–16; Felicity Heal, 'Royal Gifts and Gift-Exchange in Sixteenth-Century Anglo-Scottish Politics', in Boardman and Goodare (eds), *Kings, Lords and Men*, pp. 283–300; Sophie Cope, 'Marking the New Year: Dated Objects and the Materiality of Time in Early Modern England', *Journal of Early Modern Studies* 6 (2017), 89–111. New Year's Gift Rolls, official records of gifts exchanged between monarchs and courtiers, exist for Henry VIII, Mary I, Edward VI, and Elizabeth I. See Peter Beal, *A Dictionary of English Manuscript Terminology 1450–2000* (Oxford, 2008), p. 265. On New Year poems specifically, see A.A. MacDonald, 'William Stewart and Court Poetry of the Reign of King James V', in Janet Hadley Williams (ed.), *Stewart Style 1513–1542: Essays on the Court of James V* (East Linton, 1996), pp. 179–200, at 195–97; Jane Donawerth, 'Women's Poetry and the Tudor Stuart System of Gift Exchange', in Mary Burke, Jane Donawerth, Linda L. Dove, and Karen Nelson (eds), *Women, Writing, and the Reproduction of Culture in Tudor and Stuart Britain* (Syracuse, 2000), pp. 3–18, comments on the New Year tradition at pp. 5–6, 10–11; Theo van Heijnsbergen, 'Advice to a Princess: The Literary Articulation of a Religious, Political and Cultural Programme for Mary Queen of Scots, 1562', in Julian Goodare and A.A. MacDonald (eds), *Sixteenth-Century Scotland: Essays in Honour of Michael Lynch* (Leiden: 2008), pp. 99–122.

9 See Heal, 'Royal Gifts', p. 284. See also Linda Levy Peck, '"For a King not to be bountiful were a fault": Perspectives on Court Patronage in Early Stuart England', *Journal of British Studies* 25.1 (1986), 31–61; Simon Wortham, '"Pairt of my taill is yet untolde": James VI and I, the *Phoenix* and the Royal Gift', in Daniel Fischlin and Mark Fortier (eds), *Royal Subjects: Essays on the Writings of James VI and I* (Detroit, 2002), pp. 182–204.

10 Amy L. Juhala, 'The Household and Court of King James VI of Scotland, 1567–1603' (unpublished University of Edinburgh PhD thesis, 2000), p. 157; see also pp. 165–66. Steven Reid has identified a number of additional hitherto unpublished New Year's gifts in

to whom it was presented, the *language* of gifting is more complex than simple economic value suggests. The circumstances in which a gift was given provide telling supplementary information, revealing 'social and political obligations with which contemporary audiences would already have been familiar'.[11] Presentation of a valuable gift publicly rewards good service, but also makes a statement about the pecuniary power and largesse of the giver. Conversely, gifts could subtly chastise, underscoring the recipient's perceived neglect, as in Lady Mary Sidney's gift of a gold pelican jewel to Queen Elizabeth I on New Year's Day, 1573, an event examined by Stearn. She argues that the gift implicitly criticised Elizabeth for her lack of concern for Mary, who, when Elizabeth had smallpox in 1562, had cared for the queen. She herself then contracted the disease. The pelican was traditionally a symbol of self-sacrifice, the belief being that the mother pelican, in times of need, would pierce her breast with her beak, feeding her young with her blood and at the expense of her own life. The image was intended to remind Elizabeth that she had not nurtured as a good queen should.[12] Elizabeth quickly gave the jewel to Lady Mary's sister, the Countess of Huntingdon, indicating that she was not overly concerned about her bond with Mary.

Gift-giving between monarchs was even more loaded. Felicity Heal notes the care with which the selection and distribution of gifts was negotiated at the Tudor and Stewart courts.[13] While the process could be a public display of aggressive solvency, imbuing a symbolic gesture with broader political import, financial value was not always a significant feature. Mary and Elizabeth attempted to intellectually outdo each other via exchanged poetry, and a diamond ring Mary sent to her cousin was accompanied by some of Buchanan's poetry.[14] James VI also sent poems to his aunt, and

---

the MS Treasurers' Accounts between August 1583–May 1585 (NRS, E22/6). In January 1584, there is evidence of a range of New Year's gifts including £200 to Wm Hudson, 'his hienes master ballandin'; the king's own New Year's gift £785 8s (ff. 144r–147v); a New Year's gift for the king made by Michael Gilbert costing 441 crowns (£1,102 10s) and another by Thomas Foulis, costing 406 1/2 crowns (£986 11s); a gift to the wife of the earl of Crawford at the baptism of her son of a tablet worth 22 crowns and 'thre roiss ringis set with dyamondis and rubies' worth 130 crowns (£355) (f. 230r); a further £220 8s for gold work produced from 1 May 1583 to January 1584; £40 to lackeys for a New Year's gift in January 1585; £125 to Master Patrick Blair for going to England for James (f. 230v); and a £20 New Year's gift to the palfreymen who look after the king's 'unce' (leopard). I am extremely grateful to Dr Reid for passing these references on to me.

[11] Cope, 'Marking the New Year', p. 91.

[12] See Catherine Howey Stearn, 'Critique or Compliment? Lady Mary Sidney's 1573 New Year's Gift to Queen Elizabeth', *Sidney Journal* 30.2 (2021), 109–27, at pp. 109–10.

[13] See Heal, *Power of Gifts* and 'Royal Gifts'.

[14] Heal, 'Royal Gifts', pp. 292–93. For more on Buchanan, see Erskine and Mason (eds), *George Buchanan*. For his poetry, see *George Buchanan: The Political Poetry*, ed. and trans. Paul J. McGinnis and Arthur H. Williamson (Edinburgh, 1995). See also Robert Crawford (ed.), *Apollos of the North: Selected Poems of George Buchanan and Arthur Johnson* (Edinburgh, 2006).

these were often reciprocated – except when the tone offended her.[15] The nuanced circumstances which surrounded such exchanges – which were not always limited to New Year – and the care with which such literary gifts were composed, and read, offer a sense of the broader literary context behind New Year's gift poems.

## Literary New Year's Gifts

THE practice of exchanging poetic gifts at New Year was not confined to Scots verse: numerous examples exist in contemporary neo-Latin, English and European verse. Buettner points to the work of Christine de Pizan, adept at presenting copies of her works to multiple patrons, and who subsequently became particularly accomplished in the 'financially altogether safer strategy' of composing étrennes ('safer' because the costs of creating such literary gifts were far smaller for the poet than those associated with producing expensive manuscripts).[16] Bentley-Cranch notes the practice of giving poems as gifts in sixteenth-century France: Chappuys composed an étrenne for an unknown female recipient, while in 1532 Clément Marot gifted *Au Roy, pour avoir esté desrobé* to Francis I.[17] She records that he was rewarded with a gift from the king of 100 écus for this poetic effort. Marot's subsequent efforts were not just for the king – in 1541 he addressed a series of 44 étrennes to the ladies of court, including Queen Eléonore and Catherine de Medici, the Dauphine. These demonstrate his poetic prowess, but furthermore suggest a knowing and comfortable familiarity with courtly figures and conventions – to the king's mistress, he writes 'Sans prejudice à personne, / Je vous donne / La pomme d'or de beaulté' (Without prejudice to anyone / I give you / the golden apple of beauty).[18] Marot was writing these poems in a receptive cultural context: other examples include one by the king's sister, Marguerite de Navarre, who addressed a missive to Francis, to be presented to him along with her New Year's gift to him. He, in turn, replied with a poem accompanied by a New Year's gift.[19] Other members of the Pléiade produced étrennes: in 1552, Pierre du Ronsard dedicated one to Robert de La Haye, a neo-Latin poet and a

[15] Peter C. Herman, '"Best of Poets, Best of Kings": King James VI and the Scene of Monarchic Verse', in Fischlin and Fortier (eds), *Royal Subjects*, pp. 61–103.

[16] Buettner, 'Past Presents', p. 618.

[17] Dana Bentley-Cranch, 'Clément Marot's Étrennes aux dames de la court', in Trevor Peach and Pauline M. Smith (eds), *Renaissance Reflections* (Paris, 2002), pp. 57–83.

[18] See Clément Marot, *Œuvres complètes*, ed. C.A. Mayer, 6 vols (London, Paris, Geneva, 1958–80; vols 1–5 repr. Geneva, 1999). The *Etrennes aux Dames de la Court* appear in vol. 4, *Œuvres diverses*, cited by Bentley-Cranch, 'Clément Marot's Étrennes', pp. 62–73, who also describes the other recipients and discusses Marot's poetic innovation in these poems.

[19] Pauline M. Smith and Dana Bentley-Cranch, 'A New Iconographical Addition to Francis I's Adoption of the Persona of King David and its Contemporary Literary Context', *Renaissance Studies* 21 (2007), 607–24, at pp. 619–21.

member of the Paris *Parlement*; de La Haye and his sister Marie also received one of Du Bellay's étrennes, and Antoine De Baïf and Jean de la Péruse composed similar poems for anonymous recipients, identifiable females, their friends, and certain regal figures.[20]

In England, the association between New Year's gifts and literary presentations was common during the fifteenth and sixteenth centuries. H.W. Garrod discusses the 'strenula' of Erasmus – his translation of *Toxaris* with an accompanying dedicatory letter for Richard Foxe, the bishop of Winchester, which positions the translation as a New Year's gift for which he expects something in return.[21] Garrod quotes Erasmus' letter to Fox: '[Such gifts] are thought to be somehow of happy omen both for those who receive them and for the givers who get gifts in return.'[22] Erasmus continued to dedicate translations to potential patrons at New Year: in January 1513 Erasmus dedicated a manuscript of his translation of Plutarch's *De Tuenda Valetudine* to John Yonge, who died at the relatively young age of 49 in 1515. This was then printed by Pynson in London in August 1513; it was later reprinted as part of *Opuscula Plutarchi* by Froben in 1514, when the dedication was amended – Garrod notes that in the three surviving Froben copies he has traced, it has been removed, and suggests that this is because 'Yonge no longer counted, or because he had rewarded him [Erasmus] in an inadequate fashion'.[23] The Froben Plutarch comprises two parts: Part I, containing *De Discriminae Adulatoris et Amici*, which is dedicated to Henry VIII, and *De Utilitate capienda ex Inimicus*, which is dedicated to Wolsey, and Part II, which contains *De Tuenda* but has no dedication. The original manuscripts of the texts for Henry VIII and Wolsey survive, and Garrod posits that 'the books dedicated were intended as gifts for the New Year 1514'.[24] He identifies other New Year literary gifts, including Princess Elizabeth's offering to Queen Katherine Parr of her translation of *The Glasse of the Synneful Soule* (Bodleian Library, MS Cherry 36) on 31 December 1544 with a dedication that prays to 'garante unto your highness the sam newe yeres daye a lucky and a prosperous yere'. Other gifts include manuscript copies of George Gascoigne's *Hermetes the Heremyte* (1 January 1575) and *The Griefe of Joye* (1 January 1576), both of which were presentation copies for Elizabeth.[25] As Garrod suggests, this

[20] Bentley-Cranch, 'Clément Marot's Étrennes', provides full details of these works: I am indebted to this article.

[21] H.W. Garrod, 'Erasmus and His English Patrons', *The Library*, 5th ser., vol. 4 (1949), 1–13.

[22] Ibid., p. 6.

[23] Ibid., p. 7.

[24] Ibid., pp. 7–8.

[25] There are two other surviving manuscript translations attributed to Elizabeth, and interestingly, both are New Year's gifts – one is a translation of Katherine Parr's Prayers and Meditations into French, Italian, and Latin (British Library, MS Royal D.7.x) and the other a translation into English of Calvin (NRS, RH 13/78). These were presented as New Year's gifts to Henry VIII and Katherine in 1545/6, see: https://web.warwick.ac.uk/english/perdita/html/ms_BODC36.htm.

certainly looks like an established 'part of [English] court custom', and the tradition is further investigated by Miller in his examination of New Year presentation books.[26] He focuses on the custom of authors presenting books of their own works at New Year. For some, gifting their own compositions was a way of 'bestowing greetings and presents upon their intimates', but others had less selfless motives.[27] Miller notes Thomas Churchyard's futile attempts to impress with New Year verse. In his own words: 'I sent eche Lorde a New yeres gifte: / Such treasure as I had that tyme, / A laughing verse, a merrie ryme.'[28]

The association of literature and New Year also appears in neo-Latin Scots poems. The University of Glasgow's *Bridging the Continental Divide* project, an electronic edition of some of the *Delitiae Poetarum Scotorum huius aevi illustrium* (DPS, Amsterdam, 1637), records five 'strena'. Hercules Rollock (c. 1546–99) is the author of three (dated between 1579 and 1580), of which one is to Thomas Travers, whom he accuses of being 'bifronti' (line 1, two-faced) and two are for Francis Walsingham (Elizabeth I's secretary and head of her espionage network). An undated poem is attributed to Thomas Maitland (c. 1548–72), and directed to David Cunningham, the bishop of Aberdeen and the chancellor of King's College between 1577–1600. The fifth strena, from 1605, is by Robert Ayton (1570–1638) for James Hay, who had a number of official roles in the royal households of James VI and I and Charles I.[29]

The personal and political affiliations of the poets or recipients of these five poems show that they exist within a courtly context. But the poems themselves are not dedicated to monarchs. Their tones are beseeching, critical, or sycophantic, but they do not purport to offer advice on appropriate regal behaviour, and it is on this aspect of the Older Scots poems that I want to focus. In configuring the Scots regal poems as part of the New Year's gift tradition, the poets skilfully deploy poetic convention to make demands of their rulers which, while they are personal, at the same time serve to remind the monarchs of their political responsibilities. As such, the way this genre is utilised in Scots verse forms part of a very specific literary tradition in which

[26] Garrod, 'Erasmus', pp. 10–12; Edwin Haviland Miller, 'New Year's Day Gift Books in the Sixteenth Century', *Studies in Bibliography* 15 (1962), 233–41.

[27] Miller, 'New Year's Day Gift Books', p. 234.

[28] See ibid., pp. 234–35. Felicity Heal comments on Churchyard's similarly doomed attempts to impress the earl of Ormond in his 1580 collection *A Pleasante Laborinth Called Churchyardes Chance* (London, 1580), ff. 33v–345, cited by Heal, *Power of Gifts*, p. 69.

[29] The poems can be accessed on the project website: www.dps.gla.ac.uk/. The authors and recipients have varying degrees of association with the royal court of James VI and I: Hercules Rollock was recommended to James by George Buchanan and nominated as commissary of Dundee on 11 September 1580, and in 1584 appointed master of Edinburgh Grammar School. Some of his verses are attached to James' *Essayes of a Prentise*. See Stuart Handley, 'Rollock, Hercules (c. 1546–1599), Lawyer and Poet', *ODNB* [24030]. Thomas Maitland was the prolocutor in Buchanan's *De jure regni apud Scotos* (1579) and a courier for the Queen's Party; see Michael R.G. Spiller, 'Maitland, Sir Richard, of Lethington (1496–1586), Courtier and Writer', *ODNB* [17831]. Ayton was a noted poet and courtier at the court of James and Anne.

poetry for the monarch regularly serves a corrective function. The New Year poems below comfortably inhabit distinct but parallel literary contexts, in their advisory nature, in their adoption of political instruction, and in their use of a tone that is often at least didactic, if not accusatory. They are salutary reminders of the ways in which literary texts formed a continuous political discourse across different centuries and periods of rule in Scotland.

## Poems for Monarchs

THE majority of extant New Year's poems in Scots are addressed to kings, with one significant exception for Mary, Queen of Scots. The reign of each Stewart was marked, at different times, by conflict both internal and external. James IV's reign was bookended by the Battle of Sauchieburn in 1488, at which he led the nobility's rebellion against his father James III, and his death at Flodden in 1513, an event which virtually destroyed the Scots aristocracy. James V, his heir, was just two years old, and grew up amidst conflict between pro-English and pro-French factions, with his mother, Margaret Tudor, acting as his regent from 1513 until 1514, when she married Archibald Douglas, 6th earl of Angus, and alienated much of the Scots nobility.[30] She was replaced by John Stewart, 2nd duke of Albany, regent from 1514 to 1524. After this, Margaret again briefly exerted control over the government, this time in concert with John Hamilton, 1st earl of Arran. The minority officially ended in 1526, but James was in the power of the Angus Douglases between 1526 and 1528, until he was able to deal with the threat from the influential family of his stepfather and take control of his throne.[31] His subsequent reign was relatively stable, until the death of his mother led to increased Anglo-Scots hostilities. The Scots were defeated at the Battle of Solway Moss in 1542, and James died of an illness soon afterwards, leaving his infant daughter to ascend the throne. Mary's minority, and indeed her reign, was riven by conflict, culminating in her forced abdication in 1567. Her first regent was James Hamilton, earl of Arran (1542–54), followed by her mother, Mary of Guise (1554–60). The occasion of her return to Scotland and the chaotic royal entry to Edinburgh in 1561 is the subject of William Stewart's New Year poem for her, discussed below. Her son, James VI, was another infant king, and the nation was governed by a series of regents during his youth. First was James Stewart, 1st earl of Moray, regent from 1567 until he was assassinated in 1570. He was followed by Matthew Stewart, the 4th earl of Lennox, who took over in 1570 but was shot dead during an attack on Stirling by the Queen's Party. John Erskine, earl of Mar, was the regent

[30] See Mason, *Kingship and the Commonweal*, pp. 62–64.

[31] See Jamie Cameron, *James V: The Personal Rule, 1528–42*, ed. Norman Macdougall (East Linton, 1998), chapter 1.

between 1571 and 1572. His death was apparently of natural causes, although rumours persisted that he was poisoned by James Douglas, 4th earl of Morton, who subsequently became regent between 1572 and 1578. He was executed in 1581, accused of complicity in the murder of Darnley. It is clear, then, that the broad historical context for the poems discussed below is one which seems characterised by varying periods of monarchic security and general chaos, and this is repeatedly reflected in the poems.

The earliest is William Dunbar's, 'My prince in God, gif the guid grace' (Poem 37), dated tentatively by Bawcutt to pre-1503.[32] The prince addressed is James IV, and the poem alludes explicitly to a period of gift-giving in its refrain 'In hansill of this guid New ȝeir'. The tone is respectful (the narrator prays that God will give the king good fortune and abundant virtue) but there is nonetheless a clear advisory tenor: he is reminded that he must 'reull and … defend' (line 14) the realm with peace and justice. This expression of ideal kingship is reiterated in the final stanza when the narrator prays that God will send James happiness, 'many Fraunce crownes' (line 18), and a 'Hie liberall heart and handis not sweir' (line 19). The poem does not explicitly request reward, but the New Year association with gift-giving allows Dunbar to remind the king, without appearing impudent, that one of his many regal obligations is liberality. This emphasis recurs in Dunbar's 'This hinder nycht, halff sleiping as I lay' (Poem 75), an allegorical dream-vision which attacks courtly corruption, with Bawcutt suggesting early 1507 for the composition date.[33] Here, New Year is referenced once at line 55, but Dunbar exploits the levity associated with the period to address courtly depravity. He reminds the king of his faithful service: that he 'lange hes bene ane seruand to the king' (line 67) but remains uncompensated. Personified Witt proposes that he and Nobilnes will advocate for the poet at court, in the hope that 'sum rewaird' (line 54) will be forthcoming 'in the honour of this guid New ȝeir' (line 55). The specific association of New Year and reward reminds the king that the tone is appropriate – this is, after all, a time at which gift-giving should occur – but the poem's criticism pre-empts Sir Richard Maitland's poetic attacks on courtly corruption and paints a bleak picture of how courtly values deteriorate if the king does not intervene to correct the behaviour. 'Blind Effectioun' (partiality) is said to have 'the governance' (line 60) of the court and 'Inoportunitie' is constantly 'befoir the kingis face' (line 78). Ressoun comments that 'With gredines I sie this world ourgane, / And sufficience dwellis nocht bot in heavin' (lines 99–100), which suggests that Patience's advice to depend upon the king, for he is of 'nobill intent' (line 108), is perhaps optimistic, if not naive. Indeed, the king's intent is never tested, because at the very moment when Patience asserts that the king will not

[32] Priscilla Bawcutt (ed.), *The Poems of William Dunbar*, 2 vols (Glasgow, 1998), vol. 2, p. 367. For the poem's text, see vol. 1, p. 129. All references to Dunbar's poems are taken from this edition, and I use Bawcutt's numbers to indicate specific poems. Poem 37 survives in the Reidpeth MS, ff. 2v–3r (Cambridge University Library, MS Lines v. 10).
[33] Bawcutt, *Dunbar*, vol. 2, p. 467. The poem is extant in Reidpeth, ff. 3v–5r.

leave the poet 'vnrewairdit half ane ȝeir' (line 110), he is rudely awakened. Dunbar seems very deliberately to be exploiting the opportunities offered both by the poem's form as dream-vision (all criticism is positioned in the mouths of the personifications) and its New Year setting. Both allow him to remind the king indirectly of his personal responsibilities – responsibilities which have a clear and explicit impact on the greater good of the court and by extension, the kingdom he governs.

There are parallels here with the later work of William Stewart, specifically 'Lerges of this new ȝeir day', which survives in the Bannatyne Manuscript and the Maitland Folio. The Bannatyne text contains four more stanzas than the Maitland version, and only in that version is the king mentioned.[34] The verses common to both manuscripts refer to public figures who likely would have been identifiable to a contemporary audience: the poem is traditionally dated to 1527 (the personal rule of James V), but Alasdair MacDonald suggests the possibility of a later date of 1542, and the identity of figures for either date is indicated in what follows here.[35] 'Off galloway the bischop new' (BM line 11; the bishop in 1527 would have been Henry Wemyss; in 1542, Andrew Durie) is accused of giving the poet a horse 'but hyd or hew'(line 14), i.e. one that does not even exist. Bannatyne's extra stanzas identify more public figures whose generosity is found wanting, including 'the king my cheife' (line 1) (James V); 'the secretar' (lines 21–25; this would be Sir Thomas Erskine of Halton and Brechin, who was one of James' tutors and was in post from October 1526 to January 1543); 'my lord Bothwell' (lines 41–45; Patrick Hepburn, 3rd earl of Bothwell); 'm*ar*garet our quene' (lines 46–50; Margaret Tudor).[36] Their gifts range from the paltry (two shillings from the king) to the non-existent, with the poet disingenuously blaming the frost for freezing shut their purses.

While Dunbar's speakers reprimand unappreciative patrons for lack of reward, Stewart's tone is more pessimistic. Gifts are intentionally inadequate; the opening description of the king likens him to a thief, a resonant image: 'ffirst lerges the king my cheife / quhilk come als quiet as a theif / And in my hand sled schillingis tway' (lines 1–3). The poem is a bleakly satirical assessment, with the burden at the end of each stanza, 'ffor lerges of this new ȝeirday' emphasising that such parsimony is particularly unfitting at

[34] For discussion, see MacDonald, 'William Stewart', pp. 195–97. The poem is extant in the Bannatyne Manuscript (NLS, Adv. MS 1.1.6), ff. 95b–96b/pp. 252–54, and in the Maitland Folio Manuscript (Pepys Library, Magdalene College, Cambridge, MS 2553), pp. 220–21. The two versions are not identical: BM lines 1–5, 21–25, 41–45, 46–50 are not in the MF and neither is the attribution to Stewart. I use the Bannatyne text of the poem here; see *The Bannatyne Manuscript*, ed. W. Tod Ritchie, 4 vols (Edinburgh and London, 1928–34), vol. 2, pp. 254–57. For the Maitland text, see *The Maitland Folio Manuscript*, ed. W.A. Craigie, 2 vols (Edinburgh and London, 1919–27), vol. 1, pp. 248–49.

[35] MacDonald, 'William Stewart', pp. 196–97 identifies the individuals mentioned.

[36] Ibid. MacDonald notes that the 1527 dating stems largely from the reference to the fall of Margaret Tudor at lines 46–50, but suggests that the reference might relate to 1 January 1542, after her death, so that the verse becomes a prayer for her soul.

this time of year. The final stanza, addressed to Margaret, implies that if she 'war as scho hes bene' (line 47), she would have been more liberal than the others, and MacDonald's suggested composition date of 1542, after Queen Margaret's death, not only explains this reference, but adds an even more sombre note to the final stanza.

Attempts to refocus problematic kingly behaviour are similarly apparent in two anonymous poems, 'Schir sen of men ar dyuerss sortis' (extant in both the Bannatyne Manuscript and the Maitland Folio) and 'Princely Liberality' (Maitland Folio).[37] Explicit references to the New Year are brief, but both poems identify it as an apposite moment for verse concerned with temperate regal behaviour. The Maitland witness to 'Schir sen of men …' contains two extra stanzas that focus on lineage, noble kin and the king's power to help his subjects (lines 16–20; 46–50). James V is exhorted to recall his illustrious ancestors, and to behave in a status-appropriate way – to play dice and cards only with his mother and noble lords, because 'To play *with* puiyr men disaccordis / vnto þi princelie maiestie' (MF, lines 29–30). He is further reminded that to keep his winnings would be shamefully unprincely, and instead, such monies should be circulated amongst his servitors (lines 31–35). As MacDonald points out, poems for James tended to emphasise the 'double necessity of providing good government in the state and restraining his [James'] precocious inclination to sensuality'. [38] Thus, there is a specific context – literary and historical – for the poem's cogently expressed anxiety about the temptations faced by rulers, and its concomitant emphasis on self-control in the face of such enticements. Similar disquiet is conveyed in 'Princely Liberality', the poem quoted at the beginning of this chapter. The king is addressed respectfully as 'Excelland michtie prince and king' (l.1). 'This new ȝeir' offers a fresh opportunity for him to demonstrate his generosity, but the poem strikes an ominous note with its repeated warnings: 'Gold silver ryches and realmes of pryce / no prince makis michtie for to ring' (lines 33–34), and the reminder that the security of his position is not contingent on wealth alone – 'Men may leif *with*out ane king / Ane king but men may beir no crowne' (lines 41–42). The poem's utilisation of the New Year trope, and its advisory tone, are both fairly conventional in Scots terms, but its emphasis that 'Treu*th* m*er*cie fredome and iustice / Thir four maikis ane nobill king' (line 35) reiterates the perilous outcome for a king who forgets or chooses not to practice such virtues.

[37] 'Schir, sen of men …' appears in Bannatyne Manuscript ff. 96a–96b/pp. 256–57 and Maitland Folio, pp. 218–20. Only the Maitland text contains the New Year reference (lines 61–62); lines 16–20 and 46–50 are also omitted from Bannatyne, but Bannatyne attributes the poem to William Stewart. Craigie's edition of the Maitland Folio contains this footnote to the final lines: 'These two lines, properly the beginning of the next piece ['Larges …'], are deleted'; Craigie, *Folio*, vol. 1, p. 248. 'Princely Liberality' appears in Maitland Folio, pp. 183–85. For the poem's text, see Craigie, *Folio*, vol. 1, pp. 207–9. Pinkerton described the poem as 'not worth transcription', quoted in Craigie, *Folio*, vol. 2, p. 102.

[38] See MacDonald, 'William Stewart', p. 188.

The advice one sees in these poems for James IV and V is relatively specific, and it tends to stress the symbiotic relationship between the king's behaviour and the associated wellbeing of the realm. Alexander Scott's 'ane new ȝeir gift to the quene Mary, Quhen scho come first hame 1562', extant in the Bannatyne Manuscript, continues to manifest the advisory theme but there is a difference in tenor.[39] A less informal relationship between poet and ruler is implied, a tonal difference that surely reflects the more problematic historical and political context that surrounds (particularly) the early rule of Mary, Queen of Scots.[40] The poem repeatedly invokes the season in its title, and in 23 of the 26 verses, and it manifestly uses the New Year setting to respond to, and attempt to ameliorate, tensions arising from a specific event. During Mary's 1561 entry to Edinburgh, 'militant Protestantism' had erased the 'traditional dialogic nature of entries': the poem re-presents the customary royal entry in a positive light, but all the while reminds the Queen of her own responsibilities.[41] As van Heijnsbergen has noted, the poem self-consciously invokes the typical visual elements of a regal entry, with repeated utilisation of heraldic and symbolic imagery such as the thistle.[42] In subsequently interrogating themes of good governance and secure rule, Scott – like Dunbar before him – subtly blurs the distinction between a literary gift and an advisory piece.[43] The hope that 'This guid new ȝeir' will be one of 'peax tra*n*quillitie and rest' (line 10) is expressed with loaded terms: this year 'syll rycht and ressone rewle þe rod' (line 11). The queen is advised to remember the cardinal virtues (wisdom, justice, fortitude, temperance), and the poem's semantic field repeatedly invokes balance and stability – 'Waye', 'steidfastnes', 'steir', 'temper'. Futhermore, Mary is advised to accept counsel from the 'sage' (line 33), a word commonly associated with age (and contrasted with the recklessness of youth).[44]

The penultimate lines of many verses exhort action: 'to reforme' (line 63); 'To sett asyde sic sortis of superstitioun' (line 71); 'To mend' (line 79); 'to forbid' (line 87); 'To ceis' (line 95). These are reinforced with the assertion 'God gif þe grace aganis þis guid new ȝeir'. The tight association between the poem's advisory tone and the season emphasises the strength of the message. As van Heijnsbergen highlights, its position in the Bannatyne Manuscript – amidst poems by Stewart and Kyd that are part of the *speculum principis* tradition, and others similarly concerned with self-governance and appropriate behaviour – underscores its political significance. New Year's association with new beginnings and moral improvement is key to this poem:

[39] Scott's poem is in the Bannatyne Manuscript, ff. 90a–92a/pp. 241–45. For the text, see Tod Ritchie (ed.), *Bannatyne Manuscript*, vol. 2, pp. 235–42.

[40] On the Marian civil wars, see Hercules Rollock, 'Sylva IV', c. 1572–73, at www.dps.gla.ac.uk/electronic-resource/display/?pid=d2_RolH_006&aid=RolH.

[41] Van Heijnsbergen, 'Advice to a Princess', p. 104.

[42] Ibid., p. 109.

[43] Van Heijnsbergen highlights this 'generic inventiveness' in his essay; ibid., p. 107.

[44] See *A Dictionary of the Older Scottish Tongue*, s.v. 'Sage, adj.' (www.dsl.ac.uk/entry/dost/sage_adj).

it is not explicitly a request for preferment on Scott's own behalf, but aims to direct Mary towards 'measured but effective reform'.[45] It is particularly concerned with the state of the nation and how the newly returned queen might secure peace and stability – thus, advice about appropriate behaviour on the queen's part is directly linked to the health of the nation. The poem is critical of corruption and clerical abuses, but notably it ends on a note that iterates the security of the Stewart dynasty, citing 'the prophecie' (line 195) that one of Robert the Bruce's male descendents 'sould bruke all bretane be þe see' (line 194).[46]

John Stewart of Baldynneis' New Year poems, 'To His Maiestie the first of Ianvar. 1582' and 'To His Maiestie the first of Ianvar vith presentation of ane lawrell trie formit of gould. 1583' are written for that descendent, King James VI.[47] On the surface, they vehemently praise his worth, his resilience, and his strength. However, when they are read within the specific manuscript and historical context it becomes clear that such praise emerges from a period of strife and conflict. Anxieties around youthful kingship and self-governance are just as apparent – albeit implicitly – in Stewart's work as they were in the earlier poems.

Adv. MS 19.2.6 is the unique witness to Stewart's poetry, and is dedicated to James VI. There is, in fact, no evidence that it was ever actually presented to James or that he read any of Stewart's poetry, which makes the inclusion of these New Year poems all the more intriguing.[48] I have discussed the significance of the manuscript structure elsewhere; these are the only dated works in the collection and they immediately follow 'To his Maiestie in fascherie'.[49] The poem likely refers to the events of the Ruthven Raid of 1582, when the 16-year-old king was seized by a group of disaffected Presbyterian nobles who had concerns about the king's potential pro-French, pro-Catholic sympathies.[50] The king was held for nearly a year before he escaped in June

45 See Theo van Heijnsbergen, 'Studies in the Contextualisation of mid-sixteenth-century Scottish verse' (unpublished University of Glasgow PhD thesis, 2010), p. 138.

46 See van Heijnsbergen, 'Advice to a Princess', pp. 111, 115–16.

47 The two poems are in NLS, Advocates MS 19.2.6, ff. 73v, 74r. The manuscript was probably compiled c. 1585–87, although individual poems would have been composed earlier. The text of the poems has been published in Thomas Crockett (ed.), *The Poetry of John Stewart of Baldynneis* (Edinburgh and London, 1913), and a new edition is underway by Kate McClune. For ease of access, I use Crockett's text here.

48 See Kate McClune, 'Poetry and the In-Crowd: The Case of John Stewart of Baldynneis', in D.J. Parkinson (ed.), *James VI and I: Literature and Scotland: Tides of Change, 1567–1625* (Groningen, 2012), pp. 119–35.

49 For discussion of the manuscript's structure, see Shire, *Song, Dance, and Poetry*, p. 92; Kate McClune, 'The Poetry of John Stewart of Baldynneis (?1540–?1607)' (unpublished University of Oxford PhD thesis, 2005), pp. 19–62. For the text see Crockett, *Stewart*, p. 125.

50 See Steven J. Reid, 'Of Bairns and Bearded Men: James VI and the Ruthven Raid', in Miles Kerr-Peterson and Steven J. Reid (eds), *James VI and Noble Power in Scotland 1578–1603* (London and New York, 2017), pp. 32–56. He notes that the Raid was only one element in a tumultuous seven years, when there were at least 'six palace coups' (see

1583. Stewart's poem, which is permeated with martial imagery, advises patient and stoic resistance at times of trouble, emphasising the importance of placing one's faith in God and reminding the king that 'Thois that Induirs the vinters scharp assay / sall sie the seimlie symmer scheine againe' (lines 27–28). It is followed by a New Year poem that asserts James' strength of character in overcoming 'monie storms' (line 6) in his past, and it prays that his foes will be defeated, and that his regal power will remain strong.[51] It concludes with Stewart's iteration that he will always remain loyal to James. Stewart's deliberate decision to include the date in the title suggests that he wants the poem to be associated with the period of captivity.

The vocabulary emphasises James' nobility and multiple skills – the 'lawrer croune' (line 10) rewards martial victory and poetic skill, and he is likened to Alexander, a reference to either (or both) Alexander III of Scotland or Alexander the Great, popular exemplary figures in sixteenth-century Scotland. Interwoven with these adulatory statements are Stewart's assertions of undying loyalty to his king: 'My lyf in pledge, or this ȝeir cum till end' (line 9); I 'sall ȝow serwe maist faythfull till I die' (line 22). The New Year context is indicated through the title, but also within the body of the poem; James will be triumphant over his foes 'for new ȝeirs gift' (line 18), and will attain his heart's desire 'or ȝeir cum till end' (l.9). The explicitly advisory element of the poem exists primarily in its instruction to James to place his faith in God. Certainly the description of James as 'peirles person … / Perfyt precelling puissant prudent prence' (lines 2–3) indicates that there is little the poet can teach him in terms of self-improvement. Nonetheless, there is a didactic subtext. Likening James to Alexander is complimentary, but the death of Alexander III of Scotland – killed when he fell from a horse on an ill-advised journey to visit his new young wife – is attributed by some chronicle accounts to a lack of self-control and a failure to listen to his advisors.[52] Similarly, references to past storms (albeit overcome) remind James of the dangers of alienating his countrymen. The final stanza figures Stewart as a poverty-stricken poet, with little to offer the king but his 'treuthfull luifing hart' (line 21). He laments that he has 'no perle nor royale pretious stone, / Nor gift of gould' (lines 19–20) to offer the king, whose expenditure and debts were already becoming notorious by the early 1580s. He then asks that James take 'this thing' (the poem) as 'the vidows myt' (l. 27), a reference to the Biblical episode recounted in Mark 12:41–44 and Luke 21:1–4, where the poor widow's scant offering is said by Jesus to be worth more than all the gold of the rich because she has given all she has. Stewart does not explicitly ask the king for pecuniary reward, but the emphasis on his own parlous economic state is an indirect entreaty for aid, whether financial or otherwise. In this

p. 32, quoting Julian Goodare). One of the leading participants in the Raid was the earl of Gowrie, and interestingly, Reid notes his concern at his personal liability (as treasurer) for the crown debt, which was just over £45,000 at the time of the raid (p. 35).

[51] Crockett, *Stewart*, p. 127.

[52] See McClune, *Poetry of John Stewart of Baldynneis*, pp. 1–15 for a summary.

sense, it echoes the pleas presented in Dunbar's New Year poems above, although Stewart's tone is more serious and less intimate.

The title of Stewart's second New Year poem includes a tantalising suggestion that it accompanied a golden crown of laurel in recognition of James' poetic and martial achievements.[53] There is no evidence to support this supposition popularised by Shire, although it is reiterated in the poem proper: 'resawe this laurell sing' (line 1).[54] The approving overall tone reminds James that he 'precels in euerie thing' (line 4), hopeful that his reign will last as long as Nestor lived. Yet even within this frankly sycophantic poem there is a note of warning, in the expressed hope that God will 'all thy fois perpetuallie suppres' (line 6). The reference to enemies in a praise poem explicitly associated with New Year, a time of optimism and looking forward, reminds the reader that James' rule is not completely stable, and that its continued success depends upon fair governance, and the control of potentially rebellious magnates. In such circumstances, the professions of loyalty of even a midranking noble like Stewart become infinitely more valuable. But the manuscript was compiled long after the Raid – probably between 1585 and 1587. What, then, is the benefit of including poems designed to reassure and advise the king? If James ever received the manuscript, by the time he would have been in a position to read these poems, the dangers and challenges of the Ruthven plot might appear to have been long since past. In fact, the banished nobles returned from their English exile, and April 1584 brought the Stirling raid in which the Castle was seized by disgruntled nobles, who subsequently surrendered to the king in May.[55] In November 1585, the castle was seized once more by the surviving rebels, and James Stewart, 4th earl of Arran and keeper and governor of Edinburgh Castle, was ousted. The inclusion of such poems then speaks not only to the relative instability of James' reign at this point but also to Stewart's opportunistic approach. The poems reiterate his loyalty (albeit from a safe temporal distance), a quality never in question, even when James was seemingly at his lowest ebb. James continued to face challenges throughout the late 1580s and early 1590s from – among others – the mutinous earl of Bothwell, who was subsequently implicated in the North Berwick witch trials.[56] The events of the Gowrie Conspiracy of 1600, the 'last great noble crisis' faced by James before he ascended the

[53] Crockett, *Stewart*, p. 128: 'To His Maiestie The First Of Ianvar Vith Presentation Of Ane Lawrell Trie Formit Of Gould, 1583'.

[54] See Shire, *Song, Dance, and Poetry*, p. 101 on this. In James' 'Sonnet Decifring the Perfyte Poete', he writes 'Goddis, grant I may obteine the Laurell trie': see James Craigie (ed.), *The Poems of James VI of Scotland* (Edinburgh and London), vol. 1, p. 69, line 14.

[55] See Robin G. MacPherson, 'Francis Stewart, Fifth Earl Bothwell, and James VI: Perception Politics', in Terry Brotherstone and David Ditchburn (eds), *Freedom and Authority: Scotland, c. 1050–c. 1650: Historical and Historiographical Essays Presented to Grant G. Simpson* (East Linton, 2000), pp. 155–64, at p. 158.

[56] See Macpherson, 'Francis Bothwell', pp. 163–64; also Miles Kerr-Peterson and Steven J. Reid, 'Introduction', in Kerr-Peterson and Reid (eds), *Noble Power*, pp. 1–11, at p. 1.

English throne, are still somewhat unclear, but it seems to have comprised either the 'attempted kidnapping or assassination of the king … or the planned murder of the Ruthven brothers by James'.[57] In either case, what is evident is that James was still dealing with troublesome nobles – Stewart's advice, read or not, was still applicable.

Poems addressed to kings in more politically secure times seem to look towards broader political outcomes. The Irishman Walter Quin (c. 1575–1641), a poet and royal tutor, who was presented to James VI in 1595, apparently offered James a poem on New Year's day, 1596, that emphasised James' right to the English throne.[58] John Colville, a disaffected Church of Scotland Minister who regularly passed information to Queen Elizabeth's government (and who participated in the Ruthven Raid and subsequent exile of its main ringleaders in England),[59] notes in a letter to Robert Bowes dated 12 January 1595–96 that

> Thair is also ane other Irlandois heir, called Gualter Quin, a fyne scoler. He hes presented at New Year Day to his Majestie ane oration tuiching his titill, which is weill accepted; and he placed at the Mr Housholdis tabille, and to be rewarded, and keped. This oration is keped quiet, yit I had it about tua houris, and hes extracted the substance tharof, which salbe send be my nixt.[60]

Colville evidently viewed this allusion to James' right to the throne of England as provocative. His next letter to Bowes, dated 17 January 1595–96 records that Quin is

> gratiuslie looked on, because the mattir tuiched gratius. avdin (her Majestie) highlie, and the Lord Thresaurer; whom I so honour, I culd not keip it up. Wissing gret secrecy, for thair be sum thair that be unnaturall to .nuper-rime. (England), which wold be weill adverted unto; for thair wes never a tyme moir dangerus to your advertiseratis, nor that careeth moir necessite to advertis; alway .y. (Colville) had layid his compt, that no danger heir, nor coldness thair, shall alter his inalterabill zeall to the quatuor (service) of .avdin. (her Majestie).[61]

57 Jenny Wormald energetically proposes a new reading of the plot: see 'The Gowrie Conspiracy: Do We Need to Wait until the Day of Judgement?', pp. 194–206 in Kerr-Peterson and Reid (eds), *Noble Power*.

58 See John Flood (ed.), *The Works of Walter Quin: An Irishman at the Stuart Courts* (Dublin and Portland, 2014), pp. 47–62. 'Cease lets' appears on pp. 51–52. See also Sidney Lee and J.K. McGinley, 'Quin, Walter (c. 1575–1641), Poet and Royal Tutor', *ODNB* [22964]. Quin's poems are grouped together in TNA, SP 52/57, doc. no. 79.

59 Rob Macpherson, 'Colville, John (1542?–1605), Conspirator and Church of Scotland Minister', *ODNB* [6011].

60 D. Laing (ed.), *Original Letters of Mr. John Colville: 1582–1603. To which is added his palinode, 1600. With a memoir of the author* (Edinburgh, 1858), p. 191.

61 Ibid., p. 192.

Colville also recorded in the same letter that he had 'send heirwyth a minut of the Oration presented be Gualterus Quinus'. The poem, or a version, is probably one of those poems included in the *Anagrammata in nomen Jacobi sexti* (1595), which liken James to King Arthur and emphasise his right to the English throne, e.g.: '*Cease lets Arthur I am*, of Britain king, / Come by good right to claim my seat, and throne, / My kingdoms severed to rejoin in one' (lines 1–3).[62] None of these is explicitly connected with New Year, although John Flood, Quin's editor and translator, suggests that the poem may have been delivered on New Year's day.[63] Quin wrote many pieces about James' right to the English throne, but it is significant that New Year festivities in particular are presented as appropriate for this kind of address: Colville's apparent horror and the note that the poem was 'keped quiet' indicate that it was not a regular occurrence. Notably, though, Colville's work focuses less on the relationship between appropriate kingly behaviour and national security and more on James' future successes. Still using the licence of the New Year, Colville also exploits relative political stability to look outwith Scotland. Certainly, Quin's offering must have pleased the king, because he was appointed tutor to James and Anne's sons, later accompanied James to England, became music teacher in Prince Henry's household, and ultimately was tutor to Prince Charles.

## Poems for Regents/Absent Rulers

PERHAPS the most intriguing group of New Year poems are those that address regents and absent rulers. The mid-century poems of Sir Richard Maitland, generally composed while Mary was in France, and during Mary of Guise's regency, bespeak a clear anxiety about the absence of a strong ruler and the concomitant social chaos that he perceives. 'O hie eternall God of micht' (Poem 4 in the Maitland Quarto) echoes the concerns of Dunbar in its emphasis on the importance of 'iustice' and 'veritie' (lines 8, 21), but addresses the poem not to a ruler, but to God.[64] He prays that God will

[62] See Flood (ed.), *The Works of Walter Quin*, pp. 47–62. The poem in question, 'Cease lets', appears on pp. 51–52. For more on James VI's Arthurian associations, see David William Allan, '*Arthur Redivivus*: Politics and Patriotism in Reformation Scotland', in Felicity Riddy and James Carley (eds), *Arthurian Literature 15* (Woodbridge, 1997), pp. 185–204.

[63] Personal correspondence, John Flood.

[64] The poem, dated by Martin to c. 1557–58, survives in multiple witnesses: Maitland Quarto, ff. 5v–7v; Maitland Folio, pp. 21–23; Reidpeth Manuscript, ff. 15v–17; Drummond Manuscript, ff. 5–7. It is attributed to Sir Richard Maitland in Maitland Quarto, Reidpeth, and Drummond, while the Folio attribution is in a seventeenth-century hand. For the text of the poem discussed here, see Joanna M. Martin (ed.), *The Maitland Quarto: A New Edition of Cambridge, Magdalene College, Pepys Library MS 1408* (Woodbridge, 2015), pp. 49–52.

'keip our Quene and grace hir send / This realme to gyde and to defend' (lines 6–7), asking God to support both Marys, but more broadly praying that God gives 'ws' strength to live sincerely 'Now in to this new ȝeir' (line 5). The poem paints a picture of a country in crisis, inhabited by 'sawers of seditioun' (line 16), ignorant churchmen, and 'greit oppressouris' (line 36). Over-fashionable ladies are criticised for their flamboyant dress, while other women dress above their station, 'lyik the Quenis ladyis cled / Thocht all thair bairnis sould bleir' (lines 76–77). Workers should not be shirking their duty, but instead need to labour 'to bring furth baith staig and stirk' (line 84). Only if people's behaviour is appropriate to their station, and if they 'pray to God continuallie' (line 92), will the New Year bring peace and unity. The absence of the monarch is linked to the moral health of the nation, and Maitland's use of the New Year topos here seems designed to balance a general sense of disappointment about contemporary affairs with a (mild) sense of possibility of future improvement. Similar concerns are expressed in Maitland Quarto 7: 'Ane Ballat maid at the [ne]w ȝeirismess in the ȝeir of God 1559 ȝeiris'.[65] This poem describes a nation damaged by 'discord and inanimitie' (line 4). It was composed during a period of Reformation rebellion and conflict between the Queen Regent, Mary of Guise, and the Protestant 'Lords of the Congregation of Christ'. The poem employs the conventional New Year's request for generosity and stability in a very specific political and social context.[66] However, there is a certain non-specificity about its targets – it is addressed to God, to the corrupt 'barounis of auctoritie' (line 18), and to 'kirkmen' (line 45), but the identity of individuals is not made explicit, and the overall tone varies – beseeching when directed to God, but also censorious, with the prayerful formulation allowing Maitland to reproach all parties involved, including Mary of Guise: 'The Quenis grace, *gif* scho hes offendit / In hir office lat it reformit be' (lines 41–42; my emphasis).

Maitland's disapproval recurs in Maitland Quarto 8 (c. 1560?), 'In this new ȝeir, I sie bot weir'.[67] The potential implied by the New Year's associations with improved behaviour and new beginnings are subverted in the carol's focus on contemporary warfare and general societal injustice, cheerlessly repeating 'In this new ȝeir, I sie bot weir'. There is no cause to celebrate, because the year to come will repeat the mistakes of the one that has just passed. The poem is less didactic in nature than most of its predecessors: although it is clear from its context that it is, like its immediate predecessor in the manuscript, referring to the Wars of the Congregation, it does not

[65] Extant in Maitland Quarto, ff. 12–13; Maitland Folio, pp. 28–30; Drummond Manuscript, ff. 10v–11. The Folio gives the title 'Off the Assemblie of the Congregatioun'; and all three witnesses attribute it to Sir Richard. For the text of the poem, see Martin, *Maitland Quarto*, pp. 60–62.

[66] See Martin, *Maitland Quarto*, pp. 299–300.

[67] Maitland Quarto, ff. 13v–14; Drummond Manuscript, ff. 12r–v; attributed to S.R.M. in Drummond. Text in Martin, *Maitland Quarto*, pp. 63–64.

offer advice, but rather laments the likelihood of coming warfare. The final stanzas appear to offer a more optimistic conclusion, with the penultimate verse reminding the audience to be strong, that 'thocht we wald ly doun and die, / It will ws helpe na thing' (lines 31–32), and the poem concludes with a prayer for peace. But both stanzas are followed by the miserable refrain leaving the reader doubtful of the likelihood of any happy outcome. It is not a coincidence that Maitland is writing during a period of monarchical disruption: the poetry vividly evokes the inevitable turmoil that he perceives as resulting from both a queen regent and an absent queen.

## Conclusion

THE picture given by the Scots poems discussed above suggests a series of chaotic reigns, with the nation at war internally, as well as with the English, and with no strong monarchical figurehead. In fact, shifts in power ensured that no one individual (noble or regal) was able to consolidate control to a problematic extent, with youthful kings often punishing those magnates who had attempted to exploit minorities to aggrandise their own power (for example, James V's exiling of his stepfather Archibald Douglas, the 6th earl of Angus, and his confiscation of Douglas territories).[68] Minority rule was – to a certain degree – balanced by periods of relative security, and comparative political stability, although it is important not to over-emphasise the inadvertent symbiotic balance that resulted. Nonetheless, it is perhaps as a result of this that the New Year poems discussed above often combine a rather informal tone with authoritative strictures, advising their ruler of correct behaviour. The poetic association between the New Year and gift-giving is one with deep historical and cultural roots, as demonstrated in *Sir Gawain and the Green Knight*: 'And syþen riche forth runnen to reche hondeselle, / Ȝeȝed ȝeres-ȝiftes on hiȝ, ȝelde hem bi hond' (lines 66–67; 'And afterwards nobles ran to offer New Year gifts, / Announced New Year's gifts loudly, gave them by hand').[69] In Scotland, this cultural correlation between new beginnings and the offering of gifts was prominent enough that it was deployed ironically in Barbour's *The Bruce* (c. 1386) – describing Robert's arrival at Carrick and the resulting slaughter, the narrator laconically notes 'Sic hansell to the folk gaf he, / Richt in the first begynnyng, / Newly at his

[68] Reid notes, in his account of the Ruthven Raid, 'the classic pattern of Stewart monarchs negotiating their ascent to full power as they approached their minority, a pattern that had been established in the fifteenth century with the reign of James II and had repeated itself to varying degrees in the reigns of James III, James IV, and James V'. See Reid, 'Of Bairns', p. 33.

[69] *Sir Gawain and the Green Knight*, lines 66–67, in J.R.R. Tolkien and E.V. Gordon, 2nd edition, ed. Norman Davis. 67n (p. 74) comments that the earliest recorded reference to New Year's gifts dates to the twelfth century.

ariwyng' (V. lines 120–23; 'such a gift he gave to the people, / Right at the very beginning, / As soon as he arrived').[70]

While the poets examined in this chapter do not, perhaps, display quite the same degree of innovation as Barbour in their manipulation of the New Year trope, the broad survey demonstrates the undoubted individuality of the Scots employment of the étrenne. Certainly, their European and English counterparts took advantage of the period to make requests (or statements) that might not normally be appropriate, but only in Scotland does the license afforded by the time of year inspire poets to produce étrennes that function as advisory pieces. The sustained Scots anxiety about self-governance and good kingship recurs in the poems above, in their didactic tones, their engagement with social and political turmoil, their commentary on contemporary affairs, and their general statements about appropriate regal behaviour. Although they form part of a genre that was widely popular in England and Continental Europe, the Scots poets took care to reinterpret the link between New Year, gift-giving and behavioural changes in a way that corresponds to the thematic strands of advice and instruction so engrained in Scots literature. In doing so, they produced a series of poems that are unique in their focus not on patronage and reward, but on the correct way to govern.

70 See John Barbour, *Barbour's Bruce*, ed. Matthew P. McDiarmid and James A.C. Stephenson, 3 vols (Edinburgh 1980–85), vol. 2. The practice of giving gifts at the turn of the year survived well into the nineteenth century in Scotland, usually taking place on the first Monday after New Year's Day, a day referred to as 'Hansel Monday'. See *A Dictionary of the Older Scottish Tongue*, s.v. 'Hansel *n.*', sense 3b (www.dsl.ac.uk/entry/dost/hand). See also s.v. 'New-ȝer *n.*', sense 2b (1) (www.dsl.ac.uk/entry/dost/new_3ere). Note also that the *Oxford English Dictionary* cites one (obsolete) meaning of 'New Year, n.' as '*Scottish.* A gift of food or drink given by way of hospitality at New Year. *Obsolete* New Year, n., †c.' (www.oed.com/view/Entry/126656).

# 11

# *John Leslie, Bishop of Ross, and the Design of Mary, Queen of Scots' Defence*

Tricia A. McElroy

THREATENED with the English rack, John Leslie allegedly exclaimed to his interrogator Thomas Wilson that not only was Mary, Queen of Scots involved in the murder of her husband Darnley, but she had also poisoned her first husband Francis and then brought Bothwell 'to the Fylde to be murdered'.[1] In response, one critic has noted even-handedly that the bishop was 'subtle and resourceful but not of the stuff of which martyrs are made'.[2] Nevertheless, Leslie's desperate outburst – perhaps excusable under the emotional duress of torture – is completely at odds with our sense of his allegiance to Mary, and so it should be. For all material evidence points to Leslie's sincere and unflagging commitment to the cause of his queen. His literary efforts to resuscitate Mary's reputation and political career, spread over some 19 years, ensured that his name would be irrevocably associated with the defence of Mary. So inescapable is this connection, in fact, that referring to Leslie as Mary's arch-defender has become easy shorthand, often masking a limited understanding of the bishop's methods and principal concerns. This has had the unfortunate effect of forestalling any detailed study of Leslie's works,[3] as well as leading us to assume that Leslie sought primarily to recover Mary's damaged reputation. He was concerned about that, of course. But more than 450 years of speculation about Mary's character, fuelled in part by the wickedly clever propaganda of Robert Sempill and George Buchanan,

[1] This essay was written with immense gratitude for Roger's years of support, guidance, and friendship. Thomas Wilson to William Cecil, Lord Burghley, 8 November 1571, in William Murdin (ed.), *A Collection of State Papers relating to Affairs In the Reign of Queen Elizabeth, from The Year 1571 to 1596* (London, 1759), p. 57.

[2] D. McN. Lockie, 'The Political Career of the Bishop of Ross, 1568–80', *Historical Journal of the University of Birmingham* 4–5 (1953–56), 98–145, at pp. 109–10.

[3] In addition to Lockie, 'The Political Career of the Bishop of Ross', see the following for various perspectives on Leslie: James Phillips, *Images of a Queen: Mary Stuart in Sixteenth-Century Literature* (Berkeley, CA, 1964); Margaret J. Beckett, 'The Political Works of John Lesley, Bishop of Ross (1527–96)' (unpublished University of St Andrews PhD thesis, 2002); A.C. Southern, *Elizabethan Recusant Prose, 1559–1582* (London, 1950); Constance Jordan, 'Woman's Rule in Sixteenth-Century British Political Thought', *Renaissance Quarterly* 40.3 (1987), 421–51; and Pamela Robinson, 'John Leslie's "Libri duo": Manuscripts belonging to Mary Queen of Scots?', in R.C. Alston (ed.), *Order and Connexion: Studies in Bibliography and Book History* (Cambridge, 1997), pp. 63–75.

among others, has skewed our perception of the debate in which Leslie was engaged, for Leslie's project was deeply invested with the political possibility of Mary's restoration. Certainly, he defended her against charges of immorality, but one of his strategies in doing so was to shift the terms of the Marian debate by breathing new life into the Elizabethan succession issue. Not only does Leslie envision a recovery of Mary's political career, but he also uses her claim to the English throne – as Elizabeth's legitimate heir – to constitute her very defence. Perhaps even more startlingly, in addressing the charges against her, he uses her gender to strengthen his political argument: her femininity is a warrant both for her innocence and her place in the English succession. This chapter aims to elucidate Leslie's principal concerns and his methods for the design of Mary's defence.

Leslie was born in 1527, the son of Gavin Lesley, rector of Kingussie, Inverness-shire.[4] Although he was the illegitimate son of a priest, Leslie was nevertheless able to take holy orders with a papal dispensation. He acquired an MA at King's College, Aberdeen, and at the age of 20 became a canon of the cathedral church. In 1549, Leslie set off for the Continent to study divinity and languages, earning a Doctor of Laws in Paris in 1553. Having obtained a broad education in theology, rhetoric, and law, Leslie returned to Scotland in 1554, where he acquired several secular and ecclesiastical offices. After the death of Mary's first husband Francis II, the earl of Huntly and other Catholic nobles sent Leslie to visit the widowed queen in France, in part to counteract the mission of James Stewart, Mary's half-brother, who had been sent by the Protestant lords. Leslie 'earnestly recommended to her care and protection the interests of the tottering church',[5] and he was asked to accompany her back to Scotland. Once there, Mary made him an ordinary judge of the court of session and a member of the Privy Council, and he was inducted as the bishop of Ross. During the short period of Mary's personal rule, Leslie frequently attended the Queen: he was present in her rooms the night of David Riccio's murder, he acted as her chief advisor in ecclesiastical policy, and, near the end of her pregnancy, she entrusted him with her list of jewels and other articles of value.[6] After Mary was deposed by her nobles and imprisoned in Lochleven, Leslie retired to his diocese and whiled away his

4 Biographical details are taken from Leslie's entry in the *ODNB* by Rosalind K. Marshall [16492]; Robert Chambers, *A Biographical Dictionary of Eminent Scotsmen*, revised and continued by T. Thomson, vol. 2 (Hildesheim, 1971); E.G. Cody (ed.), *The Historie of Scotland wrytten first in Latin by the most reuerend and worthy Jhone Leslie bishop of Rosse, and translated in Scottish by Father James Dalrymple*, 2 vols (Edinburgh and London, 1888–98); David Irving, *Lives of Scotish Writers*, vol. 1 (Edinburgh, 1839); Leslie's own account of his life in James Anderson (ed.), *Collections Relating to the History of Mary Queen of Scotland*, vol. 3 (Edinburgh and London, 1727); and Lockie, 'The Political Career of the Bishop of Ross'.

5 Irving, *Lives of Scotish Writers*, vol. 1, p. 126.

6 William Forbes-Leith, S.J. (ed.), 'Bishop Leslie's Narrative of the Progress of Events in Scotland – 1562–1571', in *Narratives of Scottish Catholics under Mary Stuart and James VI* (Edinburgh, 1885), pp. 85–126, at p. 113.

time with study and ecclesiastical duties. He was summoned by the Queen when she escaped in 1568, but before he could join her at Hamilton, she had been defeated and was well on her way to an unfriendly reception by the English. Shortly thereafter, Mary appointed Leslie to act as one of her commissioners at the conferences called by Elizabeth, first at York and then Westminster.[7] When these conferences ended at an impasse, Leslie became Mary's ambassador to Elizabeth, 'to travell for the avancement and treatinge of her effaires',[8] bringing the bishop's career to the historical moment with which this chapter is concerned.

## The 'Book of the Title' and its Context

The years 1568–73 were eventful for Leslie: he spent his time as ambassador at the English court conducting ongoing negotiations with Elizabeth for the release and restoration of Mary; he was a central figure in Catholic-inspired intrigues to free her; he communicated often with the duke of Norfolk about a possible marriage with the Queen of Scots; he himself was placed under house arrest several times; when his part in the Ridolfi plot was uncovered, he complied with the Privy Council's demands for information, paving Norfolk's path to the block; and after nearly three years of imprisonment, he was granted permission to depart for the Continent, never again to set foot on either English or Scottish soil. Even more important, these years mark the commencement of Leslie's textual campaign on Mary's behalf and his emergence as her foremost adherent. The peculiar situation in which he found himself in 1569 – as ambassador for a queen without a realm – precipitated an outpouring of literature. Unquestionably, Leslie's principal contribution to the body of literature is A *defence of the honour of the right highe, mightye and noble Princesse Marie Quene of Scotlande and dowager of France with a declaration aswell of her right, title and intereste to the succession of the crowne of England, as that the regimente of women ys conformable to the lawe of God*, printed surreptitiously in 1569: it bears the false colophon, 'Imprinted at London in Flete street, at the signe of Iustice Royall against the Blacke bell, by Eusebius Dicaeophile'. Except for a few pages which may have been printed in London, the book was printed by John Fogny at Rheims (STC 15505). A second edition was printed in Louvain by John Fowler in 1571, entitled A *Treatise concerning the defence of the honour*

[7] The most thorough account of these conferences is Gordon Donaldson, *The First Trial of Mary, Queen of Scots* (London, 1969).

[8] Leslie, A *Discourse, conteyning a perfect Accompt gevin to the moste virtuous and excellent Princesse, Marie Queene of Scots*, in Anderson (ed.), *Collections*, pp. 42–43. The *Discourse* is Leslie's exhaustive account of his ambassadorial activities in England from September 1568 through March 1572. Intended for Mary and the Scottish nobility still loyal to her cause, the *Discourse* was written during Leslie's confinement in the Tower in 1571–72.

*of the right high, mightie and noble Princesse, Marie Queene of Scotland* and published under the pseudonym 'Morgan Philippes, Bachelar of Diuinitie' (STC 15506).[9] As the original vindication of the Queen of Scots, the pro-Marian *Defence* corresponds to George Buchanan's anti-Marian *Detectioun* as a 'fountainhead of all subsequent argument'.[10] All future apologies for the Scottish Queen owe a debt to Leslie's *Defence*, but none profited so much from a commensurate proximity in time and place to the turbulent events of 1567–68, to say nothing of the personal involvement of its author.

The making of the *Defence* is a convoluted story, however, and to speak of its *author* can be misleading. The better label for Leslie's role might be *mastermind*: we have every reason – and plenty of evidence – to credit him as the project manager for Mary's defence. During the autumn of 1568, the bishop of Ross – along with Lords Livingston, Boyd, and Herries, the commendator of Kilwinning, and the lairds of Lochinvar and Skirling – served as one of Mary's commissioners at the conferences at York and Westminster.[11] The purpose of the conferences was ambiguous at best, with each party trying to accomplish its own ends: the earl of Moray's party justifying their rebellion against Mary; Mary's commissioners fighting for her release and restoration; and the English delegation navigating the uncertain waters of their government's political strategy. Initially, Leslie and his fellow commissioners were encouraged by Elizabeth's professions of wishing to restore Mary to her throne in Scotland.[12] As Moray's party began their accusations in earnest, however, it became apparent that the conferences were not all they appeared to be. Mary's commissioners listened to Moray's indictment of Mary and the justifications for their rebellion, and they must have read an early form of Buchanan's *Detectioun*, which laid out the Queen's guilt in no uncertain terms. When Mary's request to defend herself in person was repeatedly denied, her commissioners realised that the conferences 'apparently tended to some other end we looked not for', and they departed without waiting for the English delegation's conclusions.[13]

9 The real Morgan Philips was the Oxford tutor of Cardinal William Allen, founder of the college at Douai and prominent supporter of the Catholic cause in England. After Elizabeth came to power, Philips settled on the Continent in Louvain and died in 1570. Leslie's choice of a pseudonym is apt and, given Philips's recent demise, convenient. This second edition is also closely associated with the discovery of the Ridolfi plot against Elizabeth, for when Leslie's servant Charles Bailly was arrested at Dover in April 1571, he was carrying copies of the *Treatise* back into England for the Bishop of Ross. Whereas the *Defence* acknowledges that Mary can claim the throne only if Elizabeth dies childless, the *Treatise* drops flattering epithets for Elizabeth and treats Mary as the only rightful heir. For the various editions, see J. Scott, 'A Bibliography of Works Relating to Mary Queen of Scots: 1544–1700', *Edinburgh Bibliographical Society* 2 (1896), 1–96. All parenthetical quotations are taken from the 1569 edition reprinted in D.M. Rogers (ed.), *English Recusant Literature, 1585–1640*, vol. 12 (Menston, 1970).

10 Phillips, *Images*, p. 88.

11 Donaldson, *The First Trial*, p. 109.

12 Ibid., pp. 85–87.

13 Leslie, *Discourse*, p. 32.

These conferences set the stage for the appearance of the first Marian apology, the 1569 *Defence*. The commissioners acting on Mary's behalf felt obligated to prepare a formal response to the arguments put forth by Moray's party. And the steady stream of anti-Marian propaganda coming from the press of Robert Lekpreuik must also have fuelled their determination to clear her name. The Lords Herries and Boyd offered assistance during the early stages,[14] with Leslie and Herries, in particular, having ample opportunity for collaboration: after walking out of the proceedings at Westminster, they were detained together at Burton-on-Trent from February to April 1569, on suspicion that they were planning to help Mary escape from English custody.[15] Leslie provides additional detail about the progress of the project once he was installed in London. According to his ambassadorial report, *A Discourse, conteyning a perfect Accompt gevin to the moste virtuous and excellent Princesse, Marie Queene of Scots* (c. 1571–72), after the dissolution of the conferences certain men opposed to a marriage between the duke of Norfolk and Mary began a crusade to discredit her claim to the English throne: 'And therefore they collected their arguments in a shorte pamphlet and treatie, wherof they sett forth divers copyes in the citty of London, tendinge to the dishonor of the Q. my Mistres'.[16] Leslie refers to a pamphlet entitled *A Discourse touching the pretended match betwene the Duke of Norfolke and the Queene of Scottes* (1569),[17] which assesses the characters of both Mary and Norfolk (neither favourably, of course) and argues that a domestic match for Mary (with Norfolk) could be more harmful than one with a foreign prince. By his own account, Leslie reacted quickly to the appearance of this pamphlet:

> And assoone as one of the copies therof was brought to my hands, I presented the same, by the advice of the Nobilitie, to the Q. of England, desiringe, that the authors therof might be tryed and punyshed, and that in the meane time it might be lesum to anie of her subiects, whoe was skilfull in the Lawes to make answere therto, *principally for the defence of the Q. my Mistres Title*, consideringe there was a treatie sett forth againste the

[14] Leslie's servant Alexander Hervey confirms the involvement of others: questioned on 14 April 1570 about the publication of the *Defence*, Hervey claimed that 'the book was made twelve month since by the Lord Herries, Lord Boyd, and the Bishop of Ross' (*CSP Scot.*, iii, no. 176).

[15] Leslie, *Discourse*, p. 43. Leslie also began work on his vernacular history during this time; T. Thomson (ed.), *The History of Scotland from the Death of King James I in the Year* M.CCCC.*XXXVI to the Year* M.D.*LXI*. (Edinburgh, 1830). See my unpublished thesis for a discussion of its relationship to the *Defence* ('Executing Mary Queen of Scots: Strategies of Representation in Early Modern Scotland', unpublished University of Oxford DPhil thesis, 2005).

[16] Leslie, *Discourse*, p. 65.

[17] STC 13869, n.d., n.p., but probably printed by John Day in London. Leslie assigns this text to 'Sampson a preacher' (*Discourse*, p. 65), but it has been attributed to Walsingham by Phillips, who follows Conyers Read. (See Phillips, *Images*, p. 252 n. 23.)

> same, in time of the laste Parliament holden in England 1565, by some evill advised persons, enemies to all justice and right.[18]

Elizabeth granted Leslie permission to formulate a response, provided he would not publish his tract until she had seen and approved the first copy. Pleased with his assignment, he began by gathering all the treatises written against Mary's title, along with some in her defence. Having carefully considered the existing arguments, Leslie began to assemble his materials into what would become the *Defence*.[19]

It is worth pausing this narrative of the *Defence*'s origins to describe the text in its final published form. As its full title indicates, the *Defence* sets out to accomplish three tasks and, accordingly, is divided into three separate books. The first book has the unenviable task of accounting for the shocking events of 1567: it attempts to clear Mary of all criminal charges by dismantling the allegations against her, arguing that she is not a depraved murderess but rather the victim of cruel slander by rebellious subjects. The second book – referred to as the 'book of the title' in contemporary documents – turns to the issue of the English succession, presenting a complex argument based on legal and historical precedent that proclaims Mary's right to the throne if Elizabeth should die childless. Finally, in the third book, Leslie defends the idea of female regiment, a debate with roots in Knox's *First Blast of the Trumpet against the Monstrous Regiment of Women* (1558) and one which had not entirely died away. Leslie acknowledges that this third book, 'maye seme perchance to some as superfluous' (†iii$^{v}$), but he feels the proliferation of treatises on this topic, as well as their gross manipulation of scripture, must be answered.[20]

18 *Discourse*, p. 65 (my emphasis). The pamphlet of 1565 to which Leslie refers is the anonymous *Allegations against the surmisid title of the Quine of Scotts and the fauorers of the same*, printed in the wake of Mary's marriage to Darnley.

19 According to Leslie's *Discourse*, after his defence was completed and printed, it 'came to the Q. and Councells hands; although I had presented a perfect copie therof longe before to the Q. at which time the Councell said unto me it was very learnedly collected and sett forth' (p. 68). Notwithstanding Elizabeth's earlier encouragement of Leslie's efforts, the book caused Leslie some trouble: 'I sustayned divers wayes trouble and injuries, by imprisonment of my selfe, my servants and others, upon the occasioun of the publyshinge therof', which probably refers to the arrest of his servant Alexander Hervey and of Leslie in spring 1570 (see note 14). The contradiction between allowing Leslie to write a defence only to censor it later would not be particularly unusual for Elizabethan policy at this time.

20 Although Leslie often mentions Knox and would have seen the *First Blast*, he also seems to address the arguments of another pamphleteer. See Amanda Shephard, *Gender and Authority in Sixteenth-Century England* (Keele, 1994), especially pp. 32–34, for a discussion of Leslie's possible targets. By the time the *Defence* was published, the debate about female sovereignty had lost some of its heat; and according to Leslie's answers to the Privy Council's interrogatories of 26 October 1571, Edmund Plowden – possibly one of Leslie's collaborators – questioned whether this section should be included in the published volume at all (Murdin [ed.], *A Collection*, p. 29).

Given the seriousness of the moral charges against Mary – adultery and murder – a reader of the *Defence* might expect Leslie to follow more strictly the declaration of the title page, that this is chiefly a 'defence of the honour' of the Queen. Yet, the prefatory letter of the 1569 *Defence* begins thus:

> It ys not vnknowen to the (gentle Reader) beinge an Englishe man what greate contention hathe of late risen in Englande ... towchinge the right heire apparente of the crowne of Englande .... Neither hathe this sturre stode with in the liste of ernest and feruente talke of eche side, but men haue gone on farther, and haue aswell by printed as vnprinted bookes, done theire indeuour to disgrace, blemishe and deface ... the iuste title claime and intereste of the noble and excellente Ladie Marie Quene of Scotlande, to the foresaide crowne. (†ii$^{r}$)

This opening passage recollects to a pointedly English audience the succession debate, which has grown into a battle of the books, and laments, in particular, the harsh treatment of Mary's just claim to the English crown. From there, the letter recounts how Mary's opponents have become so carried away with their malicious attacks that they have denied 'all womanlye gouernement' (†ii$^{v}$). Only then is the audience reminded of the 'false fained and forged reportes and opprobriouse slaunders' recently disseminated by Mary's 'rebelliouse subiectes' with regard to the 'slawghter of her late deare husbande' (†ii$^{v}$). Leslie notes the *Defence*'s arrangement into three books, each designed to touch on one of these points – the title, female regiment, Mary's honour – though not in that order. The reader is shortly made to understand that the 'defence of her honour shoulde forgoe the other two bookes', for no specific reason other than that 'yt ys thowght good' (†iii$^{r}$). Thus, the prefatory letter emphasises the issue of Mary's title, presenting the defence of gynecocracy and of Mary's reputation as secondary concerns. The overall sense of the *Defence* is that book one – the defence of Mary's honour – exists only as a means to an end, an obligatory detour on the journey to the more important issue of the English crown.[21] By introducing the succession debate in this context, he deftly moves to answer political, not moral questions.

While a defence of Mary's character may have become necessary, the idea of putting together a treatise defending her claim to the English throne was far from new. To a significant degree, the *Defence* derives from this hotly debated, more far-reaching issue, its arguments traceable to the period before Darnley's demise was plotted, the Scottish political scene turned upside down, and the material for book one became necessary. Given Elizabeth's reluctance to marry or proclaim an heir, the Elizabethan succession was, in its own right, a fraught domestic question; however, the situation was exacerbated by Mary's assumption of the royal arms of England, with encouragement from her

[21] In later editions of the *Defence* and *Treatise*, Leslie dropped the defence of her honour altogether. See Phillips, *Images*, p. 104.

father-in-law Henri II of France and her uncles, the cardinal of Lorraine and the duke of Guise.[22] The issue of Mary's claim became even more contentious in 1565 after her marriage to Henry, Lord Darnley, who had a strong claim to the same crown.[23] As a result, the mid-1560s saw the proliferation of succession tracts, many produced by able English lawyers eager to resolve the question once and for all. As I intimated above, it is unlikely that Leslie authored his 'book of the title': although he had expertise in both canon and Scottish civil law, the evidence collected and assembled for his 'book of the title' strongly suggests the pen of an *English* lawyer. The likelihood, then, is that Leslie obtained a legal document written in Mary's favour by someone else and edited it into its present form. Recognising the rootedness of the *Defence* in debates about the English succession has two important effects: its robust engagement with this issue confirms the collaborative and protean nature of Leslie's project and lays bare the political dimensions so cleverly brought to the fore by Leslie.

How did Leslie go about assembling his 'book of the title'? His London connections – a strong network of Marian sympathisers, mostly Catholics – likely provided him with the relevant arguments sketched out by English lawyers. The story begins during the parliamentary session of 1563, when John Hales composed a tract entitled *A declaration of the succession of the crown imperial of England*, which circulated widely in manuscript.[24] Hales defended the claim of the Suffolk line in Lady Catherine Grey, whom, as the daughter of the Duchess of Suffolk and by the terms of Henry VIII's will, Hales declared the lawful heir to Elizabeth's throne.[25] Mary, Queen of Scots, according to Hales, could not inherit the English crown because English common law prohibited aliens from inheriting property, and being Scottish, she was excluded. Not only did Hales's tract create a political stir – he was imprisoned by an indignant Elizabeth – but its appearance also precipitated a rash of responses, both refuting and endorsing the unfortunate Hales, several of which could have eventually reached Leslie. Edmund Plowden, a respected Catholic lawyer of the Middle Temple, wrote a lengthy and sophisticated response to Hales, one grounded solidly in legal and historical precedent.[26]

[22] John Guy gives a helpful explanation of this issue. See chapter 6, 'A Dynastic Marriage', in *'My Heart Is My Own': The Life of Mary Queen of Scots* (London, 2004). Thwarting the resolution of this problem was Mary's refusal to ratify the Treaty of Edinburgh.

[23] See Stephen Alford, *The Early Elizabethan Polity: William Cecil and the British Succession Crisis, 1558–1569* (Cambridge, 1998), chapter 2; and Phillips, *Images*, pp. 28–32.

[24] Hales's manuscript was finally printed in Georg Harbin, *The Hereditary Right of the Crown of England* (London, 1713).

[25] For an explanation of the debate about the authenticity of this will, see Mortimer Levine, *The Early Elizabethan Succession Question, 1558–1568* (Stanford, 1966), chapter 9.

[26] Plowden's tract survives in six known extant copies, two of which have been recently identified by Daniel Haywood as he prepares an edition of the *Treatise* for his forthcoming DPhil thesis. In private correspondence, Haywood has reported to me that only one witness (British Library, Harley MS 849) is definitively sixteenth century, while the other copies appear to date from the early seventeenth century or possibly the 1590s. Bodleian Library, Don.c.43 was prepared by Plowden's son Francis for presentation to James VI and

His *Treatise proveing that if our soveraigne lady Queene Elizabeth ... should die without issue, that the Queene of Scotts ... is not disabled by the law of England to receave the crowne of England by discent*, written in January 1567, argues that Mary is not barred from the succession because of her foreign birth and attempts to disprove the validity of Henry VIII's will.

A second response to Hales has traditionally been associated with Anthony Browne, another eminent Catholic lawyer, fellow member of the Middle Temple, and friend of Plowden. It too makes a strong case for Mary's claim using many of the same legal and historical arguments laid out by Plowden.[27] Of no small importance here is that Leslie's 'book of the title' in the 1571 *Treatise* is nearly verbatim the Browne tract. Nevertheless, Browne's authorship is dubious, for a variety of reasons,[28] and he died in May 1567, long before Leslie arrived in England. Moreover, the Browne tract is much shorter than Leslie's book two (by nearly 40 pages) and ends on a loyal and admonitory note: all men are exhorted to leave the succession 'to the providence of the Almightie' and 'rest dutifull to the present state without curious serch of future accidente in the misteries of princes callinge to mynde that who soo seeketh a cloude, (as the parable ys) may be stricken with the thunderbolt'[29] – odd, considering the entire tract is concerned with exploring this issue. But Leslie could indeed have been using something written by Browne – or some other unnamed individual – leading to one attractive conclusion: a recognition of the bishop's ingenuity in fingering Anthony Browne, a capable but dead English lawyer.[30]

I. Many thanks to Mr Haywood for sharing his findings with me.

[27] The 'Browne tract' exists in three known manuscript copies, two in the British Library and one in the Bodleian Library. Browne's association with this tract derives from several sources: the manuscript titles refer to 'Sir Anthonie Browne'; he is mentioned in Ridolfi plot examinations as author of a tract in Mary's favour; and book two of Leslie's 1571 *Treatise* claims that it was 'assisted with the aduise of Antonie Broune Knight, one of the Iustices of the Common Place. An. 1567'. It is difficult, if not impossible, to date the composition of the Browne tract, and space here does not permit discussion of a very complicated textual history. In my unpublished DPhil thesis (cited above), I attempt to disentangle the relevant texts and consider the arguments of other critics, especially Levine, *The Early Elizabethan Succession Question*; Marie Axton, 'The Influence of Edmund Plowden's Succession Treatise', *Huntington Library Quarterly* 37 (1974), 209–26, and *The Queen's Two Bodies: Drama and the Elizabethan Succession* (London, 1977); and Geoffrey de C. Parmiter, 'Edmund Plowden as Advocate for Mary Queen of Scots', *IR* 30 (1979), 35–53. An important collection of essays devoted to the succession issue is Susan Doran and Paulina Kewes (eds), *Doubtful and Dangerous: The Question of Succession in Late Elizabethan England* (Manchester, 2014).

[28] The hands in surviving manuscripts all appear to be English and from the late sixteenth century, suggesting that the tract is more likely to be a copy rather than a draft of Leslie's printed *Treatise*.

[29] British Library, Lansdowne 254, f. 198$^{v}$. This language does not sound like Leslie and, rather, points to an English scribe copying out a portion of Leslie's book and tacking on a pro-Elizabeth ending.

[30] Axton reminds us that when Leslie was compiling the *Defence*, Browne was dead and 'beyond the reach of the privy council' (p. 213).

There is another scenario by which Leslie could have gotten his hands on English arguments for Mary's claim. Plenty of Scots interested in Mary's title visited the English court in the mid-1560s, men who knew lawyers sympathetic to the Scottish Queen's cause. Clearly, legal arguments in Mary's favour found their way to Scotland before Leslie contemplated following his queen into exile. William Maitland of Lethington, Mary's secretary, is the most obvious candidate for importing these arguments into Scotland. Shortly after Mary's arrival back in Scotland in 1561, she dispatched Lethington to Elizabeth on a mission to propose an agreement through which Mary would be designated heir apparent.[31] The mission was unsuccessful, but Lethington was hopeful enough to continue campaigning on Mary's behalf. On 4 January 1567, years later, Lethington wrote to Cecil, outlining the 'prouffes and reasons as may declare and fortifie the Q. my sovereigns title to the crowne next to the Q. your sovereign'.[32] Though in the form of a letter, and thus abbreviated, Lethington uses familiar arguments from English law to assert that neither Mary's foreign birth nor Henry VIII's will bars her from the English crown. The similarities between Lethington's and Leslie's arguments demonstrate the currency of these ideas during the 1560s and, at this point, Lethington's – more than Leslie's – participation in and familiarity with the main arguments of the succession debate. Years later, in May 1571, when he was interrogated about the sources of the 'book of the title', Leslie said he did not know

> quha was author thairof for the same was maide at the last parliament, and that leidthingtovne & Robert Melving brought copies thairof in Scotland, befoir the coming of the Q. in to ingland and thay saie that Iustice brovne & ane carrel was in the cosell of the making thairof ...[33]

Thus, Leslie claims that a tract defending Mary's claim – with two possible authors – was brought into Scotland by Lethington and Robert Melville before her flight to England. As a member of Mary's Privy Council, Leslie might, therefore, have seen a relevant document before he began the *Defence* project, despite the fact that his later statements suggest the relevant texts came into his hands during the conferences at York and Westminster.

The issue of the title was obviously of great interest to Cecil and other English ministers, and the revelation of the Ridolfi plot in 1571 intensified their efforts to discover the makers of the *Defence*. Thus, depositions taken from various players are littered with explanations about the origins of the 'book of the title'. Imprisoned and examined after the discovery of the plot,

31 Levine, *The Early Elizabethan Succession Question*, chapter 3 talks about this mission in some detail.

32 Sir Wm Maitland to Sir Wm Cecil, in J.P. Collier (ed.), *The Egerton Papers* (London, 1840), p. 42.

33 British Library, Cotton MS Caligula C.iii, f. 78r. 'Ane carrel' is John Caryll, a Catholic and member of the Inner Temple, who died in March 1566. No book in Mary's defence written by him has been identified.

Leslie's testimony confirms the scenarios laid out here. He testified that book one of the *Defence* – the book defending Mary's honour – was a collaborative effort, under development at the Westminster conference. Leslie undertook the 'book of the title', as he claims elsewhere in his *Discourse*, by referring to several previously written tracts, both for and against Mary's claim. One Thomas Bishop, a Scot living in England,[34] helped Leslie find the men who could provide assistance with his arguments, in particular the Catholic lawyers Edmund Plowden and Nicholas Harpesfield.[35] Having previously incurred trouble because of his connection to the duke of Norfolk, Plowden hesitated to look at Leslie's work but finally did so, and suggested that the book on female regiment was not wholly necessary, or that he could make this argument more convincingly himself. Finally, Leslie reiterates the involvement of Maitland of Lethington and Robert Melville earlier in the decade.[36]

What the Ridolfi testimonies strongly indicate is the collaborative and protean nature of the *Defence*. Lethington, Melville, and even Norfolk and the host of other men named in these depositions – anyone who had access to the English court in the 1560s – could have assisted Leslie with the development of his 'book of the title' by providing access to the relevant legal arguments. The network of connections among these men and the overlapping textual histories indicate the magnitude and import of the issue under discussion. Viewed as participants in this textual conversation, Leslie and his *Defence* should look a bit different. The preponderant evidence reveals that, far from working alone, Leslie placed himself at the helm of this project for the *Defence* during the 1568–69 conferences; then, methodically and efficiently, he set about collecting, conferring, and composing. Just because Leslie – himself a capable scholar and lawyer – was not solely responsible for the content of the *Defence*, does not mean he should fall in our estimation. Rather, it is more interesting and illuminating to imagine him moving nimbly through a world of shadowy connections, ably drawing together a decade of controversy – about succession and female monarchy, not to mention murder and rebellion – into a single volume.

[34] Bishop performed various services on Mary's behalf. He is also mentioned by Sir James Melville of Halhill as an agent working for Mary's title to the English succession: T. Thomson (ed.), *Memoirs of His Own Life* (Edinburgh, 1827), pp. 175–76.

[35] Nicholas Harpsfield was an English Catholic controversialist, associated with the family of Sir Thomas More. When Elizabeth took the throne, he challenged the new regime and refused to swear the oath of supremacy, for which he spent years in prison. Thomas S. Freeman claims Harpsfield was largely responsible for the tract published under the name of Morgan Phillips in 1571 (*ODNB* [12369]). The level of Harpsfield's involvement is impossible to judge, but Leslie does make it clear that he provided expert assistance.

[36] See Leslie's detailed response to his interrogators; Murdin (ed.), *A Collection*, p. 29.

TRICIA A. McELROY

## Mercy, Motherhood, and Monarchy

THE argument for Mary's title to the English crown serves as the centre of the *Defence*, both literally and symbolically. But before Leslie can give this issue his full attention, he needs to convince his audience of Mary's innocence. Book one – which I distinguish as the 'defence' – uses several approaches to refute the charges against her: it argues for her inherent nobility, the treachery of her rebels, and the irregularity of their judicial procedure. The book of the 'defence' is largely an expression of his indignation about disregard for divinely instituted authority, hence for order and tradition. Conspicuously absent from this formulation, however, is patriarchy. Rather, with regard to monarchical right – especially Mary's – Leslie concerns himself with gratitude, legitimacy, and propriety, which for him share a common source: her feminine nature, as it is expressed in her roles as daughter, wife, mother, and queen. In this unexpected move, Leslie uses Mary's gender to her advantage by making it a key component of her political value.

The 'defence' opens with a denunciation of gossip and loose talk, reminding the reader that with good reason God furnished men 'with two eyes, two eares, and butt withe one mowthe, and one tongue' (Ai$^{r}$). He is no doubt responding to the smear campaign conducted by Mary's rebels and their supporters in London – to their 'pretensed proclamations' (Ciiii$^{r}$). No one has as much cause to complain of such 'vnbrydeled talke' as does the 'excellente Princesse ladie Marie Quene of Scotlande: whose honour manie haue gone abowte to blotte and deface' (Aii$^{v}$). Having made this point, Leslie sets about defending Mary deliberately and methodically. Broadly speaking, the 'defence' is organised in the following way.

1 Because the rebels have based their case on presumptions, Leslie offers a few of his own, such as Mary's past virtuous life and her natural inclination to mercy. People, he argues, do not suddenly 'fall to extreame lewdenes' – or become murderers (Aiiii$^{r}$). Moreover, Mary had lawful means to be rid of Darnley, if she so chose: what would she gain by his murder?

2 Next, he summarises the charges and evidence presented by her accusers, carefully considering and refuting each 'prouf' offered against her. He gives most time, of course, to their star witness, their 'singulier Iewhell [jewel], whereby they sett muche store', the Casket Letters, so-called evidence which he impugns for barefaced speciousness.

3 Leslie then examines the terms by which the nobles defend their rebellion against Mary, exposing the inconsistencies and hypocrisies in their so-called 'iust quarrell'.

4 Leslie proclaims the rebels to be 'the deuisers and procurers of the shamefull, vile vilaynouse murther of the noble younge lorde, the lorde Darley' (Dv$^{r}$).

5 Pages are then devoted to excoriating the villainy and ingratitude of the earl of Moray, above all others. *Cui bono?* Leslie asks repeatedly, citing Cicero, 'to whose advantage?'[37] Moray, the arch-villain of book one, has gained most by Mary's removal from the political scene.

It is worth noting that his characterisation of the aftermath of Darnley's murder diverges from Buchanan's not simply in its radically different interpretation of events and people. Unlike the *Detectioun*, 'narrative' does not quite describe Leslie's 'defence'. He is far more concerned with legal procedure, and his account lacks the lurid, colourful drama of the *Detectioun*. His disciplined – and mostly restrained – approach obviously harmonises with the strategy of shifting the debate away from scandal, but it is still to his credit, considering the outrageous claims and splenetic attack produced by Buchanan for the opposing side. Certainly Leslie makes his own subjective arguments, citing Mary's 'noble byrthe, her honorable state, and princelye education' as reasons to 'repell and drive awaye, all suche suspition and coniecturall presumptions' (Aiiii$^{r}$). That a noble queen so willing to show mercy to her subjects would kill her own husband, he simply describes as 'vnlikelie ... incredible' (Aiiii$^{v}$). But his main line of attack is to call attention to the vindictive and illegal means by which her enemies have brought her down.

As I have argued elsewhere, Buchanan's *Detectioun* creates the impression that 'eche man' can become a participant in the trial of Mary, a hearing in which she herself serves as a witness for the prosecution.[38] Leslie picks up this riff and, as canon and civil lawyer, expertly plays it to his advantage, charging that Moray's party have acted against the principles of justice (Dvii$^{v}$). The Casket Letters are treated as spurious evidence, for they bear 'neither subscription of the writer, nor superscription vnto whome they were directed, they are neither sealed nor signed' (Biii$^{r}$). Mary's enemies have interpreted these documents with 'vnsure and vncertaine ghesses aymes, and coniecturall supposings', which constitute no 'good & substanstiall prouf' – not even against the 'porest woman or sympliest wretched crature in all Scotlande', much less the Queen (Bii$^{v}$). Moreover, contrary to the precepts of civil law, the letters have been collated by these same enemies – 'O perfecte and worthie collation' (Biiii$^{r}$), he exclaims sardonically – who had not only the opportunity but also the expertise 'to imitate & counterfaite any character' (Biii$^{v}$). Most of the key witnesses have been conveniently executed, including George Dalgleish, Bothwell's servant, who had turned over the silver casket to the earl of Morton after Mary's imprisonment at Lochleven: 'for as muche as the verie self saide dowgleishe, whom amonge other ye haue executed and ridd owte of the waye, hathe saide and sufficientlie declared, for the Queenes innocencie' (Bv$^{v}$). Whereas all suits brought against a defendant

[37] See Av$^{v}$, for example. The Cicero reference is from *Pro Milone*, 12.32.

[38] See Tricia A. McElroy, '"Performance, Print, and Politics in George Buchanan's *Ane Detectioun of the duinges of Marie Quene of Scottes*', in Erskine and Mason (eds), *George Buchanan*, pp. 49–70.

require three 'seuerall and distincte persons' – judge, accuser, and witness – Mary's accusers have unlawfully adopted all these roles for themselves. In short, Leslie criticises Mary's opponents for failing to comply with the laws of 'well ordered common wealthes', dismissing the whole action as having no 'effecte or purpose' (Dvii$^{r}$–Dviii$^{r}$).

Leslie's legal arguments are thorough and, for the most part, well substantiated. This is not to suggest that he is never rhetorical, but he often lends credibility to his arguments by quoting ancient authorities (Aristotle, Terence, Homer) or by finding Biblical or historical analogues (the Israelites and the tribe of Benjamin, Absalom and Ahithophel, Simon of Maccabees). Even more persuasively, he frequently cites specific legal statutes, clarifying their meaning and application. As a result, the 'defence' reads as a scholarly and well-reasoned legal argument. Despite the copious legal documents appended to the 1571 *Detectioun*, Leslie's response seems far more grounded in order, tradition, and precedent, which is unsurprising given the political views of these opposing parties. Whereas the *Detectioun* derives its authority from an ostensibly populist stance, the *Defence* looks to convention and hierarchy. Arguably, this is the fundamental difference between the cases for and against the Queen of Scots.

For Leslie, one of the most shocking elements of the nobles' rebellion is their flagrant disregard for a hierarchical system from which they have benefited – or, to be more precise, their ingratitude to a clement and generous queen. Indeed, these are the very men who are 'most deapelie bownde, aswel for highe referment vndeserued, as for diuers pardons of deathe' (Dviii$^{r}$). Although all of the traitors are guilty of ingratitude, the earl of Moray bears the brunt of Leslie's indignation: he ruminates almost obsessively on Moray's ungratefulness for the honours bestowed on him by Mary. She has taken him into her confidence, relied on his advice, pardoned his conspiracies, given him preferments, even at the expense of her other nobles;[39] and, still, his 'machiuells practizes' have led him to plot Darnley's murder, contrive the marriage to Bothwell, vacate the court to avoid suspicion, secure the regency, and accuse his 'deare sister … bountefull maistresse and Souereigne' of his own dastardly deeds (Evi$^{r}$, Eiii$^{r}$). Tellingly, Leslie remarks on Moray's illegitimate birth again and again, ascribing his treachery to 'his base natiuitie, his baser conditions' (Eiii$^{r}$). Whereas Mary possesses an 'ouer good and vertuouse' nature which desires only to protect the honour of her 'self and state', Moray's illegitimacy means he has no comparable state to sully: 'the Erle of Murraye, his birthe and naturall inclination were moste apte and mete to woorke suche naughetie practises' (Fiii$^{r}$). Leslie imagines Moray as bound to serve his base nature, at the expense of his legitimate and innocent

[39] See Guy, '*My Heart Is My Own*', pp. 163–66. When Huntly challenged Mary during her northern progress in 1562, he was defeated, and Mary gave her brother James the earldom of Moray, which Huntly had been administering.

half-sister.[40] For Leslie, Mary's legitimacy as James V's true heir is the source and proof of her innocence.

Mary's femininity also corroborates her virtue. Whereas some of his contemporaries eagerly ascribe murderous tendencies to women, Leslie takes the opposite view: 'Thys sexe naturallye abhorrethe suche butcherlye practyzes: suerly rare yt ys to heare suche fowle practizes in women' (Aiii$^{v}$).[41] Moving into the particular, Leslie explores his queen's feminine and domestic roles – as daughter, wife, mother – emphasising her tenderness and benevolence. Beyond answering criminal charges or verifying temperament, however, Mary's gender transforms into an advantageous and flexible way for Leslie to support his argument about her legitimate authority. He uses her feminine roles as a measure of her political power – not as a reason to deprive her of authority. Although Elizabeth and Mary are often referred to as sister queens in contemporary texts, in the 'defence' Mary becomes Elizabeth's 'dawghter, bothe by dawghterlye reuerence she bearethe her maiestie, and by reason she ys of God called to the daughters place in the succession of the crowne' (†v$^{v}$). Obviously, Leslie invokes such an intimate family tie with an eye, as ever, on the succession, but it also reinforces a sense of mutual duty between the two queens. Leslie finds many examples in the 'monumentes of antiquitie, as well prophane as Ecclesiasticall' of one noble person assisting another in a time of need (†iiii$^{v}$–v$^{r}$). Elizabeth's kindness in helping Mary in her 'distresse and extremitie' – a natural obligation between fellow princes – is rendered even more obligatory when she is represented as Mary's mother. Elizabeth not only has made 'fayre and princelye promises' to Mary, which she should uphold, but she also, quite simply, owes this 'motherlye benefitt' to her 'dawghter' (†v$^{v}$).

This maternal argument is grafted even more strangely onto Mary's relationship with Darnley. She remains 'his owne deare wife, and dreade Souereigne' (Avi$^{r}$), yet 'thowghe they were not farre differente in yeares, she was to him not onlie a loyall Prince, a louinge and deare wife, but a most carefull and tender mother with all' (Avi$^{v}$–vii$^{r}$). To account for Mary's estrangement from Darnley after his participation in Riccio's murder, Leslie resorts to an analogy of parental discipline:

> … for a time she did dissemble and forebeare owtewardelie to shewe and vtter, her inwarde harte and affectionate loue, vpon moste iuste and good respects: As the manner and practise of prouidente and moste louinge parents oftentimes ys, towarde theire deare children, for the better reclaiminge of the wanderinge minde, and waueringe will of the yowthfull vnaduised gentleman. (Avii$^{r}$)

[40] Leslie's obsession with Moray's bastardy is made all the more curious by the fact of his own illegitimate birth.

[41] At the same time, he is no feminist: on her marriage to Bothwell, Leslie describes her as '(thowghe verie circumspecte and naturallie prudente in all her other doings) yet neuer thelesse a woman' (Bviii$^{v}$). See Shephard, *Gender and Authority*, p. 9, on the hazards of making the defenders of female regiment into proto-feminists.

Once Darnley repents his betrayal, Mary rushes to 'renewe, quicken and refreshe his sprites, and to comforte his harte, to the amendement and reparinge of his healthe lateli by sicknes sore impaired'. Leslie manages to turn the entire episode into a domestic squabble in which a wayward child returns to the forgiving arms of his mother and nurse. The happy conclusion is that Mary 'most tenderlie cherisshed him euer, eauen to the verie laste howre, that euer she sawe him' (Avii$^{r}$). Building on the respect due to a mother, Leslie also insists on Mary's other source of superiority over Darnley: he may be her husband, yet he is still 'but a membre of the Scottishe comon wealthe, subiecte to her, as to his principall and supreme governesse, and to her lawes' (Aiiii$^{v}$). Not only is he subject to her, but as a mere 'priuate man' he loses any claim to the title of king. After denying the charge that Mary observed an abbreviated mourning period following Darnley's murder, Leslie maintains that, even were this true, she was not bound by the usual conventions: although queens commonly 'mourne theire husbands who were kings, her grace mournethe after an other sorte: she a prince, her husbande a priuate man and her subiecte' (Bvi$^{r}$). Whereas wives usually receive 'honour and cheif dignitie' from their husbands, Darnley's 'encrease of aduancemente' came only through Mary – his 'deare wife', 'dreade Souereigne', and 'tender mother'.

Mary's maternal nature is invoked again later in the 'defence', this time with respect to her real son, the infant James. Used as a figurehead for the Lords' rebellion against Mary, James is now called forth by Leslie as a witness against her enemies. This 'good swete babe', had he years and understanding, would castigate Moray and his followers for their insubordination and conspiracy. Leslie imagines the infant as full of criticisms: he would cast doubt on Mary's enforced demission of the crown, condemn the legality of his 'own vnnaturall coronation', grieve over the weak foundation of his rule, lament the state of his 'poore ragged, and rent realme', and extol the generosity of his dear mother (Diii$^{v}$). Above all, James would resent being made to intrude 'against his good mother, vnto the crowne and gouernement of the realme' in order to 'colour' Moray's rise to power (Di$^{v}$). Leslie also imagines James in a more sinister role, as being used against his will to prey savagely upon his mother: 'neyther wolde be [*sic*] bye yt so deare, nor come forthe to be a king so vnnaturallie, as the vipers enter into the worlde by eatinge and gnawinge owte the mothers wombe' (Dii$^{r}$).[42] This passage simultaneously characterises James as Mary's advocate and her destroyer, invoking the power of the maternal bond, only violently to undo it again. Leslie here betrays his own ambivalence about James as a political replacement for Mary: to recognise

[42] A similar image appears at the end of a ballad inserted in Sir James Melville's *Memoirs* (pp. 268–74). See my discussion of this in '"Ane wyfis quarrel": Complaining Women in Scottish Reformation Satire', in Rosalind Smith, Sarah Ross, and Michelle O'Callaghan (eds), *Gender, Politics and Form in Early Modern Women's Complaint* (Switzerland, 2020), pp. 67–88.

James in 1569 would be to repudiate Mary's sovereignty, yet Leslie would also want to avoid insulting or casting doubt on Mary's legitimate heir.[43]

Leslie's interest in Mary's motherhood – as well as her other domestic and gendered roles – should not be abstracted from his political objectives. Moments involving Mary's gender argue for her rightful authority by firmly linking her feminine with her political roles, whether as Elizabeth's 'daughter' and heir, Darnley's 'mother' and sovereign, or James' wronged progenitor. Embedded are Mary's political past, present, and future, as reigning monarch, betrayed queen, and rightful heir; all moments exist simultaneously on Leslie's page, and all insist on Mary's uninterrupted and enduring authority. By using gender as a rhetorical tool in this way, Leslie also tries to undo traditional fears about female regiment, so often associated with the female body, by making that same body a source for legitimate and natural government. Clearly, Leslie is drawn to the idea of Mary as mother. Far from threatening or undermining her authority, however, Mary's motherhood signals the hereditary nature of monarchical politics in which her place is assured.

Even more complexly, motherhood also serves as a metaphor to signify what has happened to her and to Scotland. The image of Mary's violated womb being 'gnawed out' by her own son adds visually graphic force to the abnormality of the rebellion against her. Just as her body natural – the fertile womb of motherhood – has been metaphorically despoiled, her body politic – the realm of Scotland – has been rent by 'robberies and spoiles' committed against her subjects. In other words, Leslie stages the rape of Mary and of her country. Moray's bastardy, already noted as one of Leslie's preoccupations, can now be understood as an instigating and illustrative factor in this political rape. Because of Moray's baleful influence, James is forced to displace his mother in the natural order of succession, thereby desecrating the womb that nourished him. Though barred from the crown of Scotland and 'vncapable ... to the name and bloud of the Stewards' (Eiii$^{v}$), Moray secures the regency for himself, becoming the usurping and illegitimate ruler of Scotland. Figuratively and literally, the body politic of Scotland has become unnatural.

It would be only fair to point out that Leslie's argument does have its weaknesses. By highlighting and manipulating Mary's gender, he finds himself trapped in a conventional female dichotomy: to refute the accusations against Mary, he must reiterate her passivity, even make her into the victim of 'suche a Tragedie' scripted by her rebels, which, in turn, casts a shadow on her political effectiveness. Leslie's prevailing concern with her right and title also leads him to speculate awkwardly about Mary's guilt. For example, he says that even if Mary were guilty of 'one simple murther' (Ei$^{r}$) – not

[43] In 1569, Leslie was not prepared to deal with the claim of the newly crowned King of Scots. This tightrope Leslie continued to walk for many years. In 1584, when James was flirting with Catholicism, Leslie included his name in the title to a 1584 English edition of the *Treatise* (Scott Bibliography, item 123). When it became clear that James would remain steadfastly Protestant, 'Leslie withdrew his support of the Scottish King's right to succeed his mother' (Phillips, *Images*, pp. 104–5).

his choicest turn of phrase! – the rebels have acted illegally because 'she remainethe still theire Quene and in her full auctoritie' (Dvii$^{r}$). Here, the lingering and unsettling possibility of Mary's guilt infects his text. To underscore his opposition to the overthrow of an anointed prince, Leslie also draws an 'unhappy' analogy between Mary and the Biblical King David.[44] Although David was 'bothe an adoulterer, and also a murtherer', his subjects respected his authority; it would have been God's place – not theirs – to discipline and depose him (Ei$^{r}$).

Here Leslie enters into what for him is the heart of the matter: Mary's subjects have rebelled against an anointed prince, and regardless of what she may or may not have done, they have impugned her innate authority. As James Phillips has argued, Leslie regarded Mary's deposition 'as a blow to royal sovereignty everywhere',[45] as giving 'to the subiects of other Princes suche a wicked presidente'. Leslie scolds the Earls of Moray and Morton that 'eauen adioyninge the Quene were culpable', which 'she ys not in this matter', even then would it not have been 'muche better and more auaileable to your comon welthe, and to the state therof, prudentlie to haue dissembled the matter, (as your forefathers haue heretofore done in a greater cause then this …)'? Whatever their behaviour, he firmly believes in making allowances for the 'kings and Princes in christenedome' (Ei$^{v}$). Leslie's concern for order, tradition, and precedent makes him fear the consequences of Mary's overthrow, even beyond the irreparable damage done to the state of Scotland. His conviction is that the upshot of this little Scottish matter will reverberate perilously across the courts of Europe, calling into question the surety of all who bear 'scepter and royall dignitie' (Ei$^{v}$). If the rebels prevail against Mary, then 'princes shall haue and enioye lesse benefits and praeminences in theire owne defence, then other priuate persons' (Eii$^{r}$).

Even in its occasional moments of instability, when Leslie's personal indignation at the affront to royal sovereignty detracts from his more pressing purpose, the 'defence' still supports his view that the charges against Mary are an annoying contrivance to justify her deposition at the hands of criminals. His ripostes to the arguments of her enemies are convincing: the executions of important witnesses (Bv$^{v}$), Moray's well-timed absences from the court (Evi$^{v}$), and Mary's looming act of revocation (Fiii$^{r}$). And his citation of civil law and precedent gives weight and authority to his argument, far more than Buchanan's salacious gossip gives to the *Detectioun*. More interesting, however, is how Leslie makes Mary's sex an essential element to the argument for her innocence and for her title. All of her female roles reify her princely estate – in Scotland and in England – and thus merge abstract notions of rights and titles with a dispossessed yet worthy queen. Gender, in fact, becomes the unifying force for the three books of the *Defence*. Book one binds gender to legitimacy and political authority; book three defends female

44 Phillips, *Images*, p. 91.
45 Ibid.

rule as natural and legal. Situated at the centre, the case for Mary's title to the English crown relies implicitly on these other arguments. The *Defence*, as an independent volume, coherently asserts Mary's innocence, authority, and monarchical right.

Revitalising the succession debate in 1569, while Mary remained in English custody, was an extraordinarily clever move on Leslie's part – even if his project was not ultimately successfully. He saw Mary's title as the ideal way both to deflect attention away from the unpleasant accusations against her and to emphasise her position as a reigning monarch. That is, by turning once again to the succession issue, to arguments made on Mary's behalf, Leslie could raise the debate to the higher level of hereditary politics; he could act as if her innocence were a foregone conclusion. Using (and citing) tracts conveniently written by eminent English lawyers would not only give the sense of a range of voices but would also lend the *Defence* an air of independent authority, making it more palatable to an English audience as it corroborated Mary's political entitlements. And Leslie clearly marks this target audience: 'the (gentle Reader) beinge an Englishe man'. He had little need to convince the Scots about the merits of Mary's claim to Elizabeth's throne. Despite their mutual animosity, many supporters and opponents of Mary shared a conviction in the claims of the Stewart line. Convincing Englishmen of Mary's rightful title was the real challenge, and the obvious way to do so was to marshal a battalion of arguments based on English history and common law. The rest of the solution entailed creating the illusion that this work was an entirely English production: the false 'Flete strete' colophon set the ruse in motion; the consistently English orthography carried it along. With Leslie's masterful direction, the *Defence* became not merely a plea for Mary's innocence, but a shrewd instigator of a political discussion designed to free and restore his ousted queen.

# 12

# *Alexander Hume's* Hymnes, or Sacred Songs

Joanna Martin

This chapter offers the first full critical reading of a much overlooked but significant contribution to Scots Calvinist poetry, Alexander Hume's *Hymnes, or Sacred Songs, wherein the right vse of Poesie may be espied*, a collection of verse and prose which was printed in Edinburgh in 1599.[1] It demonstrates that the *Hymnes* is a carefully designed collection of a minister's writings, its sequence of prose and poetry precisely crafted and structured to explore the identities, roles and relationships of the 'Godly' poet and his reader, in terms both of delineating a method of private piety and of drawing the reader into a sense of community with other members of the faithful elect. By exploring Hume's collection in depth, the chapter also promotes a more complete understanding of the sophistication and complexity of Scottish devotional poetry at the turn of the seventeenth century, a period on which there is a growing body of scholarship but which remains less well-understood than later seventeenth-century religious writing.[2] Recent work on seminal Reformation writing in Scotland including *The Gude and Godlie Ballatis*,[3] on poetic and artistic masterpieces by Protestant writers such as Elizabeth Melville and Esther Inglis, on the growth of neo-Latin literature, and on post-Reformation music has done much to expand our knowledge of creative responses to the Reformation in Scotland by the turn of the seventeenth century.[4] Much of this work has been directly facilitated by Professor Roger A. Mason's illumination of Scottish Reformation culture, particularly on the

1 STC 13942. References to all of Hume's works cited are to Alexander Hume, *The Poems of Alexander Hume*, ed. Alexander Lawson (Edinburgh and London, 1902).

2 See, for example, David George Mullan, *Narratives of the Religious Self in Early Modern Scotland* (Farnham, 2010).

3 Alasdair A. MacDonald (ed.), *The Gude and Godlie Ballatis* (Woodbridge, 2015).

4 See, for example, C. Cribben and D.G. Mullan (eds), *Literature and the Scottish Reformation* (Aldershot, 2009); Elizabeth Melville, *The Poems of Elizabeth Melville, Lady Culross*, ed. Jamie Reid-Baxter (privately printed, 2010); Susan Frye, 'Miniatures and Manuscripts: Levina Teerlinc, Jane Segar, and Esther Inglis as Professional Artisans', in her *Pens and Needles: Women's Textualities in Early Modern England* (Philadelphia and Oxford, 2010), pp. 75–115 (especially pp. 102–15); Steven J. Reid, 'A Latin Renaissance in Reformation Scotland? Print Trends in Scottish Latin Literature, c. 1480–1700', *SHR* 95.1 (2016), 1–29; Jamie Reid-Baxter, Michael Lynch and E. Patricia Dennison, *Jhone Angus, Monk of Dunfermline and Scottish Reformation Music* (Dunfermline, 2011).

prominent and prolific figures of John Knox, George Buchanan and Andrew Melville.[5] His work on these individuals and the intellectual connections between them, and more generally on Reformation historiography, provides essential context for my re-examination of the *Hymnes, or Sacred Songs*, its pastoral purpose and literary context. In particular, Mason's work has frequently considered the emergence of the 'new Protestant self-image', an important concept for understanding Alexander Hume's exploration of voice, self and identity in the *Hymnes, or Sacred Songs*. In his essay 'Usable Pasts', Mason reminds us of the significance of Arthur Williamson's earlier scholarship on the anxious mental world of early Reformation Scotland and its 'tortured complexity', a particularly pertinent piece of advice for any reader of Hume's *Hymnes*.[6] Mason has also explored the manner of 'Scottish self-fashioning' through the writing of the history of the nation and mapping of its landscapes in the late sixteenth century, and the competing Protestant identities existing in Scotland and England ('protestant pluralism') at the time of the Union of Crowns.[7] This chapter demonstrates that Hume's work engages in a distinctive kind of Protestant self-fashioning which responds to the trauma of change and uncertainty, by embracing failure and the complexities of selfhood in ways which are ultimately bold and optimistic.

## Alexander Hume and His Critical Reputation

ALEXANDER Hume (d. 1609) was described by R.S.D. Jack as 'The finest of the Protestant religious poets',[8] and Sarah Dunnigan's *ODNB* entry on him refers to his 'unique but substantial contribution to the development of Protestant Poetics in Scotland'.[9] Hume, a committed Presbyterian and writer of several polemical prose tracts on matters of Protestant doctrine, was also the author of the aforementioned collection of prose and poetry, the *Hymnes*,

[5] See *Knox: On Rebellion*; Roger A. Mason, 'How Andrew Melville Read His George Buchanan', in Mason and Reid (eds), *Andrew Melville*, pp. 11–46.

[6] A.H. Williamson, *Scottish National Consciousness in the Age of James VI: The Apocalypse, the Union and the Shaping of Scotland's Public Culture* (Edinburgh, 1979). See Roger A. Mason, 'Usable Pasts: History and Identity in Reformation Scotland', *SHR* 76 (1997), 54–68, at p. 57.

[7] Roger A. Mason, '*Certeine Matters Concerning the Realme of Scotland*: George Buchanan and Scottish Self-Fashioning at the Union of Crowns', *SHR* 92 (2013), 38–65, at p. 41; 'Divided by a Common Faith? Protestantism and Union in Post-Reformation Britain', in John McCallum (ed.), *Scotland's Long Reformation. New Perspectives on Scottish Religion, c. 1500–1660* (Leiden, 2016), pp. 202–25.

[8] R.S.D. Jack, 'Poetry under King James VI', in C. Craig (ed.), *The History of Scottish Literature, vol. 1, Origins to 1660: Medieval and Renaissance* (Aberdeen, 1988), pp. 125–40. Also see, in the same volume, D. Reid, 'Prose after Knox', pp. 183–98, and A.A. MacDonald, 'Religious Poetry in Middle Scots', pp. 91–104.

[9] Sarah M. Dunnigan, 'Hume, Alexander (c. 1557–1609), Writer,' *ODNB* [14133].

*or Sacred Songs, wherein the right vse of Poesie may be espied*,[10] to which Jack's and Dunnigan's approbation relates. This slim printed volume comprises two prefatory epistles in prose, a sonnet, eight further poems composed in a variety of stanza forms (including the ballad or hymnal stanza, couplets, and six-, eight- and ten-line forms which have a long history in Older Scots), a poetic epistle, and a catechetical prose text. It was dedicated to the poet Elizabeth Melville, Lady Culross.[11] The collection was issued by the king's printer, Robert Waldegrave, in 1599,[12] shortly after Hume became minister at Logie, near Stirling. The individual texts which make up the *Hymnes* were probably composed in the two decades prior to this date: the second of the dedicatory epistles is dated to 1594 and one of the poems to 1589. No earlier complete copy of the *Hymnes* survives in manuscript form, so the nature of its earlier transmission prior to printing is obscure. However, part of it was copied, apparently from the print, into an early seventeenth-century manuscript, now Edinburgh, National Library of Scotland, Advocates MS 19.3.6. The manuscript is a collection of religious prose and verse of a Calvinist nature, including texts by John Burel, William Alexander and Robert Ayton.[13] Edinburgh University Library, MS Laing III.447, a miscellany of poetry, contains a copy of one item found in Waldegrave's print, 'The wecht of sin is wonder greitt'.[14]

Despite the claims made by Jack and Dunnigan about the importance of Hume, his contribution to Protestant poetics in Scotland remains to be fully understood.[15] The *Hymnes, or Sacred Songs* has never been examined as a whole text, though individual poems in the collection have attracted a little attention. Most celebrated of them is the Christian pastoral, 'Of the Day Estivall'. This had apparently already achieved some popularity in the early seventeenth century when it was copied into a manuscript anthology by James Murray of Tibbermuir (now Cambridge, University Library, Kk.5.30). It is still regularly included in anthologies of Scottish literature.[16] Besides

10 STC 13942.

11 Hume had graduated from St Mary's College, St Andrews, in 1574. He seems to have studied in France for some time, and then entered the ministry. As Verweij points out, the only evidence for his presence at James' court comes in his own 'Epistle' prefacing the *Hymnes* and in 'Ane Epistle to Maister Gilbert Mont-Creif'. See Sebastiaan Verweij, *The Literary Culture of Early Modern Scotland: Manuscript Production and Transmission, 1560–1625* (Oxford, 2016), p. 45.

12 STC 13942.

13 See Verweij, *Literary Culture*, pp. 45–47. Also Jamie Reid-Baxter, 'The Contents of NLS Adv, 19.3.6', private communication.

14 See Verweij, *Literary Culture*, p. 147; Hume, *Poems*, pp. lxx–lxxi.

15 On Lauder see Joanna Martin, 'William Lauder: The *Speculum Principis* in the Sixteenth Century', in Joanna Martin and Emily Wingfield (eds), *Premodern Scotland, Literature and Governance, 1424–1587* (Oxford, 2017), pp. 160–71; and on Arbuthnot see 'Alexander Arbuthnot and the Lyric in Post-Reformation Scotland', *Studies in Scottish Literature* 42 (2015), 62–87 (available at https://scholarcommons.sc.edu/ssl/vol41/iss1/10/).

16 See Priscilla Bawcutt and Felicity Riddy (eds), *Longer Scottish Poems, Volume 1, 1375–1560* (1987).

this work, Hume's most political poem, comprising verses on the defeat of the Spanish Armanda in 1588 entitled 'The Triumph of the Lord', and the apparently autobiographical poem and complaint on legal and political corruption, 'Ane Epistle to Maister Gilbert Mont-Creif, Mediciner to the Kings Majestie', which is appended to the *Hymnes* in Waldegrave's print, have also received some critical appreciation.[17] The prose 'Epistle' to the *Hymnes*, which is addressed 'To the Scottish youth', is frequently cited for the insights it provides into post-Reformation thought in its rejection of 'that naughtie subject of fleshly and vnlawfull loue' (lines 5–6) as the occupation of young poets.[18] Yet its exact relationship to the poems which follow it has been largely ignored, thus leaving a lacuna in our understanding of the intellectual and religious culture of the turn of the seventeenth century.

Hume's *Hymnes* has most often been adduced, not for its own merits, but as literary context to illuminate the writing of more prolific Jacobean poets of the so-called 'Castalian band', amongst which Hume may have found himself as a youthful courtier (with his brother, the poet Patrick Hume of Polwarth),[19] or more recently for recovered voices such as that of Hume's dedicatee, the poet Elizabeth Melville.[20] For example, Deidre Serjeantson has commented briefly on Hume's poetic practice in the wider context of English and Scottish Protestant literature. She contrasts the plain style, dependent on Biblical paraphrase, favoured in England, with the emphasis in Scottish poetry, generated in part by James VI's writing, on 'ingyne', or creativity.[21] The prose works are treated in a similar manner. While David George Mullan draws multiple quotations from Hume's prose into the wealth of writings discussed in his *Scottish Puritanism*,[22] these texts – including *Foure Discourses of Praise unto God, Ane Briefe Treatise of Conscience*, and *Of the Felicitie of the Life to Come* (all of which were printed by Waldegrave in 1594)[23]

[17] See Jack, 'Poetry under King James VI', pp. 136–37 and Gerrard Carruthers, 'Form and Substance in the Poetry of the Castalian Band', *Scottish Literary Journal* 26 (1999), 7–17, at pp. 13–14.

[18] On this common Protestant view of the corrupting nature of secular literature see Jane Dawson, 'Reading, Writing, and Gender in Early Modern Scotland', *The Seventeenth Century* 27 (2013), 335–74.

[19] On the problems surrounding this term, see Priscilla Bawcutt, 'James VI's Castalian Band: A Modern Myth', *SHR* 80 (2001), 251–59.

[20] For example, Jamie Reid-Baxter, 'Elizabeth Melville, Lady Culross: New Light from Fife', *IR* 68.1 (2017), 38–77; Sarah Ross, 'Elizabeth Melville and the Religious Sonnet Sequence in Scotland', in Susan Wiseman (ed.), *Early Modern Women and the Poem* (Manchester, 2013), pp. 42–59.

[21] Deirdre Serjeantson, 'English Bards and Scottish Poetics', in C. Cribben and D.G. Mullan (eds), *Literature and the Scottish Reformation* (Aldershot, 2009), pp. 161–89, at p. 179. She contrasts the greater concern with invention in literary art in the Scottish tradition with the preference for a plain style based on Biblical citation in the English. It is worth, however, noting that Hume avoids the highly pronounced aureate and classicising style of John Stewart.

[22] David George Mullan, *Scottish Puritanism, 1590–1638* (Oxford, 2000), for example pp. 89, 102–4.

[23] STC 13943 and 13944.

– are given no sustained analysis. While this chapter cannot fully make up for the neglect of Hume's writing, it goes some way towards revealing its literary merits, internal coherence, and wider relevance.

## The Purpose and Context of the *Hymnes*

THE concern with the '*right vse of Poesie*', as announced in the title to Hume's collection, was well-established in the tradition of Scottish devotional writing by the 1590s. On the eve of the Reformation, David Lyndsay's prologue to *The Monarche* (1553–54) rejected Classical and pagan inspiration to adopt 'That heuinlye Muse' (line 248), the Holy Spirit, God in Majesty and the crucified Christ, as the stimulus for his 'fructuous' poetry (line 297).[24] Robert Norvell's prologue to his *Meroure of a Christiane*, printed in 1561 and dedicated to the Protestant magnate, Colin Campbell, 6th earl of Argyll (d. 1584), carefully distinguishes itself from the work of poets who have wasted their time by calling on 'many sindry goddesses' rather than on 'the Lord Celestiall'.[25] Norvell was influenced by the French poet, Clemènt Marot, but another major source for such views on the religious responsibilities of the poet was the Huguenot writer, Guillaume de Salluste Du Bartas, who spent several months in Scotland in 1587, and who was a major stimulus for Scottish devotional writing and court poetry in the late sixteenth century.[26] Close in date to Hume's collection is the poetry of John Stewart of Baldynneis, whose narrator opens his devotional allegory, *Ane Schersing out of Trew Felicitie* (in part a response to James VI's translation of Salluste Du Bartas's *L'Vranie*),[27] by registering his discontentment with his previous 'scribblings', and deciding to write to 'Sum purpois mair prudent' (line 8). By the end of the century, these views on the proper religious duties of the poet received most forceful expression in the works of James Melville. His 1598 printed collection of verse and prose, *A Spirituall Propine*, contains a 'Sonnet to The Pastors', in which 'poesie' is defended as being the 'sweit

[24] See David Lyndsay, *The Works of Sir David Lindsay of the Mount 1490–1555*, 4 vols, ed. Richard Hamer (Edinburgh, 1930–36), vol. 1.
[25] STC (2nd edn) 18688, unnumbered page. On Norvell, and his translating of works, including Psalm paraphrases, by Clément Marot, see Alasdair MacDonald, 'Poetry, Politics and Reformation Censorship in Sixteenth-Century Scotland', *English Studies* (2008), 410–21; 'The Scottish Renaissance: A Rough Beast Slouching to Be Reborn', *European Journal of English Studies* (2014), 11–20.
[26] See Daniel Fischlin, '"Like a Mercenary Poet": The Politics and Poetics of James VI's Lepanto', in Sally Mapstone (ed.), *Older Scots Literature* (Edinburgh, 2005), pp. 540–59, at pp. 549–50; and Kaarina Hollo and Thomas Rutledge, 'Translation', in Nicola Royan (ed.), *The International Companion to Scottish Literature, 1400–1650* (Glasgow, 2020), pp. 237–65, at pp. 255–56.
[27] James' translation of this work was published in his *Essayes of a Prentise in the Divine Art of Poesie* (Edinburgh, 1584).

indytment [composition] of the Holy Spirit'.[28] The sub-title to the appended *A Morning Vision* also insists that 'the measures of poesie and harmonie of musick … delytes the mind and sa helpes the memorie', also stirring the 'soules affections towards God'.

The 'Epistle' 'To the Scottish youth', which begins Hume's *Hymnes*, is a careful exercise, within this tradition, in legitimising the poems that follow and explaining their purpose. Its narrator rejects the 'prophane sonnets and vaine ballats of loue' (line 9) favoured 'in Princes courts, in the houses of greate men, and in the assemblies of yong gentilmen and yong damesels' (lines 6–8).[29] Poetry is instead placed in the service of the common good as the aspiring poet is urged to put their creative gifts to the purpose of glorifying God and serving the 'weil of thy brethren' (line 42). The sonnet which follows the 'Epistle' perfectly demonstrates the harnessing of form – in this case an interlaced sonnet – to appropriate matter, in a self-consciously literary statement of the sincerity of the poetic project about to unfold. 'A Sonnet of Loue' invokes failed Classical love affairs (Pryamus and Thisbe, Jason and Medea, Demephon and Phyllis, Hercules and Iole) not to invite sympathy for their unfortunate participants, but to confirm the importance of the rejection of all kinds of folly, especially those associated with deception and pride such as 'tromperie' (trickery, wrongdoing) and 'insolence' (arrogance, licentiousness) (lines 3–4). The Sonnet warns its reader not to be 'the cause of ill' or to 'allure the heart to shame or sin' (lines 12–13). This poem is an exercise in creating a *contrafactum*, a key technique in Protestant poetics,[30] the love sonnet turned to moral ends, a demonstration of learning, and discernment, as Classical knowledge is put aside for Christian endeavours.

Hume's 'Epistle' and 'A Sonnet of Loue' have other functions in the context of the collection, besides the rejection of profane subjects for poetry. To borrow Jamie Reid-Baxter's description of Elizabeth Melville's poems, Hume's hymns are 'religious artefacts with practical application in the spiritual struggle', individually, but more importantly, as a collection.[31] In the *Christian Precepts Seruing to the Practise of Sanctification*, printed at the end of the *Hymnes*, Hume refers to the 'exercise' of 'reading and hearing' of God's law (*Christian Precepts*, lines 34–35), as well as singing,

[28] The reading found in the extant prints, 'sweit in Oyntment', is corrected to 'indytment' by Melville in the British Library copy of the print (BL C 37.e.14) which bears his revisions. See Sally Mapstone, 'James Melville's Revisions to *A Spirituall Propine* and *A Morning Vision*', in David J. Parkinson (ed.), *James VI and I, Literature and Scotland. Tides of Change, 1567–1625* (Leuven, 2013), pp. 173–92, at p. 179. There is no modern edition of these texts. References are to the BL copy of the print.

[29] These criticisms of courtly pastimes are repeated in 'Ane Epistle to Maister Gilbert Mont-Creif' at the end of the *Hymnes*. See lines 241–312. Hume laments the sensuality and idleness of the court.

[30] See MacDonald (ed.), *Gude and Godlie Ballatis*, pp. 36–43.

[31] Reid-Baxter, 'Elizabeth Melville, Lady Culross', p. 43. Also see Jamie Reid Baxter, 'Elizabeth Melville, Calvinism and the Lyric Voice', in Parkinson (ed.), *James VI and I, Literature and Scotland*, pp. 151–72.

meditating on and discussing it. Piety may be a private or internalised exercise, but also has a communal dimension as the Word is shared within households and congregations in a way that was widely recognised by Hume's contemporaries.[32] A very tangible account of the sharing of such devotional poems within a close spiritual network comes in Melville's *Spirituall Propine*: this collection was 'bedecked' (Melville's word) by clergymen who inspected the work before publication and added their own poems as liminary verse, one of which confirms Melville's confidence in 'poesie' as having the particular power to move and allure the reader to faith.[33]

To prepare us for the spiritual exercise of reading the *Hymnes*, the 'Epistle' 'To the Scottish youth' adopts some important rhetorical and interpretive strategies, particularly in the construction of the narrator's voice, and the consequent positioning of the reader. The 'Epistle' presents the poems as the author's earlier compositions, as 'a few spirituall songs, begun in my youth' (line 77), much as John Stewart presents his poems as the product or 'rhapsodies' of a youthful brain.[34] The 'Epistle to Maister Mont-Creif' is also framed in the print as relating to 'The Experience of the Authors Youth'. This kind of retrospection gives the *Hymnes* the air of a collected works: as the texts are presented in Waldegrave's print (which, as produced during the author's lifetime, surely reflects Hume's own design), with 'Ane Epistle to Maister Mont-Crief', and the prose *Christian Precepts Seruing to the Practise of Sanctification* added to the collection, they appear to comprise a confident and authoritative act of authorial self-presentation. The title page to the print clearly states Hume's name and the dedicatory Epistle to Elizabeth Melville is signed off, 'Your brother in the Lord Iesus, Alexander Hume, Minister of the Evangell'. The earlier prints of Hume's prose tend merely to bear his initials, 'A.H', on the title page or at the end of introductory epistles, and some of the works of Hume's contemporaries are printed anonymously.[35] However, although the *Hymnes* is presented as a 'collected works', with a strong autobiographical dimension (which is also evident in his earlier prose

[32] See Reid-Baxter, 'Elizabeth Melville, Calvinism and the Lyric Voice', p. 170.

[33] This sonnet, 'To the Reader' (beginning, 'Giff pleasure may perswade or mater moue'), is followed by the initials 'M.I.C.'. On the candidates for the authorship of some of these works, see Reid-Baxter, 'Elizabeth Melville, Lady Culross', pp. 66–68, and Mapstone, 'James Melville's Revisions', p. 175.

[34] John Stewart, *The Poems of John Stewart of Baldynneis*, ed. Thomas Crockett (Edinburgh and London, 1913). This is a familiar convention, dating back to patristic models. See J.A. Burrow, *The Ages of Man: A Study in Medieval Writing and Thought* (Oxford, 1986); Kate McClune, '"He was but a Yong Man": Age, Kingship and Arthur', in Martin and Wingfield (eds), *Premodern Scotland*, pp. 85–98. Also see Arnoud S.Q. Visser, *Reading Augustine in the Reformation: The Flexibility of Intellectual Authority in Europe, 1500–1620* (Oxford, 2011).

[35] Hume's earlier works were printed by Robert Waldegrave with the attribution 'A.H.'. The first 1603 print of Elizabeth Melville's *Ane Godlie Dreame* is attributed on the title page merely to 'M.M. Gentelvvoman in Culros, at the requeist of her freindes'. See STC 17811. The many later editions, from ?1605 and 1606 onwards, are ascribed to 'Elizabeth Melvill, Ladie Culros younger'.

works),[36] the book should not be read as solely concerned with Hume's 'own afflictions' or self-fashioning in the most literal and personal sense.[37] Indeed, *The Christian Precepts* draws the whole printed collection to a conclusion with a warning against 'presumption, selfe loue, and vaine ostentation' (line 6), reminding the reader that all good things accomplished are signs of God's goodness, and not of the talents of their worldly agent: 'it is the Lord that woorkes by thy hand & not thou' (line 8).

This means that the significance of the 'Epistle' 'To the Scottish youth' lies not in its biographical content, but in the way it re-establishes the positions and relationship of author and reader in a way which is vital for the efficacy of Hume's exemplary and encouraging pastoral project. The association of the *Hymnes* with a youthful self serves to connect the poems not with spiritual certainty but with vulnerability and moral struggle. The narrating voice's recovery of his youthful writing allows him both to confess his past error and offer the reader an accessible model of penitential self-reform, 'because some time I delighted in such fantasies myselfe, after the manner of riotous young men' (lines 32–34), before God 'wrought a great repentence in me' (line 35). After all, youth is a condition experienced by all of Hume's readers, in a way that physical sickness – which defines the narrating persona of some of his earlier prose works – may not be. More precisely, Hume's ideal reader, Elizabeth Melville, is described in 'The Epistle Dedicatorie' as 'a tender youth', albeit one who is 'sad, solitare and sanctified, oft sighing & weeping through the conscience of sinne' (lines 16–18). She is a model for the aspiring poets and mis-directed youth of the 'Epistle' 'To the Scottish youth'. Because Hume's poems were, the narrator notes, 'prosecuted in my wraslings with the world' (line 78), they allow the complicated and equivocal voices of the struggling sinner to remain audible, rather than privileging the self-righteous, ministerial voice of the print's title page, the opening of the 'Epistle', or even of the sonnet. If the poems offer a trajectory, it is not a linear process moving towards complete spiritual understanding, linked to an autobiographical construction of a unitary and authoritative authorial self, but one which is focused more securely on the reader, foregrounding ideas of failure, self-examination, and the need for perseverance. The eight 'hymns' as printed by Waldegrave are subtly interconnected, as the rest of this analysis will show,[38] and move from penitential self-searching to tranquility, and back to penance and self-abnegation to mirror the reader's spiritual struggles.

This kind of painstaking introspection was recommended by Hume's contemporary, James Melville, in his *Spirituall Propine*: 'Examine thy life through al the ages thou has past, bairn-head, youth-head, man head and aulde age, how God hes dealt with thee therin and how thou hes recompensed him againe' (p. 40). David George Mullan identifies in seventeenth-century

[36] For example, see 'Ane Epistle generalle' addressed 'To the Christian Reader' in *Ane Treastise of Conscience* printed in 1594, but apparently composed in 1592.

[37] Dunnigan, 'Hume, Alexander'.

[38] See especially, section 'Poetic Design in the Hymnes', below.

evangelical self-writing an emphasis on the 'deconstruction of the self-righteous subject' and the establishment of 'the authentic self, coming only by the action of grace which provides the means of resurrecting, redeeming, renewing the ruined self'.[39] The rejection of self-righteousness is very much Hume's concern too: in *Christian Precepts*, printed at the end of the *Hymnes*, he warns, 'Beware thou iustifie not thy self in thy hart: for thou knaws that thou cannot abstaine fra sinne ... without the meere mercie of God' (lines 11–13). Renewing the ruined self is a central theme in the *Hymnes*, but Hume continually acknowledges the difficulty of this task. The end of the collection is just the beginning of the reader's journey: 'if thy intention be to glorifie God, and to bee exercised in euery maner of good warke: then be assured thy regeneration is begun' (*Christian Precepts*, lines 276–78). To sum up, Hume's handling of the concept of self, that of poet and reader, is both careful and complex, and any impulses towards the biographical are also universalising and paradigmatic. The collection poses the question of how an individual life might be used in the service of God. It ponders the nature of the exemplary self in this context and asks how the sinner can reach out to other sinners, particularly in the use of poetry.

## Poetic Design in the *Hymnes*

THE construction of the Godly self, and the difficulties inherent in such an endeavour, is central to the poem that begins the *Hymnes* proper, 'His Recantation'. Here the lyric persona explains how he set out to use 'sangs and Psalmes' (line 15) to glorify God, but was held back by his sinful nature – his 'cancred carnall kind' (line 17). The poem's depiction of its persona as fissured – riven by a deadly strife between the senses and the soul – and its rhetoric of seduction by lurking sins (lines 18–19), and the polluted, wanton self ('my lasciue mouth', 'vaine polluted thought', 'speach profaine', 'fragil flesh uncleane', lines 4–7, 37) with its 'instruments of shame' (line 89) appear extreme. Yet it is paralleled in many penitential poems pre- and post-Reformation, Protestant and Catholic, all influenced, as Hume's poem is, by the Penitential Psalms. Perhaps the closest analogue to Hume's poem is the work of his contemporary, the Catholic convert, Alexander Montgomerie, and particularly *A godly prayer*, whose speaker confesses his stubborn delay in repenting, and laments his soul's imprisonment in 'filthie flesh' (line 58).[40] Montgomerie's speaker is troubled by the possibility of his repeated sliding into

[39] Mullan, *Narratives of the Religious Self*, p. 362.

[40] References are to Alexander Montgomerie, *The Poems of Alexander Montgomerie*, ed. David J. Parkinson, 2 vols (Edinburgh, 2000), vol. 1; also see Mark Sweetnam, 'Calvinism, Counter Reformation and Conversion: Alexander Montgomerie's Religious Poetry', in Crawford Cribben and David George Mullan (eds), *Literature and the Scottish Reformation* (London, 2009), pp. 143–60.

sin, but in a prayer for forgiveness promises God to 'pen thy prais and wondrous works indyte' (line 39); and in a moment of autobiographical reference, or as Lyall puts it, 'signing', he appeals for the Holy Spirit to 'be Montgomeries muse' (line 50), descending in 'forked tongues of fyre' (line 51) to inspire his verse.[41] Hume's lyric voice is precisely characterised as belonging to the tardy sinner, at last turning to God, but well aware of his belated repentance, and reluctant to give up the 'laits [behaviours] of youth' (line 2): even in appealing for clemency he admits that 'I cannot of my self, alace! / Abstaine fra vice and sin' (line 95–96). Hume, like Montgomerie, echoes Psalm 103 in the recognition that God is 'glad ... grace to shaw' (line 67) to repentant sinners, and also invokes Pentecostal imagery, calling on the 'haly spreit, / In clouen tungs of fire' (lines 127–28).[42] But while Montgomerie's speaker concludes his complaint peacefully, embracing the 'holy Ghost my gyder gude', Hume's speaker is still troubled by his unworthiness, requesting assistance rather than being assured of it: 'be my support, / My teacher, and my guyde' (lines 133–34). The authoritative Protestant poet is not yet fully formed: the anaphora of the final three stanzas, 'Then sall my singing saull reioyce', 'Then sall my sacred pen delite', 'Then they that sall thy puissance heir' (lines 131, 137, 145) suggests that the speaker still awaits divine inspiration in order to be able to fulfil his role as godly poet.

While it is tempting to attribute the subtly different endings of Montgomerie's and Hume's poems to doctrinal and confessional difference, I think the case rather is that Hume's poem is preparation for the next text in the *Hymnes*. As I have noted, the texts in the *Hymnes* are carefully arranged and interdependent. The hope expressed at the end of 'His Recantation', that once inspired he will write of 'Thy wondrous works in verse' (line 139), is fulfilled in the next poem, 'Of Gods Benefits Bestowed Vpon Man', a reflection on the creation, in part influenced by Du Bartas's *The Divine Week*.[43] An analogue may be found in Richard Maitland's poem in the Bannatyne Manuscript, 'Ane Ballat of the Creatioun of the Warld, Man, his Fall and Redemptioun'.[44] Unlike this work, though, Hume avoids the narrative of disobedience and fall, instead focusing on the wonders of God's creation, man's capacity for acquiring knowledge, and his salvation. At first, the speaker's divided self is once more in evidence: 'saull', 'reson', 'sensis', 'mind', 'memorie', and 'hart' (lines 1–4) are each in turmoil, their owner weak and wavering. As in 'His Recantation', where the speaker moves from

[41] Discussed in R.J. Lyall, *Alexander Montgomerie, Poetry, Politics and Cultural Change in Jacobean Scotland* (Tempe, AZ, 2005), pp. 298–300.

[42] Also compare John Stewart's *Ane Schersing ovt of Trew Felicitie*, part 1, lines 15–16: the narrator asks the Psalmist, to 'with thy sacred spreit my spreit inspyre / Quhilk thow send doune in toungs of flammyng fyre'.

[43] On the circulation of this text, see Peter Auger, 'The *Semaines*' Dissemination in England and Scotland before 1641', *Renaissance Studies* 26.5 (2012), 625–40.

[44] See Joanna M. Martin (ed.), *The Maitland Quarto, A New Edition of Cambridge, Magdalene College, Pepys Library MS 1408* (Woodbridge, 2015), pp. 457–62.

not knowing what it is he desires ('I knaw not what I craue', line 52), to requesting that God 'teach me what to craue' (line 86), this speaker's desire – craving – for knowledge is presented as potentially dangerous: 'I maruel mair the mair I muse, the mair I knawledge craue, / Of hid and halie things, the mair my self I doo disceaue' (lines 7–8). However, the narrator's discordant subject recedes as the poem unfolds an account of an idealised, pre-lapsarian man as 'A seemely membred microcosme' (line 61), with 'euerie member maid to haue a certaine sympathie, / Amangs themselues, and with the heauens a decent harmonie' (lines 63–64). Man is given gifts of the mind, or as Hume describes them in his *Ane Treatise of Conscience*, functions of the soul: these are 'a swift and agile thought', 'A strong imagination', a 'quick revoluing reasone', 'memorie' and 'wit' to know all things 'speedefull for his vse' of the 'naturall' world (lines 95–105).[45] Thus a craving for knowledge need not lead to self-deception but may be turned to good: man delights in 'Trew sapience and science baith' (line 158), 'hes a fragrant freshe ingyne all science to invent', a 'flowing facund tung' (lines 139–40), and 'To reason he reioysing hes, to learne, to teache, and talke' (line 161). And, although this is an account of pre-lapsarian man, Hume blurs the distinction between this and the post-lapsarian condition, to insist optimistically that man's craving for knowledge leads him to know himself and therefore his salvation: 'he knowes him selfe, and his originall, / That he mon die, and after death the heauen inherit sall' (lines 133–34). This concluding clause, of course, cannot refer to Adam before the fall.

At the end of the poem, the narrator urges his lute and lips to 'go sing a newar sang' (line 247), and it is no coincidence that 'Of the Day Estivall' is the poem which follows, opening with a reference to Genesis 1, then locating the pleasures of creation articulated in 'Of God's Benefits' in the passage of a single summer's day in a rural landscape. The poetic philosophy behind this poem reflects Hume's defence of literary language in the Preface to his *A Treatise of the Felicitie of the Life to Come* (printed in 1594), where he both laments the spiritual poverty or 'penuritie of language' (Preface, line 26) and defends the necessity of using figurative language to allow the description and comprehension of divine subjects. Here Hume explains that because 'loftie' matter of faith 'transcends so far the vnderstanding of man' (line 5), 'we are forced to speake by similitudes, and vnder shadowes of natural things which we can conceiue, that thereby the things supernatural, may be better conceived' (Preface, lines 9–12). There is no special language, he explains, for spiritual things, so we are compelled to use the same words to describe the divine as we do the worldly. In the Preface to his treatise, therefore, we are told that 'to expresse the pleasures of the life to come, comparison is made betwixt them, and the pleasures of this life, whereby the perfection of the one, more evidently appeares, by the consideration of the other' (Preface, lines 84–87). Thus, we can comprehend the nature of paradise through Biblical

[45] Compare *Ane Treatise of Conscience*, chapter 5, lines 1–2.

texts, of course, but also through the created world, 'by making comparison of the same [paradise] with bewtiful places here vpon earth, which we may see with our eies' ('A Description of the Celestiall Dwelling Place', lines 40–42).

However, despite its glimpse of purposeful activity, and ensuing tranquillity, 'Of the Day Estivall' is not permitted to be the conclusion of the *Hymnes*. Indeed, Hume's prose acknowledges the tensions inherent in the approach of that poem: its similitudes, encouraging our enjoyment of the beauty of the natural world as a reflection of the divine, may be helpful, but also root us in nature – including our fallen nature. Indeed, the first poem of the *Hymnes*, 'His Recantation', cautions the reader that God's 'wonders are not wrought to please / Mans foolish appetite' but for His 'owne delite' (lines 53–55). And, in the *Christian Precepts*, the reader is instructed to 'Craue light of God ... that thou be not guided by the light of nature, and ditement [dictation] of flesh and bloud', and not to be too much 'in nature', which is associated with the carnal and not the spiritual (lines 199–200, 276). In the context of the *Hymnes*, therefore, it is important that 'Of the Day Estivall' is followed by disquiet, in the fourth poem, 'To his Sorrowfull saull, Consolation'. The latter employs, though very distinctively, a well-used Protestant motif of the sick soul, awaiting cure by God, a trope made more popular by Calvin's sermons on Hezekiah and David. Hume had already explored the trope of physical sickness and divine cure as he set out the 'circumstances and occasion of [his] writing' in the epistle to his prose work, *Ane Treatise of Conscience*: a three-month illness precisely dated to 1592, precipitated by a 'Feuer alterne', which was caused by the narrator's preoccupation with 'warldly affaires' ('Ane Epistle generall', lines 20–22); the narrator tells us, the Lord had 'casten me on the bed, to the effect that he micht warke this his wark in me' ('Ane Epistle generall', lines 61–62).

The fourth poem of the *Hymnes*, however, is not to be read biographically. It is highly conscious of its literariness, using a 10-line stanza which recalls the form reserved for solemn complaints in earlier Scots texts, including the *Quare of Jelusy* and Henryson's *Orpheus and Eurydice*. Its manipulation of voice is particularly sophisticated too. As an address from a speaker to his 'Immortall Spirit' (line 1), the 'noble cheiftain of my manly harte' (line 3), it broadly recalls the amatory orations to the heart such as those by Alexander Scott in the Bannatyne Manuscript, and more so the devotional uses of the trope in the *contrafacta* of *The Gude and Godlie Ballatis* (such as 'Go hart vnto the lampe of licht') and Maitland Collections.[46] One of these poems 'Ceis hairt and trowbill me no moir', which is attributed to both Richard Maitland and Alexander Arbuthnot in Maitland sources, offers a useful insight into the intricacies of Hume's poem.[47] In 'Ceis Hart' the speaker lectures his heart, urging it to reject the world and trust in its election; the heart's 'blindit' wit and restless spirit are taught that suffering facilitates self-knowledge: worldly

[46] See MacDonald (ed.), *The Gude and Godlie Ballatis*, p. 206.

[47] Also see 'Vp hairt, thow art the pairt of man most souuerane', in Martin (ed.), *Maitland Quarto*, pp. 176–77.

'chaistning / Dois ws alluire our selfis to knaw' (lines 57–58). It is a rather impersonal instructional work. But in Hume's poem, the 'I' voice belongs to a fascinatingly deconstructed self: the sorrowful soul, identified as the superior part of man ('my best, maist perfite part', line 1), is addressed by its owner and urged to 'cure thy sell' (line 10). This sickness of the soul has caused a sickness of the body, yet the doubly weakened speaker turns counsellor, reminding his soul of God's promise to deliver 'his awin afflicted band' (line 47) from the exile of mortal existence 'Heare in the flesh' (line 9). [48] In a further moment of complexity, the poem's voice reveals that it inhabits a frail but nevertheless young body: 'Thow [the soul] hes not yet bein threttie yeirs and ane, / Into this fleshlie prison resident' (lines 31–32). So, despite his weakness, through despair, youth and sickness, the speaker still provides his soul with a digest of Biblical texts on the end of time, enjoining it to imagine the triumphant scenes from Book of Revelation: 'Then thou my saull with great triumph and glore … / Sall take the corps quhair thou wes first before / Unto the high and holie cietie wide' (lines 181–83). His expressions of faith are assured by the end of the poem: 'The life to come so firmely I beleeue' (line 195). The soul and heart are revived by the Biblical discourse shared with fellow readers ('I feill revert and wondrously reveif / My saull sicklike hir sorrowing she hes ceist', lines 192–93), demonstrating again that spiritual authority sometimes comes from unexpected quarters.

In poem 5, 'Thankes for the Deliverance of the Sicke', the lyric voice is once again intricately constructed: it shifts from internality and apparent biographical reference to universalising observations of its subject.[49] Despite the sense of relative resolution at the end of the previous poem, an awe-struck first-person voice begins the poem lamenting a spiritual version of writer's block: 'Quhy dois my silent tung repose and hald her peace, / Quhy dois my voice the worthie praise of God from singing cease?' (lines 1–2). The voice is that of a self-professed 'impe of Christ' (line 9), also characterised as the 'pyning patient againe to health restord' (line 16), thus offering the poem as sacrifice of praise, and as a meditation on election and reprobation, and on the afflictions God sends to the faithful as a 'needefull whipping rod' (line 60).[50] It is also styled as a personal confession: 'I mon confes (O mightie God), I haue offended thee' (line 73). But the abject penitent who utters this confession is also observed more objectively, from the outside, as the narrator 'zooms out' from what had appeared to be his own introspection (of

[48] On the use of the conceit of the diseased mind or heart, cured by God, in Protestant writing, see Anne Vaughan Lock, *The Collected Works of Anne Vaughan Lock*, ed. Susan M. Felch (Tempe, AZ, 1999), p. xxxviii.

[49] Jamie Reid-Baxter has drawn attention in private communication to the similarities between this poem and the anonymous complaints in NLS 19.3.6, especially those on folios 35–37.

[50] Compare 'Ceis hairt, and trowbill me no moir', line 159, 'The quhippis of the Lord'. The diction is generally close to Arbuthnot's poems: see Joanna Martin, 'Alexander Arbuthnot and the Lyric in Post-Reformation Scotland', *Studies in Scottish Literature* 41.1 (2016), 62–87.

the sort found in the epistle to *Ane Treatise of Conscience*) to imagine the 'sinner' more generally: 'All this and mair with broken voice and hands to heaven out-spred, / The Godly patient he powrs out, vpon his carefull bed' (lines 85–86).When the first-person pronouns return they are plural, and the voice more didactic than personal: 'This then we see: the mightie God, the crosse of sicknes sends, / Unto his awin adopted sonnes' (lines 113–14). Finally, self-reference is resumed: the pining patient is once again identified with the 'I' voice: 'I haue beene seik, and to the Lord did arily cry and call' (line 134); 'With thankfull heart this sacred sang, I dedicate to thee' (line 150). The poem, like most of the *Hymnes*, is highly performative, but this is an especially sophisticated example of how Hume often refuses a 'single subject position for the first-person voice', exploiting a range of perspectives within the single poem.[51]

Poem 5 ends with gratitude, but also the plea that God does not test his servant 'with sair assalts' (line 151) unless he also sends him renewed strength. The sixth and seventh poems are designed to inspire and encourage the reader with descriptions of God's strength. Poem 6, 'Of Gods Omnipotence', is a celebration of God's power in the natural world, but also returns to literary themes, especially the collection's central concern with the correct use of poetry. The first-person narrator reappears briefly at the conclusion of the poem to lament the folly of poets who write 'fables and fictitious leis' (line 120). These voices are contrasted with those of the Old Testament prophets, Daniel, Jonah and Elijah, who never dissimulate: 'Into the prophets mouthes the spreit, / Of lies could neuer enter in' (lines 55–56). The next poem is more complex, but continues to illustrate divine power, while also considering how best to give this expression. It is divided into three parts. The first, 'Alluding to the Defait of the Spanish Nauie in the Yeare 1588', is composed in decasyllabic couplets, and gives a description of the celebrations following the defeat of the Spanish Armada, imagining the 'buiting' (booty, line 143) won as a symbol of the vanity of worldly power and possession. The second section is entitled 'The Song of the Lords Souldiours'. It is written in six-line octosyllabic stanzas, rhyming *aabccb* and celebrating, mainly through reference to Old Testament events, 'the mightie God of weir' (line 335). This is followed by a short conclusion which reverts to the decasyllabic couplets of the first part of the poem.

The first section of the poem resounds with encouraging imperatives and nostalgic echoes of earlier Older Scots poems as the narrator calls his reader to prepare for a 'royall feast' (line 20): 'Right as the poynt of day begins to spring / And Larks aloft melodiouslie to sing' (lines 49–50) recalls the opening of Dunbar's *The Goldyn Targe*, for example. Hume is adopting the strategy used in Lyndsay's 'Epistle' to *The Monarche* in which he imitates the aureate diction of earlier Scottish poets but transfers it to a 'right vse', to address

[51] I am drawing here on Ingrid Nelson, *Lyric Tactics: Poetry, Genre and Practice in Late Medieval England* (Philadelphia, 2017), p. 49. Although Nelson refers to earlier Middle English writing, her insights enhance our understanding of later devotional lyric too.

sacred rather than secular subjects. Hume's narrator exhorts exuberant praise of God through every manner of creative and public display possible. The text's descriptive passages are highly specific and sensual, as Hume masters a range of registers from the botanical to the military in careful detail to imagine the celebration. The parading of the spoils won from the Armada, drawn through the streets in painted carts, forms an ironic royal entry, a form with a long history in Older Scots literature.[52] The entire realm, 'cities, kirks, and euerie noble towne' (line 21), is 'decked vp and downe' (line 22) in flowers, herbs, tapestries, and fine clothes, sprinkled with perfumes, polished and cleaned, and filled with 'scaffalds clare' to allow for performances of 'cumlie comedies / For pleasant plays and morall tragedies' (lines 45–47). The streets are to be lined with 'Lauender, with Thime and Cammamild: / With Mint and Medwortes ...' (lines 26–27); dozens of armaments are listed. Music from pipes and 'shouting shalms' (psalms, line 55) announce the parade of the plundered symbols of the vanquished: the crowns and banners being displayed through the streets are those of the defeated emperors and kings, who appear dressed in mourning. The presence celebrated in this festival is no worldly king or army, but the 'great God armipotent' (line 4), who has triumphed over 'many [a] puissant king' (135), flinging their sceptres from them, and turning their fortresses into ruins – 'Demolist all, into a birdis nest' (line 77). There is no virulent anti-papal rhetoric here. The narrator withholds his own views on the occasion and gives the interpretation of the scene to the voices of the spectators, who whisper the gnomic lesson:

> Heare is behald a matter maruellous ...
> Kings are bot men, men are bot wormes and dust,
> The God of heauen is onely great and iust. (lines 166–72)

The first-person narrator, then, plays relatively little part in either section of the poem, allowing the 'reading' of this military event to be made by those who watch the celebrations. A more ministerial voice appears at the end of this first section to 'set downe' (line 179) the events of 'that holy day' (line 181, the day of celebration, but perhaps also an intimation of the Day of Judgement) when the soldiers of Christ who have been dedicated to 'woork his wark, and fight into his field' (line 189) march 'in the towns / As conquerers' (lines 198–99). But even with this return to an authoritative tone, Hume's narrator does not allow his project to stand without scrutiny but inscribes humility back into this triumphant text. He warns the reader

[52] Compare Lyndsay's descriptions of the thwarted civic preparations for a young queen's visit in his *Deploratioun of the Deith of Quene Magdalene*. See David Lyndsay, *Sir David Lyndsay: Selected Poems*, ed. Janet Hadley Williams (Glasgow, 2000), pp. 101–8. In the poem see especially lines 100–75. Also see Douglas Gray, 'The Royal Entry in Sixteenth-Century Scotland', in Helen Cooper and Sally Mapstone (eds), *The Rose and the Thistle: Essays on the Culture of Late Medieval and Renaissance Scotland* (East Linton, 1998), pp. 10–37.

that whoever tries to compare the powers of God and man will simply fail: he will 'tyre his painefull pen' (line 222) because God's might 'surmounts' the might and 'craft' of men (lines 227–28).

The final penitential song of the *Hymnes*, 'The Humiliation [humility] of a Sinner', follows this pair of triumphant and optimistic poems: as we have seen, these confident works, like 'Of the Day Estivall', almost entirely avoid the complexities of imagining the self through first-person utterance. 'The Humiliation' returns the *Hymnes* almost full circle to the struggling sinful self of 'His Recantation', and strikingly it shares the stanza form of Montgomerie's *A Godly Prayer* (ababbcbc$^4$), which is such a close analogue for this first poem of the *Hymnes*. The speaker identifies himself again, as he had in 'Thankes for the Deliverance of the Sicke', as a 'pure pyning penitent' (line 8). He is 'woltring like a woefull wight' (line 13), tormented by the knowledge of his frequent relapses into sin, and fearful that he has abused God's mercy too often, as if the foregoing seven poems had offered no consolation at all. With his frailty, 'secreit sins' and 'corrupt' nature (lines 77–78), this narrator is indeed the ruined self whom Mullan identifies in later Calvinist texts, who is regenerated only through grace: 'This then (my God) of grace I craue' (line 65), begs the narrator, as he asks for God to be 'buklar and ... sure refuge' (line 59), and a 'helping hand' (69).[53]

Before *Christian Precepts* closes this collection of Hume's works, Waldegrave prints 'The Epistle to Maister Gilbert Mont-Creif', a poem about the disruption of a godly life by experience and knowledge. The speaker of the poem repeats his intentions to spend his time peacefully following God's law, yet has to accept his exposure to the polluting world around him – 'These cursed times, this wors nor irone age / Where vertue lurks, where vice dois reigne and rage' (335–36).[54] This poem intersects with several genres. It is a friendship poem, a complaint on the times, and an opportunity for Hume to offer one more 'self' for the reader's consideration and edification, besides that of the complaining narrator. Its themes of sickness and cure link it to the previous poems, recalling the weak body and sickly soul of poem four, the frail 'Godly patient' (line 86) in poem five, and the troubled sinner of poem eight. The poem's addressee, Moncrieff, 'medicinar' (line 1), is explicitly depicted as exemplary in his learning:[55] 'Thou shawis thy selfe be practise evident' (line 3) in 'knawledge singular' (line 2). He is the 'kinde', 'faithfull friend' (lines 7, 12) to whom the narrator can unburden himself. Hume's narrator addresses him throughout as an equal – one who also knows of courtly corruption 'als as weill as I' (line 266) – yet who has transcended this existence to live the 'quiet life' (line 5) the narrator yearns for. But although Moncrieff is cast as the physician, the healing in the poem comes from the narrator's own inner

[53] Compare Hume's *Ane Treatise of Conscience*: 'Be thou ever my strong rock, my bukler, and my shield' (Chapter 13, 112).

[54] Compare *Ane Godlie Dreame*, line 10.

[55] Compare Reson's appeal to Skill for knowledge and comfort in Montgomerie's *The Cherrie and the Slae*, line 1348: 'Be medciner unto this man'.

resources, especially his realisation and revelation of the wickedness of the world and the promise of salvation:

> My comfort lo, my haill felicite,
> Consists in this, I may it shaw to thee:
> To serue the Lord, and on his Christ repose,
> To sing him praise, and in his heichts reiose (lines 369–72).

This act of *showing* his revelations 'To fekfull friends' (line 384), as the last line of the 'Epistle' puts it, is one of Christian service. This idea offers the key to the practical function of this collection of texts. As 'Minister of the Evangell', Hume's ministerial duties would have included pastoral and didactic tasks such as comforting and instructing his parishioners, and the text clearly aims to soothe anxious souls.[56] But in seeking print for his work, Hume reaches beyond this immediate circle, perhaps to those at court, or the Scottish youth more generally who are named in the opening 'Epistle' 'To the Scottish youth', just as James Melville did in his *Spirituall Propine* 'of a pastour to his peple' of 1598.

Although the extent of the circulation of the *Hymnes* (and indeed of Melville's work) is now unclear, Hume's collection supplies its own evidence of its imagined readers. The first carefully idealised reader is Elizabeth Melville, addressed in the 'Epistle Dedicatorie', whom Hume hopes will be 'stirred vp & incouraged to perseuere and grow in Godlines' (lines 15–16) by reading the *Hymnes*. She is marked by 'feruent zeale' (line 9) for God, and Hume famously remarks here on her own 'compositiones so copious, so pregnant, so spirituall' (lines 44–45); these indeed, especially *Ane Godlie Dreame*, reflect her keen understanding of the many trials of the Christian's journey. Hume could be accused of preaching to the converted (though of course, in Calvinist terms, his coreligionists are the elect), and the ontological complexity of the *Hymnes* certainly requires a sophisticated reader. At the end of the collection, Moncrieff is one of the determined or 'fekfull' friends (line 384) who has the ability to carry forward Hume's message.[57] Both Elizabeth Melville and James Melville also direct their printed works to a group of friends and associates, a familiar device used by Protestant writers who often imagined themselves as an embattled minority of the elect exiled amongst the ungodly.[58]

The verse 'Epistle to Maister Gilbert Mont-Creif' stresses that shared piety is a source of strength in such an adverse world, particularly when expressed through poetry, and the resounding singing of God's praises.[59] This

[56] On the relationship between the minister and his laity see Margo Todd, *The Culture of Protestantism in Early Modern Scotland* (New Haven, CT and London, 2002), especially chapter 8; also Jane E.A. Dawson, *Scotland Re-formed, 1488–1587* (Edinburgh, 2007), on the shortage of ministers and need for worship led by the laity, p. 254.

[57] See *A Dictionary of the Older Scotish Tongue*, s.v. 'Fekfull, adj.' (www.dsl.ac.uk/entry/dost/feckfull).

[58] Compare Dawson, *Scotland Re-formed*, p. 254.

[59] See Todd, *The Culture of Protestantism*, p. 370, on the importance of the 'priesthood

is indeed the right 'vse of poesie'. The range of poetic styles in the *Hymnes* is, as noted already, exceptional: the stylistic virtuosity of the collection is a deliberate way to engage the reader's attention and to provide a spiritually challenging contrast to the catechetical prose represented by texts such as the *Christian Precepts* and Hume's earlier tracts. Only two of the ten poems in the printed collection share the same stanzaic form,[60] and each poem is also highly conscious of its identity as a song of praise. The collection accordingly abounds with references to singing. The title page bears a quotation from Ephesians which suggests that this singing is interior rather than audible or communal in a public or outward sense: 'speaking vnto your selues ... making melodie to the Lord in your hearts' (Ephesians 5:18). Community might, of course, be evoked by the prayerful interior or private act of singing. However, the poems themselves are equivocal on this point. Although the first poem refers to the 'singing saull' (line 131) suggesting internality, it ends with the narrator reaching for his lute, and desiring his tongue to be untied, as does the second poem with its preparation to sing a 'newar sang' (line 248); similarly, 'Of the Day Estivall' records the singing with 'cornet and with shalme' (line 216) to give thanks to God at the end of a productive agricultural day. Poem four suggests inward song again as the soul 'of my sang a perfite Ioy can prief' (line 194); but poem five begins by lamenting the cessation of the speaker's singing and 'sealed vp' mouth (line 4) and ends by dedicating a 'sacred sang' (150) to God; poem six is a poem of praise; and there are multiple references to celebratory songs, including the inset 'Song of the Lords Souldiours', in poem seven on the defeat of the Spanish Armada. Even in the most desperate moments of the collection, the speaker is comforted by his recollection of how he has 'Sung praise to thee with ioyfull hart' (poem eight, line 30). These references to song take us to the heart of Hume's joyful and optimistic endeavour. Hume uses the sequence of texts in the *Hymnes, or Sacred Songs* to move beyond his ministerial role, to reject the self-righteous voice of the preacher, to allow his reader to experience the journey of the self still wrestling with the world, subject to youth, frailty, doubt and failure, but also sometimes able to sing joyously of salvation.

## Conclusions

IN these references to song and singing, Hume is very much of his time, reflecting the widespread Protestant impulse to build the new community of the faithful through singing, especially of the psalms. Yet, as this chapter

of believers' and the activities of shared lay piety. On the importance of Psalm singing, see Janes Dawson, '"The Word Did Everything": Readers, Singers and the Protestant Reformation in Scotland, 1560–c. 1638', *RSCHS* 26.1 (2017), 1–37; and most recently Nathan C.J. Hood, 'Metrical Psalm-Singing and Emotion in Scottish Protestant Affective Piety, 1560–1650', *Reformation and Renaissance Review* 23.2 (2021), 151–69.

60 These are poems 2 and 5, which are composed in couplets, with 14-syllable lines.

has argued, the *Hymnes* as a carefully constructed collection of verse and prose stands out from other didactic Calvinist writing of the period. Although it is conventional in rejecting 'profane' or secular subjects as the proper substance of poetry, it also refuses other conventions including the authoritative preacher's voice as its mode of delivery. Instead, it creates a range of lyric voices and subject positions to acknowledge the reality of the audience's anxieties about spiritual failure, addressing them with compassion and encouragement. In this it is mindful of the response of this audience to the traumatic upheaval ushered into all aspects of public, private and devotional life by the Reformation, and it refuses to elide and simplify any aspect of this complex cultural situation. Nevertheless, despite the collection's refusal of a single dogmatic lyric voice, the *Hymnes* is the work of a writer confident in his own identity as a poet – a poet skilful in his mastery of form and in the careful structuring of a collection of different texts to form an intellectually demanding, yet 'affective', spiritual exercise. Thus, in this confidence Hume has produced a work of richness and complexity to match that of his most talented contemporaries, including Alexander Arbuthnot, Alexander Montgomerie, and Elizabeth and James Melville. This is not the final word on Hume: more remains to be done to further illuminate this important writer, his immediate context and literary networks in Fife and at court, and his Scots, English and European sources, in order to fully appreciate his place in the religious culture of the late sixteenth and early seventeenth centuries.

# 13

# *The Dutch in Scotland: The Diplomatic Visit of the States General upon the Baptism of Prince Henry*

Esther Mijers

On 13 August 1594, two Dutch noblemen, Jacob Valcke (?–1623) and Walraven III van Brederode (1547–1614), arrived in the Scottish port of Leith from Veere in the United Provinces. They were the representatives of the Dutch Parliament, the States General (*Staten Generaal*), who had been invited to attend the baptism of the Scottish Crown Prince Henry, which was due to take place in Stirling on 30 August. This may seem like an unlikely act of diplomacy for a number of reasons. The Dutch were in the midst of their 80-year-long war against Spain and a trip to Scotland could have been considered as an unwelcome distraction from the events at home, not to mention a financially costly and dangerous one.[1] Moreover, six of the Dutch provinces had recently assumed sovereignty, having renounced not only their Spanish overlord, Philip II, but the concept of monarchy altogether.[2] As the Scottish king James VI planned on promoting his claims to the English succession, the presence of two republican ambassadors may have appeared unusual to say the least.[3] Finally, the baptism itself, envisaged as a spectacular international projection of Stewart aspiration and power, sent a message of challenge to Queen Elizabeth I of England, with whom the Dutch had a somewhat complicated relationship. Although she was their most

1 The Dutch had been at war with Spain since 1568. The Dutch Revolt, also known as the Eighty Years' War, first saw the Dutch provinces take a stance and then rise up against their overlord Philip II of Spain, over his intrusive political and religious policies, which forced the provinces under increasingly strict Spanish control. While often labelled as a war of religion, the real reasons were to do with Philip's violation of the sovereign rights of the 17 provinces which made up his Dutch inheritance. While the southern provinces returned to the fold in 1581, the seven northern provinces of Holland, Zeeland, Utrecht, Groningen, Friesland, Gelderland and Overijssel continued their conflict until 1648, when peace was concluded as part of the Treaty of Westphalia.

2 The seventh followed in 1595. S. Groenveld, *Unie – bestand – vrede: Drie fundamentele wetten van de Republiek der Verenigde Nederlanden* (Hilversum, 2009), p. 21.

3 Following the Act of Abjuration in 1581, the Dutch became nominal pariahs for many European countries.

important ally, her position was tried when Robert Dudley, 1st earl of Leicester (1532–88), accepted the appointment as Governor General of the United Provinces. His term had come to an unhappy end in 1587, over questions of authority and sovereignty.[4] A deferential visit to Scotland might be construed as a loosening of Dutch ties with England. This chapter examines the Dutch visit, situating it within the context of the Scottish-Dutch relationship in the early modern period and their shared political and humanist culture. The questions it aims to answer are: why were the Dutch invited? Why did they accept James' invitation? How should we understand their actions before, during and after their visit? Although Prince Henry's baptism has been well documented as a grand display of James VI's dynastic ambition, particularly with regards to the English succession, as Roger Mason most recently has argued, this is an untold part of the story.[5]

To begin to understand what was at stake in 1594, we need to consider the relationship between Scotland and the Low Countries in the early modern period. Several aspects have been much studied. Originally connected by trade, Scotland and the Low Countries, the Flemish-speaking parts of the Burgundian realm, were an important axis of the wider North Sea World and the Northern European Renaissance. Following the Reformation, Protestantism and the Dutch Revolt (1568–1648) further tied the northern provinces to Scotland, while the southern Netherlands were pulled back into the Iberian orbit. As part of the economic history of both countries, their relationship has received ongoing attention, especially following the appearance of T.C. Smout's *Scottish Trade on the Eve of the Union* in 1963, in which the importance of Scottish-Dutch commerce, personified by the

[4] The Dutch had looked towards Elizabeth for political assistance, since the early days of the Dutch Revolt, and had been keen for her to become their sovereign. Initially unwilling to offer anything other than moral support, she changed her mind in 1584, when Philip II signed the Treaty of Joinville with the Catholic League. The result was the Treaty of Nonsuch which saw English troops sent to the Netherlands, led by the earl of Leicester. As surety for England's assistance, the towns of Vlissingen and Den Briel were handed over to the English as 'Cautionary Towns'. In addition, Elizabeth gained the right to appoint two councillors to the Dutch Council of State. Leicester was subsequently appointed as Governor General, much to Elizabeth's annoyance. When Leicester proved himself to be both an incompetent military commander and an absolutist ruler, the Dutch and the earl parted ways.

[5] Famously, the grand hall in Stirling castle was built for the occasion. For the contemporary account, see William Fowler, *A true reportarie of the most triumphant, and royal accomplishment of the baptisme of the most excellent, right high, and mightie prince, Frederik Henry; by the grace of God, Prince of Scotland Solemnized the 30. day of August. 1594*. Cf. Rick Bowers, 'James VI, Prince Henry, and "A True Reportarie" of Baptism at Stirling 1594', *Renaissance and Reformation / Renaissance Et Réforme* 29.4 (2005), 3–22; Michael Bath, '"Rare shewes and singular inventions": The Stirling Baptism of Prince Henry', *Journal of the Northern Renaissance* 4 (2012); Roger A. Mason, '1603: Multiple Monarchy and Scottish Identity', *History* 105 (2020), 402–21.

Rotterdam-based merchant Andrew Russell, was first brought to the fore.[6] Since then, others have examined further aspects of the Scottish-Dutch trade relationship, including the cultural, intellectual and educational exchanges that went hand in hand with goods, as well as the religious connections and the military relations, although the political connections between the two nations have been curiously understudied. While the late sixteenth and early seventeenth centuries were arguably the high point in the Scotto-Dutch relationship, much of the historiography to date has concentrated on the later seventeenth and early eighteenth centuries.[7] Recently, there has been a shift towards a chronological as well as a geographic widening, going both back in time as well as beyond the centres of Dutch seventeenth-century prosperity, the towns and cities. Furthermore, the international turn in Scottish history has provided a new lens, introducing a global perspective to the relationship.[8] As a longstanding partner, Scotland had access to the achievements of the Low Countries' Renaissance and, after 1581, of the Dutch 'Golden Age', at home and their networks further afield.[9] However, much of this is still to be researched. The Hansa, the trade hubs along the River Scheldt, the ports of Zeeland and Holland, including Scotland's own Staple at Veere, and the Dutch trading companies are all still in need of deeper scrutiny, and their transnational history awaits.[10]

Closer to home, the shared history of late Renaissance and Reformation Scotland and the Netherlands is in need of re-thinking and (re-)telling. Aside from a common story, their relationship can shed light on their political development as independent nations. It also highlights the need for closer attention to the peripheries of Renaissance Europe, if not a redressing of what we mean by peripheries and centres before the rise of the nation-state.[11] The movement of goods, people and ideas between Scotland

[6] T.C. Smout, *Scottish Trade on the Eve of Union, 1660–1707* (Edinburgh and London, 1963).

[7] For an overview of the historiography of this later period, see E. Mijers, '*News from the Republick of Letters*': *Scottish Students, Charles Mackie and the United Provinces, 1650–1750* (Leiden, 2012), Introduction.

[8] Karin Bowie, 'Cultural, British and Global Turns in the History of Early Modern Scotland', *SHR* 92 (2013), 38–48.

[9] For instance, Scots were employed by the Dutch East and West India Companies in substantial numbers. See Victor Enthoven, Steve Murdoch, and Eila Williamson (eds), *The Navigator: The Log of John Anderson, VOC Pilot-Major 1640–1643* (Leiden 2010); E. Mijers, 'A Natural Partnership? Scotland and Zeeland in the Early Seventeenth Century', in A.I. Macinnes and A. Williamson (eds), *Shaping the Stuart World, 1603–1714: The Atlantic Connection* (Leiden, 2006), pp. 233–60.

[10] For some recent projects, see Alexander Fleming and Roger Mason, *Scotland and the Flemish People* (Edinburgh, 2019) and the accompanying 'Scotland and the Flemish People' project; David Worthington, 'Sugar, Slave-Owning, Suriname and the Dutch Imperial Entanglement of the Scottish Highlands before 1707', *Dutch Crossing: Journal of Low Countries Studies* 44.1 (2019), 3–20; 'Trading Places. Exploring Scotland's Commercial Diaspora, Past and Present', www.nms.ac.uk/collections-research/collections-departments/scottish-history-and-archaeology/projects/trading-places/.

[11] See, for instance, David Worthington's work on the New Coastal History. David

and the Low Countries connected places which no longer have the same importance as they once did. Prior to the Peace of Westphalia (1648), such small nations derived importance from their transnational relations and gave meaning to their own positions within the context of larger and more powerful players' actions and ambitions. For Scotland, it was England that mattered first and foremost, whereas the United Provinces tried to carve out a space between the Spanish and the Holy Roman Empires.[12] The visit of the Dutch to Scotland in 1594 serves as an illustration or vignette, which exposes a great deal of information about the Scottish-Dutch relationship, about how the two countries viewed each other and especially about how they viewed themselves. It not only touches on some of the best-known aspects of Renaissance and Reformation Scottish History such as Stewart ideas of kingship, Anglo-Scottish Union, and the Protestant international, but it is also a Dutch story of union, provincial cooperation and competition, commercial ambition, and above all, sovereignty.[13] By recounting the events as they unfolded over the course of 1594, from a Dutch perspective, this chapter offers an analysis which joins the national with the transnational, within the conceptual framework of early modern state formation.[14]

The Dutch attendance of Prince Henry's baptism has not been examined in any detail although the background has been addressed. Aside from the now rather dated works on the Scottish Staple at Veere, the military connection has received a fair bit of attention, from Alasdair Macdonald, Jochem Miggelbrink and Adam Marks; the Jacobean literary context has been explored by Jamie Reid-Baxter and Astrid Stilma; and Roger Mason's recent project 'Scotland and the Flemish People' has looked at the relationship with the southern Netherlands.[15] As far as the specific episode

Worthington, *The New Coastal History: Cultural and Environmental Perspectives from Scotland and Beyond* (London, 2017).

[12] M. Prak, 'State Formation and Citizenship: The Dutch Republic between Medieval Communes and Modern Nation States', in Jan Luiten van Zanden (ed.), *The Long Road to the Industrial Revolution: The European Economy in a Global Perspective, 1000–1800* (Leiden, 2009), pp. 205–33, at p. 206.

[13] Roger Mason's contributions to the Scottish themes referred to in this chapter are especially significant; see for instance Mason, '1603' and 'Renaissance Monarchy? Stewart Kingship (1469–1542)', in Brown and Tanner (eds), *Scottish Kingship*, pp. 255–78. For the most recent analysis of the United Provinces' political structure(s), see David Onnekink, 'The Body Politic', in H. Helmers, and G. Janssen (eds), *The Cambridge Companion to the Dutch Golden Age* (Cambridge, 2018), pp. 107–23.

[14] State formation is considered here in the vein of composite entities, following Koenigsberger and Elliott more so than Tilly. H.G. Koenigsberger, 'Composite States, Representative Institutions and the American Revolution', *Historical Research* 62 (1989), 135–53; J.H. Elliott, 'A Europe of Composite Monarchies', *Past and Present* 137 (1992), 48–71; Charles Tilly, *Coercion, Capital, and European States, AD 990–1992* (Cambridge, MA, 1990).

[15] John Davidson and Alexander Gray, *The Scottish Staple at Veere. A Study in the Economic History of Scotland* (London, 1909); M.P. Rooseboom, *The Scottish Staple in The United Provinces. An Account of the Trade Relations between Scotland and the Low Countries from 1292 till 1676* (The Hague, 1910); A. MacDonald, *George Lauder (1603–1670): Life*

of the baptismal visit is concerned, the historiography is even more sparse. Willem Nijenhuis made mere mention of it in his *Ecclesia Reformata*, but only Cynthia Fry has paid proper attention to the visit and some of its meaning in her wider study of James VI's diplomacy.[16] In contrast, the baptism itself has received a great deal of attention, not least as a result of the contemporary printed account by the courtier William Fowler, *A true reportarie of the most triumphant, and royal accomplishment of the baptisme of the most excellent, right high, and mightie prince, Frederik Henry*.[17] As is well-known, many 'ambassadouris of sindrie Princeis and Commounwelthis, darrest and narrest freindis to our Soverane Lord and Lady' attended the occasion, including representatives from England, Denmark, Brunswick and Mecklenburg.[18] The Dutch had first been invited in May 1594, when James VI sent Sir William Keith of Delnyis as his 'ambassdour to the Esteatis of the Law Cuntreyis of Flanderis, to invite thame to be their ambassdouris to beir witness to the baptisme of the Prince, his darrest sone, and to intreate upoun certane utheris wechtie effearis'.[19] On 4 June, Sir William appeared before the States General, alongside William Murray, the provost of St Andrews, where they made a 'proposition' to the Dutch. Appealing to the longstanding peace and friendship between Scotland and the Netherlands, and their joint reformed religious outlook, they reminded their hosts in no uncertain terms of their precarious position as a newly founded state. Expressing the hope that all leagues and treaties concluded by the States General's predecessors, namely Charles V and others who had ruled over the Dutch provinces, would be honoured, they finished their letter by cautioning the Dutch over their fishing rights in Scottish waters, around the islands of Orkney and Shetland and elsewhere, which James was

*and Writings* (Cambridge, 2018); Jochem Miggelbrink, 'Serving the Republic: Scottish Soldiers in the Dutch Republic 1572–1782' (unpublished European University Institute, Florence PhD thesis, 2004); Adam Marks, 'England, the English and the Thirty Years' War (1618–1648)' (unpublished University of St Andrews PhD thesis, 2012); Astrid Stilma, *A King Translated: The Writings of King James VI & I and Their Interpretation in the Low Countries, 1593–1603* (Aldershot, 2012); Fleming and Mason, *Scotland and the Flemish People*. Jamie Reid-Baxter has transcribed the letters of Sir John Scot of Scotstarvet (1585–1670) in NLS Adv MS 17.1.9), many of which are by Dutch correspondents. These have not yet been published.

16 Willem Nijenhuis, *Ecclesia Reformata: Studies on the Reformation*, volume 2 (Leiden, 1972), pp. 253–54; Cynthia Fry, 'Diplomacy and Deception: King James VI of Scotland's Foreign Relations with Europe (c. 1584–1603)' (unpublished University of St Andrews PhD thesis, 2014).

17 For an overview of the historiography, see Mason, '1603', pp. 5–6.

18 'Stirling, 24th August. Proclamation relating to the reception of the foreign ambassadors who are in Stirling to attend the ceremony of the Prince's baptism', *RPC*, v, pp. 164, 166.

19 Edinburgh, 3 May. Act in favour of Sir William Keith, his Majesty's ambassador to Flanders, *RPC*, v, p. 144. For Keith see Miles Kerr-Peterson, 'Sir William Keith of Delny: Courtier, Ambassador and Agent of Noble Power', *IR* 67.2 (2016), 138–58. Kerr-Peterson mentions Keith's trip to 'Flanders' but does not mention the Dutch context.

prepared to continue and tolerate without hindrance, despite the fact that these privileges had been signed by previous rulers of the Dutch provinces.[20]

In addition to this ambassadorial representation, James himself had written a letter, which arrived via the Dutch agent in Scotland, Adriaan Damman van Bijsterveld (d. 1605), 'to the United Provinces asking them to send representatives, and renewed his alliance with them in order to strengthen Scottish-Dutch relations prior to the baptism'.[21] The real purpose of this episode could not be clearer: the long and ongoing trade relationship between Scotland and the Dutch Provinces was at stake.

There are several Scottish accounts that mention the Dutch visitors. *The Register of the Privy Council of Scotland* referred to Valcke and Brederode as the ambassadors of the Low Countries of Flanders, while the author of the anonymous *Historie and Life of James the Sext* was clearly more impressed, not only acknowledging them as representing the 'lords of estait in Holland and Zeeland', but also quoting, in full, the letter that accompanied the gift they brought for the young prince 'gevin in a coffer of golde', written by Cornelis van Aaersen, Heer van Spijk (1543–1627), the clerk of the States General.[22] Yet the most detailed account of the visit came from the Dutch themselves: both the States of Holland and the States General recorded the lead up to the visit and documented versions of the lengthy and extremely detailed report that Valcke and Brederode produced after their visit for the States General, along with their request for financial compensation for their trip on 7 November 1594.[23]

Following Keith and Murray's invitation, a lengthy discussion took place among the Dutch, and while the States General took their time to reach a

[20] 'Propositie. Exhibitum par les Sieurs Ambassadeurs d'Ecosse le 6 de Juin 1594 en l'Assemble de Messieurs les Estats Generaux', in *Register van Holland en Westvriesland van den jaare 1593 en 1594* (n.p., n.d.), pp. 396–97.

[21] Damman was a humanist scholar originally from Ghent who had taught at the University of Leiden before his appointment at the Scottish court. See A.J. van der Aa, *Biographisch woordenboek der Nederlanden*, 4 (Haarlem, 1858). Fry, 'Diplomacy and Deception', p. 121. Nationaal Archief, 1.01.02 Inventaris van het archief van de Staten-Generaal, (1431) 1576–1796, 3.01.14/2153. Adriaan Damman, 'Missive van Adriaan Damman, Agent van de Republiek in Schotland, Aan Johan van Oldenbarnevelt van 29 Juli 1594, Betreffende de Ontvangst van Buitenlandse Gezanten Voor de Doopplechtigheid van Karel I, Prins van Schotland, Het Verzoek Aan de Republiek Om Grotere Cadeaus En de Spanningen Tussen Hem En Kolonel William Murray' (1594). Note that Prince Henry is incorrectly described as Prince Charles; Nationaal Archief, 3.01.04.03/58.2. James VI and States General, 'Akte van alliantie tussen de Staten-Generaal en koning James I van Schotland' (26 July 1594). Cf. 'Letter from King James to the States General', 10 June 1594, in *Register van Holland en Westvriesland van den jaare 1593 en 1594* (n.p., n.d.), pp. 395–96.

[22] Holyrood House, 10 September (Convention of Estates), *RPC*, v, p. 166; (John Colville), *Historie and Life of James the Sext. Being an Account of the Affairs of Scotland from the Year 1566 to the Year 1596; with a Short Continuation to the Year 1617*, ed. T. Thompson (Edinburgh, 1825), pp. 335–37.

[23] N. Japikse (ed.), *Resolutien der Staten-Generaal, 1576–1625*, I, Rijksgeschiedkundige Publicatien (RGP) ('s-Gravenhage, 1915–), pp. 221–24. For the ambassadors' report, see below.

decision, they made sure to pay for the Scottish visitors' stay.[24] Much time was spent investigating the historic precedents for the economic relationship with Scotland, as the States General considered the United Provinces to be the successor state to the Habsburg Low Countries and wished to document this with hard evidence. The town of Veere and the province of Gelderland were both approached for copies of their treaties with Scotland.[25] Even more important than commerce was the immediate and ongoing threat of Spain, and the Dutch discussed at length the possibility of Scotland joining a Protestant league against Spain.[26] Key in all this was the Treaty of Bins, in Hainault, which had originally been concluded in 1550 between Charles V and Mary, Queen of Scots in the aftermath of the Treaty of Boulogne, to resolve the trade and piracy disputes between the Holy Roman Empire and Scotland.[27] This appears to have been the overriding agreement, and the Dutch felt that its renewal eliminated the need for the signing of any new ones, on the condition that James joined the anti-Spanish alliance. To oil the wheels of diplomacy, lavish gifts, including a set of gold cups and an annual lifelong pension for the young prince of 5,000 livres to be paid via the Staple at Veere, were to be included, although this was not without a great deal of discussion about the financial burdens this placed on the individual provinces.[28] Finally, the invitation was accepted, and on 8 July Jacob Valcke and Walraven III van Brederode were appointed as ambassadors to represent the States General. They were granted 'full power and extraordinary command' ('plain pouvoir & Mandement especial') to act on their behalf.[29] Two heavyweights of Dutch international relations, they were no strangers to diplomatic missions abroad. Valcke, Heer van Cats en Wolfaartsdijk in Goes, was Treasurer of the Province of Zeeland and an experienced politician who had been one of the men who had offered the sovereignty of the Dutch Provinces to Queen Elizabeth; he was closely associated with the earl of Leicester while Governor-General from 1586 until 1587. Brederode was from Holland and had been appointed by Leicester to the Council of State. He would later be part of the Dutch delegation sent to celebrate James' accession to the English throne in 1603. The Zeeland context is important here: it was the most westward looking of the Seven Provinces, as opposed to France-facing Holland, and was

[24] Japikse (ed.), *Resolutien der Staten-Generaal, 1576–1625*, pp. 221–22.

[25] Mary of Guelders' (c. 1434/35–63) marriage to James II had resulted in a number of privileges.

[26] 'Renovatie van de oude Tractaaten met den Koning van Schotland', *Register van Holland en Westvriesland van den jaare 1593 en 1594* (n.p., n.d.), p. 439.

[27] James D. Tracy, 'Herring Wars: The Habsburg Netherlands and the Struggle for Control of the North Sea, ca. 1520–1560', *The Sixteenth Century Journal* 24.2 (1993), 249–72.

[28] Japikse, *Resolutien der Staten-Generaal, 1576–1625*, p. 223.

[29] Their mission was to be paid by the Provinces' 'gemeene middelen' (common means). Japikse (ed.), *Resolutien der Staten-Generaal, 1576–1625*, p. 221.

home to the Scottish Staple at Veere. Around 1600 it was the most natural Scottish ally of all the Dutch provinces.[30]

On 27 and 28 July, the ambassadorial mission was set out in detail in the *Register of the States General*. The representatives were given power of attorney to propose that James establish and lead a league 'offensive et defensive' against Spain, uniting her enemies, starting with the powers present at the baptism. They were also to renew the Treaty of Bins and to present the princeling with a yearly pension of 5,000 livres to be paid annually via the Scottish conservator of the Staple at Veere. Accompanied by an Act to agree and renew the ancient treaties including the Treaty of Bins ('Akte General d'approbation & renouvellement des anciens Traitez faits entre les Princes du Pays-Bas, & les Roys d'Escosse avec insertion du Traité de Binsche l'an cinquante'), the main purpose for the States General was clearly securing the military and commercial fortunes of the United Provinces.[31] A Dutch summary of Instructions was less obvious about the ambassadors' main purpose, putting the baptism and the celebration of James' successor first.[32]

After receiving their instructions from the States General on 1 August 1594, Valcke and Brederode sailed from Veere a week later in three ships, two Zeelandish and one from Rotterdam. Although suffering some damage to their vessels along the way, they arrived in Leith on 13 August without too much trouble, where they were greeted by Damman, Sir Robert Denniston of Montjoy (1546/47–1625), the conservator of Veere, and several other notables, and were given an official welcome. The ambassadors spent the rest of the month of August in Edinburgh before travelling on to Stirling. They took the opportunity to discuss the anti-Spanish league with the other invited ambassadors and James VI's representatives. They also made headway with renewing the Treaty of Bins, and upon their departure for Stirling left Damman with instructions to follow up any further negotiations. They were entertained by the humanist and Lord Chancellor

[30] Esther Mijers, 'A Natural Partnership? Scotland and Zeeland in the Early Seventeenth Century', in Macinnes and Williamson, (eds), *Shaping the Stuart World*, pp. 233–60.

[31] 'Depeschen op Schotland. Extract uit het Register der Resolutien van myne Heeren de Generaale Staaten der vereenigde Nederlanden', *Register van Holland en Westvriesland van den jaare 1593 en 1594* (n.p., n.d.), pp. 491–505. Cf. Nationaal Archief, 1.01.02 Inventaris van het archief van de Staten-Generaal, (1431) 1576–1796, VI. C. Stukken afkomstig van de Staten-Generaal onder verschillende respecten opgenomen in de Loketkas en de Secrete kas van de Staten-Generaal 1588 juni – ca. 1795, 12589.15 Akte van renovatie door de Staten-Generaal te 's-Gravenhage uitgevaardigd van alle voorgaande tractaten, gesloten tussen de koningen van Schotland en de overheden van het grondgebied van de Republiek, met insertie van het op 15 december 1550 te Binche in Henegouwen gesloten traktaat. 1594 juli 26 1 stuk.

[32] 'Instructie voor den Weledelgebooren Edelen, Erentseste en Hoogeleerden Heere Walraven, Heere van Brederode, Vianen, Ameyden, &c. en Mr Jacob Valcke, Raad en Thesaurier Generaal van de Heeren Staaten van Zeeland, van de vereenigde Nederlandsche reisende na Schotland', 26 July 1594, in *Register van Holland en Westvriesland van den jaare 1593 en 1594* (n.p., n.d.), pp. 505–8.

Alexander Seton, 1st earl of Dunfermline, and met with a number of philosophy students at the University of Edinburgh, including 'the young Earle of Goure', John Ruthven, 3rd earl of Gowrie (c. 1577–1600).[33] When they finally set out for Stirling on 1 September – the baptism having been delayed several times – they stopped in Linlithgow for the night. Had they travelled along the east coast, they might have recognised Burntisland from Pieter Breugel the Elder's painting *Landscape with the Fall of Icarus*, which has been suggested as its location, and they would have come by the fishing villages of Fife, with their close Dutch commercial links, and St Andrews, where several students from Zeeland studied in the 1590s, at the expense of the town of Veere.[34] Had they travelled south, they might have come across Lauderdale, the landed estate in Berwickshire that once belonged to the Zeeland nobleman Paulus van Borsele (d. c. 1504), and after which he named his house in Veere *Laterdale*, which would become a favourite residence of the Stadholder, Prince Maurice of Orange.[35] In other words, the Dutch ambassadors would have felt at home, culturally, socially and visually, in their temporary Scottish surroundings.

When they finally arrived in Stirling they were put up in Argyll's Lodging, which greatly pleased them. On 3 September they had their first audience with James VI, who confirmed their common religion, friendship and alliance. He mentioned that Queen Elizabeth had been displeased with his invitation to the Dutch and the honour extended to them, explaining that she had referred to them as her subjects. The Dutch vehemently protested against this questioning of their sovereignty, at which James explained that she was merely a woman and they 'ought to forgive her her sexe'.[36] Valcke and Brederode's report states that the king invited them to act as godfathers to Prince Henry, alongside the other ambassadors. Cynthia Fry has rightly questioned this account, which after all was written for the States General and aimed at a Dutch rather than a Scottish or an international audience.[37] When the baptism finally took place on 9 September, Valcke and Brederode were embarrassed to find that, unbeknownst to them, their ambassadorial shields depicted the coat of arms of the Provinces of Holland and Zeeland, which they immediately had replaced with a single shield depicting the United Provinces. Fowler's account of the baptism contradicts this, simply stating: 'Next vnto him [the duke of Brunswick], sate the Ambassadours of

[33] *Register van Holland en Westvriesland van den jaare 1593 en 1594* (n.p., n.d.), p. 677.

[34] Christopher Harvie in *Scottish Review. Special Edition: A Backward Glance and a Look Ahead* (19 December 2018), Part 7. With thanks to Neal Ascherson for alerting me to this. For Zeelandish students at St Andrews, see Esther Mijers, '"Addicted to Puritanism": Philosophical and Theological Relations between Scotland and the United Provinces in the First Half of the Seventeenth Century', *History of Universities* 29.2 (2017), 69–96.

[35] Peter Blom *et al.* (eds), *Borsele Bourgondie Oranje: Heren en markiezen van Veere en Vlissingen, 1400. 1700* (Hilversum, 2009), passim. Paulus was a half-brother of Wolfert van Borsele, who had married Mary, the fifth daughter of James I in 1444.

[36] *Register van Holland en Westvriesland van den jaare 1593 en 1594* (n.p., n.d.), p. 682.

[37] Fry, 'Diplomacy and Deception, p. 99, n. 114.

the *Lowe Countries*, with a long faire cloth, spred on the desk before them of blew veluote, and two Cushons sutable therunto, and ouer their heades the Armes of their Countries'.[38]

Following the baptism, the Dutch delegation was keen to return to Edinburgh and conclude its business, but was kept on in Stirling for several more days, much to their annoyance. The Dutch were concerned that James and the other representatives were dragging their heels over the anti-Spanish league. James certainly used England and Elizabeth as an excuse for his position, or lack of one, undoubtedly with good reason. Valcke and Brederode had more success with the renewal of the trade treaties, which were ratified on 14 September with the exception of the Treaty of Bins, but were again confronted with the question of who they represented and on whose behalf the negotiations took place, the entire Netherlands or just the United Provinces.[39] The ambassadors clearly had some unease over this, as their instructions had lacked that level of detail, and some of the older trade treaties had been signed with specific parts of the Low Countries. Moreover, the suggestion that the United Provinces did not represent the entire country could be considered as a slight on their sovereignty. In late September they finally returned home, along the coast and via England, where they had an audience with Elizabeth, who graciously acknowledged that the States were better at running their own affairs than any other Prince.[40] They discussed the situation in France and the events in Scotland, including the Dutch wish for an anti-Spanish league, and while she assured Valcke and Brederode that she would never make peace with Spain, no concrete plans were put forward for a formal Protestant league against Spain.[41]

[38] *Register van Holland en Westvriesland van den jaare 1593 en 1594* (n.p., n.d.), pp. 684–85. Fowler, *A true reportarie*.

[39] All previous treaties were renewed by Damman in September with the exception of the Treaty of Bins, which followed the year after. Nationaal Archief, 1.01.02 Inventaris van het archief van de Staten-Generaal, (1431) 1576–1796, 12589.16A–12589.16B Akte van ratificatie te Edingburgh uitgevaardigd door de koning van Schotland van alle vroegere tractaten, gesloten tussen de koningen van Schotland en de overheden van het grondgebied van de Republiek, met uitzondering van het traktaat te Binche op 15 december 1550 gesloten en op 1 mei 1551 geratificeerd. 1594 september 14 1 stuk. Rooseboom incorrectly refers to a letter from James expressing his approval as his ratification. Rooseboom, *The Scottish Staple*, p. 120, p. CXIV, Appendix No. 101.

[40] *Register van Holland en Westvriesland van den jaare 1593 en 1594* (n.p., n.d.), p. 692.

[41] This entire account is based on Valcke and Brederode's official report for the States General: 'Relatie van het gene ons Ondergeschreeven Gesanten van myne Heeren de Staaten Generaal, aan de Koninglijke Majesteit van Schotland, op en geduurende deselve Legatie, is bejeegent en weedervaaren van daage te daage, agtervolgende den nieuwen styl', *Register van Holland en Westvriesland van den jaare 1593 en 1594* (n.p., n.d.), pp. 673–95. Cf. Nationaal Archief, 1.01.02 Inventaris van het archief van de Staten-Generaal, (1431) 1576–1796, II.B.2. Verbalen en rapporten van Nederlandse vertegenwoordigers in den vreemde: 8305 Verbaal van de gedeputeerden Walraven van Brederode en Jacob Valcke wegens hun zending naar Schotland in verband met onderhandelingen over vernieuwing van de verdragen met de Republiek, 1594 september – 1594 oktober 1 deel Exh. St.-Gen. 7 november 1594.

Despite the frustrating encounters with James and the other ambassadors, and for all their mutual flattery, perhaps with Elizabeth as well, Valcke and Brederode's visit should be considered a success. It is not surprising that the Dutch chose to attend the baptism in the first place. The relationship with Scotland was longstanding and commercially important, and friendly relations with an old trading partner and, more recently, a religious ally mattered a great deal. Clearly, diplomacy more so than the actual baptism was the Dutch purpose. This had been an ongoing policy for some time: Adriaan Damman had been appointed by the States General as their agent in Scotland on 24 December 1593 in the aftermath of a dispute over James VI's request to return parts of the Scots Brigade to Scotland, well before the invitation to attend Prince Henry's baptism reached the States General.[42] Early in the new year, Damman was issued with a set of specific instructions to protect and extend the old and existing trade relations with Scotland and elsewhere ('soo op Schotlant als elders'), which emphasised his obligation to act 'in the best interest of the United Provinces' ('vereenichde landen in 't generael') and not to be influenced by internal provincial or urban competition.[43] It is worth pointing out that the instructions for Valcke and Brederode had not been so clear. In particular, Damman was charged to look into potentially forgotten trade treaties between Scotland and any previous Dutch authorities. In addition, he was to keep an eye on James' commitment to the Reformed common cause, his relations with France, England, Denmark and any other countries, and whether any Catholic sovereigns might try to gain a foothold in Scotland. The problem of the Scots Brigade and the presence of Scottish soldiers on Dutch soil was also part of his remit. Lastly, the States worried about the confusion that might exist in Scotland between the United Provinces and the Netherlands: the Union of Utrecht (1579) had separated the northern and the southern provinces, and the former were anxious to emphasise the difference, both for reasons of sovereignty as well as to ensure that they could not be held liable for any accumulated financial debt by the south.[44]

If this looks like a story of early modern diplomacy at its most conventional, we must remember the position of the Dutch Provinces. Until very recently, they had been an agglomerate of semi-independent, semi-autonomous entities within Philip II's vast empire; as the United Provinces, they had only been in existence since 1588, after the rebellious north had come together in defiance of their Spanish overlord. While a fundamental treaty in the creation of the country, the Union of Utrecht remained constitutionally subordinate to the rights and privileges of the constituent provinces, making foreign policy as prone to provincial competition as

42 Japikse (ed.), *Resolutien der Staten-Generaal, 1576–1625*, p. 50.
43 Ibid., p. 219.
44 Ibid., pp. 218–20.

Dutch internal politics itself, for a long time to come.[45] Moreover, the Dutch had formally renounced Philip II in 1581 and, if this had not been unprecedented enough, had declared themselves independent, after several disastrous attempts at finding a new sovereign.[46] Although in the realm of foreign relations, little would have changed as far as the provinces' position in Europe was concerned – under Habsburg rule, the provinces had been able to conduct diplomacy independently from both each other as well as from their overlord, a situation which was after all confirmed in the Union of Utrecht – their open rebellion against and subsequent rejection of their rightful ruler, in the name of religion and freedom, made them stand out rather awkwardly among the monarchies and princedoms of Europe.[47] The next questions then are why the Dutch were invited at all and what were the 'utheris wechtie effearis' James had in mind when he despatched Sir William Keith and William Murray to the States General? More important still is the question of what the visit tells us about the Scottish-Dutch relationship around 1600 and how the countries saw themselves and each other.

The baptism of his oldest son was clearly an occasion for James VI to project his monarchical power to the outside world. At the same time, it was as much a diplomatic as a courtly occasion for him as well. The United Provinces, alongside England, Denmark and the German lands, were important partners in James' foreign politics. Trade with the former was very important to the Scots.[48] Dutch fishing rights, the presence of Scottish pirates in the North Sea, and the problem of the Scots Brigade recruiting men to fight abroad who might be needed at home must all be considered within this context. The Staple at Veere offered protection to this commercial relationship, as well as a diplomatic hub away from Amsterdam and The Hague where competitors and rivals could easily outdo the Scots, but by itself, a trade hub was not enough. The change in regime and form of government in the United Provinces required a formal renewal of this relationship, and James knew that this was as important to the Dutch as it was to Scotland. These were very weighty affairs indeed.

For the Dutch, despite their potential commercial success and existing international alliances with England and France, every friend mattered in the chaotic first decades of their independence. Scotland was their natural partner, commercially, religiously, culturally and even socially, especially as

[45] D. Onnekink and G. Rommelse (eds), *The Dutch in the Early Modern World: A History of a Global Power* (Cambridge, 2019), chapter 1: 'The Emerging Republic: (1579–1609)', pp. 5–50.

[46] Aside from Elizabeth I, they had also offered their sovereignty to Henry III of France.

[47] S. Groenveld, *Regeren in de Republiek Bestuurspraktijken in de 17e-eeuwse Noordelijke Nederlanden: terugblik en perspectief* (Leiden, 2006), p. 15.

[48] M. Rorke, 'English and Scottish Overseas Trade, 1300–1600', *The Economic History Review* 59 (2006), 265–88; Ian D. Whyte, *Scotland before the Industrial Revolution. An Economic and Social History c.1050–c.1750* (Milton Park and New York, 2013), chapter 15.

long as Zeeland could balance out the power of Holland.[49] Men like Valcke, Brederode, Damman, the conservators of the Staple and the many other politicians, diplomats and scholars who travelled back and forth across the North Sea shared more than a geographical space. They were part of the same Northern humanist elite who were characteristic of the Renaissance around the North Sea rim and formed part of a wider British–Flemish sphere.[50] As much as the Dutch contributed to the cultural and artistic expressions in late Renaissance Scotland, for instance through the court painters Arnold Bronckhorst (fl. 1565–83), his successor Adrian Vanson (fl. 1570s–1602; d. before 1610) and his son Adam de Colone (fl. 1622–28), and indeed Damman himself, Scotland also played a role of significant importance in the Dutch imagination of the late sixteenth and early seventeenth centuries.[51] Whether or not Breughel's *Icarus* really did depict Burntisland is not known, but it might not be as fantastical as it initially appears. Writers of Dutch history like the politician Cornelis Pietersz. Hooft (1547–1627) and poet and playwright Joost van den Vondel (1587–1679) referred to Scotland and her history in their works.[52] And James VI himself was a popular author in the United Provinces, as Astrid Stilma has shown.[53] Moreover, Scotland's Reformation was looked upon with considerable reverence by the Dutch for its perceived purity of discipline.[54]

In many ways, the States General mirrored James VI's intentions, exploiting the baptism of Scotland's crown prince to communicate political power and ambition both abroad and at home. Keen to show themselves as players on the European stage, they grabbed the chance to piggy-back onto James' diplomatic vehicle with both hands. Using their visit to re-confirm their trade relationship with Scotland, they also, and perhaps arguably more so, employed it as an international occasion to confirm their recently

[49] The powerplay between Holland and Zeeland is an underappreciated but hugely important aspect of Dutch foreign affairs throughout most of the late sixteenth and seventeenth centuries. For the rise of Holland see J. Tracy, *The Founding of the Dutch Republic: War, Finance, and Politics in Holland, 1572–1588* (Oxford, 2008).

[50] This effectively was a continuation of the North Sea culture of the late Middle Ages. J. Roding and L. Heerma van Voss (eds), *The North Sea and Culture (1550–1800): Proceedings of the International Conference Held at Leiden 21–22 April 1995* (Hilversum, 1996).

[51] Fleming and Mason, *Scotland and the Flemish People*; J. Lloyd Williams and the National Gallery of Scotland, *Dutch Art and Scotland: A Reflection of Taste* (Edinburgh, 1992).

[52] 'Redevoeringen in de Oud-Raad gehouden op 15 October 1597 en 29 Januari 1598, in zake de gevangenneming van Goosen Vogelsang: "Over de Vervolging in geloofszaken"' (1599) (Speeches to the Town Council on matters of religion), in C.P. Hooft, *Memoriën en Adviezen*, ed. H.A. Enno van Gelder (2 vols, Utrecht 1871–1925), vol. 2, p. 76; 'De Pinksterbloem van Schotland', in Joost van den Vondel, *Hekeldichtung, met de Aanteekeningen der 'Amersfoortsche' uitgave*, ed. J. Bergsma (Zutphen, 1920), pp. 110–11; cf. *De Werken van Vondel*, ed. J.F M. Sterck (10 vols, Amsterdam, 1927–37), passim.

[53] Stilma, *A King Translated.*

[54] E. Mijers, '"Holland and we were bot one in our cause": The Covenanters' "Dutch" Reception and Impact', *SHR* 99 (Supplement) (2020), 412–28.

established independence and sovereignty, as well as a performative act of unity and prestige for an internal, Dutch audience. To be part of a princely spectacle gave the Dutch the legitimacy that they much needed following their rebellion against Philip. Astute politicians like Valcke and Brederode knew the importance of outward projection – the opportunity to make it clear that they represented the *United* Provinces rather than their own Zeeland and Holland, or even more outmodedly, the Low Countries or Flanders, and gave them the chance to confirm their new country as the successor state to the individual provinces and cities which had been loosely joined under Charles V and Philip II.[55] It also offered a legal opportunity. When Sir William Keith and William Murray reminded the Dutch of their reliance on their king's goodwill the Scots tried to gain the upper hand. The Dutch, trained in legal humanism, responded in the same way as when they were confronted with Philip II's unwelcome grand strategy, turning to precedent and historic agreements.[56] By seeking renewal of the ancient treaties concluded between the Scottish monarchs and their Habsburg overlords, they ensured that Scottish-Dutch trade could continue, while at the same time enshrining into law their own sovereign position. The international implications were significant.

Far from being an exclusively international matter, the problem of Dutch sovereignty and unity also needed addressing at home. Internal competition between the seven provinces and the towns defined Dutch politics. The financial discussion over the baptismal gift was a small example of this.[57] Damman's instructions to act on behalf of the States General and the United Provinces illustrate this further. The ambassadors would have had this in mind when they wrote their report, which was after all aimed at an internal audience. Being able to negotiate with James, Elizabeth and the other ambassadors and championing their ultimate purpose, the anti-Spanish League, interpreting their invitation to the baptism as one of godfathering the princeling, confirming their position with regard to Elizabeth, categorically denouncing her claim to sovereignty, and of course insisting upon the correct

[55] The Venetian ambassador in Germany referred to them as being from Holland. Tomaso Contarini to the Doge and Senate, 8 Sept. 1594, *Calendar of States Papers and Manuscripts Relating to English Affairs Existing in the Archives and Collections of Venice and Other Libraries in Northern Italy, vol. 9: 1592–1603*, ed. H.F. Brown (Burlington, ON, 2007), p. 143. Fowler refers to them as the ambassadors of the Low Countries; see Fowler, *A True Repotarie*. Other accounts describe them as being from Flanders.

[56] Geoffrey Parker, *The Grand Strategy of Philip II* (New Haven, CT, 1998); Martin Van Gelderen, *The Political Thought of the Dutch Revolt 1555–1590* (Cambridge, 1992), chapter 4.

[57] Even after the ambassadors had returned to the Netherlands, the financial burden of the annual pension for Prince Henry continued to be debated among the provinces, with the argument centring on the question of to what extent it was the responsibility of the separate provinces to make individual contributions or whether it should be paid from the 'gemeene middelen' (common means, ie. the United Provinces' coffers). Japikse (ed.), *Resolutien der Staten-Generaal, 1576–1625*), p. 455.

coat of arms at the dinner table can all be seen as 'inward' projections of the power of the States General of the United Provinces.[58] Contemporary Dutch authors such as Emanuel van Meteren (1535–1612) and Pieter Christiaenszoon Bor (1559–1635) certainly also picked up on the mission as important enough to include in their national histories.[59] The impact in Scotland of the visit itself was smaller, while the lasting importance of the Dutch connection would continue and expand over the course of the seventeenth century. Talks with the Dutch certainly continued, and in December 1594 Sir William Stewart of Houstoun was sent as ambassador to the States General 'to intreate upoun certane utheris wechtie effearis contenit in the commissioun and instructioun gevin to him thairupoun', finally confirming the official renewal of the Treaty of Bins on 2 May 1595.[60]

So what can we then conclude from this episode in Scottish-Dutch relations? Certainly, the connection between Scotland and the Low Countries was an important link in late Renaissance and Reformation Northern Europe. Trade between the two nations was concentrated along the coastal parts of eastern Scotland and the North Sea edges of Flanders and the extended Zeeland archipelago, connecting small villages whose contemporary significance did not survive the rise of the urban centres in the seventeenth century. From this developed a lively exchange of goods, people and ideas which was held in high regard by both partners. Although its transnational history still waits to be written, its importance is clear. The invitation to attend Prince Henry's baptism was an expression of its value and a pretext to ensure its continuation. Historiographically, it provides a counterweight to the seventeenth- and early eighteenth-century relationship, which was very much tipped in favour of the Dutch. Around 1594, Scotland arguably had more to offer to the Dutch than the other way round. James unwittingly gave the Dutch the opportunity to act as a single unified entity away from the battlefield, and as such it was an early contribution to the lengthy process of Dutch state formation.[61] As a national celebration turned international event, Prince Henry's baptism helped the Dutch to position

[58] It has been argued that Fowler's contemporary account of the baptism, *A True Reportarie* 'represents a new form of political announcement, a reformed Protestant communiqué that breaks with a Catholic past, balances Scottish nationalism with British union, and asserts the cultural complexities of James's future power'; Bowers, 'James VI', p. 4. Valcke and Brederode's report certainly did not have any literary merit, but one might argue that it also was a type of political announcement, or at least statement, which balanced the concept of Dutch unity with federal union.

[59] Emanuel van Meteren, *Historie der Nederlandschen ende Haerder Na-buren oorlogen* (1614), ff. 343r–v; Pieter Christiaenszoon Bor, *Nederlantsche oorloghen, beroerten, ende borgerlijcke oneenicheyden*, vol. 3 (Amsterdam, 1679; first ed. 1621), pp. 837–43.

[60] 'Act in favour of Sir William Stewart of Houston, appointed ambassador to the Estates of Flanders', *RPC*, v, pp. 194–95. Japikse (ed.), *Resolutien der Staten-Generaal, 1576–1625*, p. 452.

[61] S. Groenveld with H.L.Ph. Leeuwenberg, *De bruid in de schuit: de consolidatie van de Republiek 1609–1650* (Zutphen, 1985).

themselves as sovereign and united amongst the divided powers of Europe, and to articulate their unity for an internal audience. In other words, it appears that sometimes state formation starts abroad. In his article 'From Buchanan to Blaeu', on Blaeu's *Atlas of Scotland* that was published in 1654,[62] Roger Mason stated that the *Atlas* was a (Scottish-)Dutch venture and a celebration of Scotland as a kingdom 'intended to make a firm statement about the country's past, present and future status'.[63] If the Scottish-Dutch relationship can be captured in vignettes, then Blaeu's *Atlas* illustrates the next stage in this relationship, and as such provided a sequel to the Dutch visit of 1594: a Scottish event used by the Dutch for their own advantage to project their Union and their unity, intended to make a firm statement about their country's present and future status.

62 *Theatrum orbis terrarum sive Atlas novus*, *Volume V* (1654).

63 Roger A. Mason, 'From Buchanan to Blaeu: The Politics of Scottish Chorography 1582–1654', in Erskine and Mason (eds), *George Buchanan*, pp. 13–47, at p. 14.

# Afterword

## *The Renaissance of Roger Mason*

Sally Mapstone

It was a pleasure to introduce the day conference in honour of Roger in which this collection of essays had its genesis, and to welcome everyone to it. It was also a pleasure to spend a day listening to the expertise of those engaging in discussion of subjects that Roger has made so much his own: Scottish historiography; humanism and literacy; Scottish political and religious thought; John Knox; George Buchanan; James VI and I; Scotland and England; Scotland and Europe; the Scottish Renaissance (if there was one); and the Declaration of Arbroath. We really needed a week rather than a day to do all of this justice.

Roger and I first met in the summer of 1985 in Edinburgh at a conference on sovereignty held by the Traditional Cosmology Society, where Roger was brave enough to be giving a paper and neither of us really had a clue about much else that was going on. The conference was largely dominated by anthropologists talking about incest and Louise Fradenburg talking about Lacan.[1] The paper that Roger was giving was to become one of his most significant contributions to the literature of sovereignty and political thought in Scotland, and I estimate that hearing it held up the completion of my doctoral thesis by a good six months – but only for the better. This was 'Kingship, Tyranny and the Right to Resist in Fifteenth-Century Scotland', published first in *SHR* in 1987, and then published again in slightly revised form in Roger's magisterial *Kingship and the Commonweal* in 1998.[2] (I have to say parenthetically here that I do – dimly – recall helping Roger celebrate the publication of that book at a conference Nicola Royan organised at St Andrews in 1999.[3] The following day there was a total eclipse of the sun, and I have rarely been more grateful for one given the size of my hangover.)

[1] This was the run-up to her highly influential *City, Marriage, Tournament: Arts of Rule in Late Medieval Scotland* (Madison, WI, 1991).

[2] Roger A. Mason, 'Kingship, Tyranny and the Right to Resist in Fifteenth-Century Scotland', *SHR* 66 (1987), 125–51 and reprinted with minor revisions in *Kingship and the Commonweal*, pp. 8–35. For some other papers from the conference see Emily Lyle (ed.), *Cosmos: The Yearbook of the Traditional Cosmology Society*, 2 (Edinburgh, 1988).

[3] This was the 9th International Conference on Medieval and Renaissance Scottish Language and Literature, held at the University of St Andrews in August 1999. Collections of essays from the conference were edited by Ian Johnson and Nicola Royan in *Forum for Modern Language Studies* 38.4 (2002) and by Nicola Royan and Theo van Heijnsbergen in

'Kingship, Tyranny and the Right to Resist' showed many of the characteristics of Roger's subsequent writing, along with the qualities that have made his work so accessible and so important to literary scholars as well as his fellow historians. These features were also well apparent in another wonderful early work completed during his celebrated tenure as Glenfiddich Research Fellow in Scottish History at St Andrews, 'George Buchanan, James VI and the Scottish Polity', in *New Perspectives on the Politics and Culture of Early Modern Scotland*, which he edited with John Dwyer and Alexander Murdoch, and which pulls off the notable bibliographical feat of omitting its date of publication in its preliminary materials.[4] Roger has both a remarkable ability to sum up the essence of a set of political or theoretical arguments while also conveying the generic reach of a work and placing it against an intellectual background which frequently involves appreciation of a wide range of Classical and late antique sources. He also contrives both to evaluate whether arguments make sense in their own terms and whether previous commentators have been fair in so judging them. In this respect in particular, Roger's work on fifteenth- and sixteenth-century Scottish conceptions of sovereignty is fundamental. It is undoubtedly the work of his to which I have returned most frequently and which affords me constant intellectual replenishment.

It is demanding to count the ways in which Roger has affected how we think about late medieval and early modern Scotland and Scottish political thought, or as Roger in his 2008 essay in Norman Macdougall's Festschrift, *Scottish Kingship 1306–1542*, might wish to put it, 'Renaissance Monarchy? Stewart Kingship'.[5] Roger's persistent embrace of the concept of Scottish Renaissance monarchy is probably one of the few areas in which I continue rather to disagree with him, though this does prompt me to say that if you are ever stuck for providing Roger with a Christmas present, a closed imperial crown is what he has been hinting he really wants for a good quarter of a century now.[6]

Roger has shown himself to be a brilliant editor. His 2004 and 1994 editions of Buchanan's *De Iure Regni* and Knox's *On Rebellion*, for example, offer so much in addition to the works they reprofile.[7] His contributions as an editor of essay collections, including his 2014 collection with Steven Reid focusing on Andrew Melville, have opened up and changed the ways in which we think about a series of major figures in Scottish political thought, as well as a series of concepts, including Scotland and Europe and indeed Scotland and England.[8] He is of

*Literature, Letters and the Canonical in Early Modern Scotland* (East Linton, 2002).

4 '*Rex Stoicus*: George Buchanan, James VI and the Scottish Polity', in John Dwyer, Roger A. Mason, and Alexander Murdoch (eds), *New Perspectives on the Politics and Culture of Early Modern Scotland* (Edinburgh, 1982), pp. 9–33.

5 'Renaissance Monarchy? Stewart Kingship (1469–1532)', in Brown and Tanner (eds), *Scottish Kingship*, pp. 255–78.

6 With illustrations in 'This Realm of Scotland Is an Empire? Imperial Ideas and Iconography in Early Renaissance Scotland', in *Church, Chronicle, and Learning in Medieval and Early Renaissance Scotland*, ed. B.A. Crawford (Edinburgh, 1999), pp. 73–91.

7 Mason and Smith; *Knox: On Rebellion*.

8 Mason and Reid (eds), *Andrew Melville*; *John Knox and the British Reformations*, ed. R.A

course a former editor of the *SHR* and of the 10-volume *New Edinburgh History of Scotland*. This kind of work is both demanding and collegial; it also does a terrific amount for the common good, or as Roger would undoubtedly want to call it, the commonweal of the subject, and I very much want to recognise this aspect of Roger's contributions as well as his magisterial essays and books.

One of the many wonderful things about Roger is that there is always more to be discovered in and about his works, and there is also more to be discovered about him. Only recently, when dining with Chris Smout and Roger's old friend Colin Ballantyne, did I find out that Roger was as a schoolboy a champion pole-vaulter. I have to say that this came as a complete surprise to me as the notion of Roger hurtling forward with an enormous pole in hand and then translating himself over a bar (sporting, rather than alcoholic) to cascade victorious on to the other side had somehow never presented itself to me as likely in all the years that I have seen Roger at conferences, in libraries, in the pub, and on very rare occasions on the dance floor. It makes you think. I have also discovered then and subsequently that Roger has a fairly extensive back history as a fire officer. His period as warden of McIntosh Hall in St Andrews was marked by a celebrated Yuletide mince pie burning which set off the Hall's alarms as if the last trump had been announced; but there was good precedent for this, which I can best express in his own words. When Roger was at school: 'I did start a fire when smoking illicitly, though it was a minor blaze in a boarded up chimney that had become overfull of fag ends. The irony was that I was a member of the school's fire brigade.'[9]

St Andrews locals may recall a touching photograph in the local paper in February 2018 of Roger and Ellen shivering in their home due to a failed delivery of their Calor gas supply, a piece of media intervention that rapidly produced the required delivery, I'm pleased to say. The picture showed Ellen lifting some of their few last wood stove logs while Roger looked on unable to move for cold, as they struggled to keep themselves warm during what was indeed a period of bitter weather.[10] One looks back on that now with different eyes, however. A) the former fire officer clearly knew what he was up to and B) of course Roger had his eye on that log for other reasons. Retirement has transformed him into a wood turner. Wands are the latest speciality, but it is surely only a question of time before Roger turns himself a specially honed wooden pole and reverts to the lost and loved pole-vaulting of his youth. This time, of course, it will all be immortalised on camera.

Returning to Roger, the historian: Roger has always had an iconoclastic streak as well as an interest in iconoclasm, and in dreadful puns, witnessed as early as his important 'Scotching the Brut: Politics, History and National

Mason (Aldershot, 1998); *Scotland and England 1286–1815*, ed. R.A. Mason (Edinburgh, 1987); *Scots and Britons: Scottish Political Thought and the Union of 1603*, ed. R.A. Mason (Cambridge, 2006); Erskine and Mason (eds), *George Buchanan*.

9 This revelation was elicited by Professor Katie Stevenson.

10 www.thecourier.co.uk/fp/news/local/fife/608505/elderly-fife-couple-face-bitterly-cold-spell-with-no-fuel/.

Myth in Sixteenth-Century Britain' in one of his edited essay collections *Scotland and England 1286–1815*.[11] He leaves the puns behind but not the capacity to dismantle convenient myths in a recent scorching essay, 'Beyond the Declaration of Arbroath: Kingship, Counsel and Consent in Late Medieval and Early Modern Scotland' (hooray, he has seen the light and ditched the Renaissance) in the marvellous Festschrift for our loved and lamented colleague Jenny Wormald, *Kings, Lords and Men*, edited by Steve Boardman and Julian Goodare in 2014.[12] Roger is probably not going to be afforded the freedom of the burgh of Arbroath as a result of this intervention. Let's recall a key part of it: 'And there's the rub. [That is Roger; it's also of course Hamlet, whom Roger chooses to modernise, even dare I say it anglicise, as the bard himself writes, 'Ay there's the rub'. Anyway.] For those who would like to see the Declaration of Arbroath as the fountainhead of Scottish political radicalism, the founding document of Scottish constitutionalism, animating Scottish political culture from that day to this, it is seriously problematic that for over 350 years after its composition virtually no one actually referred to it.'[13] But Roger of course does not leave the subject there. He goes on to set out the key traditions of political discourse that inform and profoundly affect Scottish constitutional and political history, working through from ecclesiastical conciliarism to Buchanan's 'republican moment'. It is a wonderful essay, vintage Roger, and so appropriate for his dear friend Jenny, who loved a good argument.

When I read his 'Arbroath' essay with its return to one of the figures who has featured across Roger's career, our own George Buchanan, I found myself thinking of one of the statements Roger makes about Buchanan in one of his earliest essays, to which I have already referred, 'George Buchanan, James VI and the Scottish Polity': 'Buchanan was already over sixty when his major works were written and few men radically reorientate their thought at that stage in life.'[14] This is possibly the sort of statement you can throw out and away in your twenties and thirties; I wonder if Roger would take the same view now. We are after all now in the era of Roger the wand-maker. I know Roger will continue to write and I live in hope of him jettisoning the Scottish Renaissance once and for all – but far more importantly I know that he will continue to offer us profoundly thoughtful, deeply researched, and emphatically argued challenges to and advances in the way we see Scottish history. And with everyone in this volume I want to thank him for that, most respectfully and with great affection.

[11] See n. 8; Roger's essay is pp. 60–84.

[12] Roger A. Mason, 'Beyond the Declaration of Arbroath: Kingship, Counsel and Consent in Late Medieval and Early Modern Scotland', in Boardman and Goodare (eds), *Kings, Lords and Men*, pp. 265–82.

[13] 'Beyond the Declaration of Arbroath', p. 267.

[14] 'George Buchanan, James VI and the Scottish Polity', p. 14.

# *Roger A. Mason: A Select Bibliography*

This list of Roger's works excludes book reviews, encyclopaedia entries, and other smaller works.

## Monographs, Edited Texts and Edited Collections


*Late-Medieval and Early-Modern Scotland: Literary and Historical Approaches*, ed. with Rhiannon Purdie, *The Mediaeval Journal* 10 (Special Issue, 2021).

*Scotland and the Flemish People*, ed. with Alexander Fleming (Edinburgh: John Donald, 2019), 198 pp.

*Andrew Melville (1545–1622): Writings, Reception and Reputation*, ed. with Steven Reid, St Andrews Studies in Reformation History (Farnham: Ashgate, 2014), 306 pp.

*George Buchanan: Political Thought in Early Modern Britain and Europe*, ed. with Caroline Erskine, St Andrews Studies in Reformation History (Farnham: Ashgate, 2012), 315 pp.

*A Dialogue on the Law of Kingship among the Scots: George Buchanan's 'De Iure Regni apud Scotos' with a New Introduction*, ed. with Martin Smith (Edinburgh: Saltire Society, 2006), 210 pp.

*A Dialogue on the Law of Kingship among the Scots: A Critical Edition and Translation of George Buchanan's 'De Jure Regni apud Scotos Dialogus'*, ed. with Martin Smith, St Andrews Studies in Reformation History (Farnham: Ashgate, 2004), 228 pp.

*John Knox and the British Reformations*, ed., St Andrews Studies in Reformation History (Farnham: Ashgate, 1998), 297 pp.

*Kingship and the Commonweal: Political Thought in Renaissance and Reformation Scotland* (East Linton: Tuckwell Press, 1998), 277 pp.

*John Knox: On Rebellion*, ed., Cambridge Texts in the History of Political Thought (Cambridge: Cambridge University Press, 1994), 219 pp.

*Scots and Britons: Scottish Political Thought and the Union of 1603*, ed. (Cambridge: Cambridge University Press, 1994), 323 pp.

*People and Power in Scotland: Essays in Honour of T.C. Smout*, ed. with Norman Macdougall (Edinburgh: John Donald, 1992), 240 pp.

*Scotland and England 1286–1815*, ed. (Edinburgh: John Donald, 1987), 270 pp.

*New Perspectives on the Politics and Culture of Early Modern Scotland*, ed. with John Dwyer and Alexander Murdoch (Edinburgh: John Donald, 1982), 329 pp.

## Articles and Book Chapters

'The Idea of the "Common Weal" in Sixteenth-Century Scotland', *Journal of the Northern Renaissance* 16 (2024).

'The "hodgepodge trash of *Lud*": George Buchanan on Humphrey Llwyd's Vision of Britain', in *Inventor of Britain: The Work and Legacies of Humphrey Llwyd*, ed. Philip Schwyzer (Cardiff: University of Wales Press, 2024).

'Dame Scotia and the Commonweal: Vernacular Humanism in *The Complaynt of Scotland* (1550)', in *Late-Medieval and Early-Modern Scotland: Literary and Historical Approaches*, ed. with Rhiannon Purdie, *The Mediaeval Journal* 10 (2021), 129–50.

'The Declaration of Arbroath in Print, 1680–1705', *Innes Review* 72 (2021), 158–76.

'1603: Multiple Monarchy and Scottish Identity', *History* 105 (2020), 402–21.

'University, City and Society', in *Medieval St Andrews: Church, Cult, City*, ed. Michael Brown and Katie Stevenson (Woodbridge: Boydell & Brewer, 2017), pp. 268–97.

'Counsel and Covenant: Aristocratic Conciliarism and the Scottish Revolution', in *The Politics of Counsel in England and Scotland 1286–1707*, ed. Jacqueline Rose, Proceedings of the British Academy (Oxford: Oxford University Press, 2016), pp. 229–47.

'Divided by a Common Faith? Protestantism and Union in Post-Reformation Britain', in *Scotland's Long Reformation: New Perspectives on Scottish Religion, c. 1500–1660*, ed. John McCallum, St Andrews Studies in Reformation History (Leiden: Brill, 2016), pp. 202–25.

'Debating Britain in Seventeenth-Century Scotland: Multiple Monarchy and Scottish Sovereignty', *Journal of Scottish Historical Studies* 35 (2015), 1–24.

'Beyond the Declaration of Arbroath: Kingship, Counsel and Consent in Late Medieval and Early Modern Scotland', in *Kings, Lords and Men in Scotland and Britain, 1300–1625: Essays in Honour of Jenny Wormald*, ed. Steve Boardman and Julian Goodare (Edinburgh: Edinburgh University Press, 2014), pp. 265–82.

'How Andrew Melville Read His George Buchanan', in *Andrew Melville (1545–1622): Writings, Reception and Reputation*, ed. with Steven Reid, St Andrews Studies in Reformation History (Farnham: Ashgate, 2014), pp. 11–45.

'*Certeine Matters Concerning the Realme of Scotland*: George Buchanan and Scottish Self-Fashioning at the Union of the Crowns', *Scottish Historical Review* 92 (2013), 38–65.

'Dis-United Kingdoms? What Lies Behind Scotland's Referendum on Independence', *Georgetown Journal of International Affairs* 14 (2013), 139–46.

'Scotland', in *The Oxford Handbook of Holinshed's Chronicles*, ed. Paulina Kewes, Ian W. Archer and Felicity Heal (Oxford: Oxford University Press, 2013), pp. 647–62.

'The State of Scottish History: Some Reflections', *Scottish Historical Review* 92 supplement (2013), 167–75.

'From Buchanan to Blaeu: The Politics of Scottish Chorography 1582–1654', in *George Buchanan: Political Thought in Early Modern Britain and Europe*, ed. with Caroline Erskine, St Andrews Studies in Reformation History (Farnham: Ashgate, 2012), pp. 13–47.

'Lineage and Legitimacy: Mary Queen of Scots and the Stewart Inheritance', *Royal Stuart Journal* 2 (2010), 1–21.

'Lineages of Unionism: Early Modern Scots and the Idea of Britain', *History Scotland* 8.1 (2008), 40–48.

'Renaissance Monarchy? Stewart Kingship (1469–1542)', in *Scottish Kingship 1306–1542: Essays in Honour of Norman Macdougall*, ed. Michael Brown and Roland Tanner (Edinburgh: John Donald, 2008), pp. 255–78.

'From Chronicle to History: Recovering the Past in Renaissance Scotland', in *Building the Past / Konstruktion der eigenen Vergangenheit*, ed. Rudolf Suntrup and Jan Veenstra (Frankfurt am Main: Peter Lang, 2006), pp. 53–66.

'Renaissance and Reformation: The Sixteenth Century', in *Scotland: A History*, ed. Jenny Wormald (Oxford: Oxford University Press, 2005), pp. 107–42.

'Scotland, Elizabethan England and the Idea of Britain', *Transactions of the Royal Historical Society* 14 (2004), 279–93.

'George Buchanan's Vernacular Polemics 1570–1572', *Innes Review* 54 (2003), 47–68.

'Civil Society and the Celts: Hector Boece, George Buchanan and the Ancient Scottish Past', in *Scottish History: The Power of the Past*, ed. E.J. Cowan and R.J. Finlay (Edinburgh: Edinburgh University Press, 2002), pp. 95–119.

'People Power? George Buchanan on Resistance and the Common Man', in *Widerstandsrecht in der fruhen Neuzeit*, ed. Robert Von Friedeburg (Berlin: Duncker & Humblot, 2001), pp. 163–81.

'George Buchanan and Mary Queen of Scots', *Records of the Scottish Church History Society* 30 (2000), 1–27.

'Laicization and the Law: The Reception of Humanism in Early Renaissance Scotland', in *A Palace in the Wild: Essays on Vernacular Culture and Humanism in Late Medieval and Early Renaissance Scotland*, ed. Luuk Houwen, Alasdair MacDonald, and Sally Mapstone (Louvain: Peeters, 2000), pp. 1–25.

'This Realm of Scotland Is an Empire? Imperial Ideas and Iconography in Early Renaissance Scotland', in *Church, Chronicle and Learning in Late Medieval and Early Renaissance Scotland: Essays Presented to Donald Watt*, ed. Barbara Crawford (Edinburgh: Mercat Press Ltd, 1999), pp. 77–95.

'Knox, Resistance and the Royal Supremacy', in *John Knox and the British Reformations*, ed. Roger A. Mason, St Andrews Studies in Reformation History (Farnham: Ashgate, 1998), pp. 154–75.

'Usable Pasts: History and Identity in Reformation Scotland', *Scottish Historical Review* 76 (1997), 54–68.

'George Buchanan, James VI and the Presbyterians', in *Scots and Britons: Scottish Political Thought and the Union of 1603*, ed. Roger A. Mason (Cambridge: Cambridge University Press, 1994), pp. 112–37.

'The Scottish Reformation and the Origins of Anglo-British Imperialism', in *Scots and Britons: Scottish Political Thought and the Union of 1603*, ed. Roger A. Mason (Cambridge: Cambridge University Press, 1994), pp. 161–86.

'Chivalry and Citizenship: Aspects of National Identity in Early Renaissance Scotland', in *People and Power in Scotland: Essays in Honour of T.C. Smout*, ed. with Norman Macdougall (Edinburgh: John Donald, 1992), pp. 50–73.

'Kingship, Nobility and Anglo-Scottish Union: John Mair's *History of Greater Britain* (1521)', *Innes Review* 41 (1990), 182–222.

'The Aristocracy, Episcopacy and the Revolution of 1638', in *Covenant, Charter and Party: Traditions of Revolt and Protest in Modern Scottish History*, ed. Terry Brotherstone (Aberdeen: Aberdeen University Press, 1989), pp. 7–24.

'Kingship, Tyranny and the Right to Resist in Fifteenth-Century Scotland', *Scottish Historical Review* 66 (1987), 125–51.

'Scotching the Brut: Politics, History and National Myth in Sixteenth-Century Britain', in *Scotland and England 1286–1815*, ed. Roger A. Mason (Edinburgh: John Donald, 1987), pp. 60–84.

'Covenant and Commonweal: The Language of Politics in Reformation Scotland', in *Church, Politics and Society: Scotland 1408–1929*, ed. Norman Macdougall (Edinburgh: John Donald, 1983), pp. 97–126.

'*Rex Stoicus*: George Buchanan, James VI and the Scottish Polity', in *New Perspectives on the Politics and Culture of Early Modern Scotland*, ed. with John Dwyer and Alexander Murdoch (Edinburgh: John Donald, 1982), pp. 9–33.

'Knox, Resistance and the Moral Imperative', *History of Political Thought* 1 (1980), 411–36.

# Index

# *Tabula Gratulatoria*

Kate Ash-Irisarri
Robert Bartlett
Stephen Boardman
Karin Bowie
Dauvit Broun
Michael H. Brown
Alison Cathcart
Jane E. A. Dawson
Elizabeth Elliott
Ken Emond
Elizabeth Ewan
Mark Godfrey
Julian Goodare
Janet Hadley Williams
Rachel Hart
Claire Hawes
Linsey Hunter
Amy L. Juhala
Miles Kerr-Peterson
James McAtear
John McCallum
Kate McClune
Aonghas MacCoinnich
Alasdair A. MacDonald
Alastair J. Macdonald
Catriona M. M. Macdonald
Tricia A. McElroy
Christine McGladdery
Martin MacGregor
Aonghus MacKechnie
Hector MacQueen
Sally Mapstone
Joanna M. Martin
Esther Mijers
Caroline Palmer
Michael Penman
Rhiannon Purdie
Alasdair Raffe
Norman H. Reid
Steven J. Reid
Jamie Reid-Baxter
Bess Rhodes
Nicola Royan
Charlie Spragg
Katie Stevenson
Katherine H. Terrell
Andrea Thomas
Eila Williamson
Emily Wingfield
Isla Woodman
Theo van Heijnsbergen

## St Andrews Studies in Scottish History



Sponsored by the Institute of Scottish Historical Research at the University of St Andrews, St Andrews Studies in Scottish History provides an important forum for the publication of research on any aspect of Scottish history, from the early middle ages to the present day, focusing on the historical experience of Scots at home and abroad, and Scotland's place in wider British, European and global contexts. Both monographs and essay collections are welcomed.

Proposal forms can be obtained from the Institute of Scottish Historical Research website: http://www.st-andrews.ac.uk/ishr/studies.htm. They should be sent in the first instance to the chair of the editorial board at the address below.

Professor Emeritus Roger Mason
Institute of Scottish Historical Research
St Andrews University
St Andrews
Fife KY16 9AL
UK

## St Andrews Studies in Scottish History
Previously published

I
*Elite Women and Polite Society in Eighteenth-Century Scotland*
Katharine Glover

II
*Regency in Sixteenth-Century Scotland*
Amy Blakeway

III
*Scotland, England and France after the Loss of Normandy, 1204–1296*
*'Auld Amitie'*
M. A. Pollock

IV
*Children and Youth in Premodern Scotland*
edited by Janay Nugent and Elizabeth Ewan

V
*Medieval St Andrews: Church, Cult, City*
Edited by Michael Brown and Katie Stevenson

VI
*The Life and Works of Robert Baillie (1602–1662)*
*Politics, Religion and Record-Keeping in the British Civil Wars*
Alexander D. Campbell

VII
*The Parish and the Chapel in Medieval Britain and Norway*
Sarah E. Thomas

VIII
*A Protestant Lord in James VI's Scotland*
*George Keith, Fifth Earl Marischal (1554–1623)*
Miles Kerr-Peterson

IX
*The Clergy in Early Modern Scotland*
Edited by Chris R. Langley, Catherine E. McMillan and Russell Newton

X
*Kingship, Lordship and Sanctity in Medieval Britain*
*Essays in Honour of Alexander Grant*
Edited by Steve Boardman and David Ditchburn

Printed in the United States
by Baker & Taylor Publisher Services